P9-BYD-753

Praise for *Homeschool Your Child for Free*

We purchase very, very little in the way of paid curriculum, so free resources make up about 95 percent of our curriculum resources.

—Patty Wiens,
Christian homeschool mom to six, Saskatoon, Saskatchewan

From the free printable calendars on the wall, to online video, to free audiobook downloads for our MP3 players, to unit studies . . . there is such an abundance of excellent free resources available!

—Darnia Hobson, *unschooling mum of three, New Zealand*

We have used *lots* of free homeschooling resources. Most of the free resources I have used are from online. We have found *lots* of free lesson plans that give me springboards for ideas. We have found lots of hands-on crafts and experiments to go with lessons online. We subscribe to homeschool radio shows and currclick.com and use their weekly free resources but have made purchases through them as well. We also have free posters from online resources or free Montessori cards to teach geographical terms.

—Terri Vitkovitsky,
homeschooling mom of five, Camp Lejeune, North Carolina

Free stuff? Yes, yes, and more yeses! Because of the changing economy and the addition of another baby to the family this past year, we are focusing more and more on free resources for education. We frequent the library for books on any unit we are covering, as well as for videos and pleasure reading. We use the Internet a lot as well. Our church has a library of educational videos and DVDs. I also trade out resources with friends as much as possible.

—Cheryl Lemily,
Christian, wife, mom, and education facilitator, Fleming, Colorado

I use free resources like there is no tomorrow! Especially online—
I don't accept that it's not out there, and try to find it regardless. Education is meant to be free to all, isn't it!? Our local paper prints community events each week. Our national library loans free to teachers. Companies and government organizations often offer materials for free too. Because of our flexibility, these can all be folded in wherever appropriate.

—Work-at-home mom of four
  from Jacaranda Tree Learning Co-operative, Hawkes Bay, New Zealand

We absolutely use free resources! Whenever possible. As a single parent, I have no budget for homeschooling. We've been so blessed over the years that I have no doubt we are supposed to be doing this.

—Raylene Hunt, *single home-educating mom of two, Maine*

When we started homeschooling (unexpectedly), I was not working. We used completely free resources for the first six months. We still homeschool for almost free, as I have supplemented a few things with used texts.

—Monica Allison,
  single homeschooling mom of one, Broussard, Louisiana

LauraMaery Gold
AND
Joan M. Zielinski

HOMESCHOOL YOUR CHILD FOR FREE

More Than 1,400 Smart, Effective,
and Practical Resources for
Educating Your Family at Home

 THREE RIVERS PRESS • NEW YORK

All products mentioned in this book are trademarks of their respective companies. None of the manufacturers of such products have underwritten or in any way sponsored or endorsed this book. Neither the publisher nor the authors have any financial interest in the products mentioned in this book.

The publisher and authors have worked to ensure that there are no inaccuracies or omissions in this book, but sometimes errors slip through despite our best efforts. We welcome corrections and suggestions for improvement. Contact us via the companion website for this book: http://hsfree.com.

Copyright © 2000, 2009 by LauraMaery Gold and Joan M. Zielinski

All rights reserved.
Published in the United States by Three Rivers Press, an imprint of the Crown Publishing Group, a division of Random House, Inc., New York.
www.crownpublishing.com

Three Rivers Press and the Tugboat design are registered trademarks of Random House, Inc.

Originally published in different form in the United States by Prima Publishing, Roseville, CA, and subsequently published in the United States by Three Rivers Press, an imprint of the Crown Publishing Group, a division of Random House, Inc., New York, in 2000.

Library of Congress Cataloging-in-Publication Data

Gold, LauraMaery.
    Homeschool your child for free / LauraMaery Gold and Joan M. Zielinski.—Rev. 2nd ed.
        p.   cm.
    Includes bibliographical references and index.
        1. Homeschooling—United States—Computer network resources—Handbooks, manuals, etc. 2. Internet in education—United States—Handbooks, manuals, etc. I. Zielinski, Joan M. II. Title.
LC40.G64 2009
371.04'2—dc22   2008050661

ISBN 978-0-307-45163-7

Printed in the United States of America

10 9 8 7 6 5 4 3 2 1

Revised Edition

This book is dedicated to my husband,
who rescues souls and sees to their education.
And to an entire houseful of L'il Darlin's
who homeschool us every day.

Contents

Foreword
by Kristine Farley

ARE YOU READY for a grand adventure?

In 1988, my second child was struggling with a kindergarten teacher who didn't like stragglers. A friend introduced me to homeschooling as a viable option. As I read books by John Holt, Raymond Moore, and others, I felt divinely directed to homeschool. I knew I could meet the needs of my children individually, and that we could be closer as a family. For us, homeschooling has become a lifestyle.

The world of homeschooling today is nothing like it was a couple of decades ago, when we started. LauraMaery's first homeschooling book opened the world of the Internet to me and showed me all the options that were available in cyberspace. Thanks to her, I now have almost *too* many options for materials, resources, and information.

Online resources have been a great supplement to our homeschooling effort. We have always homeschooled in an eclectic way, focusing on the children's and my interests and talents, as well as the flow of the seasons. By this I mean, our schooling takes a different twist in the late summer, when we put up the garden harvest. This becomes our unit study and a great time for us to talk.

The first week of October to late November, our studies become more academic in nature. During the holiday season we look for ways to improve our community and serve our fellow man. This sometimes has included making quilts for humanitarian aid, providing hands-on help with flood relief, coordinating donations of household items for natural-disaster victims, and coordinating and preparing Christmas Eve dinners for those in need.

After the New Year, we start another season of academic focus, along with a concentration on talent and interest projects. We use individual unit studies and hands-on activities and adventures. These have included Boy Scout merit badges, projects with our church's youth groups, tending animals, art, sports, crafts, and sewing.

Toward the end of April we begin another season of garden preparation and tending the newborn animals. Everyone has responsibilities and helps in their own way, and collectively we learn and grow—no pun intended.

The cycle of the seasons continues through the summer, with lots of outdoor projects, experiments, camping, and family fun.

The children are learning how to set goals and provide a good flow of different activities throughout the day. Sometimes children will become immersed in a particular study, and I have really tried to honor their "work" and not interrupt them. Other times, changing activities helps them to stay excited and motivated, because of the many projects they are allowed to juggle.

Throughout the year, the kids are reading books individually, and aloud to the family. Often, the books relate to what we are doing. Once, we read *Heidi* around a campfire by night while camping in the mountains, and, like Heidi, spent part of our days hiking and collecting herbs and berries.

The children in our large family have many different learning styles. We see both their strengths and their weaknesses as opportunities for learning. Reading works by pioneers such as Raymond Moore helped me to see that all of my children weren't going to be ready to read at four or five years old and that there are great benefits to developing in other ways at their own pace. As a result, we have had children who were reading by five and some that really didn't click until they were twelve or thirteen years old. That's okay, because God made each of us different, and as a homeschooling family we can each grow in our own way and in our own time.

With seven children, four grown to date, this has been a grand adventure that still excites me as a mom. I get to see children become independent, capable people who know who they are, know how to learn anything they want, and are successful in whatever they choose. I wouldn't trade our homeschooling life for anything.

Kristine Farley *is an author and homeschooling mom, as well as a master rapid eye technician and wellness coach. While she raises her family she operates Joyful Empowerment, her Web business. She lives with her children and her husband, Scott, on a mini-farm in the foothills of Mount Rainier.*

Introduction
to the Second Edition

SINCE THE FIRST edition of *Homeschool Your Child for Free,* our family has graduated four homeschoolers—all of whom are now in college and university and doing very well academically. They're even funding their own college costs (which makes us *very* proud!). Homeschooling your child for free actually works!

We continue to teach our children—even the ones in college, who still seek our academic advice from time to time—and we continue to do it without spending a penny. We love our library, and we love our co-op. But most of all, we love our freedom. We explore, we read, we use community resources, and we rely on the marvelous academic tools available to us online.

When we began our homeschooling journey, the Internet was barely a blip. The resources we used at the time were sparse, and most of them weren't very good.

Things have changed pretty dramatically in the intervening years. Now we're crazy about Wikipedia. (In fact, we generally edit at least half a dozen Wikipedia articles a week.) We love Yahoogroups and Google and a thousand other tools that didn't even rate a mention in the first edition.

In fact, there's so much available now that instead of helping you find something—anything—to teach a subject, we've spent months and months winnowing down the tens of thousands of possibilities.

Nearly every resource in this edition of *Homeschool Your Child for Free* is new. The resources are incredible, the information is deep, and the education will be meaningful.

This edition also uses much shorter URLs than we had in the first edition, making the book much easier to use.

We've also included several entirely new sections. In this edition, you'll find great tools for:

- free online courses
- public school partnering
- information literacy
- handwriting and penmanship
- business entrepreneurship
- culture and society
- graduating a homeschooler
- personal financial management
- life skills
- careers and vocational guidance

We've retained in this edition many of the interviews we conducted with professionals who work in the fields we discuss, as well as interviews with homeschooling parents who found success in teaching their children with free resources. Some of those people have moved on in their careers, and many of those parents have graduated their children and have moved on to the next stage of parenthood: watching adult children excel.

And believe us: With the strong foundation our kids received at home, this is turning out to be the best part of parenting. Join us in our journey to making cherished children into awesome adults.

—LMG
Kent, Washington

Conventions

THIS BOOK MAKES some assumptions about you and your homeschooled children:

- We assume that *you're seeking educational material for all ages.* The material here covers preschool to college. What you don't use this year will come in handy next year; if your youngest child is nearly ready to graduate, put the preschool material on the shelf for your grandchildren.

- While children come in male and female models, English doesn't. In this book, when we speak of a child, in the generic sense, we toss around some pronouns. Sometimes we use *he;* sometimes we use *she.* Except when we refer specifically to males or females, the pronouns are used alternately and interchangeably.

- We assume that because they're homeschooled, *your children may be more academically advanced than their peers are.* (Individual attention tends to have that effect on all children.) Therefore, we believe a majority of individually schooled teenagers are capable of learning well from material written at an early college level. Many of the resources in this book are designed for first- and second-year college students. Your intelligent teenager should be presented with this material, with the expectation that even if he doesn't absorb everything in a single sitting, he'll nevertheless broaden his understanding through the exposure.

- We assume *you want to cover specific subject matter* when you teach. That's why the resources in this book are grouped by curriculum area rather than by age.

- We assume *you are capable of monitoring your children's academic progress,* and you don't need day-to-day handholding to ensure that your children are making adequate educational advancement. We invite you to consider the curriculum material both for compliance, if that's an issue in your state, and for reassurance. We include in the appendix a suggested curriculum scope and sequence to help you get organized. But we don't recommend specific timetables in the belief that parents and children should make their own decisions about how and whether to incorporate their state's curriculum standards into their homeschooling.

- Who learns from the material in this book? We assume that *education is a group effort.* Whether the parent studies the material and teaches the child, or the child learns the material and reports back to the parent, the effort will educate everyone. Therefore, when we say *you,* we generally refer to the parent, while recognizing that in many families, it will be the children who take the lead in deciding how they'll be educated.

CREDITS

Much gratitude to the free URL redirector Tiny URL (**tinyurl.com**), which allowed us to convert long, complex Web addresses to something quick and easy. And yes, we made a donation to back up our thanks. The background information for some of the definitions, quotations, and biographies in this text are adapted from the following resources:

Bartleby   bartleby.com
> These include, specifically, the *American Heritage Dictionary of the English Language, Bartlett's Familiar Quotations, Columbia Encyclopedia,* and several others.

Biography   biography.com

Dictionary   dictionary.com

Easton's Bible Dictionary   eastonsbibledictionary.com

Merriam-Webster Online   m-w.com

Newbury House Online Dictionary   nhd.heinle.com

Web of Online Dictionaries   yourdictionary.com

Several of the people quoted in this text are current or former volunteers at:

Ask an Expert   askanexpert.com

All Experts   allexperts.com

Homeschool Reviews   tinyurl.com/hsreviews

HOMESCHOOL YOUR CHILD FOR FREE

Chapter 1

Why We Homeschool

ALL GOOD PARENTS homeschool their children. Some do it full time. Some do it part time in partnership with professional educators. And some do it while their kids are on break from traditional schools. If you teach your children at all, you homeschool.

Homeschoolers cut across all segments of the population. Although the movement is indisputably largest in the United States (reliable research puts the number of American homeschooled children at 1.5 million, or 1 to 2 percent of school-age children), Canadians, Europeans, and thousands of expatriated North American families in the military, in missionary service, in business, and in the civil service are also embracing homeschooling.

Homeschoolers advocate dozens of educational philosophies, ranging from strict school-at-home programs to militant unschooling. There are parents who have homeschooled from birth, parents who enroll their children in supplemental classes, and parents who embrace public or private school and supplement it with their own after-school and weekend programs.

While the homeschooling movement is often perceived as conservative in nature, a sizable number of homeschoolers are adamantly liberal. Homeschoolers cover the range of human experience. They include self-avowed

Hotlinks

Homeschool Your Child for Free!
hsfree.com

Homeschool Reviews
tinyurl.com/hsreviews

Homeschooling Step-by-Step
homeschoolsteps.com

"hippies," rural farm families, gay couples, single parents, grandparents, stepparents, and kindly aunts.

Some families homeschool in small church or neighborhood "co-ops," some are affiliated with charter or private schools, and some go it alone. Some homeschooling families are devoutly religious; some have no religious affiliation at all. The homeschooling community embraces Pagans and Catholics, Bahá'ís and Mormons, Buddhists and Sikhs, Jehovah's Witnesses and Protestant Christians, Hindus and serious atheists, Muslims and Jews.

Parents homeschool because their children are gifted, learning disabled, behavior disordered or easily overlooked, hyperactive, or just plain bored. Some parents homeschool because they feel undermined or unsafe. Most parents homeschool for smaller classes, individual attention, and customized curriculum. And most of all, parents homeschool their kids because they simply want to. Because they're good parents, and they believe it's the best thing for their children.

No matter how—or why—you homeschool, you're welcome here. And congratulations on choosing to teach your children both economically and intelligently.

Intelligently? Absolutely. In choosing this book, you're gaining access to thousands of resources that make up the best and most current information available anywhere. No stodgy, fifteen-year-old, out-of-date textbooks for your kids. By choosing to homeschool your child for free, you're also choosing to homeschool your child for *now.* For the world your child lives in today, rather than the world that existed in 1996, when many of her friends' out-of-date social studies and science textbooks were written. If you use this book properly, you'll also teach your sons and daughters how to find their independent way around modern technology to do the kind

☆ *Best Homeschooling Moment*

When kids come up to mine and say, "Aw, why don't you quit homeschooling and go to public school where you can make friends and have a social life?" I am pleased when my kids say, "Naw, I like homeschooling." Those are great moments.

—Rebecca Lynn Miller, homeschool mom who wants better life options for her kids, Hudson, Florida

of research and study that will make them successful in college and the business world.

By making wise, intelligent, frequent use of the Internet, you're teaching your children two things: one, that there are answers to all their questions, and two, that those answers are within their grasp. You'll teach them how to find information, how to work efficiently, how to avoid time-wasting dead ends, and how to focus on their educational goals. Do we guarantee that this book will make your child smarter? Yes, we do. Will your child be better off if he's homeschooled? Of course. Is homeschooling the answer to all your problems? Well . . .

Here's how it works. If you haven't yet been on the Internet, it's time to start. Visit your community library, recreation center, or YMCA and ask for assistance. In most North American locations, community Internet access is available for free. And you can get help from the librarian, the neighborhood computer geek, or a friendly family member. Ask your Designated Tutor to teach you two skills: surfing the Web and using email.

Once you know what you're doing, save yourself the headache of living at the library and get online at home. Bet you can do it for free! Here's how: There's someone in your neighborhood, congregation, or family who has an unused computer. (Our own family has to find a home for one of our old computers every year or so, as we upgrade the clunker for something more current.) Put the word out that you're looking for a PC, and offer to barter child care or some other skill in exchange for that computer. To our family, taking the computer off our hands and putting it to good use would be payment enough. Your cost may vary.

If you have your own computer, it's not hard to get online for free. Here are some options:

Juno   juno.com

Ten hours of free online time each month and a 1G email account. Access from all fifty U.S. states. It's advertising-supported, which slows down access somewhat.

NetZero   netzero.net

Offers ten hours of free access each month. It works in fifty U.S. states. Like Juno, it's advertising-supported.

Free Internet Access Providers
emailaddresses.com/email_internet.htm

Here you can find free ISPs around the world, including several regional U.S. providers. You'll also find reviews and listings for other free services.

Readers with laptop computers have even better options. Free high-speed wireless Internet access is available in nearly every community in North America, and most cities around the world. Here's how to find a nearby wi-fi hotspot:

WiFi Hotspot List   wi-fihotspotlist.com

A directory of public hotspots for wireless Internet access. Type in an address, and the site searches for the nearest wi-fi point.

WiFi FreeSpot   wififreespot.com

Another directory of public hotspots. This one is organized by U.S. state, and lists only those spots that provide free Internet access.

Whether you have your own Internet access or not, you can get free email from any connected computer. The advantage of using web-based email is that you can check your mail from any computer. Hundreds of organizations provide free web-based email accounts; these sites are my personal favorites. Visit one to set up your own free account:

Doramail   doramail.com

Email server with organizational tools. Calendar, homepage builder, greeting cards, and more. Easy sign up, easy to use.

Gmail   gmail.com

Relatively clean interface, good spam filters. Hugely popular.

Inbox   inbox.com

Absolute favorite. Easy sign-up, an incredible thirty gigs of online storage, spam filtering, easy-to-remember domain name. Plus, it's relatively unknown, so whatever name you want is probably available.

Lycos Mail   lycosmail.com

Cleanest interface, relatively unknown, easy sign-up. Stores up to 3G of email and attachments. Also provides voice mail and instant messaging services

To make good use of all the free resources in the book, you'll also need good software. Until recently, free software consisted mostly of single-purpose shareware utilities that provided pop-up clocks and calendars, or fixed your non-working mouse. Today, though, free software has grown up. Full suites of software are available in two formats: online and down-loadable. You choose.

Google Docs   docs.google.com

Everyone's talking about Google Docs. There's a reason Microsoft wanted to buy the company. Docs includes a web-based word processor, spreadsheet, and presentation tool, with more to come.

Thinkfree   thinkfree.com

Thinkfree is the least known of the three major online suites, but it claims to have the best integration with Microsoft products. The interfaces will be more familiar to Office users.

Zoho   zoho.com

An entire suite of business software, free, online, ready to go. Word processor, spreadsheet, database . . . it's all there. And more. How do they do this without charging?

Best Homeschooling Moment

The best moments for me happen when my children thank me for bringing them home to learn. It is exciting to see them become excited about learning again.

—Patty Wiens, Christian homeschool mom to six, Saskatoon, Saskatchewan

☆
*Best
Homeschooling
Moment*

We were discussing the possibility of adopting a child from the foster care system. I mentioned that a number of kids are ADHD and have behavioral problems and trouble in school. My ten-year-old son cocked his head and said, "Well, just get them out of school and homeschool them! It worked for me, didn't it?"

—**Darlene Pineda**, an intelligent, liberal family person, Elizabeth City, North Carolina

Open Office   openoffice.org

Downloadable suite of software that runs on almost any platform, including Macintosh, and is comparable to Microsoft Office. It includes word processing, spreadsheets, presentations, graphics, databases, and more.

StarOffice   sun.com/software/star

Word processor, database, spreadsheet, presentation, and drawing suite. Free to students and faculty. Runs on Windows, Linux, or Solaris platforms.

Lotus Symphony   symphony.lotus.com

The third of the three major downloadable suites. Includes a word processor, spreadsheet, and presentation application.

Now you're set to Homeschool Your Child For Free! This book focuses on four main areas. Chapters 2 and 3 give you the lowdown on homeschooling. In chapter 2, you'll find solutions to all kinds of homeschooling issues. Chapter 3 helps you pull together a full homeschool curriculum, from preschool through pre-college. Chapters 4 through 6 examine the essentials of education: readin', writin', and 'rithmetic. Chapters 7 through 11 provide a full liberal-arts education: art, history, music, social studies, and humanities. In the subsequent two chapters, 12 and 13, you'll find the hard sciences. Finally, we offer graduation guidance: a chapter on college admissions, careers, and independent living/home economics. From cradle to adulthood, your child will be homeschooled for free! Want more? The following resources are associated with this book, and will supplement and update the material you're holding in your hands. As long as this edition is in print, these resources will be available to you:

Homeschool Your Child for Free!   hsfree.com

The largest homeschool database on the Net. Thousands of sites—reviewed, rated, and updated regularly. As an owner of the most current edition of this book, you can register for access to the site, submit your own resources, search for help, participate in the Homeschool for Free discussion area, and locate additional resources.

Homeschool Reviews   tinyurl.com/hsreviews

The mailing list for homeschooling using free curriculum and educational resources. Members who contribute to the list may be eligible to win a free copy of the next edition of *Homeschool Your Child for Free*!

Homeschooling Step-by-Step   homeschoolsteps.com

The companion book to *Homeschool Your Child for Free*. Topics we touch on briefly in this survey of free homeschooling resources are covered in-depth in *Homeschooling Step-by-Step*. How to run the legal gauntlet, the finances of single-income homeschooling, creating your own curriculum materials, and developing a learning environment, along with scores of approaches to and philosophies of homeschooling that will exactly meet your family's needs at every stage of your homeschooling experience. Find an excerpt from *Step-by-Step* in the appendix at the back of this book.

Chapter 2

Homeschool How-To's

THERE ARE TWO kinds of homeschooling families: those who approach it as a right and a duty, and those who come to homeschooling out of necessity or out of frustration with the alternatives. Because of the great support available through publications, homeschool groups, and most of all, the Internet, it doesn't take long for those in the second category to convert to the first. And the successes their children experience in homeschool keep them coming back for more.

Joey Easley, a homeschooled teen from Gig Harbor, Washington, is an example of the success of homeschooling. Joey was homeschooled for the final nine years of his primary and secondary education and then went on to attend a local community college. This is Joey's take on the homeschooling experience: "Homeschooling has been great for me. Now that I am going to a community college I have been able to understand better the ups and downs of homeschooling. Probably the biggest plus for me was going at my own pace. Having to sit through sometimes weeks of class learning stuff I already knew was very frustrating. Then again, sometimes the class got going too fast and I got left behind. Another reason I

Hotlinks

Greenlance
greenlance.com

Homeschool FAQs
tinyurl.com/hsfaqs

Homeschool Journal
homeschooljournal.net

WikiHow Homeschooling
tinyurl.com/catehs

think homeschooling is so great is that it is more focused on just learning, and not on finding out how much you already know.

"The downside, of course, is the social aspect. I have been very blessed because I have so many friends who were homeschooled. If we did our work fast enough, we could get done at noon and play the rest of the day. We also have homeschool sports clubs in which I played soccer and basketball; I also have friends who played varsity sports at the local high school. So I was not lacking at all in my social interactions.

"I think homeschooling gives me the advantage over public-schoolers because I can focus more on the things that I think (actually, my mother usually makes the decisions) would be the most useful in my life, and I get to skip things that might be useful for others but have no relevance to me."

This chapter is your initiation into homeschool. In the next chapter of this book you'll begin building a curriculum and learn about various homeschooling philosophies; in subsequent chapters, you'll find resources for every academic area you'll encounter as a homeschooler.

In this chapter, though, you'll begin your homeschool journey by learning about some of the most important issues facing homeschoolers, and finding supportive answers for your questions and dilemmas. We start with a discussion of Internet safety. We then introduce some useful teaching skills, and discuss ways to motivate reluctant homeschoolers. The subsequent sections of this chapter cover homeschooling difficulties, legal issues, standardized testing, socialization, and three kinds of support: real-life support groups, email lists, and various sorts of electronic "boards."

First, though, an introduction to homeschooling. These resources introduce homeschooling, explain its appeal, and show you how to get started. Bon voyage!

10 Steps to Achieving Your Goals   lifeexcellence.com/workshop.htm
A strategy for setting and achieving goals. It's a good framework for developing your own life plan.

Active Learning Practices for Schools (ALPS)
learnweb.harvard.edu/alps/home

A Harvard University resource that will help you determine your own educational philosophies and implement them in your teaching.

Are You Considering Homeschooling?
whywehomeschool.com/hsconsider.htm

A ten-step action plan for getting started as a homeschooler. Christian oriented.

Commonly Asked Questions About Homeschooling
elainemcewan.com/hscaq.htm

An excellent list of advantages of homeschooling, along with a list of drawbacks and solutions.

Determining Your Educational Philosophy
angelfire.com/al3/merchandise/determine.html

Despite the misleading title, this article classifies homeschoolers into four groups, and suggests parents should approach homeschooling based on their family's convictions, values, and needs.

Develop a Strategy for Successful Homeschooling
crosswalk.com/homeschool

One of many channels on the Christian web portal Crosswalk. The homeschooling channel sponsors an active discussion forum and publishes well-done articles on teaching from home.

Goal Setting   mindtools.com/page6.html

Six succinct articles on goal setting, including one on why you should even bother setting goals. Consider doing an entire unit study on goal setting, making this your starting point for learning.

Greenlance   greenlance.com

Regular reviews of the "Best of the 'Net." Greenlance tracks family-friendly resources made to benefit grown-ups. The site reviews many educational resources, as well as resources for responsible parents and competent adults who need to run a home and family. If the writing seems familiar, perhaps it's because the site belongs to yours truly. If a site interests this homeschooling mom, it'll probably interest you, too.

Homeschool FAQs   tinyurl.com/hsfaqs

Frequently asked questions about homeschooling. It's brimming with good advice for newbies and for everyone else.

Homeschool Issues & Concerns
homeschooloasis.com/article_chart.htm

Visit the Homeschool Issues and Concerns link first. One article documents the regrets of a family that didn't homeschool. What they learned, and why they wouldn't do the same thing again. Another about eight motivations for homeschooling. Much to contemplate in this list of questions.

Homeschool Journal   homeschooljournal.net

Click the Member Directory link for access to an overwhelming number of homeschooling blogs—online journals where homeschool families report their journeys. You'll want to bookmark this one.

How Do We Get Started in Homeschooling?   tinyurl.com/hsstart

Six steps to effective Christian homeschooling. This is a formal approach that includes membership in a national organization and keeping a clean home.

School Choices   schoolchoices.org

Here's the research that demonstrates that school choice works, and that private education is more effective than public. Lots of articles, essays, and information on getting politically active in protecting your right to homeschool.

The Ten Most Important Things
homeschool.com/articles/mostimportant

Elizabeth Kanna responds to ten common concerns about homeschooling. An inspirational list.

Things I Wish I Had Known   tinyurl.com/thingshs

A Christian family describes what they'd do differently if they were just starting out. This mom found solace in the knowledge that God was directing her path.

Why Homeschool?   eho.org/why_homeschool

A nice collection of reassuring articles on why homeschooling is a good option. The author explains, "These resources are especially presented for those who are considering whether homeschooling is the right choice for their family."

WikiHow Homeschooling   tinyurl.com/catehs

WikiHow is younger than Wikipedia, but has the same noble goal: articles written by a community of volunteers. Read what others have said about homeschooling topics such as "How to Overcome Opposition to Homeschooling" and "How to Homeschool Yourself," then contribute your own guidelines and advice.

Internet Safety

Safety: From the Latin *salvus* (safe). To be secure from danger, risk, or harm.

YOU'VE HEARD THE horror stories. And they've probably scared you, right?

You can relax. It really is safe to go back in the cyberwater.

There are lots of good reasons why the Internet is actually a safe place for your children.

First and foremost, there's the fact that you are their parent. As a homeschooler, you already know the importance of being involved in your children's lives. Is there any real chance *your* child has a stash of weapons in the garden shed in preparation for blowing up the neighborhood?

The second safety net is related. You have taught them right from wrong, right? Many homeschooled parents report that their children are more chary of inappropriate Internet sites than they are themselves. The policy in our home has always been: "Everyone's allowed to make mistakes, to accidentally open a bad website, so long as you immediately come tell me about it. But if I find bad things in your online history, we'll have a real problem." The rare times my kids opened inappropriate websites, they made a beeline to let me know. I'd block the domain, and we maintained peace in our home.

North Carolina homeschooler Terri Vitkovitsky has a strategy for keeping her kids safe. "Keeping my kids safe on the Internet is definitely a concern. I don't really feel I should keep them from the Internet altogether because this is really a skill they need in the modern world. First off, we try to keep the computer in a visible location. We bought a rolling computer cart from IKEA, and strapped down the monitor and CPU. This way if the kids have computer time, it can be where I am and I have some control. Our computer is also password-protected, so the kids have to ask permission and have me unlock it before they can use it—this way I know they are on it. They are only allowed to go to websites we have given them permission to go to."

Missourian Lori Ramey has stronger advice: "Get a filter! We use one, and we love it." But that's not enough, she says. "Even with a filter, it is important to be with your children when they are online. They can accidentally wander somewhere they don't want to be in a moment. Plus being with them gives you an opportunity to gain insight into what they are interested in and to discuss anything that might come up that concerns or confuses them."

For Tristi Pinkston of Orem, Utah, filters have a downside. "It's impossible to keep them totally safe. Things pop up all the time. You can get a good filter, but as your children get older and start learning about racism and the Holocaust and other topics that the filters find disturbing, they won't be able to access information because of the filters." Her solution? Information. "When your children reach that age, I think that information is the best line of

Hotlinks

Be Cybersmart!
cybersmartcurriculum.org

GetNetWise
getnetwise.org

McGruff
mcgruff.com

The Internet and Your Child
theinternetandyourchild
.org

defense. Talk to them about the dangers on the Internet. Explain to them what they might see so that as soon as it comes up, they can get out of it. Tell them to reach out and shut off the monitor immediately, rather than trying to click out of it—often, the sites that come up are hard to click out of, and they've gotten an eyeful while trying to click. If they are taught to flip off the monitor, they'll see a lot less. And, of course, keep the computer in a high-traffic area in your home. You should always be nearby when your children are on the Internet. If your teen has a computer in their room, it should not have Internet access."

Maryland mom Diana Malament controls access at the connection point. "Download what you want to use and then disconnect the computer from the modem." She also finds it useful to set time boundaries. "Schedule specific limits (half an hour each day), and stick with them. Know who your child's online friends are. It might be best to have them communicate only with people they know in everyday life. Use screen savers with a password when your kids are not allowed on the Internet. If they need to use computer for schoolwork, just disconnect the Internet."

Controlling children's email access is a safety concern for homeschooler Cheryl Lemily of Colorado. "We all have the same email account, so I know who is sending mail to my son. I'm sure as he gets older and needs more privacy, he will get his own account, but we, as his parents, reserve the right to monitor it."

The following list contains some great carefully vetted tools for teaching your own kids to be safe on the Net.

Be Cybersmart!   cybersmartcurriculum.org

Lesson plans, videos, and other curriculum materials for teaching Internet safety. Safe kids are able to engage in creative inquiry, collaboration, and critical thinking.

Common Sense Media   commonsensemedia.org

Great reviews on hundreds of websites for school-age children. It provides a "content" rating system for all forms of media, including movies and music.

Connect Safely   connectsafely.org

A discussion forum, safety tips, and videos make this site worth reading with your kids.

Definitions of Privacy   tinyurl.com/defpriv

A lesson plan about the dangers of camera cell phones and the importance of protecting privacy.

GetNetWise   getnetwise.org

If you're worried about online safety, you must get netwise. Educate yourself and your children about using the Internet safely with videos and tools for reporting trouble.

K9 Web Protection   k9webprotection.com

An award-winning free Internet filtering program. It will filter content for your family.

McGruff   mcgruff.org

An informative website with tips and advice for talking to your children about the Internet. The site includes many fun safety games for children, along with stories and videos geared toward children.

Onguard Online.Gov   onguardonline.gov

The federal government and the technology industry join together to create tips for Internet safety. They even provide a few interactive "games" to help you avoid predators, fraud, and identity theft.

Safety Land   tinyurl.com/safetyland

Animated game with music and fun lessons teaching kids how to be safe online.

Surfer Beware   surferbeware.com

Shares tips on avoiding "digital hacking" and other perils that we run into as we and our children surf the Internet.

Teaching Internet Safety

Make sure that the computers are in a place where they can be watched and not in the child's bedroom. Sit with them and help them explore websites. Bookmark some of their favorite sites. Place filters through the use of software that will not let them gain access to certain websites. Periodically check where they have gone on the Web and discuss your findings for inappropriate sites.

—LA, wife of one and an M.O.M. (mother of many), Flint, Michigan

---

Teen Chat Decoder   **teenchatdecoder.com**

Finally you can decode what your teens are saying online! This site also provides articles related to teens on the Internet. Very informative.

The Internet and Your Child   **theinternetandyourchild.org**

A wonderful nonprofit organization that offers free classes taught by law enforcement officers and computer professionals. The classes cover hacking, fraud, email, sex crimes, chat rooms, and more. A must for any family with a computer.

Teaching Tips

Advice: From the Middle French *avis* (opinion). Counsel regarding an issue or a course of action.

JOYCE DOWLING, A graduated homeschooling mother of two from Prince George's County, Maryland, has something to say to parents who are afraid they can't teach their children: "If you can be a good parent, you can be a good homeschooling parent. After all, what kind of training did you have for parenting?"

Robin Goddard, raising a family of eight children in Washington state, has advice for new homeschoolers: Relax. "We've changed lots through the years and used different methods and techniques as our children have gotten older and our family has grown. I guess the most important 'technique' we've used is flexibility!"

Brenda Ulrich also homeschools a crowd. For her, teaching is a different adventure with each child. "Because I have six kids with six different personalities, I use different techniques for each," says this Washington mom. "I have some who can learn just about anything by reading a book, some who need to 'see' things to understand, and some who learn best when they can do it 'hands-on.' I've gone from very structured, to completely unstructured, to somewhere in the middle over the past eleven years and will continue to change as I see my kids' needs change."

Still worried that it's too hard? Here's a ninth-grader from the Middle East who's got it all figured out. R. J. Artty's parents are homeschoolers. English is not his first language, but his advice to parents is brilliant:

1. Always start by explaining.
2. Maintain eye contact to see whether the child is keeping up or not.
3. Head nodding does not necessarily mean that the child has understood. Other signs that the child is not focusing include repeated words like "Uh-huh, yeah, go on, I'm listening."
4. Watch out for the glazed-eye expression.
5. Do not bore your child with endless talk.
6. Try making as few mistakes as possible while teaching (i.e., go through what you say before you say it).
7. Never explain anything unless you fully understand it.
8. Do not allow your child to start fidgeting with things.
9. If your child starts to shift position while sitting, this means your child has not understood a word you said, or your child is having a hard time keeping up.
10. To make sure the child understands what you are saying, ask him a few questions while explaining what was previously said.
11. Avoid asking yes-or-no questions.
12. Keep your explanations as simple as possible and your sentences straightforward.
13. Explain things by rank of difficulty—that is, start with the basics and the easiest stuff.
14. Try to be as creative as possible when explaining or asking questions (this depends on the child's age).
15. Never stay too long on one subject.

Kentucky homeschooler Jessica Murphy advises homeschoolers to stay flexible: "Many of the ideas I have are from books that I have read

Hotlinks

A to Z Home's Cool
homeschooling
.gomilpitas.com

A to Z Teacherstuff Tips
atozteacherstuff.com/Tips

Homemade Art Supplies
artistshelpingchildren.org/
homemade.html

Teaching Tips Index
tinyurl.com/ttindex

about how this person or that person homeschooled. I take what seems like it will fit for us and modify or drop as needed. It is a little harder than following a set schedule or curriculum, but it works for us, for now. So I guess my advice would be to have fun and think about how everything we do each day can prepare our children for the future. Trust yourself but get the help you need when you need it; don't wait and then give up and trust the public school system to catch them up. It will just be heartache for all involved, in my opinion."

Robin Tompkins is philosophical about her homeschooling routines. "The first thing I did was establish a daily routine and schedule," reports the mother of two from Redding, California. "This included teaching the kids to be responsible for getting themselves ready (with some prompting), making their beds, and taking turns feeding our dogs. To encourage them to do this, I made up a job chart. Each morning they got to put on a sticker for each job completed. After about two months they forgot about the stickers, and now they usually fulfill their responsibilities without complaining."

Robin's homeschooling schedule is certainly not set in stone: "We aim to start 'school' at 9 A.M. each morning, but if we don't get started until later or are ready earlier, that works.

"I had to become more flexible so as to make myself easier to live with and make learning a fun experience. I started by writing a weekly lesson plan, which works for us very well. It was especially helpful in the beginning to keep us all on track with the learning goals for the day—though again, I have become more flexible with this and allow the educational interests of the kids to take us away from the plan."

Gina Marie (Wellman) Haugh of Tracy, California, has a practical tip for homeschooling. This is how she deals with homeschoolers who are often "on the road" during school hours: "This is my first year homeschooling. One thing I did was buy each boy a two- or three-inch binder. I cut the bindings from all the workbooks and materials that I don't have to return. Then I three-hole-punched all the pages and inserted them in the binder behind divider tabs. In the front is a tab separator for each day of the week. I go through the materials in the back of each binder and pull out the pages for each day, then put them behind each day's tab. If they have a spelling test or something to write, I add blank binder paper so they have everything (except for reading books) right there. We are in the car a lot, and it's hard to carry all their books with them. This way they just have mostly their binder with all the work and the reading books they need."

Ready to try a few homeschooling tricks of your own? We recommend consulting our companion book, *Homeschooling Step-by-Step* (**tinyurl.com/hssteps**), for in-depth explanations of more than a hundred approaches and techniques for homeschooling. To get you started, though, consider the lifesaving homeschooling advice available from the following resources:

101 Teaching Tips   help4teachers.com/tips.htm

Classroom-oriented, but most of these tips are easily adapted to the homeschool setting. An example: Use fabric, rather than butcher paper, for bulletin boards. You can hang up student work and take it down without all the pinholes that you would see in paper, "and when it gets too dirty, just wash it!" Another favorite: "Hot-glue the lids of a package of colored markers to the inside of a tuna can. The markers stay together that way and you don't lose so many lids."

A to Z Home's Cool   homeschooling.gomilpitas.com

Ann Zeise's venerable homeschooling site has been around for years, and it just gets better with time. Up-to-date information on homeschooling laws, statistics, events, and news is just the beginning. The tone is encouraging; the site is inclusive. Definitely a top-ten resource.

A-to-Z Teacherstuff Tips   atozteacherstuff.com/Tips

Though most of these tips are classroom-oriented, they're easily adaptable to homeschooling. This is part of the massive A-to-Z site

---

Homeschool Discounts

Most office supply and book stores offer discounts to homeschoolers. Bring in proof of homeschooling (your letter of intent will do) for a 10- to 20-percent discount on educational materials.

that houses thousands of online teaching resources. Go to the home-page to find links to themes, printables, lesson plans, tools, and more.

Activity Search   eduplace.com/activity

Searchable database of 400-plus original K-through-8 classroom activities and lesson plans for teachers and parents. Search for activities by both curriculum area and grade level, or browse activities by theme.

CAL Learning Strategies   muskingum.edu/~cal/database

A large database of strategies for approaching education. Organized by academic topic, by target age, by role, and by general strategies. Includes entries as diverse as memorization strategies, college options, and developing flowcharts in chemistry.

Funderstanding   tinyurl.com/engagekids

This site has virtually everything you want to know about education. The various teaching theories, influences, and history of public education are all covered.

Homehearts   homehearts.com

A website that clearly explains different styles of homeschooling. It offers information on the basics in choosing curriculum, networking, scheduling, and organization. A congenial site that makes everyone feel welcome.

Homemade Art Supplies   artistshelpingchildren.org/homemade.html

How to make your own paste, finger paint, watercolors, sticking gum, sidewalk chalk, play dough, and cookie crayons. What a great means to a good end!

Homeschool Lifetips   homeschool.lifetips.com

A collection of tips and advice for new homeschooling families. Sort of a graffiti board of good advice, most of which could fit on an index card.

Learning Style Survey   psuonline.pdx.edu/learnstyle

How do your children learn best? Are they primarily auditory, visual, or kinesthetic learners? Use this site to assess their learning styles, for free! Then learn how to incorporate learning styles into your teaching.

Meddy Bemps   meddybemps.com

To put it simply, this site makes learning fun and they show you how to make it fun, too!

Methodology vs. Content in Teaching

garlikov.com/teaching/dialogue.html

A lengthy debate over whether it's more important to know how to teach, or what to teach. While neither one can stand alone, this is a solid argument that a prepared parent can teach.

Montessori at Home   tinyurl.com/monthome

A fabulous site about "Montessoricizing" your home. The second half of this long page, under the headline "Organizing the Home," is bursting with advice for organizing every room of your home to be educational and child-friendly.

Multiple Intelligences   edwebproject.org/edref.mi.intro.html

This overview of Howard Gardner's theory of multiple intelligences is a must for every parent. It will guide you in understanding how your child learns best. It's one of scores of theories about learning styles. Learning styles are covered in depth in *Homeschooling Step-by-Step* (see Appendix).

Teaching Academic Basics

teachinghome.com/started/basics/academic.cfm

Advice for teaching reading, writing, math, higher math, and literature. Excerpts from various articles from *The Teaching Home*.

On Scheduling

"In studies, whatsoever a man commandeth upon himself, let him set hours for it."

—Francis Bacon, essayist

Teaching History   angelfire.com/al3/merchandise/history.html

Tips for teaching history in a homeschool setting. Uses various approaches, including storytelling, timelines, geography, and several others.

Teaching Tips Index   tinyurl.com/ttindex

Click the Teaching Tips Index link to view an online handbook for new teachers at the University of Hawaii. It's a complete guide to classroom teaching, but most of the material will be very helpful in motivating and preparing a home educator. Covers learning styles, teacher organization, teaching techniques, and much more.

The Feltboard Is Your Friend   bright.net/~double/feltbo.htm

Feltboards: A great teaching tool. It's inexpensive, fun, and infinitely versatile.

Tips for Arguing Siblings   contentmentacres.com/arguing.htm

Advice for Christian families dealing with bickering children.

VistaPrint   vistaprint.com

You're running a school. Make it official with free business cards, rubber stamps, address labels, announcements, and more. I can't pretend to understand the business model, but that won't stop me from taking free stuff when it's offered.

Motivators

SOME TIME AGO, a frustrated homeschooler asked me for advice. "How do you motivate kids who do not wish to learn?" she asked. "My eleven- and fourteen-year-olds act like everything is too hard, when they are very intelligent."

I had a different idea. Kids love to learn, I told her. What they're not fond of is work. That left her two options for teaching her children:

1. Persuade them that they love to work.
2. Modify the work so that it becomes something they love.

My advice to this mom? Do both. Let them learn that work is important and has intrinsic value. That a sense of accomplishment is rewarding. That work is critical to the development of character.

Motivate: From the Late Latin *motivus* (motion). To compel, induce, or incite to action.

At the same time, I said, bribe them. New York home-schooler Teena Brayen agrees. "I motivate my children by setting goals and a reward system. They especially like the field trip learning experiences, so as a reward for studying I plan a field trip for them and make it something to strive for. I also let them sign up for local sports for homeschooled children, and they really like the interaction and enjoy the time to be around peers of their same age. They also go places with the church group, but only if they have their studies up to date."

At this age, kids are still motivated by gold stars and points . . . but those gold stars and points must accumulate toward something meaningful. Start small: One day's uncomplaining work results in a new trading card or an hour of computer time. Make their "attitude" a critical component of being rewarded.

Melinda Penberthy has incentives down to a science. "We have set up a 100 percent paper graph. We have set rewards for doing an assignment correctly. We start with simple things like an extra snack or thirty minutes later bedtime for one paper, to lunch at the park and a day at the water park for more good marks collected. She collected twenty marks for a field trip. We went on a train ride (neither of us had ever been on a train) and went to Kansas City to the museum. It was fantastic." The Missouri mom recognizes that the system has its limits, though: "Of course we probably won't do that for each collection of papers, but we negotiate for what she wants to do and how many papers we think would be reasonable for it. She par-

Hotlinks

Cardboard Cognition
tinyurl.com/cardcog

Free Certificates, Period
dyetub.com

Tiger Woods' Start Something
tigerwoodsfoundation.org

ticipates in helping set up the goals, what it takes to accomplish them, and then how hard she wants to work to get to them. Then of course there are times like yesterday that we throw in a freebie and go to the park to walk the creek for some rock collecting and personal growth time—no grading involved."

Another key to success: Look for ways to encourage them to motivate one another. If the fourteen-year-old teaches the eleven-year-old how to convert fractions to decimals by noon, they both get out of doing dishes that night. This way the older child gets the math down cold, and the eleven-year-old learns to cooperate. Interdependence builds families.

"Where there is ignorance," wrote Epictetus, "there is also want of learning."

Do your children "want" learning?

Set priorities and stick to them, says Erin Goldberg, a homeschooler from Kentucky. "Praise when they do well. We always do our studies before they can play or have free time to choose their own activities."

Jo-Ann Sturko is preparing to become a teacher in Edmonton, Canada. She has several ideas for motivating reluctant learners: "Children enjoy learning when the topic being taught is relevant to them. If they can see how it can be applied to their lives in a real-world context, they are more likely to find the learning experience engaging and meaningful. When given the opportunity to learn in a 'hands-on' way, information is more easily stored and recalled for future experiences. An example of this is teaching multiple math concepts through visits to the grocery store.

"Hypothetical activity: Give your child a grocery list (a simple one for younger children, a more complex one for older children). The child must go through the store, find the items listed, and figure out the final cost, either by estimating or by using a calculator. Be sure to include multiples of items to allow for multiplication. This lesson will also qualify as a reading and language-development activity as the child reads labels and chooses the correct products."

Homeschooling mom Gita Schmitz has her own ideas about motivating homeschoolers, especially those who have spent some time in the public school system. "Parents who decide to homeschool after having their kids in public school for a number of years often find their children don't want to do anything, don't care about anything, and are basically do-nothings—for a while. The experience of traditional school squashes the interest they used to have. There are many reasons why this happens, but my point is that it's completely normal, and the common idea is to just let them be. They need to decompress and detoxify themselves from school. After several months or even a year of this, they start asking questions again and showing some interest in life, as they used to. And that means they're ready to homeschool."

Lori Ramey uses games and other activities to get her children enthusiastic about education. "I try very hard to keep school fun," says the Missouri mother of five. "We do a lot of hands-on activities, as well as some play-acting and singing songs."

If you're wondering how to get your unmotivated scholar excited about academics, these resources can help:

123 Certificates   123certificates.com

Certificate maker for progress in school, sports, Christian Sunday school classes, participation, hard work, and every other achievement. Fantastic graphics, fully customizable.

Academic Competitions   tinyurl.com/acadcomp

Let a bit of competition motivate your child. Get involved in any of scores of academic competitions in the arts, the sciences, mathematics, and nearly every other academic area. This list keeps track of what's happening on the competition front.

Back-to-School Party   tinyurl.com/backparty

Start the new homeschooling year on the right foot with a back-to-homeschool party. Fun games and other ideas for starting the year off right. Works just as well in January or June as it does in September.

Teaching Freebie

Get Involved! How Parents and Families Can Help Their Children Do Better in School is adaptable to homeschoolers. Call 877-4-ED-PUBS and request the pamphlet by name.

Cardboard Cognition   tinyurl.com/cardcog

Do your kids love board games as much as mine do? Click the Cardboard Cognition link on the left, and find a hundred or more educational board games you can make at home. Directions, printable game boards, and everything you need to educate your kids with games.

Center for Talented Youth Talent Search   cty.jhu.edu

If your children have to sit those awful tests anyway, might as well put the results to use. Johns Hopkins Center for Talented Youth identifies, assesses, recognizes, and provides educational opportunities for mathematically and/or verbally talented seventh- and eighth-graders. The site lists acceptable tests (it's a comprehensive list), and the competition also accepts parent nomination forms for students who don't have test scores available.

Cogito   cogito.org

Click the Academic Competitions link on the left for a comprehensive list of, primarily, science competitions, but also of competitions in other disciplines. Links to the National Geographic Bee, the Science Olympiad, and Model UN are among the listings.

Free Certificates, Period   dyetub.com

Certify that your child is wonderful, or hardworking, or any other attribute worth remembering. Use it to create diplomas, certificates of completion, and certificates of merit, recognition, or achievement.

Fun Brain   funbrain.com

Learning games based on grade level, or organized by curriculum area.

Hard Work and High Expectations   tinyurl.com/hardwork

Studies have shown that rewarding outstanding effort rather than academic accomplishment encourages effort by all students. These articles support this theory. Interesting reading that'll make you think.

Homebodies   homebodies.org

A community devoted to encouraging stay-at-home parents. Homebodies.org answers all your questions from finances to organization.

Kids Are Authors   scholastic.com/bookfairs/contest

Several contests, including Kids Are Authors, where children create a 21- to 29-page picture book, and compete for prizes worth $9,000. Children are required to work in teams of at least three. For grades K through 8.

Motivating Students   teaching.berkeley.edu/bgd/motivate.html

Tools for motivating your child. "There is no single magical formula for motivating students," the authors acknowledge. But here are some strategies worth trying.

National History Day Competition   nationalhistoryday.org

A year-long education program that culminates in a national contest every June. The top senior contestant wins a scholarship worth $75,000. For students in grades 6 through 12, including homeschoolers. More than 2 million students participate each year, and the program is supported by the National Endowment for the Humanities.

Parent Send-Home Activities
teacher.scholastic.com/lessonrepro/sendhome

Lots of ideas for homemade educational activities. Great fun!

Scholastic Art & Writing Awards   scholastic.com/artandwriting

For young artists and writers, in grades 7 to 12, to receive recognition and rewards for their creative achievements. Winners receive recognition, cash awards, and college scholarships.

Tiger Woods' Start Something   tigerwoodsfoundation.org

Click the Tiger's Action Plan link to access golfer Tiger Woods' curriculum for helping kids set goals, lead, and create positive changes. The self-study guide encourages youth to think about the direction of their lives and plan their futures.

Toshiba/NSTA ExploraVision Awards Program   exploravision.org

Imagine the Future competition with tens of thousands of dollars in prizes. For grades K through 12. Homeschoolers are explicitly welcome to participate. Visit links to see winning entries from previous years.

What Kids Can Do   whatkidscando.org

Articles meant to inspire our youth. Amazing stories of amazing young people. Would be great to see additional stories submitted by homeschoolers. Hint, hint!

What Really Motivates Students?   middleweb.com/StdntMotv.html

Great article about cultivating your middle-school student's curiosity.

Dealing with Difficulties

Difficult: From the Latin *difficilis* (*dis* [not] + *facile* [easy]). That which requires great effort to overcome.

DOES THE THOUGHT of teaching your children at home frighten you? Ever grow weary of the daily grind? Be honest: Do your bickering children sometimes get on your last nerve? Many of the homeschooling parents I've talked with say their biggest discouragement is children who are sometimes sulky, sometimes argumentative, and sometimes cruel to one another.

What works for us? Our children are not permitted to fight. They often debate, and sometimes do so in loud voices, but if they ever get close to a fight, they sit knee-to-knee on the back porch or in the garage or a small bathroom, where they are required to talk peaceably together until they arrive at a mutually acceptable solution.

I foresee that when kids don't learn to get along as children, they'll end up as divorced adults, living alone under a bridge. That's why this problem-solving thing is one of my Parental Articles of Faith. People sometimes express amazement at how well my kids get along with one another, but I assure you, it's not because they're good kids. It's because they've been forced by the evil mommy to resolve their differences. Since they've learned that no problem is irresolvable, what's not to get along? I never suggest solutions anymore, mostly because I've learned I don't really know the dynamics of the problem. Nine times out of ten, when I listen in on their back-porch resolutions, it turns out that one or both is actually unhappy over something entirely unrelated to what they were debating in the kitchen. Most of the time, they work out some elaborate "deal" to satisfy one another, the mechanics of which I never fathom.

Our base rule: You don't come back into the family area until you're both happy. That way, bullying, name-calling, and criticizing get no truck. Doing so just annoys the sibling, delays the resolution, and causes your feet to get tired! They always return to the house happy and laughing, the problem long forgotten, and excited about whatever new project they've devised.

I have three cautions: First, when I suspect my every-thing's-a-joke-to-me twelve-year-old is refusing to solve the problem just so he can force his older brother to stand out on the porch for a long time, I tell him he has to participate with his hands on his head. That gets old really fast, and he quickly arrives at a solution.

Second, I've also spent a great amount of energy teaching them how to be active listeners, paraphrasing one another's complaints (so that the other person is satisfied he or she has been heard) before responding or adding their own complaint to the discussion. They don't always use these skills, but when problems seem intractable, it's their final resort.

Finally, I've been doing this since they were toddlers, although I've seen other parents start when their kids were older. When they were young, I simply made them stand in one place and hold hands. My teenagers still fear I'll make 'em hold hands (yuck!) or hug each other (bigger yuck!), so the parentless back porch is considered a real privilege.

Peace is our struggle. Other homeschoolers face difficulties of their own. Susie Clawson, who homeschools five children in Clearfield, Utah, has a tale for anyone who has had to deal with the common problem of disapproving family members. Being a very opinionated and outspoken person, but hopefully kind and respectful, I've never gotten much grief from in-laws or others. One relative was a public school teacher for years, and at first he'd drill me on things, like "Are you diagramming sen-

Hotlinks

Donna Young
donnayoung.org

FlyLady
flylady.com

School Reform News
heartland.org

tences?" To which I'd respond, "Well, my oldest is only two, so we probably won't tackle that until he's much older."

When I started telling him things I'd read in books by John Holt or the Moores, he'd say, "Well, I've never heard that before." But when I offered to let him read the books, he declined and stopped drilling. Now he is thrilled with the progress my children have made and their interest in the world around them. I think he was just feeling a little insecure about his own choices.

Now that your children are learning to settle conflicts appropriately, and you know how to deal with the in-laws and the neighbors, you can move along to being an effective teacher. We recommend our companion book, *Homeschooling Step-by-Step,* as a primary resource for dealing with homeschooling issues, with three full chapters on creating a learning environment; balancing home, finances, and homeschooling; and dealing with other educational challenges. Scan the book's table of contents in the Appendix.

To get you on track, here are resources for handling common questions that arise for homeschooling families.

We address the dreaded "S" word—socialization—later in this chapter.

Chart Jungle   chartjungle.com

Some nicely done homeschool forms and printables to get you organized. The "Ready for School Chart" is working well for us right now.

Common Objections to Homeschooling
naturalchild.com/common_objections

Homeschooling guru John Holt responds to 17 questions such as "How am I going to teach my child six hours a day?" Simple answer: You're not. Neither is anyone else. Good spine-strengthening advice to parents worried about "keeping up."

Determining What Is Best for Each Child   tinyurl.com/deterbe
A fable for parents homeschooling children of multiple ages and talents.

Discusses learning styles, teaching styles, learning environments, and recommended reading.

Donna Young   donnayoung.org

Incredibly rich source of homeschooling forms such as planning calendars, household managers, chore charts, handwriting samplers, play money for math, science lab sheets, and much, much more. Bookmark this one.

Encouraging Fathers   kepl.com.au/fathers.html

An Australian site for Christian fathers. This site encourages fathers to be involved in their family's homeschooling effort.

Family Education Network   familyeducation.com

Love this site! Use the search tool to find homeschool articles. Of particular note are the dozens of well-written articles offering advice to families who teach their own. Ask your homeschool questions on the message forum. Most of the site is not specifically homeschool related, but the educational advice is useful nonetheless.

FlyLady   flylady.com

Seems to me about 50 percent of homeschooling families are incredibly organized. Their homes are clean, they never mislay their keys, and they serve fresh vegetables at every meal. Then there are the rest of us. If you're searching under dirty laundry for your youngest child, you need the FlyLady. Shine your sink; change your life.

Homeschool Dads   homeschooldads.com

Encouraging fathers to get involved with their children's education, this Christian site is home to lots of articles and a message board for fathers to exchange ideas.

National Home Education Research Institute   nheri.org

Statistics on homeschoolers. This inclusive site is dedicated to supporting homeschooling, and serves as a clearinghouse of homeschooling information. Find statistics, research, policy, and a calendar of events. Recommended reading for those who are not 100 percent committed to homeschooling.

Organized Home   organizedhome.com

Everything about this site is to love, but click the Family Ties link for specific tips about getting organized for homeschooling. You'll sit up straighter just by visiting the site.

Our Schoolrooms   bright.net/~double/school.htm

How one family organized its schoolroom from year to year. Including pictures. Share their journey.

School Reform News   heartland.org

Click the Education link and get access to numerous papers and articles supporting educational choice. The monthly 24-page *School Reform News* reports on school reform efforts nationwide. Archives from 1997. Strong support for homeschooling. And subscriptions are free to qualified subscribers.

Secrets of the One-Room Schoolhouse   tinyurl.com/hssecrets

How one homeschooling mother found success teaching all her children the same subjects at the same time. If it worked for pioneer families, why not yours?

The Homeschool Mom   thehomeschoolmom.com

Lots of freebies. The Getting Organized link at the top is particularly useful for families who have trouble keeping up with the paperwork and the mess that homeschooling brings about.

Legal Issues

I'VE HEARD ANY number of horror stories about parents who've had run-ins with local public schools. Sometimes these issues have resolved themselves; sometimes they've been the precipitating factor in a family's decision to homeschool.

The experience of Elizabeth, a Tennessee mother of three, serves as a cautionary tale to parents who get themselves entangled with local educational authorities. Her homeschooling adventure began nine years ago, during spring break. Her daughter, a learning-disabled thirteen-year-old, was enrolled in special education, and in Elizabeth's opinion, the classes were doing her more harm than good.

After a horrific debate with the school, Elizabeth ended up in court defending her daughter against a school system that, in her opinion, had gone berserk. "We even had a couple of teachers tell us in confidence that my daughter was capable of doing more, but that the system would not allow it. One teacher even told us of a lawyer who would take our case on for free." That same teacher now homeschools her children. "This went on for two years; finally the day came for our hearing, and we lost." Elizabeth and her husband were devastated by the reaction of the school personnel, who openly gloated that they now had free rein with the daughter. "My husband and I cried. The lawyer wanted to take it to the next level in the court system, for free, because he really believed that we had a case. But we told him we would have to pray first and did.

"The next day I was listening to the radio and heard the president of homeschooling for our state. It was a call-in show, so I called in and asked a few questions. He then proceeded to tell me that I could do it and where to call for more information. I did just that. That night we prayed again and put out a fleece to the Lord that if this was the way we should go, that within three days we would hear something. We had never heard of homeschooling before this, so it was all new and a step of faith. Three days later we received a call to take our children out of the school system that day. Homeschooling hasn't always been easy. We've had our bad days, but we do love teaching our children."

Legal: From the Latin *lex* (law). Rules of conduct established by a governing authority.

Hotlinks

Home School Legal Defense Association
hslda.org/laws

National Home Education Legal Defense
nheld.com

Homeschooling Laws and Legalities
tinyurl.com/hslegalities

While the homeschooling movement is undeniably finding acceptance, there are still parents around the country who have to fight in family courts for their right to homeschool. Others find themselves in David-and-Goliath battles with truculent educators, some of whom are openly hostile to homeschooling. As I was doing research for this book, most of the educators I approached for assistance and direction were very helpful. There were half a dozen, though, who responded to my requests with venom, and who refused outright to offer counsel or advice to anyone who would take their children out of public schools to educate them at home.

The tide seems to be turning, but there's still a lot of fury out there directed at people who buck the system.

Our companion book, *Homeschooling Step-by-Step,* includes an entire chapter on running the legal gauntlet. But the following sites will help you know your rights and responsibilities, and teach you what you need to know to protect yourself.

Attorneys for Homeschooling   ahsa-usa.org

AHSA's goal is to "empower homeschoolers to have the legal tools they need to meet homeschooling challenges." The group also provides a network of attorneys for legal representation, and shares informal advice via the organization's email list.

Child Abuse Law   childabuselaw.info

A prepared family is a safe family. The FAQ link on this site provides basic, commonsense guidelines for what to do when you face a capricious accusation of abuse or neglect. Know your parental rights.

Family Defense Center   familydefensecenter.net

In the unlikely event you're ever confronted by an overzealous or hostile Child Protective Services worker, there's no need to panic. You have resources, brought to you by this organization, which argues that protecting children begins with defending families.

Home School Legal Defense Association   hslda.org/laws

For each U.S. state, the HSLDA provides an analysis of current home-schooling laws. Membership in this Christian legal service is pricey, but the site has a wealth of free information for families concerned with preserving homeschooling rights.

Homeschooling Laws & Legalities   tinyurl.com/hslegalities

Useful links to homeschooling laws in each state, along with articles on legal concerns related to homeschooling. A terrific resource.

National Center for Policy Analysis   tinyurl.com/legncpa

Stay informed with the NCPA. Know what is happening with educa-tion in the United States.

National Home Education Legal Defense   nheld.com

A national legal organization that "seeks to protect and defend the rights of families who wish to educate in freedom." The organization's membership is open to all homeschooling families, regardless of reli-gious affiliation.

Legal and Legislative Info   nhen.org/leginfo

The National Home Education Network provides information on state homeschool laws and regulations, provides guidelines for home-school activists, and seeks to influence legislation when changes to homeschooling statutes come up before state legislatures. Member-ship is free and open to all.

Pacific Justice Institute   pacificjustice.org

PJI is a California-based non-profit organization with a focus on pro-tecting parental rights, civil liberties, and other freedoms for families. Articles such as "When Child Protective Services Calls" are a must-read for concerned homeschoolers.

State Laws   tinyurl.com/hsstatelaws

Actual homeschooling laws in each state, without comment or inter-pretation.

John Marshall

One of America's most influential Supreme Court justices, John Marshall, was schooled at home by his parents. Marshall was born in 1755 near Germantown, Virginia, the eldest of fifteen children. He spent his childhood on the Virginia frontier, and was taught primarily by his parents and for a short time by an itinerant preacher who lived with the family. He spent only a few months in a formal school setting, but until his death in 1835 he set the direction of the highest judicial body in the United States.

The New Jersey Incident   tinyurl.com/njincident

A widowed homeschooling dad nearly loses his children over outrageous allegations of having "quiet" children. Sheesh.

The Rutherford Institute   rutherford.org

Rutherford is a conservative Christian organization committed to the advocacy of civil liberties and human rights. Click the Parents Rights link for homeschooling-specific legal news.

Wisconsin v. Yoder   supreme.justia.com/us/406/205

Preview and full text of the 1972 Supreme Court decision that put an end to compulsory education in the United States.

Assessment Testing

Assessment:
From the Medieval Latin *assessus* (assist). An appraisal.

TO COMPLY WITH the education law in your area, you may be required to do annual assessment testing. But even if it's not required, you might wish to assess your children's academic progress with standardized tests, in-home assessments, or some other form of performance evaluation.

Patty Wiens, a homeschooler in Saskatchewan, uses standardized tests even though they're not a requirement of her jurisdiction. "I do testing yearly through our homeschool district, but that is for my own peace of mind more than anything else," she says. "Our homeschool liaison provides those testing resources to us at no cost."

Her enthusiasm is uncommon. In fact, testing may be the single most incendiary issue among homeschoolers. Those who test are viewed by some as traitorous; those who don't are viewed by others as dangerously defiant. Among those who must, there's only grudging compliance. The tests are usually administered in an environment that's unfamiliar to the homeschooled student, and there's a strong belief among homeschoolers that unless they "teach to the test"—that is, spend valuable educational time training children to parrot meaningless test-oriented trivia—the scores will suggest that homeschooled children are poorly educated.

On top of everything else, there is evidence that some test administrators have cheated in reporting scores or administering the tests.

Complying with testing laws presents an additional burden for homeschoolers such as Cheryl Lemily. "Living in a small town in Colorado, about two hours from a major city, we are, at the moment, having to use standardized testing as our method of complying with our state's homeschool law," she says. "I would much rather use the 'evaluation by a qualified person' aspect of the law, but unfortunately, no one I have spoken with feels comfortable doing this. This year will be our first year administering a standardized test, and I plan to use the California Standardized Test because the cost is lower than other tests and the requirements to administer the test are low."

Another mother, whose child has been diagnosed with attention deficit/hyperactivity disorder, explains how standardized testing fails to account for the benefits of homeschooling. "I'm a homeschooling mom with seven kids. I don't know whether my seventeen-year-old will do tremendously well on his ACT and SAT tests, but because I rescued him

Hotlinks

BBC Schools Bitesize
bbc.co.uk/schools/
revision

Portfolio Assessment
pgcps.org/~elc/portfolio
.html

Released TAKS Tests
tinyurl.com/taksrel

Rubistar
rubistar.4teachers.org

in time, he will at least be taking those exams. Before I started home-schooling, he had been kicked out of his junior high school for disruptive behavior and was in an alternative school, where he was socializing with drug addicts and criminals. Now he's being taught at home by Mom, studying for his GED (just passed the math and science sections at 94 and 87 percent, respectively), planning to attend community college this spring, and earning money so that he can go on a church mission when he turns nineteen.

"What the standardized tests don't account for is the high incidence of children who are saved from a future of drugs, crime, and unemployment by coming home to the loving, full-time attention of their parents."

Homeschooler Gita Schmitz has several reasons for not testing: "First, in my opinion, tests measure only the facts you've retained at that particular time (and if you're a lousy tester like I was, they don't even do that). I don't care whether my kids know the population of China, or what battle happened in what year. I'm much more interested in the political and historical 'big picture' of the world: why things happened, and what the effect was of those things, and whether they see similarities between those things and what's going on in this country today.

"I want them to understand issues such as how a country that started out loving liberty has been transformed to a people who seem to want government to take care of them. Government-written school tests are never going to ask the questions and demand the thinking that I would like."

Perhaps the most-used standardized achievement tests are the California Achievement Tests (CAT), the Comprehensive Tests of Basic Skills (CTBS), the Iowa Tests of Basic Skills (ITBS), the Metropolitan Achievement Tests (MAT), the Woodcock-Johnson Tests of Achievement (WJ III), and the Stanford Achievement Tests (Stanford 10 or SAT 10—not to be confused with the college-admissions test with nearly the same acronym). A number of states also administer their own tests custom-built to reflect their own curricula. Depending on state law, required tests may be administered by your local school district, or you may have to purchase your own examinations from a commercial provider.

Of course, there are other ways of assessing progress. College-entrance exams, practice tests, rubrics, portfolios, and other alternatives give objective measures of academic growth. From kindergarten through high school, scores of free resources are available for measuring progress.

Whether you embrace standardized testing, revile it, or are simply forced into it by local law, the following resources will help you stay the course. You'll find related sections on placement testing in Chapter 3 and college testing in Chapter 14.

BBC Schools Bitesize   bbc.co.uk/schools/revision

Test prep for the entire British school curriculum. Revise for the GCSE and other exams. Very well done.

Brush Up on Basic Skills

jc-schools.net/terranova-res.htm

Basic skills required for doing well on standardized tests. Includes sample questions from the TCAP test administered in Tennessee.

Classroom Assessment Models

tinyurl.com/classassess

From the British Columbia provincial department of education, tools for assessing progress in subjects across the academic curriculum.

Comprehension: Bloom's Taxonomy

tinyurl.com/blootax

Bloom's Taxonomy is a method of assessing a child's understanding. This article demonstrates the application of Bloom's Taxonomy to the story of Goldilocks and the Three Bears. The author restates each of Bloom's levels: Knowledge—the recall of specific information (who was Goldilocks?); Comprehension—an understanding of what was read (why didn't her mother want her to go into the woods?); Application—the converting of abstract content to concrete situations (how were the bears

Teaching Tips

What works for us is letting them do their work on their own (not hovering over them), checking on them, making sure they get it. Tests come back with A's and B's most of the time for my daughter. My son's work I check myself, and he gets A's and B's, too.

—Angela Petersen, homeschooling mom of two, Marseilles, Illinois

like real people?); Analysis—the comparison and contrast of the content to personal experiences (how would you react in the bears' position?); Synthesis—the organization of thoughts, ideas, and information from the content (do you know any other stories about children who escaped from danger?); Evaluation—the judgment and evaluation of characters, actions, outcome, etc., for personal reflection and understanding (why would an adult tell this story to children?).

CST Released Test Questions   tinyurl.com/relcst

Released test questions from previous years of the California Standards Tests. Questions cover language arts, math, social studies, and science for grades 2 through 12.

Florida Comprehensive Assessment Test
fcat.fldoe.org/fcatrelease.asp

Released versions of grade 4, 8, and 10 exit exams in reading, mathematics, and science, including answer keys.

How Do Homeschooling Parents Know Their Children
Are Learning?   naturalchild.com/jan_hunt/evaluation.html

The answer to this question is, to put it most simply, direct observation. An article by Jan Hunt.

Iowa Test of Basic Skills   schools.utah.gov/assessment

The national Iowa test is a bit mysterious; sample tests are generally unavailable. Utah has developed a practice test for third-grade reading, though. Click the Iowa Test link, then the Practice Test link on the right.

Legal, Testing, & Government Issues
homeschooloasis.com/article_chart.htm

Several articles on the subject of testing homeschooled children both as a legal issue and as an ethical one.

Nation's Report Card   nces.ed.gov/nationsreportcard/itmrls

A helpful testing tool. Click the Test Yourself link to access extensive online tests in civics, economics, math, reading, science, and history. Tests are administered at the fourth-, eighth- and twelfth-grade levels.

New York State Regents Exam
nysedregents.org/testing/hsregents.html

Tests are divided into subject areas (e.g., Comprehensive English, Chemistry, Biology, Physics, Sequential Mathematics, Latin, U.S. History and Government). Includes answer keys.

Portfolio Assessment   pgcps.org/~elc/portfolio.html

Portfolios are advanced versions of lapbooking and notebooking. This resource discusses their use as an assessment tool.

Professional Portfolio Development   tinyurl.com/portfoliodev

A tutorial for assembling a digital/multimedia portfolio to showcase your experience and background. Though it's designed for people applying for a very specific sort of job, the principles apply to anyone working on a multimedia portfolio.

Quizzes, Tests, and Exams   teaching.berkeley.edu/bgd/quizzes.html

When you want to prepare your own examinations, here's help. This article, from Tools for Teaching at UC Berkeley, explains exam construction methods and gives suggestions on validity and effectiveness in testing.

Released TAKS Tests   tinyurl.com/taksrel

Every two years the state of Texas releases its Texas Assessment of Knowledge and Skills (TAKS) and the Reading Proficiency Tests in English (RPTE) for grades 3 through 11. Includes answer keys.

Rubistar   rubistar.4teachers.org

An amazing rubric generator that's fully customizable, and has suggested standards pre-filled and editable. Perfect accompaniment to portfolio-based assessments. The U.S. Department of Education funds this one.

Testing 1, 2, 3 . . . 46, 47, 48   christianadhd.com/testing123.php

An inspiring article on testing kids with special needs, written by an adoptive mother of three special-needs children.

Rubric Generators   tinyurl.com/asrubric

Assess academic progress in virtually anything: notebooks, oral projects, behavior, reading, presentations, science fairs, and more.

That "Socialization" Question

AT SOME POINT, every homeschooling family has to answer this outrageous question from disapproving family and friends: "What about socialization?"

For long-time home educators, it results in some eye-rolling. "Oh, the age-old S-word," says Colorado mom Cheryl Lemily. "Three words: Forget about it! Our children are very well socialized. We work regularly on their manners and communication skills. They are comfortable communicating with anyone from babies to adults, and everyone in between. We receive compliments on their maturity all the time. Are they perfect? No. But neither am I. They participate in organized sports, story time at the library, grocery shopping, Sunday school, and church services. They are neither overly shy nor excessively hyper. They are comfortable in many different social situations. To me, this is the definition of being well socialized."

Aimee Nusz, a Texas homeschooler, laughs at the question. "Unless you lock your kids in the house and never let them see the light of day, they will be socialized. My kids have friends of many ages through their sports, worship services, and neighborhood. My in-laws were quite concerned about this aspect. After three years, they've let go of their concerns."

Homeschooling mom Tristi Pinkston points out that the word "socialization" has different meanings. When people use

Socialization:
From the Latin *socialis* (companionship). Participation in communities.

it to suggest that homeschoolers should be forced to think like the neighbor kids, she takes exception. "If I wanted my children to be just like everyone else, I wouldn't be homeschooling them in the first place," says the Utah mother. "But 'socialization' also means knowing how to converse with others, to share thoughts and feelings and opinions. Homeschooled children do this perfectly well. They also do it without fear of being teased by their peers for sharing their thoughts."

The "socialization" that goes on in schools is, for many homeschoolers, precisely the thing they hope to avoid by homeschooling. It's more than the peer expectations of drugs, sex, alcohol, and foul language. It's more than the relentless pressure to be thinner, stronger, wealthier, and more clever. It is, for many homeschoolers, the not-so-subtle undermining of values taught in the home. Homeschoolers argue that far from being a place where children meet people who are different from themselves, school is a place where children learn instead to gravitate to those most like themselves, and to create stereotypes about those who are different.

They learn that adults are the "enemy," that younger people are to be mocked, and that older people are dangerous.

Homeschooler Barbara Ritter suspects that it's only the "10 percent who had 90 percent of the fun" in high school who worry about socialization.

Homeschooling creates strong family bonds and builds a permanent social structure. The family is the "society" you keep, and it's the only one that, ultimately, makes any real difference.

That's not to say friends aren't important, too. They certainly are, and homeschoolers aren't shy about finding appropriate opportunities to be social. "Socialization should not be a concern," says Joy McConnell. "No matter where you live, there are numerous opportunities to 'socialize' your children. I live outside of a small village in the middle of rural Michigan. I

Hotlinks

How to Organize a Block Party
tinyurl.com/socpar

Is Socialization a Problem for Homeschoolers?
tinyurl.com/socprob

Learn in Freedom!
learninfreedom.org

Starting a Support Group
tinyurl.com/socsup

⭐ *Best Homeschooling Moment*

I will never forget when I was very pregnant with my third child, my son was barely four, and my daughter was barely two. We went to a bounce house warehouse. I could barely walk, let alone play with them on the bounce houses. My son put his arm around his little sister's shoulder and said, "Come on, let's go over here." He watched her and helped her attentively. They laughed and played together. They were not only siblings but also true friends. That, to me, is true socialization.
—Marisa Corless, homeschooling mom of three, Bothell, Washington

managed to find a very supportive homeschool co-op that offers field trips, sports, summer picnics, and enrichment classes. If you are having a difficult time finding one, start one of your own! In today's world, it is not that difficult to find other homeschool families. My children also participate in other free activities, such as story hour and the summer reading program at the local library, where they socialize with other children; organized playgroups sponsored by government organizations; and play dates with our friends' children. They are very social!"

Philosopher and educator John Dewey made an observation that ought to put grandparents' and neighbors' minds at ease. "Education is a social process," he wrote. "Education is growth. . . . Education is not a preparation for life; education is life itself."

Are your kids ready to make friends? Here's help. (See related information on resolving other homeschooling issues earlier in this chapter.)

Challenge to Your Thinking   tinyurl.com/socchal
The real objectives of schooling: What we call "socialization" is an attempt to turn children into compliant worker bees.

Homeschooling and Socialization of Children   tinyurl.com/soceric
Real research! It concludes, in part: "as self concept is a reflector of socialization, it would appear that few home-schooled children are socially deprived, and that there may be sufficient evidence to indicate that some home-schooled children have a higher self concept than conventionally schooled children." Hang on to this one.

How to Organize a Block Party   tinyurl.com/socpar
Meet the neighbors! Take the initiative by organizing a block party.

When the kids get involved there's sure to be some new friendships made.

Is Socialization a Problem for Homeschoolers?   tinyurl.com/socprob
An honest assessment—pro and con—of socialization issues and homeschooling.

Learn in Freedom!   learninfreedom.org
Extensive research on two questions: socialization and grade segregation. In both areas, the author argues, homeschoolers are better off than their institutionalized peers. He makes a compelling case for combining children of different ages in the same educational environment. Read his Age Segregation in School FAQ.

Projects for Your Classroom   tinyurl.com/socproj
Kids collaborate with other kids in this large collection of projects and project ideas. One recent collaboration: The International Boiling Point Project, where kids all over the world boil water on the same day and report the boiling point. Different altitudes and climates make the project results interesting.

Social Needs of Students   downes.ca/post/197
Responding to an argument against distance learning, this college professor effectively defangs all the "socialization" arguments made by institutions.

Socialization: A Great Reason Not to Go to School
learninfreedom.org/socialization.html
Writer Karl Bunday hits another home run with this well-reasoned argument that homeschooling helps self-esteem, social skills, and other measures of well-being.

Starting a Support Group   tinyurl.com/socsup
Homeschooling cooperatives and support groups are an important part of socializing. Here's advice for undertaking your own co-op.

The Socialization Question   tinyurl.com/socques

Isabel Lyman tells the stories of several homeschooled successes. And no, they didn't turn out to be twisted for lack of public schooling.

Support Groups

Support: From the Latin *supportare* (*sub* + *porte* [to carry]). To encourage a person or cause.

THE BEST KIND of support of all: friends. Make friends with a local support group, and find sustenance for your decision to homeschool, along with a good source of socialization and activities for your children. Support groups are rather a mixed bag for the homeschoolers I talked with while researching this book. Some support groups are helpful and interesting, some are silly and unsupportive, and some simply weren't a good fit for a particular homeschooling family.

"I have had both good and bad experiences with homeschool groups," says Susan Burton, a homeschooling mother of two from Somerdale, Ohio. "I have found that the ones that keep it to an educational goal are by far easier to handle." She said one of the support groups she was in degenerated into a gossipy play group. "Although having fun was important, as Mom, Teacher, Wife, and every other job I do, it really needed to be worth the time away."

Support groups are a critical part of Nola Hiatt's homeschooling program—and have been for two decades now. The Texas mother of six takes part in a faith-based homeschool support group and finds it very useful. "It helps to know you are not alone and to bounce ideas and problems off of one another and get new ideas. Even after homeschooling for twenty years, there are things I learned or used years ago that I've forgotten or didn't need then, but it comes back around and I am reminded of it by others around me. My three younger daughters are very different from the older, and have different needs and interests."

When Cheryl Northrup was a new homeschooler, support groups were very important to her. "I needed feedback and constant support."

The mother of seven lived in Denver then. "There was a group that shared my LDS faith, which was nice, but I had to drive a long way to reach them. The other group was eclectic, and I still really appreciated it. My daughter met one of her best friends at one of the first meetings we went to. We did lots of activities, field trips, and Moms' Nights Out. As I've become more secure in homeschool, my need for the group comes and goes."

For Maryland mom Diana Malament, though, working with other families is becoming increasingly important the longer she homeschools. "As my children get older, I find co-ops work well for us. My children developed an attitude that assignment deadline dates I would set did not need to be honored, because it was 'only Mom.' In our co-op situations, the kids wanted to be at their co-op and were only allowed to attend if they had done their homework first: positive peer pressure. All the parents had to agree to it, and there could be leniency if the parent wrote a note. But the parents needed to use that excuse with discretion."

Ann Glass is a homeschooler in a remote area of Washington State. A few years ago she was involved with a moms' group that would meet at a private home one evening a month to talk, share, and ask questions. One day a month, all the participants and their kids would get together for a play day. "Sometimes that would be free play," she said. "Sometimes we moms would plan a special activity. I enjoyed the moms-only evenings, and at times I miss that. The play day, however, seemed to be just one more thing to do on my list. My boys didn't need the play day for socialization; they had friends, cousins, and church. This type of support group was nice, but not something I felt really met me where I was at or what I needed. As a result, I've tended to stay away from 'organized' support groups."

That's not to say Ann doesn't find support, though. "What I have found has worked the best for me, and given me the most satisfac-

Hotlinks

Homeschool Blog Awards
homeschoolblogawards
.com

Homeschool Media
homeschoolmedia.net/
register

Support Groups
tinyurl.com/hssupport

tion, has been developing friendships with two other moms and their families."

In Santa Monica, California, homeschooling mother of three Liz deForest has found support groups to be somewhat unhelpful. "I got support on the Internet, since we were always too busy to do separate homeschooling things. Homeschool groups can also get strange and political, so it is easier for me to have my kids involved in things like scouting, music and martial arts."

But Washington homeschooler Karyn Moreno had the opposite experience: "We joined a homeschool co-op that meets once a week for ten weeks in the fall and ten weeks in the spring. We also go on field trips with the group at least once a month during the year. It's great for the kids to get together and have fun and for the parents to have some 'coffee time.'"

Bottom line? If your local group isn't meeting your needs and you can't seem to resolve the issues, don't hesitate to look around for a better fit. You're homeschooling, after all, for your kids. Don't let a bad support group experience throw you off track when there are so many good groups available.

The following links will get you connected with a good homeschooling support group, either online or in the real world:

Afrocentric Homeschooling
tinyurl.com/afrocent
Contains an impressive number of links to black-oriented and multicultural curricula.

Homeschool Blog Awards   homeschoolblogawards.com
Encouraging, informing, and connecting the homeschool community. You're bound to find a kindred homeschool spirit; just take some time to peruse the site.

Homeschool Events   home-school.com/events
An up-to-date state-by-state listing of conferences and events.

Homeschool Media   homeschoolmedia.net/register
An international homeschool registry. The possibilities are boundless

and the opportunities for making new friends endless. An absolute must-see website!

League of Observant Jewish Homeschoolers

chayas.com/homeschoolindex.htm

The LOJH focuses on meeting the needs of Orthodox homeschooling families.

Mainstreet Mom   mainstreetmom.com

A refreshing site that focuses on support, encouragement, and advice for stay-at-home moms. Support from your peers can get you through the toughest of days; sometimes you'll even smile.

National Home Education Network   nhen.org/support

NHEN provides a huge database for locating a support group that fits your needs and is in your area. Browsing through these support groups is a must. You may find something you didn't even know you needed. And don't neglect to join NHEN!

National Organizations   homeedmag.com/groups

National organizations for homeschoolers who share a focus—special needs, ethnic group, teaching style, or religious affiliation.

Planning a Homeschool Co-op

homeschoolblogger.com/writmm/142054

Inspiration for starting a homeschooling cooperative of your own.

Support Groups   tinyurl.com/hssupport

Articles about support groups, as well as a fairly comprehensive list of groups by state or province.

Support Groups and Homeschooling Law

midnightbeach.com/hs/listlist.htm

Part of Jon's Homeschool Resource Page. Look for state and regional groups, groups outside the U.S., and religious groups.

Support Groups, By State   homeschool.com/supportgroups
A small state-by-state listing of homeschooling support groups.

Email Lists

Mail: From the Middle English *male* (bag, wallet). Written messages conveyed from sender to receiver.

THE FASTEST WAY to get up and running with your homeschooling is to sign up for an email list. An email list, sometimes called a "loop" or a "group," is simply a group of people who converse via email. There are two kinds of email lists. The first is a read-only list, to which only the list owner or owners contribute, and subscribers are anonymous. These lists tend to take the form of newsletters, announcements, and bulletins.

The second type is participatory. Members are invited to contribute information relevant to the subject matter of the list, and everyone who participates reads all the mail that is exchanged within the group. These lists are sometimes moderated, and depending on the nature of the group, traffic can range from one or two messages a month to hundreds of messages a day.

You "subscribe" to a list (it's always free), and—if it's a participatory list—after reading the mail for a while and introducing yourself to the group, you simply send email messages to a single address, and the mail is automatically routed to the entire list.

Unlike the wild frontier of email list servers in existence a few years ago, virtually every active email group has converged onto just two services: Yahoo! Groups and Google Groups. Yahoo! Groups is still more popular, but the Google service is gaining followers.

"I use Yahoo! Groups," proclaims M.A., a single homeschooling mom from Louisiana. "I have found a local homeschooling group on there that keeps up with field trips and events for the kids, which has been invaluable. Probably the most beneficial was the Single Mother Homeschoolers site. There I have found like people with the same struggles in raising children on one's own, homeschooling them, and managing to work full time to support the family. We have unique situations that we have managed to share with one another. For instance, I was facing hospitalization, which sparked a whole conversation on lesson preparedness, legal documents, and backup care. Another group I belong to has started putting together a database of where we all live so that when we travel we can connect with other homeschoolers."

When I asked homeschoolers about their favorite email lists, the suggestions came flying. So many were offered, in fact, that I couldn't begin to include them all in this book. It was Misty Blagg, a homeschooler from Alexandria, Louisiana, who made the most cogent observation. She told me about a favorite list that supports her spiritual beliefs and has a non-judgmental quality, but observed, "It likely doesn't stand out as the 'best support mailing list anywhere, ever,' but it is a good one. And support lists have to be centered around the needs of so specific a segment of the population to work properly that I'm not sure there could be a 'best ever,' anyway."

She's absolutely right. In researching this book, I spent several weeks monitoring nearly every homeschooling and educational mailing list that was open to me. There are lists to support every homeschooling philosophy you can imagine. The group LDSCMC (**yahoogroups.com/group/LDSCMC**) is an example of how narrowly focused an email list can be. The list is specifically for Mormon homeschoolers who use the Charlotte Mason approach to education. The list "AHomeschoolReview" (**yahoogroups.com/group/AHomeschoolReview**), on the other hand, is open to anyone, anywhere, who has ever considered homeschooling, or whoever might do so at any time in the future. This high-traffic list is the *USA Today* of homeschool lists. In a single month, list members exchanged more than 2,000 messages.

Email lists are a lifeline to homeschoolers like Raylene Hunt from Maine. "We live in a pretty rural part of our state. There are lots of

Hotlinks

Google Groups
groups.google.com

Homeschool Reviews
tinyurl.com/hsreviews

Yahoo! Groups
groups.yahoo.com

homeschooling families, but they are spread out and are often a half hour to forty-five minutes away. We use Yahoo! Groups to connect with each other, share curriculum ideas, and plan field trips. We're all pretty independent, too, so this works well. It keeps me in touch with others, but the group isn't so close-knit that you feel like you're missing out when you can't take part in something."

When Lori Ramey moved to Sikeston, Missouri, far away from her strong support group, email lists made it possible for her to continue homeschooling. "I was able to find support online at some amazing homeschool groups. One of the groups I belong to is strictly for homeschoolers with the particular disability that my daughters have. It is so wonderful to be able to have someone who has been where you are who can tell you that it is worth it and that you are not going to go crazy. What is even more wonderful is being able to turn around and do that for someone else."

You, too, can help and be helped, without ever leaving home. Here are some of the most popular email lists on the Internet, along with a few interesting pages on joining lists. Some lists are announcement only; others are very participatory. Something here will help you on your way.

Homeschool Your Child for Free!

There's a popular mailing list associated with this book. Sign up by sending an email request to 0-homeschoolreviews-subscribe@yahoogroups.com.

Flat Travelers Homeschool

tinyurl.com/flatman

Send your flat traveler to a home far away; receive photos or journal pages when the little guy comes back home.

Free Homeschool

tinyurl.com/hsfbooks

A free curriculum exchange for ebooks, curricula, and lesson plans. No money changes hands.

Google Groups   **groups.google.com**

If Yahoo! Groups isn't your thing, explore Google Groups. The volume is much lower, but keep an eye out. In some quarters, Google is wildly popular.

Home Education Magazine   homeedmag.com

Provides support, blogs, networking, and discussion groups. Access the discussion lists by clicking the Network link.

Homeschool Form Share   tinyurl.com/hsformshare

A list for sharing the homeschooling forms you created. Members are invited to share planning ideas, curriculum, schedules, and teaching styles.

Homeschool Reviews   tinyurl.com/hsreviews

The companion list for this book. Brief reviews of free homeschooling resources. No chatter, no arguments. Just reviews and tips, and you're on your way.

Homeschooling Special Needs Kidz   tinyurl.com/hskidz

A support group for parents of kids with ADHD, learning disabilities, dyslexia, emotional or neurological disorders, or any other type of handicap.

HSTUAC   hstuac.org

Home School Train Up A Child is a collection of Christian homeschooling email lists. This page has links to many other Christian homeschooling resources.

Military Homeschool   tinyurl.com/hsmilitar

A well-traveled egroup. Many users translates into more support for military homeschoolers from military homeschoolers.

Unschooling Basics   tinyurl.com/unshome

If you want to learn more about the everyday life of an unschooling home then this is the place for you! It's a very active list that promises to help you along the path that is unschooling.

Yahoo! Groups   groups.yahoo.com

Your starting point for searching out a support group that fits your needs. From the Search box, type "homeschool" and your city, your religious affiliation, your teaching approach, or any other need. Then sign yourself up for a list.

The Boards

Board: From the Middle English *bord* (plank). Table at which a council meets.

LIKE EMAIL LISTS, discussion boards, chat rooms, newsgroups, and forums all provide different kinds of online support. Participants are relatively anonymous, discussions occur in threads that sometimes go on for years, and participation is generally a bit sporadic. With few exceptions, participants on discussion boards tend to come for a while, then leave without ever coming back.

Unlike email lists, where conversation comes to you, boards require a special trip to the group's website or other resource. If you want to know what people have said in response to your comments, you have to return to the site and investigate the new traffic.

They also require a bit more caution than email lists. Anything said on a newsgroup is both public and permanent. (Email lists, on the other hand, tend to be of no interest to anyone outside the group, and it's unlikely that anyone has the time, disk space, or energy to maintain a permanent searchable public archive.)

Nevertheless, your Internet experience isn't complete until you've experienced the entire spectrum. And who knows? You might actually enjoy it. Here are some of the top newsgroups and forums for homeschoolers.

Hotlinks

Homeschool Forum
forum.homeschool.com

Homeschool Talk and Swap!
vegsource.com/
homeschool

Homeschool Channel   crosswalk.com/homeschool
One of many channels on the Christian web portal Crosswalk. The homeschooling channel sponsors an active discussion forum and publishes well-done articles on teaching from home.

Homeschool Forum   forum.homeschool.com
Possibly the most active discussion group on the Internet. The support forums and the religion forums are quite heavily traversed.

Homeschool Spot   **homeschoolspot.com**

A fairly active homeschooling discussion forum. Topics are very general.

Homeschool Swap

groups.google.com/group/homeschool-swap-board

Homeschoolers offer curriculum to sell or swap on this newsgroup.

Homeschool Talk and Swap!   **vegsource.com/homeschool**

Discussion boards for military homeschoolers, single parents, adoptive parents, special-needs homeschoolers, and other communities of families. Lots of support and good advice from people who've been there. Access boards for swapping curriculum, as well.

Homeschool World Forum   **home-school.com/forums**

This site accommodates more than 14,000 homeschool forum posts. Have something you just need to share? There is probably a spot here just for you.

Chapter 3

Curriculum Core: Scope and Sequence

T HE FIRST TASK for a homeschooling family is deciding what and how to teach. Eventually, every homeschooling family chooses its own path. That's not much reassurance, though, to families who are just starting out.

Initially, our family's homeschooling experience overseas was more a matter of necessity than of choice. I had a special-needs child who was becoming increasingly disruptive in class, and it eventually became necessary to bring him home to ensure that he got an education at all.

I knew many homeschoolers overseas, but didn't realize the growing size of the movement in North America until we returned to the States and started meeting homeschoolers everywhere we went. The movement fascinated me, and I felt a strong desire to continue homeschooling. But the homeschooling curriculum materials I was reading were unimpressive, and I had difficulty imagining how I would incorporate them into a program for our family.

When we eventually decided to go ahead and homeschool in the United States, we were required by the local school district to submit a curriculum plan. I read many

Curriculum:
From the Latin *curr-* (course) and *-culum* (method); the British equivalent of résumé, *curriculum vitæ*, means "course of one's life."

homeschooling resources and realized that lots of families were choosing to avoid formal curricula altogether, in favor of an eclectic approach. I had been conditioned, though, to think in more formal terms, so I had a bit of a dilemma.

I continued to research. Eventually I found lots of curriculum resources, including the educational outcome goals for our own school district, available online. As I read through the district's curriculum, I realized that everything there was available to me without purchasing a full-scale set of curriculum materials from a professional developer. It was a go.

Curriculum development needn't be as difficult for you as it was for me. You have, essentially, three choices: use prepackaged curriculum materials, build your own curriculum, or take the eclectic approach, doing a little bit of both. The prepackaged route has traditionally been the most popular, but there are many ways to do it for free—or nearly so.

Two studies from National Home Education Research Institute (NHERI) indicate that 71 percent of homeschooling programs are designed by parents. Just less than a quarter are complete, off-the-shelf curriculum packages. Ten percent of parents use a combination or some other method. The NHERI surveyed 1,657 families with 5,402 children.*

Homeschooler Gita Schmitz advises parents to do a bit of planning before spending anything on pricey curriculum materials. "Parents need to first figure out what their teaching style will be, and the best way their kids learn."

Kentucky mom Erin Goldberg agrees. "First of all decide what subjects you want to include in your curriculum. I downloaded the core content for each subject from our state's Department of Education website and used it as a

* See our website, **hsfree.com,** for citations for this and other statistics in this chapter.

Curriculum

Hotlinks

Ambleside Online
amblesideonline.org

An Old Fashioned Education
oldfashionededucation.com

Content Knowledge
mcrel.org/standards-benchmarks

National and State Standards
education-world.com/standards

Simply Charlotte Mason Home
simplycharlottemason.com

On Teaching

The best teacher is the one who suggests, rather than dogmatizes, and inspires his listener with the wish to teach himself.

—Edward Bulwer-Lytton, English author

starting ground for my curriculum. A lot of homeschoolers have set up websites filled with their own experiences and links to resources, and there are so many awesome educational sites out there.

"Most important," she advises, "I would say, trust yourself. Most parents decide to homeschool because they know what is best for their children, so when it comes to building your curriculum you *can* do it. Don't overwhelm yourself and try to create your year of curriculum in a day. Give yourself about a month to collect materials, form ideas, and organize your home.

"And don't put your schooling on a super-strict time schedule; you will drive yourself crazy. If you need to focus more on a subject, cool, the other projects you have planned will wait. I promise. And unit studies are really one of the best things ever thought of. To spend a whole day, week, or whatever on a subject they are interested in is wonderful. They learn when they are interested, so keep the kiddos' ideas in mind, but keep to your course of must-haves as well. We should always seek the balance, because that is where they learn."

To save money on curriculum, Luanne, a homeschooling mom from Virginia, organized a consortium of homeschoolers who exchange curriculum materials. Here's how she did it:

"Shortly after I started homeschooling, I became keenly aware of my inability to get the books and other resources that I wanted for teaching with my very limited budget. I also learned there were families homeschooling in our area, part of our group, who had used books and things packed away in boxes and sitting collecting dust on shelves. These could be sold at used-book sales or conventions, but the profit was small for the sellers; and for me, the opportunity didn't come very often to make it to these events to buy. Also, even that much money was hard to come by at times.

"On the other hand, I had collected quite a few nice books at the high-school level—teacher's manuals and assorted books that had been given to me by family members. We could use these later, but at that time my son was in the first grade.

"Sounds like bad timing, but it isn't if other homeschoolers are willing to put their collections together for common use. This we did, and it has grown into a marvelous organization. Our library is small; we call it the Home Education Consortium because it is a place for us to share our common resources. It has grown in many ways other than just the sharing of used curricula and other books.

"Now our group does the Weekly Reader program and earns free books, which go into the consortium for all to use. When we want to honor one of our members, we donate to the consortium a book that is meaningful to that member. We keep this collection at the church where we are so graciously allowed to have our weekly meetings and activities, so all members can use its resources freely."

Buying curriculum materials is a practical matter for Debbie Hostetler, a homeschooling mother of three in Newport Beach, California. She attends every local used-curriculum fair she can find, and buys used books for her family's curriculum. "When we're finished using the curriculum, we pay anywhere from one to five dollars for a space at the next used-curriculum fair, and sell the items we're finished with. I have always come out even by careful shopping, even after paying for the space. I just increase the price of the item by five to ten cents. We end up selling about three half-days per year, but are able to have a rich and varied curriculum at no cost!" She also recommends the fairs as a great place to preview curricula, "so you don't waste money in the first place."

For homeschooling mom Susie Clawson, buying curriculum materials has been nothing but a waste of money. She has several tips for dealing with the expensive curriculum materials that you've already purchased:

- Put the curriculum on the shelf.
- Sell it.
- Adapt it to suit the needs of your kids.

- Skip the boring stuff.
- Supplement with fun library books and videos.
- Add lots of field trips, even if they don't relate to what you're learning.
- Use the Scouting and 4-H projects as their curriculum.
- Use a unit study approach.
- Allow each child to pick a project, and help the child find materials to learn.

On Education

It is possible to store the mind with a million facts and still be entirely uneducated.

—Aleck Bourne, A Doctor's Creed

The Clearfield, Utah, mother of five says her family used this last system to do a science fair project one year. She and her children read the library books together, and each child worked individually on his or her display.

Several homeschooling families make use of some incredible full-curriculum resources available for free, online.

Maryland homeschooler Diana Malament is one. "I am currently homeschooling using Ambleside (**amblesideonline.org**). This has been very helpful, financially. Many of the books used are available for free online. If I cannot afford to buy them, I sit with my laptop and read from the screen, or print out the pages I need. Reading from the laptop is less expensive, though. If I were going to print all the material out, it would cost about the same as just buying the book, but at least you can spread the cost of ink cartridges out over the year."

Brenda Ulrich, a Washington mother of six, was happy to find a similarly complete online curriculum. "My favorite free resource is a website called Old Fashioned Education (**oldfashionededucation.com**). It has a complete K through 12 curriculum laid out using classic literature that can all be found for free online. I absolutely love their recommended math curriculum from CIMT (Center for Innovation in Mathematics Teaching). I use it for all my kids!"

Diana Malament supplements her teaching using two other resources. "I found a site, Google Books (**books.google.com**), where I can search for books that have been digitized online. I have found many of the books I needed that were previously unavailable are now available there. I also use PortaPortal (**portaportal.net**) to set up a set of files of free resources, and when I have time I add new resources I find."

Donna Lee Spruill, a homeschooling mother of four in Estancia, New Mexico, has taken the eclectic approach in an effort to get around the flexibility issues. "We've used curricula from noted entities, such as Calvert, International Institute, Bob Jones University, and A Beka. And we've designed our own and combined ideas and books. This has been a labor of love for us . . . all of us. And we wouldn't have done anything differently."

Another eclectic philosophy, of sorts, is that of an Englishwoman named Charlotte Mason. She lived in the early 1900s and advocated a gentle form of teaching that involved nature walks, journals, and reading classic literature. Christine Blair, a homeschooling mother of two in Massachusetts, has taken Charlotte Mason to heart. "I have started homeschooling the Charlotte Mason way, using the book *The Gentle Art of Learning*. We are enjoying school immensely, and I feel like my life is also being enriched."

Susan Clawson has also embraced the Charlotte Mason approach. "We use some Charlotte Mason ideals in our schooling, but we're very eclectic and approach unschooling. We get totally engrossed in various projects and spend the entire day working on something like a notebook. 'Whatever works' is our motto!" She has also used what she calls a Scout curriculum. "For a while, the only way I could motivate my oldest was to make her studies part of a badge or belt loop award for Scouts. I'm my daughter's Brownie leader as well, and her sash is covered with her Try Its. Our troop used to be mostly homeschooled girls, but now it is open to the girls at the private school where we meet. The homeschoolers usually end up with more badges simply because they work on things with their family and friends as part of their learning. Many moth-

Self-Determination

Only the educated are free.

—Epictetus, A.D. c. 55–c. 135

Curriculum

On Success

Success is the sum of small efforts—repeated day in and day out.
—Robert Collier, author

ers told us in advance that they wouldn't be involved except to bring their girls to the meetings. Sad but true."

Another Scout curriculum user is Susan Amiot, a homeschooling mom of five in Orlando, Florida. "I used some of the Scout badges for 'homeschool' stuff. My daughter didn't think of it as school. This is a great way to do homeschool, at least a part of it, very cheaply without buying all the books on the market."

Annie Glass, on the other hand, has figured out how to do everything for free, using nothing but the resources of the Internet as her curriculum. Annie lives near the Canadian border in Everson, Washington, where she teaches music lessons and homeschools her two boys. "I think homeschoolers are becoming much pickier as they gain confidence in what they are doing. Most of us are living on a single income, many with large families to support. We want the best for our children but can't afford to spend much in dollar amounts. That's why I think this book is much needed and will be welcomed by the homeschooling community."

This chapter introduces everything you need to build a curriculum of your own, whether you're trying to supplement a set curriculum or devise one of your own from scratch. Whether you're a devout "school at home-er" or a committed unschooler or something in between, this is where you get started.

We begin with a section on placement testing, so you'll be able to evaluate your child's current educational level. Then we locate some great resources for lesson plans and for worksheets. The next section discusses unit studies, an alternative educational philosophy in which multidisciplinary units rather than single subjects are taught. After that come sections on field trips, preschool, special education—and unschooling, a philosophy of natural, or child-led, learning. Finally, we've added two sections for online courses and public school partnering. We've got you covered.

First, though, are a few of the best curriculum links on the Internet. Use these resources to build a traditional curriculum that parallels the public school system, or build your curriculum around any mixture of alternative philosophies that fit your family's learning style. In the Appendix, page 445, you'll also find a suggested Scope and Sequence that may help you in devising your own curriculum.

19th-Century Schoolbooks   digital.library.pitt.edu/nietz

A collection of more than 140 old American textbooks, digitized and searchable, in virtually every subject area, including accounting, spelling, penmanship, civics, science, and much, much more. My favorite is the geography textbook, containing such ditties as this: "Ohio is the most populous of the Western states" and "St. Louis, in Missouri, is one of the three largest cities in the West." Utah and Washington are territories, and Los Angeles doesn't rate a mention on the map.

Adam Smith Academy   adamsmithacademy.org/titles.html

Dedicated to producing original audiovisual educational content and distributing it through the latest technology such as iPods, iPhones, DVDs, and online streaming videos. Using these short narrated and illustrated movies of classic literature, history, economics, and philosophy, parents can increase interest, comprehension, and retention of difficult subject matter by delivering it to kids in their favored formats. Short movies such as *Aesop's Fables* are on demand.

Ambleside Online   amblesideonline.org

Done in the tradition of Charlotte Mason. There is no cost to use their information or join one of the support groups. One mom writes, "I love this one. It is way more intense than what we could handle, so I pick and choose. I love their booklists. This is what I use the most. It also has the material laid out for you."

An Old Fashioned Education
oldfashionededucation.com

A complete online curriculum for K through 12. "It uses all public domain books," one homeschooling mom writes, "and I love the old books. The developer

On Child-Led Learning

The art of standing aside to let a child develop the relations proper to him is the fine art of education.

—Charlotte Mason, educator

Curriculum

On Education

I have never let my schooling interfere with my education.

—Mark Twain, author

lays everything out, with weekly lesson plans, and a free lesson planner book. It is an excellent free resource for those who like everything planned out for them."

Baltimore Curriculum Project Lesson Plan Index
tinyurl.com/bcpscope
Lesson plans that follow the Core Knowledge Sequence for grades K through 5.

BBC Schools   bbc.co.uk/schools

An entire British curriculum, with games, revisions, examinations, videos, lectures, teachers' guides, and much more. Covers every subject—and then some. The only place it falls short: American history and government. But what would you expect?

Classical Christian Homeschooling

classical-homeschooling.org/curriculum.html

A recommended sequence of courses for Classical homeschoolers who use the Trivium. Though links on this site are poorly maintained, the sequence of courses is itself invaluable.

Content Knowledge   mcrel.org/standards-benchmarks

Wow. A complete set of standards and benchmarks for education at all grade levels, and for virtually every topic: math, science, history (including U.S. history and world history), language arts, geography, the arts, civics, economics, foreign language, health, physical education, technology, behavioral studies, and life skills. And there are lesson plans to back it up.

Crickweb   crickweb.co.uk

A U.K.-based resource for students aged four to eleven, Crickweb provides scores of graphic flipboards for teaching maths, English, science, history, geography, religious education, design technology, information technology, French, and Spanish. See the Water Cycle presentation for an example of how the charts teach concepts.

Curriculum Core: Scope and Sequence 65

Curriculum

Cultural Unliteracy   books.google.com

The actual link is too long to type, so search on Cultural Unliteracy at Google Books to read a chapter from an online textbook on learning, where the author, Roger Schank from Northwestern University, decries so-called "literacy lists" and proposes what he believes are superior alternatives for education. An excellent argument.

Ed Pubs   edpubs.ed.gov

Free educational materials published by the U.S. Department of Education. The most popular publications discuss reading, college funding, and crisis management, but there are hundreds more on every conceivable subject. Order online or by phone at 1-877-4-ED-PUBS.

ExpertVillage   expertvillage.com

Click the Education link for homeschool-specific videos, but browse the entire site for how-to videos on just about any conceivable subject. Make vegan chocolate mousse, predict the weather, organize a convention.

Federal Citizen Information Center   pueblo.gsa.gov

The U.S. government prints hundreds of free and low-cost brochures on everything from changing a tire to changing your diet. Bet you can't think of a subject—academic or otherwise—that's not covered by some government publication. What a way to supplement your curriculum.

I Know That   iknowthat.com

Cross-curriculum activities for pre-K through grade 6. Play animated games and work on activities in the arts, language, math, science, and social studies. A bit slow loading.

MeritBadge   meritbadge.org

This fully redesigned site is now a wiki that stays up to date with changing requirements. If you want to design your own curriculum, you really should consider the Scouting program as a model. At this site you'll find a listing of all the BSA merit badges, along with the requirements and resources for earning them. The site is gradually incorporating requirements for all youth organizations.

National and State Standards   educationworld.com/standards

Here it is, every state and national standard, by subject and with links to the actual curriculum pages from the departments of education for each entity. Perfect.

PBS Teachers   pbs.org/teachers

Don't you just love public television? This site is a gold mine for educators and students. It has thousands of lessons tied to your state's curriculum standards. It's there, just waiting for you and your child to enjoy.

Pete's PowerPoint Station   pppst.com

A full curriculum of PowerPoint presentations covering every academic area. Each presentation is professionally executed, and serves as the foundation for a lesson or an entire unit study. Lecturing from PowerPoint is a very parent-intensive undertaking.

Simply Charlotte Mason Home   simplycharlottemason.com

A more gentle and flexible form of classical education, Charlotte Mason educators seek living books, good habits, and broad learning based on experiencing life. This page provides a curriculum guide, along with lots of tools for teaching the CM way.

SOL Enhanced Scope and Sequence   ttaconline.org/staff/sol/sol.asp?

Better than a mere curriculum planner. This resource has both scope and sequence and lesson plans combined in individual, very large documents. Mathematics, English, science, history, and social science are all covered for grades K through 12.

SparkNotes   sparknotes.com

Cross-curriculum study guides for high-school and college-level learners. Extensive summaries of literature (and Shakespeare in particular), poetry, history, psychology, economics, math, film, drama, writing, philosophy, chemistry, biology, and physics. Use the study guides to refresh your own understanding, or to prepare to teach the material.

Teachertube   teachertube.com

YouTube for teachers! Need to teach a lesson on chemistry, but have no idea how? Just type "chemistry" in the search box and sit back with a bowl of popcorn.

The Kids Know It All   kidsknowit.com

Educational movies are just one of the many great resources on this site. Interactive high-end graphics teach animal science, geology, astronomy, history, biology, human anatomy, chemistry, math, dinosaurs, memory, geography, and spelling.

Typical Course of Study   tinyurl.com/scotyp

A proposed course of study for preschool through high school. Use it to design your own curriculum. This course of study covers math, social studies, science, language arts, and health and safety.

Video Placement Worldwide   vpw.com

Free educational videos. One mom writes, "Video Placement Worldwide is a great service that we have used since starting homeschooling (especially if you are part of a co-op where the videos can be seen by multiple kids and 'teachers')."

Wonder How To   wonderhowto.com/education

Hundreds of educational podcasts in the humanities, math, science, and legal/consumer education. Another section is home to multimedia videos teaching how to teach. Beyond the education section are podcasts on music and instruments, fine art, film and theater, computers, programming, finance, and crafts.

Curriculum

Placement Testing

PLACEMENT TESTING HELPS you get a handle on your child's educational level in reading, math, science, and other subjects.

For our purposes, placement testing is a specific procedure that new homeschoolers can use to determine their children's academic strengths or educational gaps. It's also for parents making decisions about formal homeschooling for their kindergarten-age children.

Placement testing is different from the assessment testing required by some states (see the assessment testing section of Chapter 2 for more information on assessment testing). For homeschoolers, placement testing is strictly for your own information, so it can be as formal or as informal as you wish.

Homeschooling mom Joyce Dumire in Akron, Ohio, explains how placement testing worked for her and her son: "We started late with homeschooling. My son was already a teenager. He was the one that really wanted to do the homeschooling. I wanted to, but since I had a full-time job, it just didn't seem possible. He really wanted this to work, because if it didn't, he'd have to return to public school.

"When we started, I tested him in all subjects with a test purchased from a commercial supplier called Alpha Omega. The results were not pretty. He had a lot of catching up to do. But I went to the appropriate grade level and started from there. He whizzed through his work at first, but it slowly (and sometimes rapidly) got harder. He'd walk away and then come back—maybe in a few minutes, maybe in a few days. If he didn't return to his work I'd put it aside and go back a bit.

"Today he proudly will announce, 'I love math, I've always been good at math.' He's right, it's always been a successful subject for him."

The placement-testing material in the following list isn't as formal as the prepackaged set Joyce used. It will, nevertheless, give you good information about your young child's school readiness, and your older child's comprehension of basic academic subjects.

Level: From the Latin *libella* (*libra*: balance). The line at which everything is everywhere parallel.

Erin Goldberg does homemade placement testing. "I create my own grade-level-appropriate tests for each child using the free Kentucky Department of Education website downloads," she says.

Another Kentucky mom, Jessica Murphy, follows a similar course. "I don't test them as much as I try to make sure they are on track with public school children. I use the *World Book* site and follow the Typical Course of Study." (**tinyurl.com/scotyp**)

Missouri mom Lori Ramey was surprised when her placement testing showed that her kids were ahead of the game. "I do not do any formal testing of my children. I prefer to allow them to learn at their own pace. However, when I sent my oldest two daughters back to public school, they had to undergo placement testing. Both did so well, we had the option of moving them up a grade level or letting them stay with their own age group."

If you want independent confirmation that your kids are on schedule academically, or need to decide at which level you should begin teaching, consider the following resources:

Advanced Placement Testing Program
tinyurl.com/mathplace

Intermediate and advanced placement tests for high school math. Self-scoring.

Apsoft IQ Test   tinyurl.com/applace

Answer 30 questions in 15 minutes. The test is challenging, but there are no answers available, and the score is given only as the number of correct responses.

Assessment Assistance
internet4classrooms.com/assistance.htm

This nearly overwhelming collection of test-prep materials for every grade level and every skill set will give you a good feel for your children's academic strengths and weaknesses.

Hotlinks

Florida Kindergarten Readiness Checklist
tinyurl.com/floplace

NWREL's Assessment Program
nwrel.org/assessment

Test Your Level
tinyurl.com/britcent

Calvert's Placement Services   tinyurl.com/calplace

Free tests by commercial curriculum developer Calvert help parents determine their children's appropriate grade levels. Complete the assessments at home and evaluate your children's responses using the guidelines provided.

COMPASS Test   act.org/compass

Placement and diagnostic testing in mathematics, reading, and writing. Required by many colleges and universities as a prerequisite to admissions or for enrollment in college-level math, reading, or writing classes.

Florida Kindergarten Readiness Checklist   tinyurl.com/floplace

Click the link at the bottom of the page to access a seven-part checklist for school readiness. Each portion covers a different developmental area, and includes helpful advice for parents who are preparing their young children for academia.

Introduction to Motor Behavior and Control   tinyurl.com/motplace

An interesting PowerPoint slide presentation describing the acquisition, classification, and development of motor skills.

IQ Test   iqtest.com

The IQ test is free—though definitely geared toward older kids and adults. Take the test, give an email address (hello, **mailinator.com**?), and receive your score. Pretty straightforward.

Kindergarten Readiness Checklist   tinyurl.com/kinplace

Use this checklist to see whether your child is prepared to do kindergarten-level coursework.

Math-U-See Placement   mathusee.com/placement.html

Primarily a commercial site, but the assessment test will be helpful in determining your child's math placement level. Covers each math curriculum from beginning through geometry and algebra II.

NWREL's Assessment Program   nwrel.org/assessment

Everything you need to know about assessing your child's reading, writing, and oral communication, as well as other aspects of learning. This is really a tremendous resource, and should be bookmarked if you need to evaluate your child's progress in nearly any subject.

Online IQ Test   gallagher.com/iq.htm

Download this free 30-minute IQ test. It's a good one.

Sample Math Placement Test   mdtp.ucsd.edu/test

A self-scoring pre-calculus placement test for incoming college freshmen.

Study Skills   teachingonline.org/studyskills.html

A placement test for New Zealanders, but it's just as helpful to parents of other English speakers. These tests are a series of "quiz cards," with teacher guides. They cover a variety of subjects.

Test Your Level   tinyurl.com/britcent

How's your (British) English? Test your grammar, vocabulary, listening, and reading skills. Designed for non-native speakers, this test will nevertheless expose areas that require further study.

Lesson Plans

NOW THAT YOU know your children's academic levels and have developed your curriculum program, it's time to start teaching.

What you want is to avoid getting into the situation experienced by Sherrie Rosenau of Van Dyne, Wisconsin. Sherrie, a mother of six, is in her first year of homeschooling. She says that with her set curriculum, she's spending more time making agendas and corrections than teaching.

Melody Daisson, an Orem, Utah, mother of three, has a

> **Lesson:** From the Latin *lection* (reading). Exercises or readings given as part of a course of instruction.

similar struggle. "I guess my biggest frustration is that I never feel on top of things. I started out wanting to plan lessons for three months; now I'm just happy to have it for a week at a time!"

Throughout this book we focus on specific curriculum areas and provide a comprehensive, focused selection of research resources, lesson plans, and teaching tips.

The following collection of lesson plans is slightly different. Here we look at several broad-based sites that combine multiple curriculum areas in a high-quality library of lesson plans.

Homeschooling mom Karyn Moreno thinks online lesson plans are the way to go. While she purchases her math curriculum, "as for the other subjects, many lesson plans can be found online for free that work just as well as any store-bought curriculum."

These lessons tend, for the most part, to be either fairly interactive, meaning that the parent becomes highly involved in the teaching process, or fairly independent, meaning that focused students will be given rough guidelines, a start-up list of resources, and time to absorb the material. With either approach, your burden as a teaching parent goes from agenda-focused to education-focused. Dive in!

Hotlinks

AskERIC Lesson Plans
ericir.syr.edu/Virtual/
Lessons

Scholastic Lesson Plans
teacher.scholastic.com/ilp

**Smithsonian Education
Resource Library**
smithsonianeducation
.org/educators

Teacher's Edition Online
teachnet.com/lesson

10 Steps to Developing a Quality Lesson Plan
lessonplanspage.com/WriteLessonPlan.htm
Step five: Write the step-by-step procedures. Helpful if you're working with a co-op to develop lessons. From the site's main page, access any of about 3,500 lesson plans in every academic area.

Adprima Lesson Planning   adprima.com/lesson.htm
The author of this excellent resource writes, "Think of a lesson plan as a way of communicating." Offers help on writing lesson plans, along with links to online lesson-plan collections.

AskERIC Lesson Plans   ericir.syr.edu/Virtual/Lessons

Some two thousand lesson plans across the curriculum. Search by grade level and subject.

Columbia Education Center   www.col-ed.org/cur

No bells, whistles, or bright colors, but they do share lesson plans galore for K through 12.

Core Knowledge Lesson Plans   coreknowledge.org/ck/resrcs/lessons

Excellent hands-on interdisciplinary lessons to supplement the Core Knowledge series. Most don't require the actual books, but they're always available at your local public library if required.

Designing Performance Assessments

geocities.com/athens/parthenon/8658

A wealth of information and templates for designing performance assessment tasks for your children.

Discovery Education   school.discovery.com/lessonplans

Lesson plans to accompany Discovery Channel programs in science, social studies, math, language, and the fine arts. If you're not a cable subscriber, many public libraries carry the videos.

Ellen McHenry's Basement Workshop   ellenjmchenry.com

This "educational inventor" creates objects games, activities, and much more. Click the Free Products link on the left for downloads in life sciences, earth sciences, chemistry, energy/machines, history/social studies, geography/maps, math, Latin, and drama.

Federal Resources for Educational Excellence   free.ed.gov

Hundreds of resources for teachers. Find U.S. government-sponsored lesson plans and teaching tips in art, music, health, language, math, science, language, social studies, and history.

How to Develop a Lesson Plan   eduref.org/Virtual/Lessons/Guide.shtml

This guide explains how to write formal lesson plans. While you probably won't spend this much energy on a single lesson for a single child, parents with large families, and families that share lesson plans, will find this format helpful.

K–12 Core Lesson Plans   tinyurl.com/K12uen

Lesson plans in all the usual curriculum areas, along with a large number of specialized technology plans covering topics such as agricultural education, family and consumer sciences, marketing, and technology and engineering.

Learn NC Lessons   learnnc.org/lessons

From the state of North Carolina, hundreds of lesson plans organized by grade level, then by subject area.

Lesson Plan Study   lessonplans.com/study.htm

Part A explains how to make a lesson plan; Part B contains a link to Teach-nology's actual lesson-plan generator. Use it to write your own lesson plans for sharing or documenting your academic process. Additional links take you to a thought organizer, a rubric generator, a worksheet generator, and a timeline generator.

Lesson Planning   educationworld.com/a_lesson

Diversity is good, right? If you agree, you'll enjoy the diversity of the lessons found here. Teacher Lesson Plans is a changing, eclectic collection of lesson plans submitted by educators. This entire site is a great place, so start here and spend a few hours.

Louisiana Lesson Plans   mconn.doe.state.la.us/lessonplans.php

Hundreds of teacher-written lesson plans on subjects from arts and business to trade and industrial education.

PIGS Space: Cooperative Learning Modules
cspace.unb.ca/nbco/pigs/modules

A small collection of co-op lesson plans related to the New Brunswick Curriculum. Find sections for language arts, math, science, and social studies.

Scholastic Lesson Plans   teacher.scholastic.com/ilp

The entire Scholastic site is a treasure hunter's dream, but this subpage of Lesson Plans and Skills and Strategies is the most valuable. You'll find hundreds of lesson plans for reading, science, social studies, math, and several other categories, with grade-level recommendations. Most include reproducibles taken directly from Scholastic's published materials.

Section Six: Lesson Planning   tinyurl.com/sectsix

Learn about the three types of lesson plans: Informational (focuses on the development of cognitive knowledge), Manipulative (focuses on the development of psychomotor skills through the application of knowledge), and Affective (focuses on the development of attitudes and/or values that are directly related to successful job performance). The site also covers the six characteristics of a lesson (Unified, Contains Some New Element, Properly Related to Other Lessons, Reasonable in Scope, Provides for Practice, Measurable), the five stages of the lesson (preparation, presentation, application, evaluation, review), and ever so much more. You'll want to read it several times.

Smithsonian Education Resource Library

smithsonianeducation.org/educators

Lesson plans that teach art and design, science and technology, history and culture, and language arts. Very well done.

Teacher's Edition Online   teachnet.com/lesson

Far more than just lesson ideas, Teachnet provides a collection of lesson-planning resources. The site also offers brainstorming ideas, micro-activities, classroom management strategies in the How-To section, and a free email newsletter for sharing ideas.

Teachers.Net Lesson Plan Exchange   teachers.net/lessons

More than four thousand lesson plans submitted by teachers. Organized by subject matter or grade level.

TeachersFirst Content Matrix   teachersfirst.com/matrix.htm

Teacher-written reviews of lesson plans from around the Web. The reviews are grouped by subject and grade.

World Lecture Hall   web.austin.utexas.edu/wlh

An amazing lesson library covering even obscure subjects.

Worksheets

IT'S REAL SCHOOLWORK. It's how you reinforce learning and test understanding. It's the dreaded worksheet!

Actually, when Mom and Dad tailor the learning, worksheets needn't be the boring make-work you experienced when you were in school.

Homeschooling mom Barbara Jermstad from Hampton, Virginia, says her oldest son loves worksheets. And workbooks were the very successful foundation of Joyce Dumire's homeschooling. When the Ohio mom took her teenage son out of public school, "the school let me keep the books that were assigned to him for that school year—until the end of the year. We worked on them and finished out his school year with what he had been using. My son loved the workbook method for math and hated it for everything else. That's when we started mixing it up to make it more fun for both of us."

Kentucky homeschooler Jessica Murphy is making more use of worksheets as her kids grow up. "We use worksheets and workbooks that I get at the local discount store. We actually sit and do lessons. We are working on getting more formal, since the kids are getting older and need more than fun to learn some things. I think some formal training is needed but it is not the end-all. Don't get too caught up in the formalities of lessons and trying to play school at home and just love your children the way God intended, with Grace."

The worksheet resources in this section cover almost

Work: From the Ancient Iranian *varEzem* (activity). Specific task or assignment that is part of some larger project.

Curriculum

every academic subject, as well as a lot of subjects that are fun but probably only marginally educational. Some even allow you to create your own worksheets, so you're covered from every angle.

ABC Teach   abcteach.com

Printable worksheets with thousands of free activities, games, unit studies, shapes, and puzzles. Your younger children in particular will enjoy these resources.

Freeology   freeology.com

Memorable address for some memorable worksheets. The graphic organizers are particularly well done. There is much here to love. Access the site with Internet Explorer for best results.

Homeschoolmath Worksheets
homeschoolmath.net/worksheets

An excellent collection of math worksheet generators that can create a variety of worksheets for subjects like telling time, factoring, decimals, and more.

Learning Page   learningpage.com

A collection of about 1,500 worksheets for grades K through 3. You must register, but it's free. The worksheets are very well done, and cover a range of subjects: alphabet, calendar, money, senses, time, measurement, and numbers. There are also numerous theme worksheets for older children on oceans, zoo animals, dinosaurs, reptiles, and insects. You'll also find links to lesson plans, clip art, ebooks and much more.

Printables and Worksheets   atozteacherstuff.com/printables

Pages and pages of worksheets, primarily for younger grades. Most of these worksheets are supplements to lesson plans linked from the worksheet page.

Hotlinks

Freeology
freeology.com

RHL School
rhlschool.com

School Express
schoolexpress.com

Teach-nology Worksheets
teach-nology.com/
worksheets

Curriculum

Curriculum

RHL School   rhlschool.com

Worksheets for reading comprehension, English basics, math problem solving, research skills, and math computation. Answer keys included.

School Express   schoolexpress.com

More than 11,000 worksheets across the curriculum. Includes answer files, which is always helpful. Includes a worksheet generator to make your own worksheets, awards, flashcards, and word scrambles. Genius!

Softschool Worksheet Generator   softschools.com

Generate worksheets, games, puzzles, and quizzes in many subjects, including handwriting, geography, phonics, and math.

Teach-nology Worksheets   teach-nology.com/worksheets

A collection of some 6,000 free printable K–12 teacher worksheets. Rubrics, critical thinking, graphic organizers, and research skills, along with all the usual academic subjects.

TLS page   tlsbooks.com

Free printable worksheets for preschool to fifth grade. Covers handwriting, spelling, reading, holidays, and more.

Toytown Treasures   toytowntreasures.com

A fairly large collection of worksheets and forms for math, grammar, social studies, science, and Bible studies. The math game templates are particularly useful for drilling math skills.

On Work

Man hath his daily work of body or mind Appointed.

—John Milton, 1608–1674

Worksheet Generator   worksheetworks.com

Create PDF-formatted worksheets in math, English, and geography. Choose your own criteria to make custom maps, crossword puzzles, and word searches.

Worksheets from Kiddy House   kiddyhouse.com/Worksheets

A small collection of worksheets on phonics, amphibians and reptiles, farm animals, holidays, social studies, geography, and history, colors, musical instruments, earth science, and life science. Black and white with line drawings.

Unit Studies

MANY HOMESCHOOLERS TAKE an entirely new approach to education: rather than teach a subject, they teach a unit. Unit studies is an educational philosophy that uses a single topic—seeds, for example, or the Civil War—to teach multiple curriculum areas.

> **Unit:** From the Latin *unitas* (one). A group of items combined as a single entity.

Unit studies inspire Robin Goddard's kids. The Maple Valley, Washington, mom of eight highly recommends them "because you can cover almost every subject (with the possible exception of math, although you can include it too with some doing) for every age at the same time. You can put together a wonderful unit study for free by picking a subject, going to the library for a pile of books on the subject, and searching out information, worksheets, coloring pages, quizzes, and so forth on the Internet. Have the kids write about what they learned, slap it all in a binder, and before you know it you've done a unit study!"

Lori Larson, another Washington mom, makes unit studies an integral part of her homeschooling program. "We work best when we work together. I have a hard time trying to fit four different schedules into one day. We start our day together: scriptures, prayer, breakfast, unit study, and then I pass out the math and they kind of work at their own pace after that.

"By lunchtime we are ready to play together, work together, or find time for individual projects while the others are playing. I always have a one-hour break in the day for 'quiet time,' when they can work on whatever they choose, but they must be in their rooms and quiet. This gives me time to recharge, or get something done, and it gives them time

Hotlinks

Highland Heritage Home School
highland.hitcho.com.au

Ignite the Fire
ignitethefire.com/fuel.html

Jessica Hulcy
tinyurl.com/hulunit

Templates by Donovan
bydonovan.com/
templates.html

alone (many of my children will still take a small nap during that time, even the older ones). We come back together for dinner, scriptures, and prayer, then whatever the evening holds for individuals."

One important component of unit studies is keeping a record of what the kids learn. Techniques such as lapbooking, notebooking, and portfolio creation serve this need quite nicely.

"When we found lapbooking, things really became alive in our home," says Wisconsin homeschooler Sarah Bull. "All three of my children began to understand more of the fundamentals of history and science."

Diana Malament from Gaithersburg, Maryland, is equally fond of lapbooks. "I have loved the free lapbooks that various companies offer at different times throughout the year. So far I have saved many and only worked with my son on one. Lapbooking is a learning experience, and my son is still fairly young for getting much out of it."

Ann Crum's homeschooled daughter understands the principle behind unit studies. Ann says, "The other day my twelve-year-old daughter told me, 'Mom, you know what I really like about homeschool? The fact that if I want to I can breeze through a subject as fast as I need to. But if something stumps me, I know you are there to help me through it, to learn it, and I can take what time I need to really learn it without a class leaving me behind.'" That, says Ann, is exactly the point of homeschooling.

These popular unit studies resources will engage your children's attention, and will probably teach them something as well!

Curriculum in a Click   currclick.com

Each week a new—and very well done—unit study. This is primarily a commercial site, but the free offerings are worth coming back to again and again.

Eclectic Homeschool   eclectichomeschool.org

An online magazine that bills itself as "for creative homeschoolers, published from a Christian perspective." The site is rich with excellent unit studies covering a variety of topics. You'll also find here curriculum reviews, and articles proffering advice and opinions.

Educationworld Interdisciplinary   tinyurl.com/ewunit

A small collection of lesson plans covering cross-curriculum teaching.

Emints   emints.org/ethemes/resources/by-grade.shtml

Hundreds of themes, organized not by topic but by grade level. Despite that, these themes are actually very, very good and worth investigating. Each theme consists of a description, a list of reviewed resources, and a tie-in to curriculum standards for various states. Someone's done your research for you. Take it!

Highland Heritage Home School   highland.hitcho.com.au

A genuinely useful page for unit studies, forms, and notebooking advice. Click the Forms link to find well-done forms for unit studies, nature journals, portfolios, field trips and general academic subjects. There are hundreds of homeschooling forms all over the Web; this is one of the few worth holding on to.

Homeschool Journaling   lacellefamily.com/journal.html

About a dozen different ideas for subject-oriented notebooks.

Homeschool Share   homeschoolshare.com

Literature-based unit studies developed by a consortium of sharing families. The multi-book thematic units are particularly well done.

Homeschool Unit Studies   oklahomahomeschool.com/unitstudies.html

Unit studies in history, social studies, science, and music, along with general instruction on how to use unit studies in your homeschooling, from a homeschooling family.

On Excellence

We are what we repeatedly do. Excellence then is not an act but a habit.
—Aristotle, 384–322 B.C.

Curriculum

On Success

The only place success comes before work is in the dictionary.

—Vince Lombardi, football coach

Homeschooling Lapbooks
homeschoolhelperonline.com/lapbooks.htm

How to create and fold lapbooks, along with dozens of lapbook ideas and templates. Click the Notebooking link on the left for even more ideas.

How to Plan a Unit Study   tinyurl.com/abunit
Thirteen steps to creating and using a unit study.

Ignite the Fire   ignitethefire.com/fuel.html
Terrific notebooking ideas that explain what notebook is and how can it be used to educate your kids.

Interdisciplinary Lesson Plans   tinyurl.com/interlp
Dozens of easy-to-use unit studies. These units were prepared for classroom use but are easily adapted to homeschooling.

Jessica Hulcy   tinyurl.com/hulunit
This homeschooling writer explains why she believes unit studies are the best approach to home education. A series of articles.

Learner Interactives   learner.org/exhibits
Very well made interactives with strategies, content, and activities to teach math, science, language, history, and the arts. Each resource makes up a complex web quest that would make a great foundation for a unit study.

Making Books with Children   makingbooks.com
Teach bookmaking to encourage literacy and creativity, says the creator of this site for teachers and families. Advice, ideas, and activities.

Mr. Donn's Lessons & Learning Modules   mrdonn.org/#ours
History-based unit studies covering ancient history, world history, and U.S. history. Very thorough.

Multidisciplinary   learnersonline.com/weekly/subject/multi.htm
Web quests. Extremely well done, with photographs, links, explanatory text, and illustrations.

Notebooking Pages   notebookingpages.com

Explanations and examples of notebooking as a teaching technique. Mostly a commercial site, but the educational pages make for a good starting place.

Paso Partners   tinyurl.com/sedunit

Bilingual unit studies for grades K through 3, integrating mathematics, science, and language.

Templates by Donovan   bydonovan.com/templates.html

Templates for building lapbooks with envelopes, pop-up cards, folios, and mini-books.

Themes and Topics   pppst.com/themes.html

PowerPoint presentations on hundreds and hundreds of academic topics. Introducing a unit study topic to small co-op or sibling groups is easy with the help of these pre-made presentations.

ThinkQuest Library   thinkquest.org/library

More than 7,000 websites created by students around the world who have participated in a ThinkQuest competition. This is what a completed unit study might look like.

Unit Study Index   easyfunschool.com/IndexUnitStudies.html

Unit studies on everything from Aesop's Fables and Ancient China to Wilderness Survival and Women's History. The Hot Chocolate study may not have any educational purpose, but it's a lot of fun!

Field Trips

FIELD TRIPS, SAYS North Carolina mom Terri Vitkovitsky, are what homeschooling is all about. "We do lots of field trips and I certainly find it a very effective way to teach."

Sometimes the zoo, sometimes a museum, sometimes online . . . but always educational. How do you handle field trips?

Curriculum

Field: From the Germanic *feld* (field). A setting for practical learning outside one's usual place of education or work.

"To get the most out of a field trip, plan, plan, plan!" says Angela Jones from Dry Fork, Virginia. "I always look for ways to fit the field trip into multiple subject areas and the child's particular interest. I also look for other nearby learning experiences, in case the first plan falls through for whatever reason. Mostly, just get creative and you can make any trip, from a routine trip to the grocery store to a drive down a country road, into a fun, enjoyable learning experience."

Field trips needn't cost more than the price of getting there. Free resources abound. "For me," says Amber Neal of Fredericksburg, Virginia, "the best field trips are the free ones. I use the library's programs, the trip to the grocery store, and my local farms or parks, to name a few. I always recommend joining a local homeschool email chain, because you get the best ideas from other moms."

California mom Liz deForest has taken plenty of free field trips, too. "Once we visited a cake-decorating business by accident because we were passing it and stopped in and asked if the kids could watch the work in the back. They made very large numbers of cakes and the workers were very fast. One showed off for the kids and flipped a cake in the air. We recently went to the Exxon refinery and that was not only free, they gave the kids bags of loot. That tour was fascinating."

For Darnia Hobson, a New Zealand homeschooler, field trips are best when they involve a group. "We have a ball on our field trips!" she says. "Most of the children in our group are between four and ten years of age. Usually we have around twenty to thirty attending, plus parents and younger siblings.

"The children have gained a wide range of skills from these trips, but, more important, they have been exposed to a variety of perspectives, including those of experts in their fields, and had firsthand learning experiences. They have learned to communicate with a wide range of adults, in a big

Hotlinks

Museumlink
museumlink.com

National Register of Historic Places
nationalregisterof historicplaces.com

U.S. Forest Service
www.fs.fed.us

range of circumstances, and had social contact with their friends, too. And the Mums have had a chance for a natter and coffee, which is also invaluable. Of course we are in New Zealand, so our experiences will vary but the principles are the same! We use free services where possible, or at least heavily discounted rates.

"My advice is to just ring and ask! Most people have bent over backwards to accommodate our group, and once you talk to one person, news of your groups spread and more opportunities crop up. Many organisations offer pre-visit information packs, so use these or do a little Google research before you go. Not too much, mind; part of the fun is discovering something new!"

Make ID cards and get discounts, advises Shari Ramsey, an Illinois homeschooler. "We have printed homeschool ID cards from the homeschool buyers' co-op (**homeschoolbuyersco-op.org/homeschool-id**). With these ID cards, we can get into any museum or attraction that offers teacher discounts or free admission. We have taken our son to the museum campus in Chicago and plan to continue to take him there as he gets older. We can get into all of those museums for free all year long."

Robin Tompkins recently had a tremendous field trip for her two young children. During a unit study of homes and neighborhoods, the Redding, California, mom covered fire safety. She explained to her children the importance of developing and practicing a fire escape plan, and had each child practice opening windows, removing screens, jumping to the ground, and meeting at the designated location. She followed up with a field trip to a fire station, where the kids were told how the firefighters lived at the station. They also saw the tools of the trade and watched one of the firefighters get dressed in gear, including full mask and oxygen, which prepared the children not to be afraid should they ever need to be rescued.

To make the trip more enjoyable, Robin invited other homeschool families to join in. "There were seven families with a total of about fourteen kids in attendance, and they had many good questions," she says.

Some homeschooling parents are overwhelmed by the notion of trying to teach their children about the arts. If you've considered making your field trips more cultural, more focused on the arts, you may have dealt with the same concern. Michael Brownlee, a professional actor and playwright living and working in Chicago, offers suggestions for homeschoolers visiting the theater or a concert for the first time: "I think the first thing to remember when approaching the subject of seeing a play or a concert is to make it fun," Michael says. "Try to incorporate the play or music into the lesson plan. If it's a play, then have the children act out some of the scenes."

Michael says living the play is the best way to teach kids to appreciate the drama. "I remember reading *Romeo and Juliet* in high school and being bored to tears because that's all we did—read it. Get them on their feet and into the play. I think you learn a lot about a play if you are suddenly one of the people in it. It doesn't have to be Broadway-worthy; just have fun. The same thing goes for attending a concert or visiting a museum: Find some way to make them a part of it, not just spectators. Ask what their favorite songs are and what it is they like about those songs. Then put it all in context with what they are going to see. Bach was the Bon Jovi of his time."

Stephanie Coomer, an unschooling mother of four in Michigan, is a committed field tripper. She and her husband Ron, whom she says is as much into homeschooling as she is, love to take the family camping. Her husband is home a great deal of the time, which means the family can go camping anytime they want. "This is great bonding time, and we can look for berries, flowers, types of rocks, animal tracks, and fossils."

Ron and Stephanie have made virtually everything an education for their family. "We go to museums, zoos . . . we even went to Kansas to buy a home and to see places along the way in all the different states. We have been camping with other homeschool families, gone to Home Depot to build items (for free, by the way), and have seen The Wonders of Egypt at our tiny local museum."

Stephanie operates a local homeschooling support group that has gone on many field trips together. Her group operates a mailing list to discuss field trips a few months in advance, and one person actually does the organizing. "The one originating the visit sets up a time, a date, and a price. Four to six weeks before the trip, that person sends out a memo and starts posting the names of those who have confirmed. Someone makes the nametags and works with the originator. A week ahead, they remind those who have not paid, confirm new people, send out a map and directions, name a meeting place, and send out reminders about all the little details. We all meet, pass out nametags, and enjoy!"

The unschooling experience means anything is possible. As an unschooling family, Stephanie says, they try to make every field trip fun but educational. "Our life is a learning experience, and that's how we make it fun for the children. It's not unusual to find one of the children talking about the different colors in the clouds, or why the water is different today than yesterday." She and her husband make it easy for all questions to have answers, she says, "and if that means looking up a word before answering a question, we do it."

Dena Anderson is in her second year as the field trip coordinator for her Alabama support group of more than 150 homeschooling families. Dena has found that the best field trips are the free ones. "They're available in all shapes and sizes, if you just look," she says. Factory tours tend to be free of charge, for example; Dena's group has visited factories making Bud's cookies and Golden Flake chips. "All sorts of that stuff is available, from pizza to donuts." State parks often offer naturalist tours for free. "We have gone to two of those. One was a killer hike uphill to an indoor wild animal rescue-and-rehabilitation facility. The other was a watershed tour where they took us to a creek and we had a hands-on look at creek life. Both were wonderfully done."

Susie Clawson has been homeschooling her five children from the beginning. She belongs to a local homeschool support group that is very active with field trips. "For us, they aren't 'extracurricular' but a part of our learning. We have a very relaxed approach to learning, and we do it as a family. When we visit a place, we usually review proper behavior while en route, and sometimes we'll read a book or watch a video in preparation or in review."

She tries to keep up her children's enthusiasm. "I try to not ruin the fun with too much preparation. I try not to force their focus, as I've seen done in public school field trips. I allow the kids to explore on their own at times and we explore together at times, depending on the place we visit. I don't press them to move on before they've had their fill of a display or gallery or project. Being blessed with no time constraints (as opposed to a public school field trip), we have this luxury.

"Our family's philosophy of life and learning is that they're interconnected. You can compartmentalize learning, but why would you want to? Everything in the world is educational in one way or another, and the joy of learning is to find that and use it to enrich your own life. I see my children learning to do this. They glean and grow from their experiences."

Many of the following Internet resources will help you prepare for field trips. Others will serve as field trips of another sort, by taking your children on an online trip to places far, far away.

Association of Zoos and Aquariums   aza.org/FindZooAquarium

The AZA accredits zoos, aquariums, and wildlife refuges throughout the U.S. and in various international locations. Use this resource to find locations near your home and near your vacation destinations.

Botanical Gardens   tinyurl.com/ftbot

Arboretums and botanical gardens all around the world are listed on this Wikipedia page. No matter where you go, there's a great garden awaiting your kids' visit.

CitySearch   citysearch.com

Mostly an adult-oriented resource, but there are still enough family-oriented events to make the site worth visiting. Most U.S. metropolitan areas are represented.

Designing a Virtual Field Trip   tinyurl.com/virfie

How and why to use virtual field trips. Explains how to plan the "trip" so the kids can learn more from it.

Field Trip Factory   fieldtripfactory.com

Find field trips in your area and learn how to schedule them. The focus is on commercial enterprises. Just enter your zip code and see what's available.

Museumlink   museumlink.com

Great site with links to museums all around the United States and Canada, as well as to several international museum. New to the site: virtual museums, where you and your kids can see exhibitions of toasters, the Beatles, and chocolate cats. Chocolate cats?

National Park Service   nps.gov/findapark

Turns out there are nine national parks within 100 miles of my zip code. Can you do better? Click the Kids and Teacher link on the left for curriculum links to make your visit even more educational.

National Register of Historic Places
nationalregisterofhistoricplaces.com

More than 85,000 registered historic places in the United States. That oughta keep you busy for a few days, yes? Don't limit yourself to the neighborhood. Every vacation deserves at least one historic side trip.

Trail Database   traildatabase.org

An immense database of hiking trails around the world.

U.S. Department of the Interior   www.doi.gov/teachers

The teacher's section. Learn about the government's conservation initiatives, and visit the resources for individual parks near your home. There is a lot of information on these sites.

U.S. Forest Service   www.fs.fed.us

Locate forests and grasslands managed by the forest service. Click the International link to learn about the department's work outside the U.S. The Recreational Activities link describes special events and programs.

When We Get There   whenwegetthere.com

Click the Tourist Attraction Search button at the top of the page to find local activities.

Preschool

THE WHOLE "BABY" thing was behind me: The baby clothes were long gone, I was planning a tenth-birthday celebration for my youngest, and my only concern was getting my kids into college.

So why was I pregnant?

Now that we have a baby again, and our home is filled with blocks and duckies and Dr. Seuss, I'm finding that the Internet is even more fun than I'd thought. And homeschooling a one-year-old is an entirely different experience from teaching her older siblings. For one thing, she has a whole house full of "teachers."

Jenny McComber, homeschooling in Texas, finds it challenging to teach with a little one at her feet, but has found ways to make it work. "How do I homeschool with four children of varying ages?" she asks. "I take one day at a time. I try to include my two-year-old during our art projects, even though the cleanup time triples when she's involved. The boys and I installed foam square flooring in the schoolroom so at least I don't have to worry about messes. I try to do some lessons with the boys together, but because they are seven and eleven, they are at different learning levels, which makes this difficult. My eleven-year-old is a great help. He can discipline, control, distract, or play with my two-year-old as well as, and sometimes better than, I can. He has an infinite amount of patience. He is teaching his brother how to play the piano."

Early: From the Old English *ær* (before). An initial stage of development.

North Carolina mom Terri Vitkovitsky is taking it easy with her preschool homeschooler. "Curriculum is definitely unnecessary for preschoolers," she says. "I use life experience, reading books, field trips, exploring outside, and so forth. I love *Teach Your Child to Read in 100 Easy Lessons* (**tinyurl.com/read100**) to teach them to read. When they are ready to write, get them writing things pertinent: the ingredients to scrambled eggs, family members' names, and so forth."

Other moms are equally unstructured. Shari Ramsey, mother of a two-year-old, says, "We're a little early in our homeschool adventure to be planning too many field trips with structured educations, but we take our son everywhere we can whenever we can."

Melody Daisson's preschool is more formal. "I have set up a preschool for my kids teaching religion, self-care, manners, music, reading, math readiness, social studies, and science," she says. "My theme this year is 'Learning Together Is Fun.' I teach the subjects according to ability and interest."

This year, Melody's goal is to determine each child's learning style. "I am in the 'this works, that doesn't work' stage," she says. "Our mistakes are definitely learning experiences. For example, I started out teaching five days a week. We were all overwhelmed! So now we cut down to three days of formal school and just enjoy playing together the rest of the week. I think what I want to accomplish by homeschooling is to teach them that we love them and we are their parents and their best friends."

Teresa Cavender from Tennessee is homeschooling her eighteen-month-old son. "I know you may think I'm crazy for saying that I homeschool," she says, "but it's a way of life for us. And since his life began eighteen months ago, we've been homeschooling." Teresa also runs a very small educational child care program from her home, where she teaches a three-year-old girl and a set of five-year-old twins. Her experiences are instructive to any parent of a preschooler:

"We recently read 'The Little Hero of Holland' out of the book *The Children's Book of Virtues,* edited by William Bennett. I explained a couple of words I thought they might not know (such as 'dike') before we began

Hotlinks

Homeschooling with a Preschooler
contentmentacres.com

Perpetual Preschool
perpetualpreschool.com

Poisson Rouge
poissonrouge.com

Yakaberry
yakaberry.com

Curriculum

Preschool Freebie

Helping Your Preschool Child suggests activities for families with children from infancy through age five. Call 877-4-ED-PUBS and request pamphlet number ED004453H.

the story, and asked them if they knew where Holland was located. Of course they said no, so I told them we would look it up after we read the story. After a couple of pages, they wanted to act it out (I guess they realized their little brains were filling up), so we stopped and they acted and then we continued. When we finished the story and narration (very short story), they jumped up and said, 'Okay, let's look up where Holland is.' We went to the big map I have mounted on the wall. We looked and looked and looked and couldn't find the country called Holland. So we went to the computer to see what we could find. I allowed them to use the mouse, type, and browse the Web. We found that another name for Holland is the Netherlands. We went back to the map and looked for the name Netherlands, and we found it. I must sheepishly admit that I didn't know that they were one and the same. I, of course, didn't let on anything of the kind and made it seem as though that was part of the lesson! It does remind me that I will be learning as much as the children will, though.

"My son was in the thick of the whole lesson. He wanted to 'play' on the computer, run back and forth with us from computer to map, and sat a little bit through the story. It was great fun and a great experience watching the children get so excited about learning."

Ready to homeschool your own preschoolers? Here are the best resources for getting started.

BBC Preschool   bbc.co.uk/schools/websites/preschool

The BBC's amazing, colorful resource for children eighteen months to five years old. A bottomless collection of learning activities, games, and stories. Some of it even involves Teletubbies.

Coloring Pages   free-coloring-pages.com

If you're teaching your preschooler about colors, these coloring-book pictures will amuse and educate.

Educational Activities for Children   dltk-teach.com

A gold mine of educational materials for the little ones. The Mini-Books section, for example, has illustrated books that teach the alphabet, Bible stories, colors, the body, and many others.

Educational Preschool and Kindergarten Teaching Activities
kidschalkboard.com

Dozens and dozens of great hands-on ideas for activities using common household items. You'll find the article entitled "Expectations of 3, 4, and 5 Year Olds" especially interesting.

Games Lessons and Activities   easyfunschool.com/IndexGames.html

A collection of real-life educational games for families to play together—off the computer.

Homeschooling Preschoolers   tinyurl.com/prebon

Loads of advice from moms who've been there. Homeschooling little ones is an entirely different pursuit from teaching big kids. Here are suggestions for guiding preschool learning to prepare them for a lifetime of learning.

Homeschooling with a Preschooler
contentmentacres.com

Click the Homeschooling Tips link on the left, and find several excellent articles about homeschooling with young children, from infants to preschool.

Kendra's Colouring Pages   colorbook.tripod.com

Pictures and an alphabet book to color online or print out and color by hand.

Kiddie Records Weekly   kiddierecords.com

New presentations of old recorded children's stories, including such classics as Robin Hood, Uncle Remus,

---

Motivation

My son is only two, but I'm lucky because he still loves to learn. I think making learning fun is definitely key.

—Shari Ramsey, homeschooling mom of one with another homeschooler on the way, Loves Park, Illinois

☆ Best Homeschooling Moment

When Daddy comes home from work our three-year-old will often give him a verbal rundown of everything I taught the older ones in the day. Didn't know she was paying attention and I never realized until then that she could grasp what we were learning.

—Sarah Bull, a guide to three educations, Wisconsin Dells, Wisconsin

and Paul Bunyan. The website also shows the jacket covers from the old recordings.

Kids CBC Preschool   cbc.ca/kidscbc

Enter the Play section to load fun, colorful online games that teach cooking, numbers, art, writing, weather, and so much more. From the Canadian Broadcasting Corporation.

Online Coloring   Bookcoloring.com

Every one of my kids—even the seventeen-year-old—loves this darling little page. We use it to entertain the baby.

Perpetual Preschool   perpetualpreschool.com

Woodworking, art, blocks, and so much more in the Learning Center. Tons of lessons for the little ones. Click the Themes link and choose new themes for each school day.

Playtime for Toddlers   tinyurl.com/tmplay

Recipes for bubbles, papier-mâché, paints, play dough, and cooking, as well as coloring, craft, and indoor gardening projects. All projects use inexpensive recycled materials. The sidewalk chalk and soap crayons were especially popular with our three-year-old daughter.

Poisson Rouge   poissonrouge.com

Extensive multilingual educational printables, colorful games, lots to talk about with your preschooler. The user guide explains how to navigate the site.

Preschool   themes.pppst.com/preschool.html

PowerPoint presentations that teach parents how to teach preschoolers. One of the lessons, Thinking Skills for Littlies, explains "Thinker's Keys" that help young learners begin to expand their thinking skills.

Others discuss counting, art, ABCs, and many other preschool topics.

Preschool Lessons and Activities

easyfunschool.com/IndexPreschool.html

Fun educational activities for your littlest learners. Colored play dough, Pooh butter, and Lapbooks for Everyone are highly recommended.

Sprout Online   sproutonline.com

PBS Kids Sprout is a 24-hour cable channel for preschoolers. This companion website has videos that teach preschool skills such as exercise, sign language, art, and nature studies.

Universal Preschool   universalpreschool.com

Preschool already *is* universal; it's what we call "home." This site provides research demonstrating that there's no better place for toddlers than at home with loving parents.

Yakaberry   yakaberry.com

Story-hour lesson plans and activities designed to help children become better readers. Fun, brightly colored graphics. Tools are organized by age group and theme.

> ☆ *Best Homeschooling Moment*
>
> We have just started informal homeschooling with my two-year-old. He gets so excited when he learns something new. He really is a sponge and always is asking for more new things. I guess a recent great moment was when we sat down to talk about letters and numbers while playing and my son was just not in the mood for it. I told him that we could do it later. He got a little upset thinking we would not do it at all. I explained to him that this was the great thing about doing school at home and that we could come back to it later.
>
> —**Shari Ramsey,** homeschooling mom of one with another homeschooler on the way, Loves Park, Illinois

Special Education

I'M THE MOTHER of an entire houseful of "special-needs" children.

Some are "special-needs" because of attention or behavior disorders; one has a slight learning disability; one was classified as "special-needs" by the local government because she was two years old when she was adopted; some are "special-needs" because they're gifted; another is "special-needs"

Curriculum

Special: From the Latin *species* (kind). Surpassing the common or usual.

because she's an entire decade younger than anyone else in the house and believes the world rotates around her whims. (She's right, of course. It's a handicap, being exceptionally cute and spoiled rotten.)

Whether you're dealing with learning disabilities, behavior disorders, physical or mental disabilities, gifted children, or a combination of "exceptional" educational issues, your homeschooling takes on a different cast from the norm.

Some of the most difficult children to homeschool are those with behavior disorders. Dr. K. Ross is a Texas psychologist who specializes in classroom management and working with the "problem child." Dr. Ross was hired by the Dallas Independent School District to run a high school-level alternative education program after they lost control of their "problem kids."

Dr. Ross offers some advice to parents who are homeschooling children with behavior disorders: "You don't need to reinvent the wheel. I have observed, and made a lot of mistakes working with, kids. The following is what I have found (through observation, education, and experience) that works, even with the toughest kids.

Hotlinks

Accommodation Strategies
washington.edu/doit/ faculty/strategies

Born to Explore
borntoexplore.org

Mommy Speech Therapy
mommyspeechtherapy .com

Uniquely Gifted
uniquelygifted.org

"Kids seek pride from adults they respect. They want us to be proud of them. Sometimes I see well-intentioned teachers and parents with big hearts make the biggest mistakes. If you love your children, make them mind. Expect proper behavior, acknowledge and appreciate them when you see it, and when you see willful disregard and disobedience, take swift action. Set clear rules and expect them to follow them. Inappropriate behavior will not stop without consistent consequences. The rule for consequences is consistent, non-hostile action that immediately follows any willful disobedience to the rule.

"This is easier said than done. However, one of the worst things parent-teachers do is threaten with no action.

All you do is reinforce their behavior and wear yourself out till you're angry and have some unhealthy resentments. The worst thing teachers do is lose their temper. Do not ever lose your temper, or you will lose all respect and ability to manage your students. This is particularly true the older they get.

"The important thing to remember is to take some action, even if it is small. Talk is not action. Kids are used to the 'lectures' and usually stop for only a short time. Other kids don't even wait for the lecture to end. Remember: Kids learn from experience, and if they don't receive a consequence, they didn't learn not to repeat their mistake. They will cease the inappropriate behavior when it is easier to choose to comply.

"If you have shown them you will do these things and follow through, they really do begin to understand that you care. Your words begin (in time) to have real value to them, so when you do say, 'Great job, Johnny,' it means something. It means you're proud of them; and kids, like the rest of us, tend to take care of things they are proud of."

For Sarah Bull, a Wisconsin mom of three, homeschooling addresses special needs at both ends of the learning spectrum. And does it better than public resources can: "Our public school and local schools do not have a gifted/talented or accelerated classes in the elementary years. I have one child gifted and one child with ADHD. I can better reach them and be more patient with their learning styles," she says.

On Giftedness

What is called genius is the abundance of life and health.

—Henry David Thoreau, 1817–1862

Massachusetts mother Christine Blair is dealing with a problem even more severe. "I am homeschooling two boys, ages nine and six, both with autism. This is my second year of homeschool, and we now just love what we are doing.

"I started out homeschooling because I believed my boys need individualized educations. I wanted to meet them where they were and move forward from there. I wanted the freedom to move through areas quickly if they 'got it' right away, but stop and sit on a subject if they needed more time. I bought a packaged curriculum and they were going to keep the records and grades. I quickly found out that this was not the way for

Curriculum

Tip

Get a free copy of *Achieving in Spite Of*, a booklet on learning disabilities, by calling 800-323-7938.

us. You would have thought some form of medieval torture was going on at our house during school hours. I forced my older son to do every problem because that was what was required from the school. We did this for more than half of the school year until I finally gave up in frustration. I bought a unit study and a few other things and finished out the rest of the year that way.

"I started to learn about the Charlotte Mason way of teaching: short lessons, little or no workbooks, narration as a way of checking comprehension, nature walks and nature journals, and good books. We have been doing this for the last few months, and my boys are thriving and absolutely loving school. We are still doing our A Beka math, although I pick and choose from the page what I want them to do. I will be getting *Making Math Meaningful* soon, which is more hands-on with manipulatives. We are reading great books like *Robinson Crusoe* and biographies of people like Corrie Ten Boom."

Ann Glass has discovered lots of tricks for making homeschool work for her "squirrely" five- and seven-year-old sons: "First, we have rules and expectations in the area of listening, just as we have rules and expectations in all the other areas of family life. My firm belief is that learning cannot take place if there is no discipline—and I don't necessarily mean punishment, but rather training.

"We intersperse 'seatwork' with more active, hands-on learning. When I am actively teaching or reading aloud, I ask questions, and the boys offer their suggestions and speculations. Often they really do know the answer. I keep my explanations short. I also have them repeat back to me any instructions that I've given.

"If they're really stumped, I step in and help them think through it. It all comes back to listening. The boys have found that it pays to listen carefully the first time and ask questions at that time to clarify it, rather than to be without a clue later and left to struggle for a while.

"We also insist that they listen in church. We've had wonderful discussions on the way home. We've asked our pastor to let us know his scripture and the topic of his sermon beforehand, so the boys are somewhat prepared. They listen eagerly to see what Pastor has to say, since they've already formed their own opinions on the topic. We're also fortunate that our pastor has the ability to preach about profound things in simple terms."

No matter what the needs of your exceptional child, the following resources will contain something useful. Give them a try!

Accommodation Strategies   washington.edu/doit/faculty/strategies

Tons of strategies for accommodating various disabilities while teaching. Very resourceful.

ADHD and Other Learning Challenges

highland.hitcho.com.au/learningchall.htm

This homeschooling family offers tested teaching strategies for ADHD children, many of which will work with other learning challenges as well.

Born to Explore   borntoexplore.org

Alternatives to medication for ADD/ADHD children.

Bry-Back Manor   bry-backmanor.org

Lots of fun ideas and activities to keep young children and children with special needs productive and engaged. From activity pages to garden fun, this site will provide many busy hours for your child.

Family Education   familyeducation.com

From the Your Child links at the top, click Special Needs for great articles and advice on teaching for learning disabilities, gifted and talented, Asperger's syndrome, and ADHD.

Gifted Children   gifted-children.com

Is your child gifted? This site offers articles about identifying whether your child is gifted and encouraging

---

Special-Ed Freebie

Identifying and Treating Attention Deficit Hyperactivity Disorder provides helpful hints on how to deal with ADHD at school and at home. Call 877-4-ED-PUBS and request product number ED004463P.

Curriculum

their talents. It is a networking site to help parents meet the needs of their highly capable children.

GT World   gtworld.org

A support community for gifted and talented individuals and those who support and nurture them. Mailing lists, glossary, testing information, and articles. Quite useful.

Homeschooling Gifted Students   tinyurl.com/nswspec

Describes academic, social, and legal considerations in homeschooling gifted children.

Homeschooling with Special Challenges   hsc.org/143.html

Three moms who have found their own solutions to special-education challenges share some helpful advice. Collected by the Homeschooling Association of California.

It's the Biology, Stupid   tinyurl.com/biospec

Transcript from a radio program that asks "Are little boys naturally brattier than little girls? And how should the answer to that question affect public policy?" Fascinating reading, and a strong repudiation of drugging boys.

Learning Abled Kids   learningabledkids.com

Encouragement for parents teaching children with disabilities.

Learning Disabilities Resources   ldonline.org

Claims—with some believability—to be the "world's leading website on learning disabilities and ADHD." Good support, and answers to questions, for parents and educators dealing with childhood learning disabilities.

Learning Disability: A Rose by Another Name
naturalchild.org/jan_hunt/learning.html

You say tomato; I say dysteachia. The author argues that latin-ate gobbledegook doesn't make an illness. Unless there's clear evidence of neurological damage, the problem is probably not the child.

Mommy Speech Therapy mommyspeechtherapy.com

An entire blog about providing at-home speech therapy, written by a mom who is also a trained speech/language pathologist.

Smart Kid at Home smartkidathome.com

This site offers sage advice on homeschooling your gifted children and about meeting their needs.

Special Education Resource Documents tinyurl.com/sedocs

From the government of British Columbia, suggestions and advice for teaching children with a wide variety of learning disabilities, giftedness, syndromes, disorders, and other special needs.

Special Needs tinyurl.com/bbcspec

A collection of special-education resources from the BBC's Education Web Guide. Each review suggests ways to integrate the site into your teaching.

Tinsnips tinsnips.org

A good resource for parents and teachers of autistic children and those with similar special needs. They provide information and links about autism along with plenty of ideas and activities to help children learn.

Uniquely Gifted uniquelygifted.org

A plethora of resources for parents of gifted children with special needs. Informative articles and personal stories offer support for parents.

Unschooling

I'M NOT AN unschooler. Not for any philosophical reasons, mind you; I simply lack the courage. Other homeschoolers are braver and are openly embracing the unschooling movement, which has children directing their own educations based on their academic interests, rather than following a set curricu-

Un-: From the Greek *an-* (not). Prefix meaning to reverse or undo an action.

lum. Texas homeschooling mom Jenny McComber is one. "Some days I ask myself, 'Are they learning anything?'" But then she remembers that her kids are learning wonderful life skills. "I try to turn everyday activities into learning opportunities, whether it is cooking, writing out bills, balancing the checkbook, caring for the baby, or gardening. My eleven-year-old used a map in the truck the other day to help us get to a farm we were visiting. When we arrived, only a little late, and after being a little off course, he said, 'That was fun.' I asked him if he thought he learned more about maps during our trip to the farm than if he had been sitting at a desk studying simulated map scenarios. His choice was obvious.

"I may not be able to have sit-down lessons with my children all the time at this point in our lives because of the demands of having an infant and a toddler, but I feel it will be okay. I have faith in my children that they are learning every day."

California homeschooler Liz deForest has been home-schooling for nearly seventeen years and believes she has it down to a science. "I unschool them when they are little, then gradually introduce some reading and math. Then around age twelve we get more serious. At thirteen the party is over, and at fourteen they do college prep and/or community college."

For Nola Hiatt, homeschooling six daughters in Texas, unschooling is just more practical than rigid adherence to a tight curriculum. "We have gravitated to a combination of general curriculum plan and unschooling. I have seen this same pattern in other friends I have who have also homeschooled for long periods of time. I make a yearly plan or a semester's plan, and work at it, but I'm afraid I don't usually stick to it very consistently. That's one of my weaknesses, but it seems to work anyway.

"We have actually done a lot of unschooling along with the plan and between new plans. There are a lot of times when I think we need to start school and I look at what they are doing and find them playing an edu-

Hotlinks

Experiential Education
wilderdom.com/
experiential

Life Without School
lifewithoutschool
.typepad.com

cational game on the computer or creating something. Why should I stop them from their chosen learning to do something I have decided on? I just tell myself, 'There's math for the day.' We do have some structured time that is maybe two hours a day three to four days a week. I use it for building their testimonies of God, and reading lots of things from history, science, or math. I try to use it to introduce new things that they might not look at themselves or to follow some of the plan I made. Then they have just a little seatwork—some math, journaling, or whatever else we are working on. We rarely spend more than three hours a day on structured schoolwork."

Lauren Frazer, an unschooler from New Jersey, has plenty of advice for new unschoolers. "I think one thing I have had to do is remember that this is homeschool; you can do it your way. Homeschooling parents sometimes get caught up in grading and following a curriculum. As long as my son learns what is required by the end of the year, it doesn't matter how I do it."

Heather Hada, an unschooling mother of three, is an advocate of unschooling and believes it's the best way to teach children. "Unschooling is hard to explain. I know this because a few years ago I would have thought these ideas crazy. But now what I don't understand is why schools still operate as they do, and why they totally ignore child education research. Learning is a natural process and can't be forced."

Heather didn't start out unschooling. "When I first started homeschooling I bought a book full of worksheets that was supposed to cover every subject for first grade. I figured that that would do until I could find a suitable curriculum. My son hated it. It was like pulling teeth to make him do the worksheets. I found out about de-schooling, so I figured I'd let him recover for a while. He had a bad experience with his first-grade teacher, which is why I chose to take him out of school."

Heather's approach illustrates the difference between homeschooling and unschooling. "Most unschoolers don't do school at home, unless that's what their child wants to do. There is a lot of open communication between the parent and the child. The parent acts more as a facilitator.

We do a lot of field trips. We also explore the Internet together. My husband buys lots of educational software, and I buy a lot of hands-on stuff such as science kits and models.

"I don't look at my son as an empty vessel whom I have to fill with knowledge, but rather as a growing plant that just needs love and care. Everything that children do is educational." Thinking about unschooling for your own family? These resources provide a good foundation for making the decision:

Can a Christian Be an Unschooler?   tinyurl.com/unmid

Patrick Farenga, publisher of John Holt's *Growing Without Schooling*, says there's little distinction between relaxed homeschooling and unschooling. The family structure issue is a parenting question, he says, not an educational one.

Experiential Education   wilderdom.com/experiential

A resource page describing the philosophy, theory, and practice of experiential learning, the belief that actually living life is more educational than learning about living life.

Francis W. Parker's Concentration Pedagogy
san.beck.org/Parker.html

The original unschooler—though John Holt is credited with coining the word—Civil War–era educator Francis Parker defined education as "the science of the soul and the laws of its development." Parker, a devout believer in God, did not want to see the naturally active and curious child being forced to become passive. Besides his pioneering work in child-led learning, he may also have been the founder of the idea of learning styles, positing that there are three modes of "attention": observation, hearing-language, and reading.

Gardening with Kids   tinyurl.com/ungar

Click the link to "A Visit with Mary Hood," where she advocates creating a natural learning environment. Don't hide materials away in cupboards. Out of sight, out of mind. Instead, create learning centers where materials are out in the open, and available. And don't attempt

Mark Twain

Samuel Clemens was four years old when his family moved to Hannibal, Missouri, on the bank of the Mississippi River. He spent his childhood playing alongside the river, fascinated by the romance of steamboats, keelboats, and the river life all around him. Hannibal's wooded hills, fishing, and nearby island fired the imagination of the man who grew up to call himself Mark Twain, in honor of the river that so influenced his childhood. When he was thirteen, Samuel was apprenticed to a local printer, and when his older brother Orion established a newspaper, the *Hannibal Journal,* Samuel became a compositor—the beginning of his professional life as a newspaperman and author.

to dole out knowledge in little bits, year after year. Learning binges are a good thing.

HLN Homeschool Approaches
homeschoollearning.com/approaches
Discusses ten of the most popular philosophies of homeschooling, including unschooling.

Home Educate's Unschooling   home-educate.com/unschooling
Dedicated to the unschooling method of education. Offers unschooling as a relaxing alternative to a stressful life.

Life Without School   lifewithoutschool.typepad.com
A collection of blogs that support life without school, diversity of perspective, choice, the family, and the child.

Natural Learning Initiative   naturalearning.org
The Initiative seeks to get education moved . . . well, outdoors, where children can regain contact with the natural world. Kids without trees don't get their developmental needs met.

Natural Nature Learning   seedsofknowledge.com/learning1.html
How to keep a nature diary, even when you're living in the city.

Six-Lesson Schoolteacher   cantrip.org/gatto.html

The six lessons that public schools teach—which happens to coincide with the six reasons unschooling advocates unschool. By John Taylor Gatto. Cynical, but it rings with truth.

Unschooling Philosophy   tinyurl.com/unphil

A series of eight lessons on natural schooling from Suite 101, home to hundreds of articles on every conceivable subject.

What Is Unschooling?   naturalchild.com/guest/earl_stevens.html

Unschooling isn't a method, says writer Earl Stevens. "It is a way of looking at children and at life." Stevens' method: Children do real things all day long, and in a trusting and supportive home environment. He says it is natural for children to read, write, play with numbers, learn about society, find out about the past, think, wonder, and do all those things that society so unsuccessfully attempts to force upon them in the context of schooling. Includes advice on compliance with legal requirements.

Why Should I Make My Child Take Science?   tinyurl.com/unviol

An argument against child-led learning, and in support of requiring children to learn subjects they may not initially like.

Online Courses

Course: the French *cours*, for a series of academic lectures, is from the Latin *curus*, a running race.

ONLINE LEARNING HAS exploded. And it's way, way bigger than you can imagine. It's because the commercial sites get all the publicity and the debate (Oh no! Are traditional schools in danger? Is the Internet putting the schoolhouse out of business?) and so nobody's paying attention to the noncommercial education revolution called open courseware.

Suddenly, and without a lot of fanfare, colleges, universities, and educational foundations have begun making their resources available—for free—to anyone who wants to plug in, watch, and learn. It's astonishing. It is now possible to get an entire college education—including the special campus speakers and guests—on line for absolutely free. (Unfortunately, that piece of paper that earns you big money is still going to cost you and your kids four years and thousands of dollars.)

But why not jump-start it by learning it all at home before the first day of college?

Here is some of the best cross-curriculum courseware currently on offer:

Annenberg Media   learner.org

Educational videos on demand from the Annenberg Foundation. You've seen 'em on educational TV. Annenberg has developed a vast number of educational videos that span the curriculum. Here they are, online and free, with corresponding curriculum materials. The videos were designed for K–12 teachers, but the material will be helpful to parents and older teenagers seeking to understand nearly every academic subject.

Free Web Courses   tinyurl.com/byucis

Though most of its independent-study classes are offered for high school and college credit, Brigham Young University also provides more than fifty free online courses to families and college students. The free classes cover family life, history and government, music, recreation, personal and professional development, genealogy, and religion. Begin anytime and set your own pace.

Hippo Campus   hippocampus.org

Designed for high school and college students, Hippocampus offers multimedia AP and introductory courses in algebra, American government, biology, calculus, environmental science, physics, psychology, religion, and U.S. history. The courses are somewhat slow-loading and clumsy, but that may change as the site matures.

Hotlinks

MINDsprinting
mindsprinting.com

OpenCourseware Consortium
ocwconsortium.org

UCCP College Prep
www.ucopenaccess.org

Webcast Berkeley
webcast.berkeley.edu

Wonder How-To
wonderhowto.com

Curriculum

MINDsprinting   mindsprinting.com

An entirely free tutoring program in math and reading. Use the assessment tools to determine your child's grade level, then print out worksheets and other instructional materials so your child can work through the program independently. The program is tailored to each student's abilities and needs, as determined by the assessment tests.

Open Courseware Consortium   ocwconsortium.org

A collection of colleges and universities from around the globe—including such luminaries as MIT, Notre Dame, Tufts, and Johns Hopkins—offering free online classes of varying degrees of quality. The news articles make for especially interesting reading.

Open University   openlearn.open.ac.uk

Britain's OU offers free college-level courses in the arts and history, business and management, education, health and lifestyle, IT and computing, law, mathematics and statistics, modern languages, science and nature, society, study skills, and technology. These are serious classes with in-depth learning, but some of the courses—such as "Maths Everywhere"—are introductory-level classes that will interest middle- and high-schoolers.

Open UW   outreach.washington.edu/openuw

At the time of this writing, the University of Washington's free courses are offered in the areas of history, health, literature, and information technology. Other offerings appear to be on the way.

Open Yale Courses   oyc.yale.edu

Free and open access to a selection of introductory courses taught by distinguished teachers and scholars at Yale University. Courses are offered in the departments of astronomy, English, philosophy, physics, political science, psychology, and religious studies.

Stanford on iTunes University   itunes.stanford.edu

This is the one that finally motivated me to install iTunes. Audio and video broadcasts of Stanford University lectures over a wide variety of subjects.

Suite 101 University   suite101.com/suiteu

Homeschooling 101, anyone? It's here, along with nearly 200 other free online courses in parenting, religion, business, careers, film, cooking, health, history, homemaking, literature, science, technology, and performing arts.

UC Podcasts   podcast.ucsd.edu

Audio recordings of college lectures at the University of California–San Diego. The offerings expand as more professors get on board. The full podcast must download to your computer before it begins to play.

UCCP College Prep   www.ucopenaccess.org

The University of California offers college prep courses, both introductory and Advanced Placement, in the areas of math, science, history, and social studies. Great slide shows, video clips, and audio lectures. Online examinations provide immediate feedback.

Utah Open Courseware Alliance   uocwa.org

Most of Utah's state colleges—College of Eastern Utah, Dixie State College, University of Utah, Utah State University, Utah Valley State College, Weber State University, and Western Governors University—have joined together to present free online college classes.

Virtual Homeschool Group   virtualhomeschoolgroup.com

Free online classes for homeschoolers. Some classes are unattended—meaning all the materials are available for you to teach yourself—and others are offered live by volunteer teachers. Volunteer to teach a class of your own, or just sign up and let your kids start learning with other homeschooling families.

On Learning Online

I use online courses for my college. It is similar to homeschooling but quite a bit like public schooling. I am a public-schooled person but chose to homeschool my children because of the overpopulation and because the way the kids are nowadays scares me.

—Teena Brayen, stay-at-homeschooling mom of three, Rome, New York

Curriculum

Webcast Berkeley   webcast.berkeley.edu

Not just podcasts and webcasts of UC Berkeley's courses, dating back to 2001, but also podcasts of prominent speakers and on-campus events, live and on-demand. What a world.

Wonder How To   wonderhowto.com

Video lessons on how to do almost anything. How-to videos teach skills as varied as Tie the Monkey's Fist Knot. Make Cheddar Soup, Save Paint Brushes, and Impersonate Christopher Walken. Watch and learn.

World Wide School Library   worldwideschool.com

A collection of more than 2,000 public-domain textbooks and classic works of literature from every area of the curriculum.

Public School Partnering

IF YOU LIVE in one of the many states that offer virtual schools, or any of the other states that permit homeschoolers access to school resources, you have a decision to make. Will you, or won't you, use the public school system as a partner in teaching your kids?

"I have mixed feelings about this topic," says homeschooling mom Marisa Corless of Washington State. In college, Marisa studied to become a schoolteacher, and was so put off by what she was learning about the school system that she decided she'd educate her own children herself. But she believes there may be a role for public school partnerships in a homeschooling curriculum—if you're careful. "I think for the most part, most of them are too invasive. They require the parents to report too much to the state and they still make too many decisions about what the parent should teach. However, there are some that are not as invasive. I still don't like aligning with the public schools in any

Public: From the Latin *pūblicus* and akin to the Old French *pueple*, people.

fashion, but if the school gives curriculum funds, that money is the money you paid in property taxes for the education of your child. Therefore, *if* the school requires little oversight and *if* the school will give a curriculum fund that the parent can use as he sees fit, and *if* you can still retain homeschool status as opposed to "alternative education" status, then I say use it. It is your money."

Maryland homeschooler Diana Malament worries that getting involved with public schools in any form might be politically unwise. "I have concerns that if you start using public school materials, the public schools will begin to get their finger in the door and begin to push for more overregulation of homeschooling. It is better for each family to be free to pursue the education suited for each individual child. When public school has a struggling student, they work with the student as appropriate. When a homeschooler has a struggling student and works with the student as appropriate, the public school wants to make the homeschooled student leave the home and go to the public school."

Another mom, Sarah Bull, shares those concerns, and worries about losing independence, though she sees a possible upside. She says, "We chose not to use the virtual school in Wisconsin. I wanted the complete autonomy of teaching. When using public school resources you still fall under the laws and rules of the government-run school. We did research it well. If we ever get to a point where I am unable to spend the time creating their curriculum, the virtual school would be a possibility. It would still keep them home, which is half the battle."

But other homeschoolers see public schools as a useful resource for homeschooling families. Coloradoan Cheryl Lemily thinks it's beneficial to use public school resources while homeschooling. "I do know of some people, however, who feel you are not a 'true' homeschooler if you rely on public schools in any way. I certainly do not agree with that. We are friendly with our local teachers and our local school. We have nothing against the school itself. Our children cur-

Hotlinks

Alliance for the Separation of School & State
schoolandstate.org

List of Virtual Schools
tinyurl.com/wikivs

Virtual School Trends and Benefits
nacol.org/resources

rently participate in sports organized by the school and have been invited to stop by for recess. If one of our children chose to take a class at the school, we would discuss the pros and cons and would make the decision as a family. I hope to homeschool our children through high school if possible. While in high school, I'd encourage my children to take whatever classes are of interest to them, either online or at a community college." Washingtonian Robin Goddard agrees. "I personally think that the more options available to families the better. I have no problem with accessing educational opportunities through the public schools and love to see public schools and homeschooling working together for the best interests of our kids."

Many states have embraced homeschooling by offering virtual schools that allow students to study at home using school-provided curricula, either through online methods or in some cases by providing full commercial curricula. And for several years now, more than half of all U.S. colleges have enrolled high-school students in courses for college credit, commonly called dual enrollment, concurrent enrollment, joint enrollment, or running start. Tuition in most cases is covered by the state or the local school district.

Chapter 14 has a section on earning college credit while in high school. And the Legal section of our companion book, *Homeschooling Step-by-Step,* includes an in-depth survey of state rules for homeschoolers using public-school resources. To get you started, though, here are some of the best resources for homeschooling in partnership with public schools:

Alliance for the Separation of School & State   schoolandstate.org

Why is the government involved in education at all? asks the Alliance. An adamant argument for completely detaching the government from education, and leaving parents—who don't ask the government to change diapers for them—in charge of their children's educations, as well.

At the End of the Day   tinyurl.com/dayend

Rebecca Miller writes: "I feel so strongly about partnering that I created an email list. I think we all are just trying to do our best to educate the children that we are responsible for. It is a resource group specifically for private, public, and homeschool educators. It is moderated by a homeschool mom and a public school educator. In less than a year, we have over 400 members and are still growing. People who join write that they like the concept, and it seems to be working."

Dual Enrollment   tinyurl.com/psdual2

One advantage of homeschooling: Your academically minded teenagers can take college classes at a young age. This article explains the advantages and disadvantages.

How Public Schools Harm Children   tinyurl.com/psharm

The other side of the coin. Articles that argue that public schools are a menace, and ought to be avoided. Full stop.

List of Virtual Schools   tinyurl.com/wikivs

Well, when you can't find a comprehensive list online, you go write one on Wikipedia. We couldn't, so we did.

Virtual Public Schools   k12.com/getk12

Families partnering with virtual schools in their state often can choose the curriculum they'd like for their children. K12, a major commercial provider of online curriculum, maintains this list of the virtual academies currently offering its curriculum.

Virtual School Trends and Benefits   nacol.org/resources

A collection of articles and interviews supporting the notion that traditional schools are crippling students who need to compete in a modern, technology-driven economy.

Chapter 4

Education Essentials

FOR MANY YEARS we lived on a small island off Hong Kong, where my children were enrolled in the local public school. It was an interesting experience for them. There was a small, two-room schoolhouse buried in a jungle of trees. During the day, island children would sit quietly under the drone of fans, dressed in their uniforms of shorts and short-sleeved shirts. My children—the only blondes in their class—would chant along with their Chinese classmates the lessons they learned each day. Then they would sit for hours and work through their daily routine of writing Chinese characters with brushstrokes, answering math problems, and reading their reading books. Their social studies, English, and science lessons were brief and to-the-point, because the main purpose of school for Chinese children is: Reading. Writing. Arithmetic. And these tiny children would come home from school at lunchtime, backpacks loaded down with books, ready to start their afternoon of homework.

They were getting a first-class education.

Then we moved back to the States.

Imagine my dismay when my kids came home from public school with stories about what they had learned that day in their drug-abuse class, or during their AIDS-prevention discussion in health class. Or about the horrible things that took place on the playgrounds during recess. Or the pep rally they had attended that day. Or any of the hundreds of time fillers assigned by overburdened teachers who were spending days dealing with discipline problems in the classroom. What I came to realize was that public school for my kids meant they were doing anything but learn to read or write or do arithmetic.

When I finally got the courage to homeschool, guess what my first priority was? You got it. Reading. Writing. Arithmetic.

In this chapter and the following two chapters, you'll be introduced to everything you need to get your kids through the essentials of education. This chapter covers the basic educational skills that will make your children lifelong learners, Chapter 5 covers language literacy, and Chapter 6 presents the entire spectrum of mathematics.

We start this chapter with tools for teaching the most essential skill of all: the value of service. Then we locate resources for teaching listening skills, logic and critical thinking, and library and media skills. We investigate the field of information literacy, and list some great sites for reference materials. Then we look at tools for teaching research and reporting skills, study skills, and most important: values, standards, and ethics.

Community Involvement and Public Service

HOMESCHOOLING FAMILIES ARE amazing. Far from being the recluses they're sometimes portrayed as, homeschooling families are out working in and serving their communities in a multitude of ways. "We get our kids involved in the community with public service, 4-H clubs, and church groups," says Sarah Bull, Wisconsin mother of three.

It's not hard to get involved, says Raylene Hunt, a single home-educating mom of two in Maine. "When it comes to community involvement and public service, volunteer at a local nursing home, hospital, church ministry, food pantry.

Community:
From the Latin *communitas* (common). A group having common interests; society as a whole; the public.

Hotlinks

Community Service
communityservice.org

Do Something
dosomething.org

Learning to Give
learningtogive.org

Education Essentials

No curriculum needed; just practical hands-on, real-life experience."

Georgia homeschooling mom Priscilla Pike is one of thousands who volunteer. "I have organized and run a food pantry at our church," she reports. "My daughter goes with me and helps me work in it each week. She helps give out food, stocks shelves, and is learning to help people in need." Priscilla is also planning to take her daughter to a larger food bank to help sort food.

Other homeschoolers get involved in political groups and in community organizations such as Scouting and 4-H. Cheryl Northrup, a Colorado homeschooler, describes some of the many ways her family gets connected: "Our sons have always been involved in Scouts, and for rank advancement they are required to do much service," Cheryl says. "We now live in an area where there are few members of our church, with lots of move-ins and move-outs, so again, my sons get many opportunities to serve." Her daughters get involved in their church community by cleaning, babysitting, and providing meals for shut-ins.

Volunteering also has a religious theme for the central Arkansas family of Ann Crum, a homeschooling mother of two: "Our children are heavily involved in several aspects of our church's ministry, including visiting nursing homes, assisting with church services or singing, taking food to less fortunate members of the community, caring for the church grounds, and helping during church camps. We feel that these activities take our children's minds off themselves and make them aware of others around them in a real way. They volunteer to help with cleanup in the kitchen at church, to decorate for special occasions, to visit folks in the community. Helpfulness has become such a habit that they readily open doors for others and even help folks inside when it's raining by taking an umbrella out to them—without being told."

Donna Lee Spruill's Estancia, New Mexico, family gets politically connected: "Our family has been involved in the political process for years. We take our children to rallies and attend our political party's meetings; they have always gone with us to vote in elections and learned the process. After the polls close, we meet at the courthouse to check the winners and losers." Donna Lee says that when she serves on jury duty, her daughters sometimes tag along to observe the court process.

Shea Wilkinson's young children are already learning about the importance of taking a political stand. "My children are still very young, so civic involvement hasn't really been an issue," she says. "But we are talking to our four-year-old son about what elections mean. We have been very clear to him that we vote and that we think voting is a great privilege. We are hoping that our boys will grow up with the desire to vote and participate in politics on all levels."

The Huntington, Virginia, mother of two also participates with her children in service functions at their church. "We have served dinner to families following funerals and visited shut-ins at nursing homes. We want them to realize that all people are important, not just the ones in our immediate or even our church family."

Tracy Jenkins is a homeschooling mother of two in Hagerstown, Maryland. She is a member of a local homeschool support group, and she and another member of the group lead a girls' club that does acts of service within the community. "We go to a nursing home twice a year, and we take homemade gifts and serve a snack and sing songs. The residents love it! We also brought in gently used toys and cleaned them up and sent them to Romanian orphanages and the Dominican Republic. In addition, the girls also made Valentine's Day cards to send to the VA hospitals this year. We also participated in the American Heart Association's Jump Rope for Heart and raised $1,366.80!"

Joyce Dumire from Akron, Ohio, has had her homeschooled son volunteer to teach younger kids. "Teaching something is the best way to really learn," she says.

North Carolina's Tracee Stewart takes her family out to do some hands-on service. "We clean up our streets and roadsides, and go to the town square to help clean it. My son is involved with the Scouts, so he

Education Essentials

Franklin D. Roosevelt

One of the best-loved and most powerful presidents in United States history was homeschooled. Franklin Delano Roosevelt was an only child, born into a wealthy family that traveled frequently between Europe and New York. Roosevelt, reared to be a gentleman and to be responsible to those who were less fortunate, was taught at home until he was fourteen, at which time he entered a private school in Groton, Massachusetts. In his late thirties he was struck with a crippling case of polio and through sheer force of will regained partial use of his legs. He eventually led the United States out of the Great Depression and through World War II and in so doing became the only president to be elected to four terms in office.

Education Essentials

does a lot of community service. My daughter and I are involved with our church group that provides services to the elderly and handicapped. We help out where we are needed and meet all kinds of people."

Jennie Littrell, who homeschools two children in Michigan, says service doesn't always have to be planned out. "We were out on a walk tonight. It had been a windy day, and my seven-year-old observed that there was a lot of garbage blowing around. She asked if we could go around the neighborhood with a garbage bag and pick it up. So that's what we are doing in the morning."

Annie Glass, a homeschooling mother of two from Everson, Washington, looks for innovative ways to involve her children in service. "We live in a small community, about 1,800 people. There are two senior centers where we regularly sing. I play the guitar and love the old folk, band, and vaudeville songs. We're the only group with young children that sings the songs the older people like, and so they request us often. We sing about twice a month for them. We're certainly not professional, but we can carry a tune—sort of. Our reward is the joy and delight on these people's faces.

Free Videos

Libraries and many Blockbuster video outlets around the United States offer free rentals of community-service videos.

"When the gal who had usually put together our church's weekly bulletin had to quit, our boys (five and seven) were asked if they would like to take over the job as a way to serve the church. The congregation has been very understanding when bulletins aren't folded as straight as they should be or inserts are missing from some. Over the past few months the boys' work has much improved and they feel thrilled to be 'needed.' "

Kim Eckles' high-school freshman-aged daughter Heather "is on the committee for the century celebration for our community, where she gathers information about the schools and meets with people who have lived here all their lives. Heather is also a junior docent at the Neville House, the historical home of General John Neville, where she gives tours and participates in fundraisers."

Looking for ways to help out in your own community? Here's what you need to know about volunteering:

Community Helpers   themes.pppst.com/communityhelpers.html
A collection of PowerPoint presentations that teach about community and service. One of the lessons, "Types of Communities," uses pictures to explain urban, suburban, and rural. Another discusses police officers, firefighters, farmers, and other people who make up a community.

Community Service   communityservice.org
Enter your zip code to locate volunteer service opportunities in your own neighborhood. Quite a large database.

CyberActivism Tutorial   tinyurl.com/sercyb
How to get involved. This step-by-step tutorial doesn't take a stand on what you should involve yourself in. Just suggests, step by step, how to get involved.

Do Something   dosomething.org
Search for volunteer opportunities in your own community, and participate in conversations about volunteerism. CelebsGoneGood (see

Education Essentials

link at bottom of the page) may be the first worthwhile celebrity gossip site ever created.

Food Force (World Food Programme) food-force.com

Click the Teachers link to access educational resources about solving the world hunger crisis. Lesson plans and games are both on offer. From the United Nations.

Habitat for Humanity habitat.org

Get your hands dirty by volunteering to build homes for needy people right in your own community.

Helpful Hints for Volunteering volunteerinfo.org/volhints.htm

A list of things to consider when volunteering.

☆ Best Homeschooling Moment

A disabled woman drove a block and hailed me over to her car to tell me that she had been sitting and watching for someone to pick up a top that had fallen off a sale rack outside a retail shop. Our ten-year-old had been the fifth person by but the only one to stop. She complimented me for her upbringing. I certainly don't get that every day.

—Work-at-home mom of four from Jacaranda Tree Learning Co-operative, Hawkes Bay, New Zealand

---

Learning to Give learningtogive.org

Click the Lesson Search link at the top of the page to find hundreds of well-done lesson plans on philanthropy and service.

US Freedom Corps usafreedomcorps.gov

The USA Freedom Corps is a government-operated service organization initiated in response to volunteers asking to serve following September 11. Click the Educators link to find current learn-and-serve opportunities for individuals and small groups.

WikiSpaces wikispaces.com

A terrific—and free—wikibuilder. Create your very own version of Wikipedia, and use it to plan events or build a community. Your club, service group, or co-op can use it to coordinate classes and activities, advertise for new members, and improve communication. I use it as a freestyle database for storing information and research. Endless possibilities.

Listening Skills

"SSSHHHH! LISTEN!"

"You're not listening!"

"Be quiet and listen to me!"

It's the universal call of the parent and the teacher. Whether you're the kind of parent who commands order and attention, or the sort who spends time on your knees talking eye to eye with the short people in your home, you've probably been frustrated by your kids' inability to follow instructions and absorb meaning from what they hear. So why is it that kids all over the planet aren't listening to their parents? Perhaps they just haven't been taught.

To teach her own children the skill of listening, Cheryl Northrup, a Colorado homeschooler, took inspiration from a motivational speaker. "We have tried, with varying success, to use inspirational speaker John Bytheway's idea of a 'church journal' to teach the kids to take notes as a speaker speaks and learn to outline on the spot."

She's been a bit more pragmatic about day-to-day interaction with her older boys. "When faced with teenaged boys who would act as if they were listening to me, then completely forget what I told them to do, I found that having them repeat the instructions back to me helped a great deal. A 'narration' approach, I guess!"

For Tracee Stewart, the skill of listening is a more formal lesson. The North Carolina homeschooler of two says her family uses books as their listening resource. Tracee reads, and her children answer her questions at the end of each chapter. She also uses chapters of books or paragraphs. "I read them the paragraph in a set time, and they write answers to questions that I make up," she says. "Mostly I give them three minutes. This helps them listen well, because they don't ever know what I'm going to ask." When they were younger, she says, she did the same thing using colors

> **Listen:** From the Sanskrit *srosati* (he hears). To give consideration and thoughtful attention.

Education Essentials

Hotlinks

Effective Communication Techniques
okvoices.org/
communication.html

Learning by Listening?
ldshomeschoolinginca
.org/audio.html

Love and Logic Institute
www.loveandlogic.com

Education Essentials

and shapes. "I might say (and only one time), 'Color the square blue. Draw a circle in red.' This helped them learn their colors and shapes as well. It's great to know they're learning two or three things at once!"

Storytelling also plays a large role in Kim Eckles' lessons in listening. Her five daughters range from five years old to college age. She's repeating tried-and-true skills with her youngest daughter: "I have found that reading them a story, then having them retell it at a later time, helps with the listening and comprehension skills. If we come across a word that I feel my youngest may not understand, we talk about what it might mean. At the upper levels, we tear apart the sentence to find the meaning."

For Seattle-area mom vanessa ronsse, teaching her toddler to listen involves simply not talking too much. "The best thing I can do to help my son to hear and follow directions is to KISS—Keep It Simple, Stupid. The other thing is to not raise my voice—a difficult thing when he is doing the same thing for the fifteenth time in a row! But I hate hearing my own voice raised, and it just seems to shut him down."

Ready to do some listening of your own? Here's what the experts want you to hear:

On Repetition

Attention and repetition help much to fix ideas in the memory.

—John Locke

Effective Communication Techniques
okvoices.org/communication.html

A list of rules for listening actively and communicating without being adversarial.

How Can Parents Model Good Listening Skills?
focusas.com/ListeningSkills.html

Several bullet-point tips for improving communication with your children, and in the process teach them to be better listeners.

Improve Your Listening Skills: Three Steps   tinyurl.com/lisimp

A brief article on improving listening skills. Useful tips that will help older teens.

Improving Listening Skills

coping.org/dialogue/listen.htm

Teach your kids the three types of effective listening, reasons to improve listening skills, and role-play activities . . . and more.

Learning by Listening?

ldshomeschoolinginca.org/audio.html

Ways of teaching children better listening. Includes putting it all on a podcast. This site explains how to use technology to teach. Auditory learners will benefit greatly. Listen to the podcasts listed at the bottom of the page for practice.

Listening Skills   tinyurl.com/liskill

Tips for being a good listener, and the three basic steps of active listening. Quick, numbered article is a good backgrounder for teaching the skill.

Love and Logic Institute   www.loveandlogic.com

Model good listening and communication by practicing it. Hear L&L podcasts or watch video clips from the website. Most public libraries carry the books and tapes that will absolutely improve communication in your family.

Teachable Moment   teachablemoment.org

Collection of lesson plans for helping children understand another person's point of view, becoming peacemakers, listening well and affirmation interviews. Click the Elementary or Middle School links for the best resources.

Teaching Communication Skills   tinyurl.com/liscom

Lesson plan for teaching communication and teamwork skills such as taking turns, praising without putdowns, sharing, asking for help, staying on task, resolving conflicts, paraphrasing, and managing materials.

On Listening

Let a fool hold his tongue and he will pass for a sage.

—Publilius Syrus, c. 45 B.C.

Education Essentials

Teaching Guide: Listening to Others   tinyurl.com/lisgro

A complete lesson plan for teaching listening skills. Though it's designed to accompany a video, the lesson plan is easily adapted to a homeschooling environment. Make your own sock-puppet show to demonstrate good and bad listening.

Logic and Critical Thinking

Logic: From the Greek *logos* (reason). The science of reasoning through a sequence or relationship of facts to arrive at a conclusion.

IF YOUR FIRST duty as a parent is to teach your children to be ethical, then your first duty as their teacher is to teach them to evaluate. If you accomplish nothing else as an educator, you must, of course, teach them to think. "It is not enough," said French philosopher René Descartes, "to have a good mind. The main thing is to use it well." The skill of critical evaluation arises in part from simply being part of a family. Whether your only child learns to debate social issues with her parents, or your seventh son learns to solve problems with his younger brother, logic, evaluation, and critical thinking are essential life skills.

Greeley, Colorado, computer programmer Bryan Smith, who earned his degree in philosophy, explains the importance of understanding the principles of logic in the real world: "Logic is a unique skill in that it almost never is directly or consciously invoked in common everyday interactions, but it is, in fact, one of the most important skills one can have in those interactions.

"An intimate knowledge of logic so changes the thought process that, once a person has acquired it, it is applied constantly with little or no knowledge of the fact that it is being applied. Very few people ever, in everyday conversation, construct Aristotelian syllogisms out of what other people say in order to fully understand them. After acquiring the

Education Essentials

skill of constructing such valid argument forms, however, you find things that are invalid strike very discordantly with you. Hence you are much less likely to be fooled by trickery and scams.

"A professor I once had would hand out arguments from advertisements to the students and ask them if there was, based on the evidence given, a reason to believe the conclusion (or what the ad was trying to make you believe). He proved every time that people not schooled in logic will often say that there is good reason to believe things in support of which there is absolutely no evidence.

"An ingrained knowledge of logic often spawns the desire for more proof in everyday life. After taking even an intro class, I have had students tell me that they no longer find it possible to accept things they hear with no supporting evidence.

"Sadly, most people (those not schooled in logic) will accept something as true with no proof or very faulty 'proof.' With most people, learning logic creates a deep desire to seek truth in everyday life; they will beg for reasons when told something and point out contradictions in beliefs held by others. So logic is a unique skill. It's not like carpentry, which you use only while building stuff, or computer programming, which you use only while programming computers. It's a skill that permeates and infects your very life and being."

Logic and critical thinking skills will carry your children through college and life. These resources will help them get started. (Find related information in the section on public speaking in Chapter 11.)

20Q.net   20q.net

Amazing use of artificial intelligence. Users can play 20 Questions against the computer on topics as varied as British television and the Old Testament. The program learns as players participate.

Hotlinks

20q.net
20q.net

Mighty Optical Illusions
moillusions.com

Silva Rhetoricae
humanities.byu.edu/
rhetoric/silva.htm

Why Study Logic?
tinyurl.com/logwhy

Education Essentials

On Logic

Histories make men wise; poets, witty; the mathematics, subtle; natural philosophy, deep; morality, grave; logic and rhetoric, able to contend.

—Francis Bacon

Discovery Education Puzzlemaker
puzzlemaker.discoveryeducation.com
Free puzzle maker for your word lists. There are lots of other great things on this site; the puzzle maker is the one we use the most.

Essential Logic   home.honolulu.hawaii.edu/~pine
Click the Essential Logic link for access to an online logic textbook for college freshmen.

Levels and Types of Questions   tinyurl.com/loglev
How to ask questions that cause children to think at higher levels, using examples from Bloom's Taxonomy.

Mighty Optical Illusions   moillusions.com
When your kid begs for the address, you know a website is cool. Dozens and dozens of weird optical illusions that will fascinate you and your children. Our favorites are the Escher style illusions.

Silva Rhetoricae   humanities.byu.edu/rhetoric/silva.htm
Gideon Burton's awe-inspiring resource for learning everything there is to know about logic, rhetoric, and argumentation. A child—or adult—who absorbs the information on this site will be smart. By definition.

Socratic Method   thomasaquinas.edu/curriculum/socratic.htm
Thomas Aquinas College specializes in using what it calls the discussion method—as opposed to the lecture method—of teaching. Students "give birth" to learning; teachers act only as midwife. This article discusses the nature of education and the importance of the Socratic method.

Tests, Tests, Tests   teststeststests.com
Tests, Tests, Tests lets your older kids break their brains against career tests, Bible tests, typing tests, personality tests, and even IQ tests. There are plenty of fun quizzes here, too. What's your Hogwarts House? Are you a Neat Freak? How Jealous are You? It's all good fun.

The Socratic Method: Teaching by Asking Instead of by Telling

garlikov.com/Soc_Meth.html

A discussion of questioning, the key to effective learning. In the article, the writer, a schoolteacher, uses the "pure" Socratic method, in which questions (and only questions) are used to arouse curiosity and at the same time serve as a logical, incremental guide to help students to resolve a complex topic or issue using their own thinking and insights.

Using Questions to Teach Better

garlikov.com/teaching/usingquestions.html

Brilliant. Writer Rick Garlikov says questions are generally misused in the education process: "Tests of mere memory . . . have very little practical meaning though vast importance is imputed to them." Two better uses: (1) to develop interest in a topic, and (2) to give students a map for self-recognition of reaching milestones of understanding as they study a unit. (The questions are presented up front, and learners check their own progress by their ability to answer the question.) He also suggests teachers ask direct questions to find out what a learner was thinking when responding to a question incorrectly. Direct questions in this situation tell the teacher what was missed in the teaching process.

Using the Socratic Method

garlikov.com/teaching/smmore.htm

What kind of questions should be asked? Questions that meet these four criteria: (1) they must be interesting or intriguing to the students; they must lead by (2) incremental and (3) logical steps (from the students' prior knowledge or understanding) in order to be readily answered and, at some point, seen to be evidence toward a conclusion, not just individual, isolated points; and (4) they must be designed to get the student to see particular points.

Education Essentials

Teaching Tips

We use the library of course. Kids can play Bridge free at most clubs, and the older people enjoy them. They learn a lot from the Bridge players about all kinds of things.

—**Liz deForest**, housewife and homeschooling mom of three, Santa Monica, California

---

What to Do When You Get the Wrong Answer
ops.org/reading/wrong_answer.html

Prompt, says this teacher. Don't let a wrong answer get "bested" by another kid with the right answer.

Why Study Logic?   tinyurl.com/logwhy

An essay on the social and the cognitive reasons for learning the tenets of logic.

Library and Media Skills

ANOTHER MARK OF a well-educated person is the ability to use all the resources of the library. "Borrow materials from the library," counsels Diana Malament of Gaithersburg, Maryland. "I taught my first child how to read using Romalda Spalding's *The Writing Road to Reading,* which I borrowed from the library month after month. Many other moms have great success using *Teach Your Child to Read in 100 Easy Lessons* (**tinyurl.com/read100**), which is also available at the library."

Florida homeschooler Rebecca Lynn Miller knows how to take full advantage of library resources. "I request a free copy of a public school educating type of magazine, such as *Instructor,* and then sent away for free catalogs of books, curricula, and books on CDs that they advertise throughout the magazine. This put me on mailing lists for such items. I then looked through these catalogs for educational DVDs that I wanted my children to see. Rather than purchase them, I requested that my library interloan them through the county. Through this, I found that by having a library card in my county, I could apply to get a card in the next county. This gave me an even greater database to find educational DVDs/VHSs. Sometimes it might cost me a dollar for postage, but considering that some of the material might be forty dollars to buy, I'm okay with spending the dollar."

The library is Washington mom Marisa Corless' most-

Library: From the Latin *librarius* (of books). A collection of literary and artistic materials.

Education Essentials

used free tool. "Interlibrary loan gives me just about anything I want that my library doesn't have or won't buy. I
also use the library and interlibrary loan frequently. I have
very few materials that I have bought, and usually I buy
things only if I use them over and over and over and over
again from the library. Most fiction and subject matter
books aren't needed more than a month or two, so the library is perfect for those."

Lillian Haas, who homeschools two children in
Audubon, New Jersey, takes her kids to the library at least
two or three times a week. "My kids can take out as many
books as they can take care of," she says. "I never taught
my eight-year-old to use the library; he just figured out the
computer system when he wanted to find specific books.
He had a bit more trouble learning to find the books on the shelves, but
he can do that now, too."

For the Bridgeville, Pennsylvania, Eckles family, the library is a weekly
destination. Mom Kim says her five children really enjoy their library experience. In the early days, though, teaching them to use the library
meant getting their hands a little dirty: "I taught the girls to use the card
catalog (shows my age), but now we use the computer for information.
The computer was a big tool in our learning and still is."

Kim's family is getting an eclectic education from their library experience: "We borrow the classics as well as fun books to read about
crafts, vacation spots, languages (using the free audiotapes), history,
and more. The video collections are great, particularly eyewitness
movies like *Schindler's List.*"

Kim has a great suggestion for making good use of the library: "After
we read a classic, we check to see if there is a movie version of it, and we
critique the movie compared with the book! It's lots of fun to see what
the director of the movie did in comparison with the original book."

Michigan's Jennie Littrell has lots to do with her two young children.
"I had the librarian give my daughter a tour of the library. She showed

Hotlinks

Bogeybear's Slideshows
slideshare.net/bogeybear

Library Skills
pppst.com/library.html

Propaganda Techniques
propaganda.mrdonn.org/
lessonplans.html

Education Essentials

Dame Agatha Christie

Author Agatha Christie turned her homeschooling experience into a life of mystery. She was educated at home by her mother, and began writing detective stories while she was a World War I nurse. She published her first novel, *The Mysterious Affair at Styles*, at age twenty-nine and over the course of her life published some seventy-five novels. Her books have sold more than 100 million copies and have been translated into more than a hundred languages.

her everything." Jennie lets her daughter check out free movies for fun. "We watch fairy tales a lot, because they get her imagination flowing. She usually writes something about each movie for composition or draws a picture of her favorite scene."

The following resources will help your kids get familiar with the library, and get smart about media in general. Ready to make the library a big part of your homeschooling experience? Here's what the experts say.

Advertising and Promotion   themes.pppst.com/advertising.html

Dozens of well-made PowerPoint presentations on propaganda and advertising gimmicks. Use the media to teach your kids to get media-savvy.

Bogeybear's Slideshows   slideshare.net/bogeybear

Part of a project for sharing slide shows, this collection of presentations is an excellent introduction to library literacy. The show "Taking Care of Books," for example, gives a good, very watchable overview of proper care and feeding of library books. For younger learners.

Teaching Tips

The library. We use the library for almost everything.
—Dawn Nelson, happy homeschool mom of three, Kent, Washington

Don't Buy It   pbskids.org/dontbuyit

A PBS site that teaches kids to access, evaluate, analyze, and produce both electronic and print media by thinking about pop culture and advertisements.

Guide to Library Research

homeworktips.about.com/od/libraryresearch

The Using the Library link urges college-bound kids to get familiar with the library in order to excel at their university studies.

Learning to Learn   tv411.org/learning

Click the How to Use a Library link for a slide show explaining library resources and literacy.

Library Instruction

libraryinstruction.com/literacy-education.html

A resource for lesson plans, bibliography, and links to library instruction resources. Articles such as "The Role of Libraries in Literacy Education" are especially helpful.

Library Skills   pppst.com/library.html

PowerPoint presentations that teach how to get oriented in the library. One of the lessons, "Parts of a Book," explains everything you need to know to locate books on shelves or in card catalogs. Another teaches the Dewey Decimal system.

Media Literacy Starting Points

edutopia.org/media-literacy-starting-points

Parents should plan their family's media consumption in the same way they plan meals to achieve a balanced diet, argues this author. Great tips for making your family smarter about its media choices.

PBS Media Literacy   pbs.org/teachers/media_lit

Quizzes, activities, and PBS resources that answer these questions: How do you succeed in a media-filled world? How is media created? Can you analyze the messages that inform, entertain, and sell to us every day? How can you create your own media messages?

How We Homeschool

The world is our resource! Libraries are awesome! We use any learning situation in our everyday life as a lesson of some sort. My resources are about half free and half low-cost.

—Erin Goldberg, homeschooling mother of two, ages five and seven, Bardstown, Kentucky

---

Education Essentials

Propaganda Techniques   propaganda.mrdonn.org/lessonplans.html

Lesson plans and other resources that teach kids to be wary of advertising and slogans. Critical thinking is key.

Why Media Literacy Matters   mediachannel.org/classroom

It involves getting smart about consumerism, propaganda, and privacy. Click the link to learn about "The Seven Great Debates in Media Literacy."

Information Literacy

Education Essentials

Information:

From the Latin *informationem*, meaning "outline, concept, idea."

INFORMATION, COMPUTERS, TECHNOLOGY—kids homeschooled in computer-literate homes can grow up with a real advantage over their traditionally schooled peers. Kids who have access to the family computer don't suffer from being limited to outdated technology labs and fifteen minutes a week of hands-on computer time.

To give your kids an edge, consider making information literacy part of your own educational curriculum. A computer-literate child, one prepared for a technology-savvy world, will be adept at keyboarding, business software, networking technology, Internet safety, and the use of communication tools such as weblogs, podcasting, and social networking.

Following are some of the basic tools for teaching kids and teens about information literacy. Related sections in this chapter cover Research Skills, and Library and Media Literacy. The Design section of Chapter 7 teaches kids how to build their own web pages and use graphics software. Chapter 5 contains a section on Computer Math. And Chapter 2 contains a section on Internet Safety.

Here, then, is everything your family needs to get started learning about basic computer literacy:

Burlington County Library

burlco.lib.nj.us/Classes/Intforkids

How to teach basic Internet skills to younger children. Mousing, scrolling, hyperlinks—it's all very cute.

Computer Lab Favorites

teacher.scholastic.com/activities/clf

Cross-curricula games and activities. For young and middle readers, these graphic-intensive games will enliven computer time. Let your child spin a dial and choose the curriculum topic that sounds most interesting.

Computer Literacy

www.uni.uiuc.edu/library/computerlit

All about Netiquette, using search engines, and working with online catalogs.

Computer Science Lesson Plans   tinyurl.com/cslesson

Lesson plans in information literacy designed by classroom teachers. Most are easily adapted to homeschooling programs.

Computers and Technology   technology.pppst.com

PowerPoint presentations that teach how computers work. One of the lessons, "The Rabbit Hunt," explains Java. Another discusses turning photos into writing. Keyboarding, digital cameras, and Internet safety are all covered.

Dance Mat Typing   bbc.co.uk/schools/typing

Animated games from the BBC teach typing skills. Colorful and fun.

Ed & Technology   tinyurl.com/infoed

A collection of lesson plans for online scavenger hunts, keyboarding, and other skills that teach technology literacy.

Good Typing   goodtyping.com

Easy-to-use keyboarding teacher. Requires easy registration to track progress.

Hotlinks

Computer Literacy
www.uni.uiuc.edu/library/
computerlit

Dance Mat Typing
bbc.co.uk/schools/typing

How to Start a Blog
wikihow.com/Start-a-Blog

Internet for Classrooms
internet4classrooms.com

Education Essentials

How to Start a Blog   wikihow.com/Start-a-Blog

Wikihow is a collection of how-to manuals that teach everything from asking for autographs to making a miniature zoo. In this how-to, users go step by step through the process of building and maintain a weblog.

Information Literacy Lesson Plans   tinyurl.com/infolitles

Library and information literacy lesson plans designed by teachers. Though they're intended for the classroom, most are easily adapted to homeschooling programs.

Internet for Classrooms   internet4classrooms.com

Start with the link for Online Practice Modules, where you'll find tutorials for operating more than a dozen computer programs and technologies, including MS-Word and Excel. Use the tutorials to teach everything from basic skills to the most advanced tools.

Jan's Computer Literacy 101   jegsworks.com/lessons

Teaches an array of computer literacy topics, beginning with computer basics and moving through operating systems, business software, and building websites. Each project includes a summary, quiz, and exercises.

Learn Excel the Easy Way   microsoft-office-excel.com

Excel is my specialty. I've written books on the subject. Websites like this could put me out of business. Online videos demonstrate most—but not all (whew)—of the basics of using spreadsheets.

Peter's Online Typing Course   typing-lessons.org

Developer Peter Hudson writes: "free online typing lessons and typing exercises for beginning typists, and frustrated hunt-and-peckers who want to move from four-finger typing to full-blown touch typing." His "Principles for Effective Learning" are worth reviewing with your beginning typists.

Technology and Instruction Interwoven   its.leesummit.k12.mo.us

A full curriculum of information technology skills. Separate sections cover digital ethics, digital media, Excel, game resources, graphic organizers, graphics, Internet, keyboarding, PowerPoint, resources, sounds, tutorials, virtual activities, webcams, web page design, web quests, Windows, and Word.

Technology Tutorials   teach-nology.com/tutorials

Designed specifically for teaching classroom teachers about the Internet. Brief articles, lots of links.

Tutorials   pppst.com/tutorials.html

Presentation on how to make a presentation. Colorful, fun, well executed.

TypeSpeed   mytypespeed.com

Typing lessons and speed tests. Registration is required so that users can track their progress through the lessons.

Reference Materials

ISN'T TECHNOLOGY GREAT? What took you and me hours and hours—and a trip to the library—to look up in our childhood is now available to your children with no more effort than typing a few words and clicking in the right places.

Over the past two years, there has been an amazing improvement in the research material available on the Internet. Just a short time ago the best online encyclopedia, *Britannica,* charged a subscription fee, and all the other general research sites were hardly worth the energy it took to look at them.

No more.

There are now hundreds of great reference sites on the Internet. Dictionaries, thesauri, encyclopedias, translators, atlases, almanacs, and much more are all available, free, on the Internet.

> **Reference:** From the Latin *re-* and *-ferre* (to carry back). A source of information containing usual facts.

Before they start doing research, your kids will probably want to know where they can go to find the information they need. Whether they want to know how to spell rutabaga, find a synonym for "earthy," or learn about cetaceans, the following resources are the places to start.

AllExperts   allexperts.com

Communicate with experts on every imaginable subject. This is the pioneer "free experts" site, staffed by volunteers willing to share their expertise for free.

Bartleby: Great Books Online   bartleby.com

Just keeps getting better. In one place: A searchable database of encyclopedias, dictionaries, thesauri, gazetteers, quotations, style guides, and books on religion, mythology, literature, anatomy, etiquette, cooking, and government. And that's just the reference section. There are also anthologies of poetry, fiction and non-fiction orations, essays and journals, and much, much more. What a collection!

Biographical Dictionary   s9.com

Links to databases of biographies. Some of the categories include Nobel Prize winners, astronauts, mathematicians, and political figures. There are many others. A great jumping-off place for biographies.

Law by Source or Jurisdiction
www.law.cornell.edu/soj.html

Cornell maintains these links to sources of U.S. state, U.S. federal, and international law. A good central source for researching laws and bills.

Learning Island   learningisland.org

More than 300 printable books, most with extensive illustrations and well-written text. Alphabet books, history, health, biography, and many other academic subjects are covered.

Hotlinks

Bartleby: Great Books Online
Bartleby.com

Law by Source or Jurisdiction
www.law.cornell.edu/ soj.html

Martindale's Reference Desk
martindalecenter.com

Wikipedia—The Free Encyclopedia
wikipedia.org

Education Essentials

Martindale's Reference Desk   martindalecenter.com

There's pretty much nothing that's not here. Every conceivable reference tool for health, science, language, math, entertainment, photography . . . There's even a hearing test.

Merriam-Webster's Open Dictionary

www3.merriam-webster.com/opendictionary

Add your own words to the venerable (that's a word, right?) Merriam-Webster dictionary. New slang and text-messaging abbreviations make up many of the entries.

One Look Dictionaries   onelook.com

Almost 13 million words in more than 1,000 specialized dictionaries. Search 'em all in one keystroke. Even takes wildcards. And try the reverse dictionary for fun. It's weirdly thesaurus-like.

Quotations   quotationspage.com

More than 26,000 quotations. Who says there's nothing new under the sun? No, seriously. Who said it?

Quoteland   quoteland.com

Who said what, and when? Includes step-by-step instructions for identifying a quote, and your older children might benefit from the writers' club or the debate forum that are part of this site.

Repositories of Primary Documents

uidaho.edu/special-collections/iil.htm

More than 5,000 websites from around the world describing holdings of manuscripts, archives, rare books, historical photographs, and other primary sources for the research scholar.

Unit Converter   digitaldutch.com/unitconverter

Unit converter from almost anything to almost anything. Nobody, however, can convert grams to cups—an ongoing struggle for those of us who read food labels.

Education Essentials

U.S. Census Bureau   census.gov

Population clocks and fact finders. Find statistics on U.S. population, genealogy, housing, businesses, geography, and more.

Wikipedia—The Free Encyclopedia   wikipedia.org

It's almost as ubiquitous as the telephone. No reference list would be complete without it.

Wordsmyth Children's Dictionary   wordsmyth.net

Simplified dictionary entries for younger users, along with a standard dictionary for older learners. Need a thesaurus? Each definition includes a synonym list.

Research Skills

NOW THAT YOUR kids know where to find the information, can they figure out what to do with it? Kim Eckles' kids can. The mother of five teaches her children to write research papers—lots of them—from about the fourth grade on.

"One research project I remember doing was about Wisconsin. We called the capital of Wisconsin, told them we were doing a research paper, and asked them to send information to us. (This was before computers or the Internet.) Then we got books out of the library about the state. We read and took notes. I taught my daughter how to take notes and compile them in some kind of order on index cards.

> **Research:** From the Middle French *recerche* (to search). To investigate thoroughly.

"Since the Internet, we have used computer programs, websites, the Library of Congress, the library online, and real books. We compile information and write reports on numerous subjects. Some of our topics in the past have been abortion, teen suicide, Generation X, states, Y2K, and various diseases. My children have grown greatly by doing the research, and it is essential if they are going to attend college. My daughters in college do, on the average, four research papers a term."

New York mom Teena Brayen uses field trips as the foundation of her family's research. "For free field trips we have gone to the library and taught the kids how to use the card catalog, then we have gone to ponds and taught them about the wildlife and flowers. We took pictures and then looked them up in the encyclopedias and other material that had what we took photos of to learn more. Kind of like a research project."

Other research trips have included fishing and garbage cleanup along a local waterway. "Fishing taught the kids what the fish like to eat and won't eat and taught them patience. We cleaned garbage up along the Erie Canal as an Earth-friendly field trip. My kids loved each one. We are working on finding out when the Canal Village is open so they can learn about things that happened back when the Canal was a big waterway."

Nancy J. Rose, a homeschooling mother in West Palm Beach, Florida, turned a business trip into an educational experience for the family by researching the history of the place they had visited. Nancy homeschools two children, ages ten and eight. "A few months ago, my husband had some meetings near Daytona," she said. "We were able to visit a historic battleground, and then we came home and looked up the site we had visited on the computer encyclopedia. It made it so much more tangible, and helped us relate to the event by being able to see where it took place."

Research is the basis of Ann Crum's homeschooling method. "Yes! We do research!" she says. "Researching a topic draws out details that might otherwise be left out. I try to do a bit of pre-research to ensure that what I have assigned them can truly be found. But I merely suggest to them where to look or what to type into a search engine."

As a result of their research, the central Arkansas family

Research Tip:
From your browser's address line type "www.state.xx.us" —using a state's two-letter abbreviation for xx— to link to any state's official website. Similarly, type "gov.xx.ca" with any province's two-letter abbreviation, to link to the official site for each Canadian province.

Education Essentials

Hotlinks

Kids Research Portal
tinyurl.com/rekids

Materials Center
readwritethink.org/
materials

Son of Citation Machine
citationmachine.net

Wayback Machine
web.archive.org/web

On Knowledge

It is only the ignorant who despise education.

—Publilius Syrus, c. 45 b.c.

has gained a broader vision. Ann says her two kids "have learned so much about people around the world and can now view them not as statistics but as real people—just like themselves. They have learned the histories of different countries and how it is that a country lives by a certain philosophy or what their cultural base is. Sometimes they will come to me and say, 'Did you know thus and such?! Wow, I never knew that before!' They really get excited. Writing the research paper is another step in getting it embedded in their brains. So reading, writing, and telling all help to reinforce what they are learning."

Even though her six children are very young, Mary Batchelor of Sandy, Utah, is already getting started on teaching them the basics of research and helping them get familiar with the resources in the library. "I have shown the kids how to find authors and names of specific books on the library computers," she says, "and they have helped me locate the books on the shelves."

Mary says her children are still very young for in-depth research projects, "but we go to the library regularly, sometimes every week. I let them pick out several books each, and they are responsible for their particular books. I steer them toward books at or above their reading level so that they can be challenged but not disheartened, and for every educational book they choose (for reading time or for studying), they can pick out one non-educational book for fun."

Whether your children are young or old, they'll benefit from the great research guides below. Related information, including style guides and basic research resources, are located in the Reference Materials section, above, and in the Writing section of Chapter 5.

A Checklist for Evaluating Web Material
lib.nmsu.edu/instruction/evalcrit.html

Is a website a legitimate research source? Maybe. If it meets these five criteria.

Citing Electronic Sources   memory.loc.gov/learn/start/cite

The Library of Congress' online guide to citing sources in research papers. Guides for MLA and Chicago citations for cartoons, photographs, maps, and more. Includes examples. Part of the American Memory collection of historical documents.

Conducting Historical Research   cnx.org/content/col10291

Using a case study, this online course guides users through the process of conducting research using library and online sources. Most important, it teaches older students how to ask questions when they research.

Conducting Primary Research   tinyurl.com/resowl

An in-depth series of lessons on how to do research—part of Purdue's impressive writing laboratory. Ethical considerations, interviewing techniques, analysis techniques. Any kid who masters this material will breeze through college.

Copyright and Fair Use Guidelines for Teachers
www.sandhills.edu/blackboard/copyright.html

A chart describing what you can and cannot legally copy and use.

Factmonster   factmonster.com

Facts and stats, lists and lesson plans. In the homework center, find resources listed by academic subject.

Google Scholar   scholar.google.com

If you're looking for scholarly research on any particular topic, here's your tool. Find peer-reviewed papers, theses, books, abstracts and articles, from academic publishers, professional societies, preprint repositories, universities, and other scholarly organizations.

Guidelines for History and Archaeology Students
ubh.tripod.com/ub/h403g.htm

University of Botswana guidelines for quoting historical information, including good guidelines for citing scriptures.

Education Essentials

Education Essentials

Kids Research Portal   tinyurl.com/rekids

The Kentucky Virtual Library uses colorful graphics to explain the six steps of conducting research, using the library, and online sources.

Materials Center   readwritethink.org/materials

This collection of more than 50 research tools is awe-inspiring, but of most interest are the timeline maker and the biocube, which puts biographical information onto a printable, foldable cube. Enter data, print the results. Very professional-looking. And each tool comes with accompanying lesson plans.

Our Timelines   bright.net/~double/timelin1.htm

A unit-study idea involving creating a timeline as a history project. This homeschooling family made its own history timeline and has the photos to prove it.

Reading, Writing, and Researching for History
bowdoin.edu/writing-guides

A fabulous guide to writing history papers. All about how to research, how to write, and even how to read and analyze historical sources. The writing advice is thorough and well done.

Research Skills Worksheets   rhlschool.com/research.htm

Original-research skills worksheets that teach using a dictionary or thesaurus and fact finding. A link at the bottom of the page gives answer keys.

Scholastic Research Skills   teacher.scholastic.com/ilp

To connect to several dozen lesson plans that teach specific research skills, click the Reading tab, then go to the Research Skills link on the left. For pre-K through eighth grade. The "Home Sweet Home" lesson plan is particularly good for introducing young learners to the idea of research.

Son of Citation Machine   citationmachine.net

Web tool to help students properly cite sources in research papers—

an invaluable skill when they get to college, or build a portfolio. Just enter the citation information into a form, click the style, and bingo. Cite anything from anthologies to websites, in MLA, APA, Turabian, or Chicago style.

Top Tips for Research Skills   bbc.co.uk/keyskills/extra

Good research skills help kids find answers to every question. The BBC provides guidance to honing those skills.

Visit to Copyright Bay   stfrancis.edu/cid/copyrightbay

An entertaining way for educators and students to learn the meaning of "copyright" and "fair use."

Wayback Machine   web.archive.org/web

Want to check a web page to see whether it's legit? Start by looking at its history. WayBack Machine allows you to travel back through time to see the history of pretty much any website.

Writing and Analytical Resources   tinyurl.com/resrice

This is the front page of—incidentally—an online biology course, worth visiting in its own right. But click the Writing and Analytical Resources link for access to four independently useful resources: Notebook provides guidelines for keeping a laboratory record. Research Papers describes guidelines for writing research papers. Both Statistical Methods and Analytical Resources may be beyond the cognitive skills of most teenagers, but your smartest kids will find them educational.

Study Skills

ONE OF THE most challenging parts of homeschooling may be the part where you teach your children how to study. The casual atmosphere at home makes it difficult for many parents who want to establish some structured study.

Education Essentials

Study: From the Latin *studium* (to apply oneself). Careful consideration of a subject in order to acquire knowledge.

M.A., a single homeschooling mom in Louisiana, has a system that works for her family. "I work full-time during the day, so a lot of his homeschool is self study. We use interactive websites, text, and field trips. I go over work with him at night and we keep in touch through instant messenger during the day. That way, if he has trouble he just sends a message and I look for a link that explains the subject better."

If you think your children's education could be better served with a little more structure, this is the section for you.

Whether you do "school at home" or are simply preparing your older children for college, there comes a time when everyone, even the most unschooled child, needs to learn basic study skills.

The following sites contain scores of handouts, articles, tests, and lessons on improving study skills. As your children work through these resources, they will learn the essential skills of note taking, exam preparation, outlining, sticking to task, and many other critical educational skills.

So pull out a pencil. It's time to learn.

Hotlinks

Academic Tips
academictips.org

Effective Study Skills
adprima.com/
studyout.htm

Study Guides and Strategies
studygs.net

Study Stack
studystack.com

Academic Tips   academictips.org
College will be a change. Here's how to help your kids prepare. Academic Tips is full of tips and tricks to help students manage their time, take better notes, study more effectively, improve memory, take tests, and handle the stresses of college life.

College Success Seminars
www.wmich.edu/asc/collegesuccessseminars.html
College-prep articles outlining note-taking techniques, research, test-taking techniques, reading speed, time management, and more.

Effective Study Skills   adprima.com/studyout.htm
Well-written advice on topics such as setting schedules, finding workable strategies, and taking notes.

Education Essentials

Learning Strategies elc.polyu.edu.hk/cill/strategy.htm

Very specific clues for how to study an unfamiliar subject. It's directed at learners of English as a second language, but the skills apply to any subject.

Note Taking languagearts.pppst.com/notetaking.html

PowerPoint presentations that teach kids how to take effective lecture notes. Use these skills while watching online lectures or public television programs, or when participating in co-op classes. One of the lessons explains summarizing and note taking. Two others discuss the Cornell Note-taking System.

Revision & Skills bbc.co.uk/schools/studentlife/revisionandskills

Chock-full of helpful articles such as How to speed read, Eat your way to exam success, and Do you have a critical mind? Covers revision, exams, study skills, and stress. By the BBC.

Strategies for Success mtsu.edu/~studskl

A full online course in test preparation, time management, goal setting, and more helpful information on studying effectively. Especially useful for college prep.

Study Guides and Strategies studygs.net

Strategies and study guides that will help motivate you and your student.

Study Skills Self-Help Information
www.ucc.vt.edu/stdysk/stdyhlp.html

All about attitude, organization, time management, establishing an environment, note taking, reading and memorizing, writing and editing, and test-taking strategies. Designed for college freshmen, but the information applies equally to middle- and high-school ages.

Study Stack studystack.com

Flashcards were never this good. Use the Study Stack the way you'd use regular flashcards, but take advantage of all the improvements:

On Study

If you think education is expensive, try ignorance.

—Derek Bok, former president, Harvard University

Education Essentials

Education Essentials

Motivation

Rewards usually motivate my children to study.

—L.A., wife of one and an M.O.M. (mother of many), Flint, Michigan

Use the study table to see all the data in a single place. Print data or export flashcards to your cell phone, PDA, or iPod. Play games with the flashcard data. This is what computers were made to do. Use any of hundreds of existing card stacks, or create your own.

Survivor Algebra   **coolmath.com/Survivor-Algebra**
Teaching algebra—or any other subject—gets more fun when kids are motivated to learn. Here's a way to help kids teach themselves. Includes tips on being a successful student, and steps for studying for a math exam.

Values, Standards, and Ethics

THE FINAL AND most critical area of education essentials: Teaching your children to be good human beings.

Teaching ethics may be the best argument for homeschooling. Public schools have their hands tied when it comes to teaching values. "We decided to homeschool for many reasons," says Terri Vitkovitsky from Camp Lejeune, North Carolina. "Primarily, we wanted to have the leading role in shaping our children's character. We wanted to provide a very hands-on, experiential education where there would be many field trips, games, and activities, and not all books and workbooks."

Kentucky homeschooler Jessica Murphy had a similar motive: "My husband and I decided we wanted to teach our children Biblical morals and values that are not taught in public schools and to protect our children from the many dangers that are becoming so prevalent in public schools. I wanted to teach them. Why should that stop at age five?"

Fifty years ago, there was a good likelihood that parents and teachers shared the same values, and so parents felt safe sending their kids to school, confident that the values they

Ethics: From the Greek *-ethikos* (character). A system of moral values and standards.

taught at home were being reinforced in the classroom. Now, though, whether your family members have strong religious values or are devout believers in secularism, there's a good chance that your position won't find support in the public schools. In many—if not most—school districts, teachers are discouraged from taking a position on any ethical issue that is not part of the approved curriculum.

Fortunately, you have no such problem: You have boundless opportunity to teach your kids right and wrong.

The Internet has some terrific resources for parents looking for a framework for teaching moral behavior. Here's where you can start:

Appleseeds   www.appleseeds.org

Quotations and blessings from a Franciscan monk that promote positive attitudes and human dignity.

Becoming a Brilliant Star   chiron.valdosta.edu/whuitt/brilstar.html

A high-quality guide to developing homeschooling curriculum, written by a college professor who is an educational psychologist. This system encourages children to develop positive beliefs about themselves, and to act on those beliefs.

Bonner Center for Character Education
education.csufresno. edu/bonnercenter

Click the Promising Practices link on the left to access excellent curriculum materials, including the article "Sixty-five Suggestions," which is a helpful start for teaching ethics and morality.

Character Counts!   charactercounts.org

The Josephson Institute's "Six Pillars of Character" teach the basics of ethical behavior. Find here commentaries and lesson plans to back up the pillars. Throughout the site you'll find great information on teaching character and integrity.

Hotlinks

Character Counts!
charactercounts.org

Character Education
tinyurl.com/valchar

Kindness Lesson Plans
actsofkindness.org

Morality in Media
moralityinmedia.org

On Virtue

The very spring and root of honesty and virtue lie in the felicity of lighting on good education.

—Plutarch, A.D. 46–120

Character Education   tinyurl.com/valchar

The state of Utah developed this character-education site to teach public school students moral behavior. You'll find the lesson plans helpful in developing your own character-education lessons. If you haven't thought through what you expect of your effort to develop character in your children, the rubric under Lifeskills will be useful.

Humanistic Psychology and Education
tinyurl.com/valpsy

An investigation into the dire results of non-directive approaches to public education. Non-directive approaches say, "We're not going to call anything wrong, we're not going to call drug use wrong, because we'll make some of the kids in this classroom feel bad because they are already using drugs. Let's see if we can help people without identifying for them what they're doing wrong." What happens is that the kids who are always looking for the objective standard—so that they can meet it—are left without one.

Kindness Lesson Plans   actsofkindness.org

The Random Acts of Kindness foundation offers more than 50 lesson plans and teaching guides to encourage kind behavior in everyday life. Click the In Your Classroom link at the top of the page to access these excellent educational materials.

Kohlberg's Theory of Moral Development   tinyurl.com/valkl

Based on the premise that at birth, all humans are void of morals, ethics, and honesty. Kohlberg identified the family as the first source of values and moral development for an individual. He believed that as one's intelligence and ability to interact with others matures, so do one's patterns of moral behavior. Kohlberg argues that each of the six stages is progressive, and that there's no functioning on a higher level until a lower level is mastered. This article includes links to real-life classroom applications of Kohlberg's theory.

George Washington

George Washington, the first president of the United States, grew up on a Virginia farm on the Rappahannock River. From age seven to fifteen he attended school sporadically, but appears to have spent a large part of his childhood learning on his own. At the age of fourteen he transcribed in his copybook a set of moral precepts, called Rules of Civility and Decent Behaviour in Company and Conversation. During these years he became conversant in practical math and enough trigonometry to become a qualified surveyor. In addition, he learned a little Latin and geography and read some of the classics. Some of his best training came through his outdoor vocations—tobacco growing and stock raising. By his early teens he had already begun surveying, which served as the beginning of his distinguished career as a farmer, military leader, politician, and statesman.

Lifeskills at ppst   facs.pppst.com/lifeskills.html

PowerPoint presentations that teach conflict resolution, feelings, etiquette, character building, and decision making. One of the lessons, "Don't Gross Out the World," teaches proper table manners while traveling. Another, "Friends," teaches social skills as illustrated by Norman Rockwell paintings.

Meaning and Cancer   tinyurl.com/valmean

Quotations from Man's Search for Meaning, and an essay on facing life's most difficult times with courage.

Morality in Media   moralityinmedia.org

Fight obscenity in the media. This organization tells you how.

Quotes from Man's Search for Meaning

webwinds.com/frankl/quotes.htm

Quotes on choosing one's attitude, committing to values and goals, discovering the meaning of life, and fulfilling one's task. They're my favorite quotes, too.

Education Essentials

Table Manners for Toddlers   sk-infotech.com/19120.html

A tutorial on teaching etiquette to youngsters. Links at the bottom of the page go to related toddler teaching sites.

The Glory of Books: A Guide for Homeschoolers
tinyurl.com/glorybooks

A guide to choosing literature based on moral values.

Education Essentials

Chapter 5

Language Literacy

WHEN I WAS twelve years old, I decided I'd grow up to become a writer. A book called *Harriet the Spy*, by Louise Fitzhugh, had inspired me. The book's title character is an adolescent girl determined to be a famous writer when she grows up, and in preparation she maintains a notebook of candid observations of her friends, family, and neighbors. The book set the course for my entire life.

Harriet was a rather unattractive, frumpy little girl, and even though her wealthy East Coast private-schooled life was completely different from my middle-class West Coast upbringing, Harriet was someone I could identify with. In preparation for her career, Harriet carried around a book and made notes about the people on her daily "spy route."

I recently did an Internet search on *Harriet the Spy* and was astounded to find that lots of people had decided on a career while in grade school because they'd been inspired by the book (e.g., **tinyurl.com/authint** and **francesdowell .com**).

"You cannot teach a man anything," said Galileo. "You can only help him find it within himself." It was literature that taught me to find the potential within myself.

This chapter introduces two of the three R's ('rithmetic is covered in Chapter 6).

Hotlinks

English Grammar Online
ego4u.com

Language Arts Presentations
languagearts.pppst.com

Technology Tips for Classroom Teachers
edzone.net/~mwestern

Traci's List of Tens
tengrrl.com/tens

Language

Here you'll find everything you might ever need to teach English to your kids. We begin with a discussion of etymology: the origin of words. The second section covers grammar, usage, and punctuation. The subsequent sections cover handwriting, literature, reading skills, spelling, vocabulary, and written expression.

To get you started, here are some of the most helpful sites on the Internet for pulling together a general English curriculum.

Busy Teacher's Café   busyteacherscafe.com/printables.htm

Worksheets for math, science, and social studies, but the primary focus is printables, themes, and other resources that teach literacy and language arts. Click the Teacher Resources link for an especially good section called Literacy Strategies.

English Grammar Online   ego4u.com

Grammar is just part of this information-heavy resource. The Study Tips section is filled with good advice, and the writing and vocabulary sections contain lessons in punctuation, essay writing, and business English.

Language Arts   tinyurl.com/lawebq

Web quests on topics such as spelling and literature. Extremely well done, with photographs, links, explanatory text, and illustrations.

Language Arts Lesson Plans   tinyurl.com/lalessons

English and language arts lesson plans designed by classroom teachers. Most are easily adapted to homeschooling programs.

Language Arts Presentations   languagearts.pppst.com

PowerPoint presentations that teach language arts across the curriculum. This is an extensive collection, and you'll find something for every subject you teach.

Language Arts Teaching Themes   teach-nology.com/themes/lang_arts

Another cross-curriculum resource for language arts. Unit studies for handwriting, grammar, phonics, public speaking, creative writing, and individual literature series such as Harry Potter and the Wizard of Oz.

Literacy   tinyurl.com/lalit

English by the English. The BBC offers literacy lessons for younger learners. Lots of interactive games teach writing, spelling, reading, and grammar.

Literacy Web   www.literacy.uconn.edu

The Effective Teaching link is particularly helpful, but this University of Connecticut site includes resources for many areas of English instruction.

Six Features of Effective Instruction
cela.albany.edu/publication/brochure/guidelines.pdf

Six important research findings on teaching reading and writing at the middle- and high-school levels. The first: "Students learn skills and knowledge in multiple lesson types."

Skillswise Words   bbc.co.uk/skillswise/words

A BBC resource for teaching literacy to older learners. Click a tab in the Words section for quick courses in grammar, spelling, reading, listening, writing, and vocabulary. Other links go to quizzes, games, glossaries, and a place to submit your own writing to the BBC.

Teachnet's Language Arts   teachnet.com/lesson/langarts

A collection of short lesson ideas in several areas of English-language instruction—journalism, writing, reading, spelling, ESL, poetry, and others.

Technology Tips for Classroom Teachers   edzone.net/~mwestern

The section entitled Handouts is particularly good. One of the handouts is 101 ways to integrate technology into literacy activities. It directs you to alphabet sites, vocabulary games, make-your-own word puzzles, contractions, spelling games, handwriting worksheets, and my current favorite: create online flashcards.

Language

The Mysteries of Language Arts   tinyurl.com/lamys

Why the catchall "language arts" isn't a useful way of teaching unrelated skills. An article for homeschooling parents.

Traci's List of Tens   tengrrl.com/tens

Lists of Ten are articles about teaching language arts, each with ten tips for addressing subjects such as grammar, literature, media literacy, and the writing process.

Way Out Communication   tinyurl.com/wayouc

All about the history of communicating. The links begin with lessons on cave paintings and papyrus, and progress straight through the printing press and telegraphs to the Internet. Are we now at the end of communications history?

Writing Handouts   tinyurl.com/writeho

From a university student learning center, printable handouts to reinforce writing and language skills. Many handouts include problem sets with answers. Handouts cover grammar, spelling, punctuation, ESL, documentation, and the writing process.

Etymology and Linguistics

IT'S ONE OF the newer sciences.

Rather than learn a lot of languages (which is what polyglots do), linguists learn a lot about languages. They study word origins and language acquisition, the structure of language, and its usage.

One of the most interesting branches of linguistics is etymology. (No, not the bug science—that's entomology.) Etymologists trace the history and origin of words.

Why is the origin and construction of language worth studying? I have found this to be true: The more my children

> **Etymology:**
> From the Greek *etymon* (word). The branch of linguistics that deals with word origins.

Language

learn about the origin of words, the better they become at spelling, vo-cabulary, grammar, and all the other elements that go into making them good writers.

Want another reason? It's just plain fun.

Discovering the etymological relationship between words such as "hippopotamus" and "feather" (**tinyurl.com/fhippo**) is as much fun as solving any Arthur Conan Doyle mystery.

Some of the subcategories of linguistics—other than etymology—include phonology (the study of sounds), syntax (the study of sentence structure), morphology (the study of word parts), and semantics (the study of meaning). We also cover some excellent resources for speech re-mediation, and a handful of helps for teaching English to children who are speaking it as a second language.

If you'd like to turn your own kids into expert word sleuths, investi-gate these fun websites:

Cockney Rhyming Slang   cockneyrhymingslang.co.uk

Your brussels sprout is earning merit badges, and your bricks and mortar is in the bin laden. While they're out, p'haps you can pick up an uncle Bert for the old pot.

Dr. Goodword Linguistics Minicourse

alphadictionary.com/articles

"Dr. Goodword" introduces a plethora of information on how words and language came to be. "Mama teached me talk?" and "Can colorless green ideas sleep furi-ously?" are two of my favorites. You'll enjoy the rest.

ESL Teachers Board   eslteachersboard.com

Click the Short Stories link under ESL resources to find stories for reading aloud or individually. See, for exam-ple, the Coloring Page Crayons History, a short tutorial on the history of crayons. Teaching Tips and ESL Print-ables are also useful resources.

Hotlinks

Cockney Rhyming Slang
cockneyrhymingslang
.co.uk

Dr. Goodword Linguistics Minicourse
alphadictionary.com/
articles

Fun with Words
alphadictionary.com/fun

Word Origins
wordorigins.org

Language

Fun with Words   alphadictionary.com/fun

Word games and other entertaining resources that teach kids of all ages about the beauty of language. The bottom link, Word Fun Across the Web, is particularly good, with sections on Fun with Words, Word Origins, and Say It in Another Language.

Interesting Things for ESL Students   www.manythings.org

Quizzes, word puzzles, grammar fun, and lots more to entertain students studying English. It's not a very pretty site, but the more you use it, the better it gets.

Learning English Online   englisch-hilfen.de/en

Lessons, examinations, explanations, and exercises explaining English to non-native speakers. The idiom lists will be particularly interesting to anyone seeking to understand the language.

Linguistics and Semantics   tinyurl.com/lingsema

An eight-lesson course that teaches about the properties of language, articulation, word formation, syntax, semantics, pragmatic language, text, and poetry.

Mixed Metaphors   tinyurl.com/ggmixed

I once heard a speaker talk about how a new idea hit him like a light-bulb. Ouch. Be smart; learn about mixed metaphors so you don't ever make the same mistake.

Online Etymology Dictionary   etymonline.com

Shows the etymology (and often the original pronunciation) of words, but also of words related to the one you're investigating. "Genesis," for example, also explains parthenogenesis, biogenesis, Eden, chaos, and apple.

The Phrase Finder   www.phrases.org.uk

Find the origins and meanings of phrases and sayings. Includes a list of dictionaries, thesauri, and etymology books.

Language

Verbivore verbivore.com

The very funny language columnist Richard Lederer is the Verbivore. Read some of his thoughts on linguistics and language, or follow any of the hundreds of links to related resources.

What If They Don't Speak English?
http://misd.net/bilingual/resources.htm

I've adopted from, and raised children, overseas, so ESL was once a big part of our homeschooling. Whether they're your own or a neighbor's, if you work with non-native English speakers, this guide, one of several on this site, will help. The desuggestive learning techniques are particularly interesting.

Word Origins wordorigins.org

Interesting, and well-documented (that's important!), explanations of common colloquialisms and slang terms. Is it aluminum or aluminium? Burma or Myanmar? Here's proof.

Word.A.Day wordsmith.org

Wordsmith Chat is the most educational feature on this site, featuring live chats with authors, lexicographers, and thinkers. But Word a Day will be the most immediately entertaining for younger kids. Features a new word each day, along with a definition.

On School

School days, I believe, are the unhappiest in the whole span of human existence. They are full of dull, unintelligible tasks, new and unpleasant ordinances, brutal violations of common sense and common decency.

—H. L. Mencken, journalist, 1880–1956

Grammar, Usage, and Punctuation

WE MOVE FROM the simple origin and history of language to modern English usage. Grammar is . . . well . . . listen in on a conversation we had in our house, as I was teaching my seven-year-old daughter about parts of speech:

Me: "A noun is a person or a place or a thing."

Language

Grammar: From the Greek *grammatikos* (of letters). The art of using language with propriety and correctness.

Daughter: "You mean like Nebraska?"

Me (stifling a laugh; didn't realize she'd ever *heard* of Nebraska): "Yes! Good! Now, sometimes, a noun isn't so much a thing you can touch, but it's more like an idea, a thing you can't touch."

Daughter: "So it's like romance? Or electricity?"

Fist pump!

If you once endured hours of sentence diagramming in school, this is probably the stuff you used to hate. Despite the tedium of watching a sentence being diagrammed, however, grammar really does have important real-world applications. Brent Ayers, a copy editor and sports writer in Greensboro, North Carolina, explains, "Grammar is extremely important in my field. Because no one is perfect, my job is to correct problems with grammar, among other things, when reporters send stories to me.

"As a reader, I see things in a document that others may not. Grammar and style are two of the most important things in a newspaper. They give it consistency, clarity, and power to inform.

"I am very qualified to address how to prepare for this job in high school, because that's exactly what I did. First, I had a teacher who was a stickler for grammar. Then I began working for my high school newspaper, writing as much as possible. You may be embarrassed to have others read your writing, but that's something you'll have to get over sooner or later.

"To prepare for this field of work, find a small local newspaper—preferably a weekly, but a daily would work, too. Find a way to be around the office as much as possible. If you can get a paying job doing something, great. If not, volunteer for an internship; it may turn into a paying job."

Samuel J. Sackett, Ph.D, a career counselor in Oklahoma City, says grammar can make all the difference when it comes to getting a well-paid job. "I help my clients pre-

Hotlinks

Bitesize Games
tinyurl.com/labite

English Basics
rhlschool.com/english.htm

Grammar Gorillas
funbrain.com/grammar

KISS Grammar Course
tinyurl.com/lakiss

pare résumés and other documentation that supports their efforts to get jobs. Since nothing makes a worse impression on a prospective employer than a résumé with grammatical errors, my work frequently involves correcting these documents and explaining to my clients just why what they wrote is wrong—hoping that they won't make the same mistakes again."

Here are some great grammar, usage, and punctuation sites. Rest assured, they're considerably more fun than watching Mrs. Grumpy's backside as she diagrammed sentences on a squeaky chalkboard!

An Elementary Grammar

englishinstitute.co.uk/intro.html

A clear explanation of various elements of English speech. Despite the name, it's probably most appropriate for older students.

Bitesize Games   **tinyurl.com/labite**

The BBC's collection of language games to teach literacy, narrated in a plummy British accent. Various games teach phonics, rhyming words, alphabetical order, spelling, using pronouns, using conjunctions, synonyms, use of punctuation, and sentence construction. It's slow-loading, because it's high quality.

Common Errors in English   **wsu.edu/~brians/errors**

Is it "forego" or "forgo"? What does it mean to "beg the question"? The supplementary page Non-Errors lists usages the people believe are errors, but aren't.

English Basics   **rhlschool.com/english.htm**

Grammar worksheets for teaching, reinforcement, and review. Worksheets cover analogies, parts of speech, proofreading, and many grammatical principles.

Best Homeschooling Moment

I have so many "Yes!" moments where I have realized that the time we spend homeschooling and the way we are educating our children is so worth it. For example, my almost-three-year-old loves to pick out quotation marks on signs and packages. And she knows exactly what they are.

—Terri Vitkovitsky, homeschooling mom of five, Camp Lejeune, North Carolina

Language

Grammar Gorillas   funbrain.com/grammar

The Grammar Gorillas need help identifying parts of speech. Feed them bananas by clicking the correct answers. An interactive game for young learners.

Grammar Handbook   cws.illinois.edu/workshop/writers

The Writers Workshop includes a link to an amazing Grammar Handbook. This handbook explains and illustrates the basic rules of speech, phrases, clauses, sentences and sentence elements, and common problems of usage. Includes teaching sections for various elements of the handbook.

Grammar Rock   schoolhouserock.tv/Grammar.html

The old School House Rock grammar videos are collected here, including my favorite: Conjunction Junction. Use music to teach your kids about parts of speech such as pronouns, interjections, verbs, and nouns.

Guide to Grammar and Writing
grammar.ccc.commnet.edu/grammar

Three levels of grammar (including a terrific graphic resource on diagramming sentences), questions, quizzes, and more.

Home for Abused Apostrophes
www.suepalmer.co.uk/apostrophes.php

"A haven for little punctuation marks which have been cruelly misused by greengrocers and other uncaring notice-writers." After amusing yourself with the photos of bad punctuation, click the Articles link for some good articles on literacy education.

KISS Grammar Course   tinyurl.com/lakiss

Free, non-credit, self-paced grammar course taught by a professor at the Pennsylvania College of Technology. Includes exercises and answer keys.

Punctuation: A Brief History   tinyurl.com/lahist

Did you know that putting spaces between words didn't come into

Language

vogue until after A.D. 800? Or that paragraphs used to be separated by horizontal black lines? The history is fascinating; the punctuation rules are helpful.

Punctuation Made Simple   tinyurl.com/lapunc

Simple rules for using the five most-misunderstood punctuation marks: colon, semicolon, comma, dash, and apostrophe.

The King's English   bartleby.com/116

The ultimate grammar primer: Fowler's 1908 treatise on vocabulary, syntax, punctuation, and affectations of English has set the standard for better than a century.

Handwriting and Penmanship

IS PENMANSHIP DEAD? Not with homeschoolers. With little pressure to teach to artificial test standards, families who learn at home have the leisure to teach the fine art of handwriting. And they do. Many families spend part of each day doing copywork or seatwork, which teaches memorization, language acquisition, and—of course—handwriting.

The method is simple. Children manually copy out selections of text from classic literature, from scripture or from textbooks.

Other families enjoy teaching with handwriting worksheets, or spend time learning calligraphy as part of their art or foreign language curriculum. No matter which path you follow, you'll find helpful resources here for teaching penmanship, cursive writing, printing, and calligraphy.

Cursive Writing Worksheets   tinyurl.com/hwcurs

Printable cursive worksheets for each letter of the alphabet. Each sheet begins with a single letter, then progresses to using the letter in short words.

Calligraphy:
From the Greek *kalligraphia*, from *kallos* (beauty) and *graphia* (to write)

Language

Draw Your World   drawyourworld.com/dnealian.html

A single page comparing penmanship styles. The styles are cursive, manuscript, Italic, D'Nealian, Handwriting Without Tears, Palmer, and three Australians hands: New South Wales, Queensland, and Victorian.

Handwriting for Kids   handwritingforkids.com

Writing numbers and letters is an important task for children. This site attempts to make it more fun with activities and advice to reward their success. Worksheets teach manuscript and cursive writing.

Handwriting Printables   tinyurl.com/hwprint

Free printable worksheets, flashcards, and more using D'Nealian, Zaner-Bloser, Handwriting Without Tears, and other alphabets. This page includes dotted practice sheets, letters to color, and cursive activities. You'll find it quite useful.

Helping Your Child to Better Handwriting   tinyurl.com/hwhelp

In-depth articles explaining how to teach penmanship, and how to work with disabilities such as dysgraphia.

Hotlinks

Incredible Handwriting Worksheet Maker
handwritingworksheets.com

Lessons in Calligraphy and Penmanship
iampeth.com/lessons.php

YoungMinds Handwriting
donnayoung.org/penmanship

Incredible Handwriting Worksheet Maker
handwritingworksheets.com

Make custom handwriting worksheets at the click of a button. Select a handwriting style—basic print, D'Nealian print, or cursive—and watch the magic unfold.

Lessons in Calligraphy and Penmanship
iampeth.com/lessons.php

The keepers of the calligraphy and penmanship flame offer video demonstrations of calligraphic methods and styles. Guide sheets, tips, and history lessons are included.

Notebooking Pages   tinyurl.com/hwnote

The printable notebooking pages have plenty of space to practice penmanship. Most come decorated with icons and graphics to inspire your reluctant writer.

Language

Remember Penmanship?   tinyurl.com/hw20th

No, it's not "So Twentieth Century." An article decrying the loss of handwriting instruction in the school curriculum.

YoungMinds Handwriting   donnayoung.org/penmanship

Print handwriting paper to accompany the many printing and cursive lessons housed on this site. The Rules of Civility book posted on this site is useful for copywork lessons.

Literature

IN THIS SECTION on literature—which could easily be expanded to a book of its own—we locate resources for teaching children to comprehend and appreciate literature.

If you have a grudging reader, it might help him or her to understand how a thorough knowledge of literature is important to gaining a complete education.

"I believe that the study of literature serves several purposes in the 'real world,' " says P. Timothy Ervin, a professor of English at Yasuda Women's University in Hiroshima, Japan. I view literature in the following ways: Literature provides a basic background to human cultures, both past and present (Emily Dickinson's 'There is no frigate like a book / To take us lands away'); it provides a basic education, a language with which to communicate (the 'traverse even the poorest take / Without oppress of toll'); it gives us a deeper understanding of human nature ('How frugal is the chariot / That bears the human soul')."

Teaching kids to love literature has become significantly easier in recent years, with the advent of free audiobooks online. "We have just recently found audio files of *Shakespeare for Children* (**tinyurl.com/litshake**), and many other audiobooks, all free online," says a mom of four from Jacaranda

Literature: From the Latin *litteratus* (lettered). The study of written works with a high and lasting artistic value.

Hotlinks

Aha! Poetry!
ahapoetry.com

Children's Literature Site
carolhurst.com

LibriVox
librivox.org

Literature Lesson Plans
litplans.com

What Makes a Good Short Story?
learner.org/interactives/ literature

Tree Learning Co-operative, Hawkes Bay, New Zealand. "As our children love music and listening to stories, we will use these as a complement and they'll be very handy when travelling, too, as you have a captive audience!"

The Internet simplifies teaching literature in other ways, as well. Most publishers now publish free reading group guides on their websites. These guides provide lots of great questions that can be incorporated into a discussion after reading.

This section doesn't list works by individual authors (That's a whole 'nuther book!), though it does take you to several very large collections of literature. Nor will you find material on basic reading skills; that's covered in the following section.

What you will find here is an amazing selection of literature resources. That will help you teach your children to love literature.

1000 Good Books List   tinyurl.com/lit1000

A reading list organized by reading level. The creator of this list uses a classical Christian approach to education.

30 Days of Poetry   tinyurl.com/lit30days

Thirty poetry lessons. Each gives a format to follow and student examples.

Aha Poetry   ahapoetry.com

All sorts of fun challenges and adventures related to Japanese poetical styles. Add your own work to this online anthology and meeting place for poets.

American Literature, 1820–1890   wsu.edu/~campbelld/amlit

A very thorough resource on American literature. Each segment is a unit study on a literary period. By Donna Campbell, Gonzaga University.

Language

Children's Books Online   editec.net

Some four hundred antique children's books published in the nineteenth and early twentieth centuries. Free, illustrated, beautiful!

Children's Literature Site   carolhurst.com

Teaching ideas using children's books. An award-winning page. This is a collection of reviews of great books for kids, ideas of ways to use them in your teaching, and collections of books and activities about particular subjects, curriculum areas, themes, and professional topics.

Chinese Poetry Reading   chinapage.org/poetry9.html

Classical Chinese poetry, read by native speakers. Of particular interest is the "Du Fu," which is translated into English by numerous translators, each with astounding variations. The last translation is the most literally accurate.

Classic Audiobooks   freeclassicaudiobooks.com

More than fifty well-known books, including such classics as *Tom Sawyer, Heidi,* and *Robinson Crusoe,* narrated by readers, not by text-to-speech. For auditory learners, listening while reading is an aid to comprehension.

Critical Reading: A Guide
brocku.ca/english/jlye/criticalreading.html

Professor John Lye writes: "a guide to what you might look for in analyzing literature, particularly poetry and fiction. An analysis explains what a work of literature means, and how it means it; it is essentially an articulation of and a defense of an interpretation." This excellent guide is written for college students, but it's easily adapted to preteens and teens.

Twain Says

Training is everything. The peach was once a bitter almond; cauliflower is nothing but cabbage with a college education.

—Mark Twain,
Pudd'nhead Wilson

Asimov Says

I know less of anything practical than anyone else in the world. When I say I know everything, I mean everything useless.

—Isaac Asimov, *Yours, Isaac Asimov: A Lifetime of Letters*

Language

Reading Freebie

Dad's Playbook: Coaching Kids to Read discusses the importance of teaching children to read, and explains how fathers can use simple skills to help their children be even better readers. Call 877-4-ED-PUBS and request product number ED002542P.

Kids' Corner Books   wiredforbooks.org/kids.htm

Classic, illustrated children's stories from Beatrix Potter, along with audio stories from Potter, L. Frank Baum, and others.

Language Arts Lesson Plans

easyfunschool.com/IndexLanguageArts.html

A collection of language arts lessons, activities, and literature units. Most of the lessons are designed to increase understanding of specific works of classic literature such as *Alice in Wonderland* and the *Velveteen Rabbit.*

LibriVox   librivox.org

Hundreds and hundreds of books—classic, mostly—in audio form. Listen to podcasts, subscribe in iTunes, or hear them using the media player on your computer.

Literature Lesson Plans   litplans.com

Some 30,000 literature lesson plans for teaching Chaucer, Shakespeare, Twain, C. S. Lewis, and virtually every classic author you've encountered.

Literature Study Guides   tinyurl.com/litsg

Study guides for a dozen or more works of classic modern literature, prepared by a high school English class. Useful in their own right, but in addition, useful as an intelligent format for book reports.

Multimedia Book Report Rubric   ncsu.edu/midlink/bk.rep.fic.htm

If you're wondering what makes a good book report, or how to determine whether your kids are getting anything out of their reading, this grading rubric may help you set the standards.

Poetry Archives   emule.com/poetry

The works of hundreds of poets, from Ovid and Virgil to Jorge Luis Borges and Robert Frost. This ever-expanding archive of classical poetry contains more than 5,000 poems.

Language

Poetry Lessons for Teachers and Students   tinyurl.com/litpogui

Twenty-five online lessons in poetry. Teach your little ones about poetry with lessons on subjects such as figurative language, famous poems and poets, the art of poetry; and purpose: Write with a Porpoise.

Project Gutenberg   gutenberg.org

Tens of thousands of volunteers have taken out-of-print older books and put them online as free ebooks. Subscribe to the RSS feed to keep an eye on new offerings.

Renascence Editions   darkwing.uoregon.edu/~rbear/ren.htm

An online repository of works printed in English between the years 1477 and 1799. Roger Ascham, Bacon, Defoe, Elizabeth I, Hobbes, Hume, Milton, More, Shakespeare, Adam Smith, and all your classical favorites.

SCORE CyberGuides   tinyurl.com/litscore

How do you follow up when your daughter finishes reading *Sarah, Plain and Tall*? The Cyber-Guides will help. These lists of recommended literature are tied in with a California standards curriculum. The list is divided by grade level. Each recommended book has an associated study unit. These units teach several hundred specific works of literature, from *Charlotte's Web* and *Velveteen Rabbit* to *Animal Farm* and *Julius Caesar.*

Story Online   storylineonline.net

Well-known actors read well-known children's stories. Your younger kids will be fascinated for hours.

Storynory   storynory.com

Audio versions of children's stories, read in an English accent. Classic stories from Kipling, Dickens, Lewis Carroll, and Wilde, along with famous

Best Homeschooling Moment

Having three boys over from another homeschooling family, playing in the backyard with my ten-year-old daughter, and overhearing them casually but enthusiastically discussing and critiquing the Greek and Roman gods "outside of school."

—Work-at-home mom of four from Jacaranda Tree Learning Co-operative, Hawkes Bay, New Zealand

Language

poetry, fairy tales, fables, Bible stories, myths, and original stories. Transcripts of the audios are viewable for reading along.

StudyStack Literature   studystack.com/category-25

Online flashcards—including the space to build your own—that re-inforce literature lessons. Uses traditional flashcard format, as well as games and other tools for teaching.

The Lifetime Reading Plan   interleaves.org/~rteeter/grtfad3.html

A great-books list in several categories. Work through the list and you'll have a thorough grounding in the classics.

What Makes a Good Short Story?   learner.org/interactives/literature

An exploratory journey through a short story. "Like a great journey, literature can show you things you have never seen before and will never forget."

World Wide School Library   worldwideschool.org

Click the Library link for access to works of classic literature about history, geography, social sciences, science, philosophy, and religion. Includes lots of fiction, as well, such as Bobbsey Twins stories and Lamb's *Tales from Shakespeare.*

Reading Skills

RECENTLY, I EXCHANGED letters with a mom who was worried that her kids weren't "keeping up with the Joneses" when it came to learning to read.

I advised her to do what my mother did to get me reading by the time I was four. The three components of my mother's very successful 1960s early reading program were letters, words, and stories. Oh, and there was also a fourth component: sibling competition. (I was the oldest child and, as such, had to show up my little sister, who was picking this stuff up as fast I was; she started reading at three.)

This is how my mother got her daughters reading almost before they were out of diapers: She put capital letters on flashcards, and hooked them together with a metal ring so they never got scattered.

Then she made a competition out of learning those letters and their sounds. Whichever kid shouted the sound out first would win.

To teach words, she would place the names of household objects in block capital letters on strips of paper, and tape each strip to the appropriate object. For the longest time, I thought the thing our family calls a couch was a sofa, because that's the word my mom taped to the couch. Over the few months we learned to read, our entire house was labeled; to this day, though, I remember going around the house "reading" the word strips. Every once in a while my mom would change them around to see whether she could catch us out, but eventually we got to where we could spot the changed words. That's how it happened that the first English word I learned to read was "refrigerator." I always knew when the long word got moved!

Finally, stories. The first one I learned to read was a Dr. Seuss–like story called *Nose Is Not Toes*. It was clipped together with a metal ring and had about twenty-five words written in all capital letters. Now I make up my own silly stories for my own kids. I use simple rhyming words to get them reading: "The cat is fat. The bat is not fat. The cat is not the bat. The bat is not the cat. The bat sat on the cat. The cat sat on the bat. Fat cat! The bat ran away from the fat cat. What's that? Uh-oh! Flat cat. The bat saves the cat. The cat is not flat. Happy bat. Happy cat." Get the kids to sit on your lap and read homemade stories with you over and over until they recognize all the words. Then repeat the flashcard system, this time with all the story words clipped together, until they recognize them. Presto! You've got successful readers!

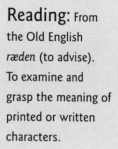

Reading: From the Old English *ræden* (to advise). To examine and grasp the meaning of printed or written characters.

Hotlinks

Learning to Read
succeedtoread.com

Literacy Connections
literacyconnections.com

Online Phonics Course
reading.indiana.edu/
www/indexoe.html

Star Fall
starfall.com

Language

For many families, reading provides the most tangible proof that homeschooling is working. "The most rewarding thing for me so far has been watching my children learn to read," says Washington homeschooler Robin Goddard. "It's just amazing to watch them have that 'aha' moment when it all clicks."

She's not the only one. "My most wonderful and favorite moment thus far was when my four-year-old son picked out a book in the library, sat down at the table, and proceeded to read," says Kentucky mom Jessica Murphy. "It was not a book that we had at home so I knew it was not memorized. It was such a blessing! My baby could read! By himself! He taught himself to read using **starfall.com**. I was so impressed I started to cry! There have been many occasions that my seven-year-old daughter has told me that she is glad that I homeschool so that we have a closer family. That is very heartwarming!"

Darlene Pineda, in North Carolina, was likewise encouraged by her child's reading progress. "My ten-year-old son was reading a book called *The House of Sixty Fathers* (**tinyurl.com/hsixty**) as we studied China and Japan. There's a heartbreaking moment in it where the boy has to abandon his three ducks. My son put down that book, called me over, and as he was telling me about it he started to cry, and then we were both holding each other, weeping for the baby ducks. He said, 'I didn't know books could be so real!' It was the first time a book really touched him like that, and his approach to books changed. He holds them in more awe, and has realized their power. He now respects reading in a way he never did before. And he worries about baby ducks!"

Mary M., raising seven children in Tennessee, says teaching her kids to read was a high point in parenting. "My best moment was the day that my son, who had made it to second grade in public school not able to read, came to me so excited because he was able to read his reading assignment. Or when my daughter—who

Reading Freebie

Helping Your Child Become a Reader includes activities for teaching reading using materials found in the home or for free at public libraries. Call 877-4-ED-PUBS and request product number ED004450H.

Language

had been in high school and barely reading—was sitting at the kitchen table reading *Pride and Prejudice*."

If you still have trouble motivating your kids to tackle reading, Maureen Supple, a distributor of literacy materials and the mother of two young sons in Indian Head, Maryland, says she has a proven strategy for helping children develop a love of reading from the very start. "My major strategy for motivating children to read is to find reading material that they are interested in. I think it's important to follow the child's interest as much as possible, particularly for homeschoolers. Parents, with their broader knowledge of the world, can then steer the child to information that will broaden his or her horizons.

"For example, if a child is interested in martial arts, find a how-to book first. That could be followed by fiction that features martial arts as part of the story. Then the exploration could follow several paths: history of China or Japan, Oriental cooking (using recipes to support math lessons), travel guides to place the development of martial arts geographically, and so on. Many times, providing reluctant readers with material of interest to them will help them to develop a greater love of (or tolerance for) reading."

The following resources will help you teach your babies to read. They cover topics such as phonics, word attack, and comprehension. The literature section, which covers teaching kids what to read, is located earlier in this chapter.

Book It! Program   bookitprogram.com

Pizza Hut sponsors this fun program to encourage kids to read 20 minutes a day. Participants can earn free pizza.

Edward Fry's Readability Graph   tinyurl.com/readgraph

One of the few resources around that aid in determining the reading level of a particular piece of writing.

Motivation

There have been so many ways to motivate! I am brought to tears (of happiness) almost weekly. I was thrilled when my oldest learned to read, and I helped! Now, our middle son (age five) is expressing interest in reading as well and I can't wait to help him along. The best days are when they get along well and enjoy each other's company.

—Cheryl Lemily,
Christian, wife, mom and education facilitator,
Fleming, Colorado

Language

Language

☆ Best Homeschooling Moment

I have loved teaching the boys to read. Starting out very basic and then seeing them unlocking that code and figuring it out. We always do our reading snuggled up on the couch. Seeing them get excited over being able to read a story to *me* is so fulfilling!

—Dawn Nelson, happy homeschool mom of three, Kent, Washington

How to Help Your Child with Reading Problems
elainemcewan.com/readingcaq.htm

A very helpful Q&A on resolving reading issues. "How important is reading aloud?" "It's more important than brushing your teeth!" Questions with in-depth explanations.

Learning to Read   succeedtoread.com

Teaching the teacher. All the research, all the advice, all the methods you need to teach reading to even the most reluctant reader.

Letter Sounds   yourchildlearns.com/lettersounds.htm

Free software for learning beginning phonics. Download software that speaks the letter sounds. Other free software teaches the letters of the alphabet, and phonics blends. Help your preschooler hear and see the relationship between sounds and letters.

Literacy Connections   literacyconnections.com

The section called "All About Reading Aloud" is particularly helpful, as are the sections under "Especially for Reading Teachers." Learn about sight words, reading comprehension, and more.

Online Phonics Course   reading.indiana.edu/www/indexoe.html

Register for free to gain access to two online courses, one in phonics and the other in reading for information. The required texts may be available through your local library.

Phonological Schedule   tinyurl.com/reapho

A schedule for teaching phonics, along with links to helpful articles on how to teach phonics.

Reading   tinyurl.com/restrat

Activities and good materials for teaching reading. Includes forms such as creating reading plans and maintaining a reading log.

Reading Strategies   tinyurl.com/restrat

A brief lesson in teaching reading to students of a second language. The information applies to anyone teaching reading.

Reading with Ms. Danielle   tinyurl.com/dolchlit

Learn the 220 most-frequently used words in children's books. Includes links to online flashcards and audio files.

Short Books   tinyurl.com/shortbooks

Short little books to print and read together. "What Grade Am I In?" is a sweet little guide to teach children how to answer homeschooling questions.

Starfall   starfall.com

High-quality black-and-white printables and graphics-intensive games that teach the alphabet, prereading, and elementary reading skills.

StudyDog   studydog.com

One reader reports that the company "has an inexpensive curriculum available online. If you speak directly to a representative, you will find it is free to low-income families. If you are not low-income, you can get the program for $25 a year, if you don't need to have the feedback from the company on how your child is doing."

Teaching Preschoolers to Read

welltrainedmind.com/wtmchap4.html

A sample chapter from The Well-Trained Mind, this advice on teaching preschoolers to read is the first step in accelerated learning. One unusual piece of advice: "Talk, talk, talk—adult talk, not baby talk. We have found that children from silent families struggle to read."

Best Homeschooling Moment

My children are all small on the charts. So it was so funny when my articulate, early-reading, tiny six-year-old daughter approached the librarian asking for a particular book. "Do you have a copy of *The Clue of the Tapping Heels*? It's a Nancy Drew book, by Carolyn Keene. I prefer the older editions, if you have one, because the new ones have been edited."

—Diana Malament,
a mom homeschooling one with two graduated,
Gaithersburg, Maryland

Language

The Book Whisperer   tinyurl.com/rdwhisp

The "Book Whisperer" blog has lighthearted articles about the deep subject of reading. Ms. Miller has the ability to motivate the most unenthused reader. Well worth your time to peruse her site.

Words and Pictures Scrapbook   bbc.co.uk/education/wordsandpictures

Teach phonics with the BBC. From this page you can print out pages and create a phonics scrapbook, write poetry, and play great phonics games.

Spelling

I LEARNED TO spell in college, when I was a copy editor for a daily newspaper. It was learn or lose a job, so I learned. I sat there with one hand on a dictionary and the other at the ready, and looked up every single word that caused me any doubt at all.

When I realized I was looking up the same words rather often, I began making marginal notes in the dictionary. Once I'd looked up the same word three times, I would manually copy and recopy the word during my breaks until I had it memorized. Eventually, I became a pretty good speller. Your kids may not be so motivated, but perhaps they should be.

Retired high school and college teacher Harry Livermore, from Valdosta, Georgia, describes the importance of learning to spell: "Have you ever noticed, after having dinner with friends at a nice restaurant, that you had a tiny piece of green spinach right smack in the middle of your front tooth, and you knew that everyone at the table saw it? Have you ever been listening to a choir at church sing the most beautiful music you have ever heard, and the organist hit a wrong note, loudly? Have you ever seen the most beautiful girl in the world or the most handsome guy in the world, but when she or he opened her or his mouth, there was a deep black gap where two front teeth should be?

Spell: From the Middle French *espeller* (to spell). To write or speak the letters that make up a word in their correct order.

Language

"If any of these strike a chord with you, you know what misspelled words do to a person with a reasonably good eye for our language. Misspelled words are a sign of either ignorance or carelessness. Frankly, as a teacher, I would rather work with ignorance than with carelessness. Ignorance can be corrected. Carelessness seems to be a congenital disease that affects us all, to some degree, but affects some more than others. I do not want anyone who may be careless to handle anything that is critical to me.

"I'm not talking about the misspelled word that shows up in a quick note you dash off to a friend or to yourself as a reminder. I'm talking about misspelled words that show up in business letters, job applications, accident insurance reports, formal and informal essays, and school reports."

Washington mom Dawn Nelson finds that simply being positive motivates her children in academic areas like spelling. "Right now they are still young enough that I haven't had to motivate them to study on their own, but I always try to phrase things in the positive, like, 'We get to practice our spelling words today!' instead of they 'have to.' Plus, I put a time limit on things. They have a certain amount of time to finish copywork or writing, then they are done. I try to set reasonable goal times to make sure they are able to finish the work I give them, but force them to finish it in a timely manner. (Otherwise they would sit and daydream and take all day on some things.)

"If you have a few words that you always misspell, sit yourself down and memorize their spelling. Don't let your poor spelling cast a shadow over your character and personality."

The following resources are already helping to change my bad spellers into—if nothing else—adequate spellers.

AAA Spelling   aaaspell.com

For each grade level, thirty short spelling lists, along with games, vocabulary lessons, and recommended activities for teaching the words.

Hotlinks

AAA Spelling
aaaspell.com

Basic Cozy Spelling Course
splashesfromtheriver.com/spelling

Spelling City
spellingcity.com

Language

Teaching Spelling

My most favorite homeschooling resource would have to be spellingcity.com. I guess it's my fav because we've been focused a lot on spelling right now.

—Michelle Rucker, homeschooling mom of two boys, Springfield, Ohio

Basic Cozy Spelling Course
splashesfromtheriver.com/spelling

For your sixth- to eighth-graders, a free spelling course with spelling rules and lesson plans to last an entire school year.

Everyday Spelling   everydayspelling.com

Affiliated with the commercial product, this site also contains a Reference Room with 25 frequently misspelled words for each grade, review tests, and spelling strategies. The most useful feature may be the spelling file lists, with 36 lessons and other helps for each grade level, 1 through 8.

Facts: On the Teaching of Spelling
tinyurl.com/teachspell

What research demonstrates about teaching spelling. One finding: Learning strategies is more effective than simple memorization.

Grammar, Punctuation, and Spelling
owl.english.purdue.edu/handouts/grammar

In addition to rules about punctuation, capitalization, sentence construction, and parts of speech, you'll find here several good handouts covering the rules of spelling.

Harcourt Brace Spelling   tinyurl.com/hbspell

Unscramble misspelled words and identify missing words in this animated game that categorizes spelling words by grade level.

HM Spelling and Vocabulary   eduplace.com/rdg/hmsv

Choose a grade level from one to eight to access hands-on spelling activities such as Spelling Word Charades and Word Bingo.

National Spelling Bee   www.spellingbee.com

For kids in the sixth through eighth grades, it's the National Spelling Bee. Follow these tips to help them improve their spelling.

Language

SpellingB   literatefolk.com/spellingB/index.htm

Hundreds of frequently misspelled words. Pick ten and create a spelling test.

Spelling City   spellingcity.com

Enter your spelling list and hear the words spoken and used in a sentence as you test yourself. Includes spelling games for your word lists or theirs.

Spelling Mnemonics   tinyurl.com/mnemon

Spelling mnemonics for difficult words: receive, separate, rhythm, and more.

Vocabulary

WHEN I WAS a little girl, I loved to go to my grandparents' house. The food was okay and my grandpa told funny stories, but mostly, I'm afraid, I liked to go because they kept a stash of *Reader's Digest*s that went back for decades.

Anytime I could get away from the notice of my keepers, I would sneak away with a handful of *Reader's Digest*s to hide in a corner and read.

The anecdotes and stories were great, but one of my favorite sections in the entire magazine was "Improve Your Word Power," the monthly vocabulary test. Each issue I'd pit myself against the experts, and come away determined to earn a perfect score the next time.

I don't know that all the test taking helped me improve my score much—the words never seemed to repeat—but I do know that the experience had a beneficial effect on my own Word Power.

Maine homeschooler Raylene Hunt has a tip for teaching vocabulary as part of the spelling curriculum. "Keep a journal of words that are consistently misspelled in writing projects; use these words to create your

> **Vocabulary:**
> From the medieval Latin *vocabularium* (verbal). The sum of the words an individual is able to use.

Hotlinks

100 Most Often Mispronounced Words
yourdictionary.com/library/mispron.html

Banished Words List
lssu.edu/banished

Free Rice
freerice.com

Literary Devices
literatefolk.com/literarydevices.htm

own spelling lists. In the same journal, or a different one, have the child keep a list of words that he or she doesn't understand when reading or listening to a story. Then look them up in the dictionary."

Following are some of the best resources anywhere for developing and expanding your kids' word knowledge—including, of course, a link to the *Reader's Digest* site, where your own kids can play games to improve their Word Power.

100 Most Often Mispronounced Words

yourdictionary.com/library/mispron.html

It's "probably," not "probly," and "library," not "libary." Some of my own pet peeves are missing from the list: "Anyways," "Could of," "Statuate," "Suppose to," and "Try and (v.)."

Alice in Wonderland   tinyurl.com/alicevoc

Nobody had more fun with words than Lewis Carroll. This lesson compares Carroll's absurd words with the visual work of surrealist painters.

Banished Words List   lssu.edu/banished

Since the late 1970s, this university has been tracking overused words that it believes ought to be banished from English. It serves as a tracker of last year's slang. Great fun.

English Vocabulary   studystack.com/category-12

Online flashcards—including the space to build your own—that reinforce the subject matter. Uses traditional flashcard format, as well as games and other tools for teaching vocabulary.

Free Rice   freerice.com

Get smart, end hunger. For each vocabulary question you answer correctly, the program donates 20 grains of rice to the UN World Food Program.

Literary Devices

literatefolk.com/literarydevices.htm

From allegory to zeugma, and everything in between, all the figures of speech and other devices of rhetoric are listed here. It's a how-to-use-language resource that will build vocabulary.

The Word Detective   word-detective.com

One of the oldest vocabulary sites on the Web, it continues to be updated with humorous columns, articles, and bits of trivia.

Vocabulary Building   vocabulary.co.il

Wonderful, colorful games to teach vocabulary skills. Letter Blocks is a Tetris-like game where players must create words from adjacent letters before new letters drop down from the sky.

Vocabulary Development   languagearts.pppst.com/vocabulary.html

PowerPoint presentations that teach language acquisition. One of the lessons, "Looking at Vocabulary," explains principles for teaching vocabulary—an excellent research for parent teachers. Another, "WordSmart—Vocabulary," is a collection of presentations created by students to teach specific vocabulary words to their classmates. Your co-op might enjoy undertaking a similar project.

Vocabulary, Dictionaries, Glossaries   eleaston.com/vocabulary.html

Fascinating collection of lists of common words, categorized words, abbreviations, homonyms, mondegreens, oxymorons, quizzes, quotes, Shakespeare, and synonyms—and so much more you've just got to take a look.

Word Games   storyit.com/wgames/wgames.htm

Colorful vocabulary-building games that involve shooting cannons, choosing words that don't belong, and a Scrabble-like game that involves making words out of tiles.

Best Homeschooling Moment

It's hard to narrow this down to one or two moments, but I love it when my children amaze people with their vocabularies. They frequently slip long words into their conversations, as a matter of course, and I enjoy seeing the surprised looks on people's faces.

—Tristi Pinkston, an eccentric yet lovable mommy, Orem, Utah

Language

Written Expression

Language

Write: From the Old English *w r-itan* (to scratch or draw). To produce or inscribe words in a manner that creates meaning.

AT THE BEGINNING of my senior year in high school, I fancied myself quite a writer. I was, after all, on the staff of our school newspaper and was even writing a column for the city paper.

I suspect I walked with quite a swagger.

One of the required courses for graduation was a senior-level composition class. I wasn't the least bit worried; I had, after all, gotten easy A's in every writing class I'd ever taken.

So as Mrs. Kelleher, the toughest English teacher in the western United States, explained how to write a composition, I sat back and contemplated my fingernails. I tossed together my first essay on its due date, on the bus, on the way to school. And a couple of days later, Mrs. Kelleher returned my essay to me, marked with a big fat D–.

I'm still embarrassed. I got the courage to talk to her after class and asked for an explanation.

"That's not a composition," she told me. "That's a bunch of garbage you probably threw together on the bus, on the way to school!" She had my number.

She gave me permission to try it again, and this time, she said, she planned to grade me harder than she'd graded anyone else. If I wanted to make the grade, I had to figure out how to write.

That was some pretty serious motivation.

I buckled down and worked my tail off. I learned the structure of an essay, learned how to do research, and figured out how to use transition statements, cobble together a strong thesis statement, and build supporting arguments.

I think I actually earned the A I got out of that class. And more important, I learned how to write.

Teaching writing to your own children needn't be as difficult. As a homeschooler, you have the freedom to experiment. Aimee Nusz, who teaches two children in Texas, found a workaround for a son who hated writing. "My son does not like to write," she says. "We started a 30-days-of-poetry program, and he produced some true sparks of talent. He then took his favorite poems, typed them out, printed and illustrated them, and produced a wonderful book of poetry."

For Jenny McComber, another Texas homeschooler, writing is just a part of everyday academic life. "My advice for teaching individual subjects is to try to combine as many as possible using unit studies. Practice writing by copying words and sentences from the current book you are reading; practice spelling using words taken out of the books you are reading; teach writing structure by writing about what you are reading and then edit. In the younger years, 'study' math by playing games!"

English teacher Carl M. Sharpe of Westborough, Massachusetts, says the skills learned in composition are useful in all walks of life. "I would say that a knowledge of composition is useful virtually every day, even outside of the academic environment," he says. "Right now, for example, as I write these thoughts, I do not believe that electronic communication or modern technology will ever replace or change the need for clear written communication.

"I use my writing abilities on a day-to-day basis in everything from memo writing to press releases. I have written for a newspaper, and I do a lot of writing and editing for people who seek my assistance." This section describes the best resources for teaching expository, fictional, and critical writing. For those in need of additional resources, see the section on grammar, earlier in this chapter, which discusses usage and style guides; the section on literature, also earlier in this chapter, which covers literary analysis and various genres of literature; and the research section of Chapter 4, which covers writing research papers.

Hotlinks

A Site About Writing and Stuff
people.whitman.edu/
~hashimiy

Blast Writing Tips and Tools
bbc.co.uk/blast/writing/
tipsandtools

Graphic Organizers
eduplace.com/
graphicorganizer

NaNoWriMo
nanowrimo.org

Purdue Online Writing Lab
owl.english.purdue.edu

Language

Sophocles

The ancient playwright Sophocles was raised by parents of modest means. It appears that, unlike the wealthy Greeks with whom he associated as an adult, Sophocles was raised by a father who was either a carpenter or a bronze worker. Despite his humble beginnings, Sophocles became perhaps the most influential playwright in all of history, as well as an important politician.

A Site About Writing and Stuff   people.whitman.edu/~hashimiy

Tremendous collection of articles on how to teach writing, and how to write. Includes a section on poetry, and links to the Whitman College Writing Center. Drill down through the Writing Classes links to find sample essays.

Blast Writing Tips and Tools
bbc.co.uk/blast/writing/tipsandtools

Interactive tools to help you get started on your journey to creative writing, courtesy of the BBC. Tips on writing, publishing in various genres, editing your own work, and finding an agent.

Eight Useful Essay-Writing Tips   tinyurl.com/wreight
For writers who have mastered the five-paragraph essay, advanced tips for better writing.

Essay Conventions You Should Know
tinyurl.com/wrcon
How to format an essay or research paper. For students preparing for college.

Express Writing Worksheets   tinyurl.com/wrela
Worksheets that teach creative writing, journal writing, sentences, and writing activities.

Museum Writing

Collecting Their Thoughts: Using Museums as Sources for Student Writing is a Smithsonian pamphlet that suggests ways to use museums to teach writing. Smithsonian Institution, OESE, Arts and Industries Building, Room 1163, MRC 402, Washington, DC 20560; 202-357-2425.

Graphic Organizer Lesson Plans   tinyurl.com/wrorg

A collection of links to lesson plans that use graphic organizers such as Venn diagrams and T charts to prompt nonfiction writing.

Graphic Organizers   eduplace.com/graphicorganizer

These graphic organizers will help your writers organize their ideas. The Five Ws chart, the Clock, and the Sandwich are particularly useful, but each of these 40-some organizers will be an aid to writing.

Helping Students Write Better in All Courses
teaching.berkeley.edu/bgd/writebetter.html

Written for new college professors, this material will nevertheless be adaptable to the homeschooling environment with explanations of tips such as "Let students know that you value good writing" and "Explain that writing is hard work."

> **Tip:** Want a free booklet on your child's language development and hearing? Call 800-587-DAYS.

Help Your Child to Write!   ed.gov/pubs/parents/Writing

The government wants you to teach your child. Here's proof. And for a government document, the advice isn't half bad.

How to Write a Dissertation   tinyurl.com/wrdis

Dissertation: Bedtime reading for people who can't sleep. Lots of good advice for writing a serious dissertation. Your older teenagers will benefit.

NaNoWriMo   nanowrimo.org

Each November thousands of writers take the month to write a book during National Novel Writing Month. Your older teens who love to write need to be involved. For younger writers, click the Our Programs link to access a sister site, Young Writers Program.

Paradigm Online Writing Assistant   powa.org

An online writing course. Terrific! How to write four forms of essays, getting organized as a writer, and other resources.

Language

Language

Teaching Writing

We are pretty free around here. We use a variety of things: workbooks, puzzles, games, Brainquest cards, flash cards, word wall, library books, used school reading textbooks, copywork, hands-on science including microscope usage, and free writing time.

Once you have a good idea of what you want to teach, figure out how your kids learn best. Mine get bored if they have too much writing to do in one day, so we may do a small amount of writing (quality), but much more time spent on art projects or science, etc.

—Erin Goldberg, homeschooling mother of two, ages five and seven, Bardstown, Kentucky

Principles of Composition
grammar.ccc.commnet.edu
It's an entire college-prep course in writing, beginning with the basics of nouns and verbs and progressing to organizing principles for composition.

Purdue Online Writing Lab   owl.english.purdue.edu
Mostly college-level writing advice, but click the "Grades 7–12 Instructors and Students" link for an entire six-year online writing course. That's some serious college prep.

Resources for Writers & Teachers
writing.colostate.edu
A resource for learning about writing and for teaching about writing. The Writing Center provides tutorials, demonstrations, writing guides, and activities. Register and gain access to a world of helps for teaching college-prep writing to your teens.

Story-It   storyit.com
Not a particularly well-organized page, but mine it for ideas to prompt story writing. Includes picture prompts, story starters, write-on shapes, border pages, children's poems, and other resources to spark creativity.

Writing and Literature   tinyurl.com/wrocw
Highlights for High School provides resources from MIT to improve writing instruction at the high school level. Watch video demonstrations; study for AP exams; and view sample college coursework.

Writing Plans from the Teacher's Desk
teachersdesk.org/writing_plans.html
The Paragraph a Week yearly writing program will be

particularly interesting, but you'll find here many well-considered writing ideas for younger writers and those of middle-school age.

Writing Techniques Handbook   cws.illinois.edu/workshop/writers
This guide offers lots of advice on the writing process, including developing a thesis statement, editing principles, parallelism, practical writing advice, transitions and connective phrases, using commas correctly, writing summaries, overcoming writer's block, and handling quotations. It also offers tips on taking an essay exam, writing about film, writing abstracts, writing about poetry, writing cover letters, writing a literature paper, writing a thesis for a literature paper, writing a philosophy paper, writing personal statements, writing résumés, writing proposals, and writing standardized essay exams.

Language

Chapter 6

Mathematics Mastery

I CONFESS: I was a mathematical idiot. Oh, I managed—somehow—to get through the usual high-school mathematics courses. But when I took my college entrance exams, it certainly wasn't the math that got me admitted.

Hotlinks

Math TV
mathtv.com

Mathematics Activities
quia.com/shared/math

Maths Is Good for You
mathsisgoodforyou.com

SMILE Program Math Index
iit.edu/~smile/mathinde
.html

XP-math
xpmath.com

That's why during my first year at university, I was required to take the dummies' math class; it turned out to be one of the smartest things I ever did. Here's how the class worked: The first day, the teacher told an auditorium full of math dummies, "Get this packet. When you finish, take the test. Dismissed." You can imagine the shock. There I was, a proven idiot, and this teacher expected me to learn math without anybody holding my hand . . . and he expected me to learn based on a book that didn't even have a cover!

That packet of math papers changed my life. I went home and got to work. The packet started at 1 + 1 and worked straight through to trigonometry, in a systematic fashion that made everything completely clear. Fractions, decimals, polynomials, factoring . . . By the time I finished the packet, math made sense. And that's how a math dummy ended up studying finance in college.

Math—more than any other subject addressed in this

text—would seem to require the formalized, disciplined use of a book. Don't let that slow you down.

Formal texts are available at public libraries. But there are so many tremendous math resources online—including full textbooks—that there may be no need. And for younger kids, just living life may be the best curriculum. "I prefer a structured math program for our oldest son," says a mom of four from Hawkes Bay, New Zealand. "Our middle son may go the way of manipulatives, who knows? The baby just wants to put everything in his mouth for now! When they are young, under the age of ten, let life be their teacher. Would they like one half the bag of M&M's or one quarter of the bag? Play games, construct tangrams, bake, or go shopping."

Washington homeschooler Brenda Ulrich, raising six children, agrees. "It's really not necessary to have a formal math curriculum when kids are very young. You can teach them so much math by just doing everyday things: numbers, counting, sorting, measuring, shapes, addition, subtraction, multiplication, and division can all be taught through cooking, grocery shopping, and helping with laundry."

Here's how you can still teach math—and teach it well—for free. First, borrow a math book. It might come from a co-operative local school district, or you might check one out from the library. Math hasn't changed dramatically over the past century, so any age-appropriate book you choose will suit your purpose. When you've got your book, put it on a shelf and leave it there for one reason: as a backup to the great Internet resources found in this chapter. Use your borrowed book to double-check your progress and to ensure that you're covering all the material. Let it be a backup when you find your own explanations inadequate. In any event, even if you're as weak at math as I once was, you'll rest easy knowing that your kids are on track.

Math Freebie

Helping Your Child Learn Mathematics helps families make math-learning experiences out of everyday routines. Call 877-4-ED-PUBS and request product number ED004449H.

In this chapter, you'll find resources for teaching your children basic math, pre-algebra, algebra, geometry, computer math (including calculator math), trigonometry, calculus, and statistics. We begin with resources and tools for teaching the entire spectrum of mathematics. Use them as your primary text or as a supplement to that borrowed book. Either way, with these interactive, well-written materials, your kids will learn to love numbers:

Motivation

I use everything we do as a field trip! The grocery store is my favorite; I combine math, science, and home ec all together!

—Amber Neal, homeschool mom of four, Fredericksburg, Virginia

Centre for Innovation in Mathematics Teaching
www.cimt.plymouth.ac.uk

A complete British maths program with lesson plans, copy masters, and practice books for primary grades through the GCSE and A Levels. The site features such resources as interactive tutorials, short quizzes, posters, and transparencies.

Color Addition   coolmath.com

Middle-school and advanced math on a fun, colorful site. Algebra, trig, geometry, and more.

Countdown   countdown.luc.edu

Televised math program from Chicago. Each week the program introduces a different math concept. More than 300 segments of the program are archived here.

Exercises in Math Readiness   math.usask.ca/emr/menu.html

Quizzes and drills to improve math speed and skill, beginning with mental arithmetic and progressing through two levels of algebra, geometry, trigonometry, calculus, and logic.

Illuminations   illuminations.nctm.org

The National Council of Teachers of Mathematics presents math activities, lessons, and web links for teaching math to kids of all ages. The Standards tab provides a recommended scope and sequence for high school math.

Interactive Mathematics   cut-the-knot.org

Well over 900 games, puzzles, and resources for every area of the math curriculum. In the Algebra section, try the Candy Game for an eye-opening exercise in distribution.

Math   tinyurl.com/ocwmath

Highlights for High School provides resources from MIT to improve math instruction at the high school level. Watch video demonstrations, study for AP exams, and sample college coursework.

Math Central   mathcentral.uregina.ca

Teacher resources, puzzles, and bios of mathematicians, but the best resource here is the Quandaries and Queries section, where mathematicians answer hundreds of questions submitted by math students.

Math Formula Sheets   tinyurl.com/mathform

Printable sheets with formulas required for working on algebra, trigonometry, and calculus.

Math Study Guides   sparknotes.com/math/

Guides to every math subject from pre-algebra through advanced calculus. Look here for in-depth explanations of every math subject your child needs to learn prior to—and during—college. Includes problems and solutions for each subject.

Math TV   mathtv.com

Math teachers teach math—on video. This large collection of professionally done math videos explains principles of basic math, algebra, trigonometry, and calculus.

Mathematics   tinyurl.com/mathlps

A collection of lesson plans covering algebra, applied math, arithmetic, geometry, measurement, process skills, and statistics.

Motivation

Lots of nagging. It doesn't really change too much from public school. It helps my son for me to do his math lessons with him. It then becomes a competition for him.

—Aimee Nusz, teacher and fellow student of two, Amarillo, Texas

Mathematics

Mathematics

☆ *Best Homeschooling Moment*

When my son goes from saying that adding four-digit numbers with regrouping is "hard" to "This is easy, I want more," in the span of a few days, I am thrilled to watch the development.

—Marisa Corless, homeschooling mom of three, Bothell, Washington

Mathematics Activities   quia.com/shared/math

A selection of hundreds—maybe thousands—of games, activities, and quizzes to teach math across almost every subject area.

Mathematics How-to Library

tinyurl.com/howmath

Step-by-step how-to-do-it instructions for solving most math problem areas, from algebra to trig and calc.

Mathematics Lesson Plans   tinyurl.com/mathles

Math lesson plans designed by classroom teachers. Most are easily adapted to homeschooling programs.

Mathematics Videos   tinyurl.com/mathvid

A large collection of educational videos that teach math at every grade level. One section, for example, explains pre-algebra in simplest terms. Another demonstrates math in real-world phenomena. From the Annenberg CPB series.

Maths Is Good for You!   mathsisgoodforyou.com

A history of math for young mathematicians. Consider, for example, "Famous conjectures, theorems, and problems." Good lessons accompany each math subject.

MathWire   mathwire.com

Standards-based math activities, games, and worksheets in diverse areas of the math curriculum. Organized not by curriculum area but by posting date.

Skillswise Numbers   bbc.co.uk/skillswise/numbers

A BBC resource for teaching math literacy to older learners. Click a tab for quick courses in whole numbers, measuring, fractions, and data handling. Each section includes fact sheets and help to improve skills. Other links go to quizzes, games, and glossaries.

Smile Program Math Index   iit.edu/~smile/mathinde.html

Want to teach memorable lessons about geometry and measurement, patterns and logic, probability and statistics, recreational and creative math, practical and applied math, arithmetic, graphs and visuals, algebra and trigonometry, and more? Choose from among this collection of almost 200 single concept lessons. Very well done.

The Lesson Plans Page   lessonplanspage.com/Math.htm

Choose a grade level to find hundreds of math lesson plans, for pre-K through high school, of varying quality. Includes resources for worksheets and flashcards for grades 1 through 4.

Tutor-USA   tutor-usa.com

Math tutoring and homework help. Click the Free links on the right to find worksheets and solutions, lesson plans, videos, games, and tools to supplement or reinforce math studies. The algebra worksheets section, for example, explains algebraic principles such as graphing, solving, factoring, and quadratic equations.

What Good Is Math?   tinyurl.com/whatmath

Planning a party, going shopping, budgeting a trip, filling a piggy bank. That's just for starters. Math has lots of applications in everyday life. Help your kids see why they're studying it.

What Is Math Night?   orion.math.iastate.edu/mathnight

Make your next family night a math night. A Math Night is an event that allows kids and their parents to explore and enjoy areas of mathematics they wouldn't encounter in everyday schoolwork. Kids can show off their math skills and discover new ones. Includes lots of fun games you can do as a family.

XP Math   xpmath.com

Downloadable math ebooks from Cambridge University Press, worksheets, games, and videos featuring the Standard Deviants. Who can deny "The Pumped-Up World of Pre-Algebra"?

Basic Math

IT'S ARITHMETIC TIME! Teaching math to younger children requires a lot of interaction. But it can be very rewarding. One homeschooling mother, Joanna Francis from Newark, Delaware, says her best homeschooling moment came while teaching math to her young daughter. "I was working with my first-grader in math and I was talking about money. I started talking about what the decimal places mean and realized she was listening to me and understanding what I was telling her. I knew then that all she needed was my time and attention and she would do just fine."

Keeping them motivated can be a challenge, though. Mary Batchelor from Sandy, Utah, says she motivates her young math students by using a variety of materials: "I have all kinds of manipulatives, such as pattern blocks, interlocking cubes, links, dominoes, and geoboards. I have mostly used the cubes, blocks, and boards when teaching primary ages. We purchased a very nice clock with a descriptive face, but you can easily use your own clock right off the wall. It is especially good if you have one with a second hand.

"I use manipulatives—countable objects—to show my kids what they need to learn in math. We also work regularly with worksheets and with educational software. I do not require them to do all the problems on their worksheets. I usually pick and choose what I want them to do ahead of time, and then, as we progress through that day's work, I might cut or add some problems. From time to time, I also let the kids negotiate what they want to learn or practice."

Ready to extend your kids' learning? Use this information to teach your elementary- and middle-school-aged children basic mathematical operators, multiplication tables, fractions, decimals, and percentages, so they'll be well prepared to learn more advanced math.

Arithmetic:
From the Greek *arithmein* (to count). Adding, subtracting, multiplying, and dividing positive real numbers.

Mathematics

A Maths Dictionary for Kids

amathsdictionaryforkids.com

Animated dictionary for children explaining more than 600 math terms.

Abiator's Times Table Emporium   tinyurl.com/abiemp

Online flashcards help to practice multiplication tables. Select speed and specific multipliers or select random.

Bitesize Games

bbc.co.uk/schools/ks1bitesize/numeracy

The BBC's collection of math games to teach numeracy, all narrated in a Potter-esque Brit accent. Various games teach addition and subtraction, multiplication, division, number ordering, number sequences, place value, money, length and weight measurement, telling the time, 2D and 3D shapes, and organizing data. It's slow-loading because it's high quality.

BrainisH   brainish.com

Your children log in and it keeps track of their progress with "credit card" points. If they excel at a certain lesson they can skip pages and still get all the points. There are multiple levels of each math topic for the kids to work through. It can be progressive or you can skip to topics that you want to work on. For pre-K through grade 5.

Coolmath for Kids   coolmath4kids.com

An amusement park of math. Very bright, colorful site that includes math motivators such as Number Monster, Lemonade Stand, and more.

Count On   counton.org

A good variety of games. Click the Maths Magnet link for counting games for younger children.

Hotlinks

Bitesize Games
bbc.co.uk/schools/
ks1bitesize/numeracy

Brainish
brainish.com

**Houghton-Mifflin Free
Math Course Online**
eduplace.com/math/mw

Math TV
mathtv.org

**The Math Worksheet
Online Generator**
themathworksheetsite
.com

Mathematics

Houghton-Mifflin Free Math Course Online
eduplace.com/math/mw

Basic math lessons and activities for grades K through 5. The Math at Home section makes a good supplement to the main site.

Instructional Mathematics Resources   tinyurl.com/mathinstruc

A curriculum for studying basic math—covering number recognition, measuring, mental math, and other basic skills. Find sample problems, classroom strategies, vocabulary, and related concepts and skills. Designed for grades K through 2.

Internet Educational Workbook   inew.com

A large database useful for practicing math skills for kindergarten through grade 6. Covers concepts such as time, calendar, money, rounding, word problems, geometry, and order of operations. Includes answer keys.

Math at the Grocery Store
ed.gov/pubs/parents/Math/grocerymath.html

Great math activities for kids and parents at the grocery store. Grades K–5.

Math Readiness Suggestions
ed.gov/pubs/parents/LearnPtnrs/math.html

Tips from the U.S. Department of Education on teaching math at home.

Math TV   mathtv.org

Incredibly fun games and tutorials using animated videos to explain how to solve problems. Math Playground is filled with logic games and games that teach math skills; Math TV uses animated videos that show, step by step, how to solve problems; and thinking blocks uses animated blocks to show problem-solving skills.

Teaching Math

I am learning that there are many ways to teach the same subject. For math, my six-year-old wants to do worksheets and math book pages. My oldest shuts down completely at the sight of those things, but is happy to count the brushes in a car wash and figure out how many minutes it takes for the car to go through. My advice is take the time (for me it's been a couple of years!) to observe your kids and really get a handle on how they learn and what they love. It makes the teaching process so much easier.

—**Dawn Nelson**, happy homeschool mom of three, Kent, Washington

---

Math-U-See Drill   mathusee.com/drill.html

An easy-to-use drill maker for learning addition, subtraction, multiplication, and division facts. Get all the answers right and win a blue ribbon.

Mathematics Lesson Plans   www.col-ed.org/cur/math.html

A single page of easy to use lesson plans for K–5 math. Intermediate- and high-school lessons are also included.

Mathematics Overview   nsf.gov/news/overviews/mathematics

An overview by the National Science foundation: "Mathematics is the natural language of science and engineering. It is about numbers, shapes, symmetry, chance, change, and much more. Mathematics is deeply interwoven into all of modern life."

Multiplication Rock   schoolhouserock.tv/Multiplication.html

Gotta love those old Schoolhouse Rock videos. Here are catchy songs about each of the 12 times tables. Includes the lyrics and animations.

NumberNut   numbernut.com

Activities, lessons, quizzes, and games that cover all the basics: shapes and colors, numbers and counting, addition, subtraction, multiplication, division, order of operations, dates and times, activities, fractions, decimals, percentages, estimation and rounding, ratios, and money math.

The Math Worksheet Online Generator   themathworksheetsite.com

Generates worksheets with all the basic operators, fractions, measurement, and graphing. A separate Hundred Chart teaches prime numbers and place values.

Two Plus Two   funnymathforkids.com

Download and install this award-winning educational software for hours of learning fun. Designed for young children.

Pre-Algebra

WHEN SHOULD YOU start teaching algebraic concepts? Early, say the experts. "The concepts of algebra, most specifically the concepts of variables, should be introduced as early as possible, even before junior high school. This helps prepare the student for being able to start a regular algebra curriculum by the time he or she reaches seventh or eighth grade," writes Gary McMurrin, a high school math teacher from Valencia, California.

"But very clearly, the foundation must be established in the grade schools with the skills of the four basic operations and an understanding of variables."

Why learn algebra? For one thing, it's the basis of all higher math.

Retired thermodynamics and heat-transfer engineer Jim Taylor, who lives in southeastern Pennsylvania, tells homeschoolers about some real-life applications for algebra: "Because I'm an engineer, mathematics has always played an important role in my work. Early in my career, I specialized in thermodynamics and heat transfer, and a great deal of algebra was involved with calculating heat flow in designing such things as heat exchangers. I also worked on our country's missile programs in the early days and found a great need for math in the design of missile nose cones, which are subjected to terrific heating upon re-entry into the atmosphere. And of course, everyone is familiar with the Apollo program and the landing on the moon; I used a lot of mathematics on all sorts of design and operational problems that had to be solved when I worked on that program. Much of this was advanced mathematics, but algebra was more or less the building block from which all other forms flowed."

McMurrin worries that teenagers don't appreciate the need to learn mathematics: "In my previous careers in financial services as a stockbroker and life insurance agent, I used math skills every day to analyze various investments and life insurance policies for clients. Without the analytical skills

Pre-algebra:

Introduction to formulas and measurements.

Mathematics

learned in high school and college, I would never have been able to perform my job duties."

This section presents a collection of resources for teaching pre-algebra to your middle-school-aged children. When they're well grounded in the basics, they'll be ready to move to the next section.

AAA Math   aaamath.com

Interactive arithmetic lessons for pre-algebra students. Don't let the terribly unattractive layout put you off. The material here is actually very useful.

Algebasics   algebasics.com

Audio lessons with video explanations. The 16 sections cover the basics of algebra; the final section provides real-life applications of algebraic principles.

Arabic Mathematics   tinyurl.com/preara

Discusses contributions to the math sciences centuries before the discoveries were recorded in Europe.

Babylonian Math   angelfire.com/il2/babylonianmath

The Babylonians made significant contributions to the field of math. Read about it here and follow it up with an activity page.

Basic Math Lessons   hanlonmath.com/basic-lessons.html

Nineteen mini pre-algebra lessons explain fractions, decimals, exponents, integers, percents, ratios, and proportions. Quickly covers the material with explanations and charts.

Counting to Infinity

scidiv.bcc.ctc.edu/math/infinity.html

An article on the origin and development of the concept of infinity.

Hotlinks

AAA Math
aaamath.com

Algebasics
algebasics.com

Free-Ed Pre-Algebra
free-ed.net/
free-ed/math/prealg01

Pre-Algebra Help
algebra-help.info/
pre-algebra.php

Free-Ed Pre-Algebra   free-ed.net/free-ed/Math/PreAlg01

An online textbook containing an entire pre-algebra curriculum. One parent writes, "We used this as the basis for our math and it was a life-saver."

Hex Headquarters   intuitor.com/hex

A great page for learning about mathematical bases. This teenager-friendly page explains why the base-10 system we use is less efficient than a base-16 system. Lots of articles and easy explanations. Once your children have a basic grasp of mathematical bases, teach them to count to 1023 on their fingers, at the companion page, **intuitor.com/counting.**

Instructional Mathematics Resources   tinyurl.com/preins

A curriculum to prepare kids for studying algebra. Games and activities reinforce multiplication tables, fractions, and other math skills. Find sample problems, classroom strategies, vocabulary, and related concepts and skills. Designed for grades 3 through 5.

Lesson Starters   tinyurl.com/mastart

Hundreds of fun little "warm-up" activities for math students of middle-school age.

Starting Young

Some students don't seem ready for algebra because there is a lack of good instruction at the earlier stages of schooling.

—Gary McMurrin, high school math teacher, Valencia, California

---

Math Handouts

www.txstate.edu/slac/subject-area/math.html

From a university student learning center, printable handouts to reinforce mathematics learning. Many handouts include problem sets with answers. Handouts cover pre-algebra principles such as real numbers and operations. Additional subject areas explain algebra, calculus, and math study skills.

Math League   mathleague.com/help/help.htm

Definitions of algebra terms for new learners. Starts with the properties of whole numbers and continues to an introduction to algebra and positive and negative numbers.

Neufeld Learning Systems Math   *neufeldmath.com/worksheets*

Pre-algebra-level worksheets teach algebra, probabilities, and graphing.

Pre-Algebra Help   *algebra-help.info/pre-algebra.php*

A thorough understanding of pre-algebra help topics is essential to kick-start your way toward learning algebra, says this site. Separate sections explain fractions, absolute value, negative numbers, scientific notation, and order of operations.

Algebra

MOVING FROM THE rote memorization of basic math into the philosophical concepts of advanced math can be a tough leap. A high school math teacher, Eugene Karel Pilouw, of Harlingen, Texas, told me that even when algebra seems difficult, it's important not to give up. Mr. Pilouw spent three years touring Alaska, Japan, Korea, and West Germany "as a guest of the U.S. Army" and has taught secondary English and math since 1968. This is what he says about the importance of learning algebra:

> **Algebra:** From the Arabic *al-jabr* (reduction). The branch of mathematics in which symbols are used to represent all numbers in a set.

"Algebra—a word that strikes fear into the hearts of the bravest of the brave. The truth of the matter, however, is that we all use algebra every day in our lives without calling it by that distasteful name. (Remember what Shakespeare had to say about names.)

"Did you ever:

- budget your spending for the week or month?
- plan which bills will be paid out of this week's paycheck and which will be paid from next week's?
- determine the area of the walls in a house so you could buy the right amount of paint?
- decide which size of a certain product in a store was the better buy?

- calculate how much herbicide, pesticide, or fertilizer you would need to treat your yard, a flower bed, or a field on a farm?
- figure out, at a theater or game, which candies or drinks you could afford after you had paid for the tickets?
- purchase a certain amount of material to make an article of clothing and base the amount on the dress size you wear and the money in your budget?
- place a bet on an event after you had carefully weighed the odds?
- plan how much you could place on layaway for a gift according to the amount of disposable income you had left in your household budget or allowance?
- arrived at a solution after using numbers in any way?

"If you said yes to any of these or to similar situations, then you have used algebra in the real world. The actual study of algebra formalizes these procedures and puts them in a logical sequence. Sometimes we have difficulty with the rigor involved, but don't let it frighten you into quitting before you begin. Sometimes algebra, or any subject, can seem to be a frustrating ordeal, but that is usually true of anything we preconceive as insurmountable. Whatever you do, don't quit!" Sometimes it helps to understand how algebra is useful in the here and now. An algebra-loving student, Chhoeun Sann from Fall River, Massachusetts, explains how algebra is useful to teenagers: "I do algebra just for fun. I love to develop my own video games," says the junior at Massachusetts Institute of Technology. "I design my characters using 3D transformations, using my knowledge of geometry, algebra, and some calculus. I program my keyboard to correspond to the actions of each figure with complex mathematical formulas. This way I can move the figures easily without any further programming. When I add intense graphics, I use even more complex geometric figures.

Hotlinks

Practical Algebra Lessons
purplemath.com

Totally Free Math
totallyfreemath.com/
math.html

Understanding Algebra
jamesbrennan.org/
algebra

Virtual Math Lab
tinyurl.com/algvir

"I also use the basic I = PRT formula to budget and to find the status of my investments. I use algebra for shopping, when I use ratio and proportion to determine which item is cheapest. There are many other ways to apply algebra. It can actually save you thousands of dollars a year if you use it right, maybe even more. I'm glad there's algebra." Would you like your own kids to be "glad there's algebra"? Here's how you start.

Algebra Help   algebra-help.info

Two sections—Basic Algebra and College Algebra—introduce every topic from completing the square and solving quadratic inequalities to linear algebra and matrices.

Algebra Lessons   hanlonmath.com/algebra-lessons.html

Here you'll find 35 mini–algebra lessons that explain the material found in a high school algebra class. Quickly covers the material with explanations and charts.

Algebra Review in Ten Lessons   tinyurl.com/algrev

From the University of Akron, an online textbook that reviews algebra principles for students preparing for college. Well written, easy to read.

Algebra Videos   mathpower.com/video.htm

Video snippets from a math professor help algebra students remember principles such as Order of Operations and Combining Like Terms.

Chameleon Graphing   mathforum.org/cgraph

Introductory lessons on coordinate planes and graphing.

Create a Graph   nces.ed.gov/nceskids/createagraph

Nice tool from the National Center for Education Statistics. Helps to organize data and display it in many different graph formats. Includes a basic tutorial on how to use the tool. Not a curriculum by itself, but a good supplement to any other curriculum.

Equation Sheet   equationsheet.com

A cheat sheet for remembering how to factor and other equations. Provides many standard equations for math disciplines—including algebra, geometry, trig, calculus, and statistics—and for science disciplines, including chemistry and physics.

Free Online Graph Paper   incompetech.com/graphpaper
Allows you to design your own graph paper in dozens of different formats: number lines, music notation, notebook paper, many kinds of grids, and straight-up graph paper.

Graph Paper Printer   pharm.kuleuven.be/pharbio/gpaper.htm
My son tried to get out of an algebra assignment one day by complaining that he had no graph paper. I put an end to that! This free software program prints any kind of graph paper, in lots of groovy colors. Supports Cartesian, Polar, Triangular, and Mercator coordinates, along with custom margins, size, automatic centering, and more. It can also print music paper.

Instructional Mathematics Resources   tinyurl.com/instmath
A curriculum for studying algebra, covering numbers and operations through first-year algebra. Find sample problems, classroom strategies, vocabulary, and related concepts and skills. Designed for grades 6 through 8.

Introduction to Algebra   mathleague.com/help/algebra/algebra.htm
Quick overview, with solved examples, of how to solve equations. Combining like terms, simplifying, and word problems as equations are all covered.

Practical Algebra Lessons   purplemath.com
Nice, well-organized and well-written site with a full algebra curriculum. Includes pre-algebra topics for those who need them.

Print Free Graph Paper   printfreegraphpaper.com
Easy templates for printing your own graph paper.

Rationality   cnx.org/content/co110350/latest
Algebra students really and truly need to understand graphing. This site is an entire online course in rational functions and graphing them

in 2D and 3D. Includes interactive quizzes to test kids' understanding of how equations create graphs, and how graphs represent equations.

SOS Mathematics   sosmath.com/algebra/algebra.html

The whole durned book, right there online. Step-by-step instructions, beginning with fractions. Great stuff with a good logical sequence of lessons. Also of interest will be the separate section on Matrix Algebra.

Totally Free Math   totallyfreemath.com

A high-quality, fully illustrated online algebra textbook. Includes a student solutions manual and an instructor's resource manual. What a deal.

Understanding Algebra   jamesbrennan.org/algebra

Good curriculum from beginning algebra to advanced concepts. Can be done online or downloaded and printed.

Virtual Math Lab   tinyurl.com/algvir

A series of three college-prep algebra classes, each with a year's worth of math learning. The first-year course begins with number sets. The work continues sequentially through the third-year course, which ends with principles such as the binomial theorem, logarithmic equations, and probability.

Geometry

GEOMETRY MAY BE the most practical of all the maths. Mathematics and chemistry teacher Kari Farrell Matthews, from Rossville, Illinois, explains how before she became a teacher she worked for a large agricultural company. A large part of her job involved training farmers and other agricultural professionals to use satellite receivers to track the exact global position of tractors and other farm implements in their fields. "This technology is being used in many industries, including cartography, trucking/shipping, aeronautics, and real estate." She says, "Under-

Geometry: From the Greek *geometria* (to measure land). The study of the properties of points, lines, angles, planes, and objects.

standing how to use the satellite receivers was contingent on a solid knowledge of geometry.

"In my personal life, I find that geometry comes in handy regularly. For instance, my husband has built some of our furniture, and he remodeled the kitchen. If you want to tackle furniture and remodeling projects on your own, geometry knowledge is indispensable! We used geometry to determine how to get our new countertop into the house and between two walls. These are just a few of the ways that I use geometry in everyday life. Geometry concepts really do permeate our lives."

When your own kids are ready to take the geometry challenge, here's where they should start:

Ask Dr. Math   mathforum.org/dr.math

The standard geometry formulas are all available here (click the Formulas link), along with archives of hundreds of math questions for every math subject, plus there is a place to ask questions of your own.

For an unattractive site, there's an awful lot of fascinating information here.

Hotlinks

Geometry
tinyurl.com/tqgeo

Geometry Help & Lessons
hanlonmath.com/
geometry-lessons.html

The Pythagorean Theorem Lesson
arcytech.org/java/
pythagoras

Figures and Polygons
mathleague.com/help/geometry/polygons.htm
Descriptions and examples of various geometric shapes and concepts.

Geometria   tinyurl.com/geomet
A tool for calculating lines, surfaces, and volumes of the main plane and solid figures, through direct and indirect formulas.

Geometry   tinyurl.com/tqgeo
Euclid have you stumped? Archimedes run rings around your head? This great collection of geometry tutorials will get you sorted out. Written in a breezy, easy-to-read style.

Geometry Help & Lessons

hanlonmath.com/geometry-lessons.html

Thirty mini–geometry lessons explain the material found in a high-school geometry class. Quickly covers the material with explanations and charts.

Geometry Topics and Lessons

aaaknow.com/geo.htm

Each lesson includes a brief explanation of a geometry principle, followed by a practice test and games for reinforcing learning. Explore other math topics by subject or grade level by following the links in the left-hand column.

Index for Geometry

mathwords.com/index_geometry.htm

The geometry vocabulary resource. Find math terminology from plane and solid geometry, including basic triangle trigonometry, as well as a few facts not traditionally taught in basic geometry.

Introduction to the Works of Euclid   obkb.com/dcljr/euclid.html

An unpublished paper about the founder of geography.

Math Formulas

mathconnect.com/math-formula.htm

Many of the formulas for geometry: area, volume, and circumference. Also has a page with more complex electrical engineering formulas.

Math League Geometry

mathleague.com/help/geometry/geometry.htm

Basic terminology, with graphic explanations of geometry principles.

The Everlasting Pi   freewebs.com/abishek

A small site about the history and uses of pi.

Best Homeschooling Moment

Once, my almost-four-year-old and my barely-two-year-old were sitting at the kitchen table, and noticed that the light fixture was a shape larger than a square. They began to debate whether or not it was a hexagon or an octagon and *why*.

—Marisa Corless, homeschooling mom of three, Bothell, Washington

Mathematics

The Pythagorean Theorem Lesson   arcytech.org/java/pythagoras

How to figure out the Pythagorean Theorem. An in-depth lesson that reviews concepts and background necessary for understanding the measurement of right triangles.

Computer Math

IF YOUR KIDS are going to be competitive in the adult workplace, they'll need to know how to handle the technology. And that includes understanding the principles of computer math.

In colleges today, five-dollar calculators are as much an anachronism as slide rules and abacuses are. Your children need to know how to handle scientific or business calculators with some dexterity. They also need to know how to operate computers, of course. But of equal importance is their ability to understand the basic principles of mathematical operations as those operations relate to computers.

Here's how the work world looks for people who understand computer math: "In the nine years that I've been with my present employer, I've moved up the ladder higher than many of my peers who have two or three times more experience," writes Scott "Warlock" Windhorn, a systems control technician in New Ulm, Minnesota.

Computer math: From the Latin *putare* (to consider). Binary and hexadecimal systems, calculator math, and other math processes that integrate technology.

"Many people with experience in electronics say, 'You don't need to know any of those equations.' That's only true if you just want to get a job, never move up, be the first in line for layoffs, do the same thing every day, and basically have a boring life. The best service technicians are those who understand the machines they're servicing. To truly understand a machine, you must know the electronics, mechanics, and mathematics that make it work."

Your math-literate offspring will have a great time at the following sites. Don't have a graphing calculator? Don't worry. There are loaner programs available from major manufacturers (see the following links), and there are plenty of online calculators on the Internet.

Abacus—The Art of Calculating with Beads
tinyurl.com/abacom

The original computer is still in wide use in Asia. Learn how to work those beads with this terrific tutorial.

Calculator Tips   **tinyurl.com/calcvid**

A video lesson with general tips on how to better use your calculator.

Computer Math
arachnoid.com/lutusp/computermath.html

"Imagine that a person is brought forward from the year 1500 and you are to tell him the advantages of literacy," this article proposes. All about mass storage and other advances that make humans more "numerate."

Computers and Electronics   **tinyurl.com/elecom**

Highlights for High School provides resources from MIT to improve computer instruction at the high school level. Watch video demonstrations, study for AP exams, and sample college coursework.

Elementary Computer Mathematics   **tinyurl.com/elmath**

An ebook on the math that underlies modern technology. Requires a firm understanding of algebraic principles.

GCalc   **gcalc.net**

Free graphing calculator. A basic, easy-to-use set of graphing functions for algebra, pre-calculus, and calculus.

Online Calculator   **tinyurl.com/matcalc**

Enter an expression, find the answer. Expressions can contain complexities such as exponentiation, square roots, sin, cos, and ch.

Hotlinks

Abacus: Calculating with Beads
tinyurl.com/abacom

GCalc
gcalc.net

Quick-Start Guide to Common Calculators
tinyurl.com/calcguid

Scooter Computer and Mr. Chips
schoolhouserock.tv/
Computer.html

Mathematics

Quick-Start Guide to Common Calculators
tinyurl.com/calcguid

For nearly every graphing calculator on the market—even Microsoft Excel—this tutorial explains how to enter data (both one and two variable), how to compute mean, standard deviation (both population and sample), correlation, linear regression coefficients, combinations, permutations, and (important) how to turn the calculator on and off. Each calculator model gets its own page.

Scooter Computer & Mr. Chips   **schoolhouserock.tv/Computer.html**

Schoolhouse Rock gets technical. Memorable songs about number crunching, software, hardware, and data processing. Includes the lyrics and animations. What a great way to learn.

Seeing Math   **seeingmath.concord.org/sms_interactives.html**

A free graphics calculator with advanced functions such as a Function Analyzer, a Linear Transformer, and a Qualitative Grapher.

Technical Mathematics Resources   **tinyurl.com/teccom**

A curriculum for studying computer math, covering advanced functions, modeling, and pre-calculus. Find sample problems, classroom strategies, vocabulary, and related concepts and skills. Designed for grades 9 through 12.

Wolfram Demonstrations Project   **demonstrations.wolfram.com**

Computerized demonstrations—and you can contribute your own—of mathematical concepts such as spline curves, helices, and my favorite: Three Ways to Fold a Net of Eight Triangles.

Trigonometry

THE REALLY FUN stuff! Do your children know interesting words like sine, cosine, tangent, cotangent, secant, and cosecant? No? Then it's time to learn some trig.

Trigonometry is important stuff. Really. John Reed, an electrical engineer in Oak Ridge, Tennessee, explains why: "I actually use much more algebra and trigonometry than calculus. Vector algebra and matrix inversions come up pretty often. In control systems, Laplace transforms and Z transforms are very important.

"I think the emphasis on rushing students into calculus is a big mistake. A lot of math that needs to be absorbed is omitted. They learn the quadratic equation, but how many 'advanced placement' students can solve a cubic or quadratic equation? How many understand where the roots of a quadratic equation have gone when a parabola doesn't cross the x-axis? Can they calculate the volume of an irregular tetrahedron knowing only the edges?

"They do simple trig problems with shadows and trees, but how many could take an aerial photograph and determine the time of day and the day of the year when it was made? How many understand spherical coordinates well enough to have navigated a ship back in the eighteenth century? How many could operate a theodolite or understand the geometry involved in aligning the front wheels of a car?

"None of this involves any calculus, and it represents a huge gap in understanding engineering problems. I suspect that a lot of students today fail in engineering not because they weren't given a head start in calculus, but because they were shortchanged in other areas. A little exposure to calculus is okay, but don't skip the other stuff."

Wanita Talbot is a homeschooling mother in St. Louis. She is studying to be an electronics engineer technician, and she uses trig every day for such things as figuring out the phase angle of current and voltage to troubleshoot circuits. "The phase angle is theta, and to find it, you have to solve for a right triangle," she said. "It's not difficult, nor is it too challenging, but it is a process that technicians have to do. You have to know every aspect of circuitry to find and fix the problem."

Persuaded yet? Let's hit the books.

Trigonometry:
From the Greek *trigonon* (triangle). The study of triangles and angles and their functions.

Mathematics

An Introduction to Trigonometry   tinyurl.com/inttrig

Another online textbook that provides, primarily, a review of principles for students who've already studied the basics.

Dave's Short Trig course   clarku.edu/~djoyce/trig

A sixteen-chapter course that begins with an explanation of why trig is worth studying, and ends with a summary of identities. The lessons are brief but cover all the basics.

Frequently Asked Questions About Trigonometry   catcode.com/trig

One man's online project to make trig accessible to everyone. Requires a Java plug-in.

Marlene's Trigonometry Calculator
marlenesite.com/math/trigonometry

An ebook of basic trigonometry functions. Some pages have interactive features that allow students to input data and find solutions to trig problems.

Hotlinks

Dave's Short Trig course
clarku.edu/~djoyce/trig

Frequently Asked Questions About Trigonometry
catcode.com/trig

Trigonometry Functions
syvum.com/math/trigonometry.html

Technical Tutoring   hyper-ad.com/tutoring/math/trig

A quick review of trig principles, along with more in-depth explanations of functions, sines, cosines, and identities.

Trigonometry Functions
syvum.com/math/trigonometry.html

An online trig textbook—albeit, a short textbook—with ten modules teaching functions, identities, and properties. Includes word problems.

Trigonometry Help   trigonometry-help.net

Trigonometry involves questions on ratios and angles. This site provides in-depth explanations of radian, ratios, functions, identities, values, sines, and cosines. There's even a humor section that may baffle non-trig learners.

Trigonometry Tutorials and Problems
analyzemath.com/Trigonometry.html

Interactive trig tutorials to help you explore angles, functions, inverse functions, and unit circles. Following the tutorials are questions with solutions, articles about trigonometry applications, formulas, tables, and worksheets.

Trigonometry Videos   tinyurl.com/trigvid

A large but not terribly well organized collection of videos teaching trigonometry principles.

What Is Trigonometry?   oolong.co.uk/trig.htm

A definition and a basic introduction to the material found in a trig course.

Calculus

AND NOW, THE really advanced stuff. If you get your child through calculus, you'll have a well-grounded college applicant on your hands.

Calculus is most useful to students who plan to enter the hard sciences, technology, or mathematics fields. Engineer John Reed explains the real-world application of calculus principles: "Calculus is important for understanding relationships involved in engineering. A competent engineer will want to understand why and under what circumstances an equation is valid, not just plug in the numbers and crank out an answer. If the student aspires to a career in development, then in-depth knowledge is essential. Sometimes you face a situation that is different from what is covered by a handbook equation. Then you have to have the mathematical competence to analyze the problem or you can't handle it."

Your pre-college students will be more competent to analyze problems if they take advantage of these resources:

Calculus: From the Latin word for stone. A mathematical field that involves calculations using logical notation.

Mathematics

A History of the Calculus   tinyurl.com/calhist

Understanding the history and development of calculus helps introduce students to the subject.

Better Explained   tinyurl.com/calbet

Two articles, one of which is "A Gentle Introduction to Learning Calculus"—a guide to teaching a difficult subject in a fun way.

Calculus Help   calculus-help.com

Here you'll find more than a dozen video lectures explaining limits, continuity, and derivatives. There's music, too, and a flash movie that explains calculus formulas.

Hotlinks

Calculus Help
calculus-help.com

Karl's Calculus Tutor
karlscalculus.org

Video Calculus
tinyurl.com/vidcalc

Doing Well in Calculus   tinyurl.com/calwel

Advice for college calc students will help any student studying higher math.

Geometry Tutorials, Problems, and Interactive Applets
analyzemath.com/geometry.html

Tutorials on all sorts of geometry topics: reflection, perpendicular bisector, central and inscribed angles, circumcircles, sine law, and triangle properties to solve triangle problems. You'll also find problems and solutions. Polar coordinates equations, conversion, and graphing are also included.

HMC Calculus Tutorial   math.hmc.edu/calculus/tutorials

A series of tutorials explaining pre-calculus, single- and multi-variable calculus, linear algebra, and differential equations. From the text "How to Ace Calculus."

Karl's Calculus Tutor   karlscalculus.org

Click the Tutor link for an online calculus textbook. Look up what you need by topic or search the site for help.

Honda Soichiro

Japanese auto executive Honda Soichiro was a self-taught engineer. The some-time mechanic and race car driver founded his renowned motorcycle company in the 1940s and began producing cars in the 1950s. He started a revolution with his clean-burning CVCC engine, which won Honda cars a prominent place in the U.S. market.

Mathematics Tutorials and Problems
analyzemath.com/calculus.html

Interactive calculus tutorials to help you explore and investigate derivatives, graphing, differential equations, and other calc problems. Check the links in the left-hand column for other calculus help: questions and answers, worksheets, and graphing functions.

Problem of the Week   tinyurl.com/calpro

Years' worth of archived problems and their solutions.

The Calculus Initiative   geom.umn.edu/education/calc-init

Calculus labs that teach how calculus properties apply to real life.

Video Calculus   tinyurl.com/vidcalc

More than 50 Quicktime videos explaining calculus principles with graphics and audio.

Visual Calculus   archives.math.utk.edu/visual.calculus

A cool collection of tutorials and tools from the University of Tennessee, Knoxville, takes students through the steps of learning precalculus and calculus. Ordered by topic.

Why Do We Study Calculus?   tinyurl.com/calwhy

"Calculus is not just a vocational training course," says the author. Find out why it's a valuable course of study.

Statistics

STATISTICS LITERACY GETS far, far too little attention in most educational curricula. And it may be one of the most critical literacies of all. For one thing, the media are rife with misused statistics. Unless your kids are knowledgeable about what they're reading, they're liable to get sucked into foolish agendas and social "problems" that aren't problems at all.

A good understanding of statistics will also help your kids in their personal lives.

Statistics: From the New Latin *statisticus* (statecraft). The study of population samples.

Barry Richardson, a senior lecturer in psychology at Monash University, in Australia, says statistical analysis played a very important role in a major decision in his life. "While living in England a few years ago, I was unemployed and found that at fifty years of age, nobody wanted to hire me. I noticed that many newspaper job ads had age limits (e.g., 'You will be between 26 and 35'), but I needed to quantify this and compare the frequency of such ads between publications and countries. Using the chi-square statistic and others, I was able to show that Britain showed significantly more age discrimination in employment than the United States, Australia, and Canada."

For Luis Enrique Demestre, a university professor and a psychologist with a master's degree in organizational development, a working knowledge of statistics is critical. Luis teaches statistics at the Catholic University Andrés Bello in Venezuela. "I find statistics quite useful in carrying out my three jobs: father, teacher, and social scientist," he says.

"When my children were small, I used statistics to understand their grades in school. Our grading scale is from 1 to 20. I used to take down their grades in each subject, and then I obtained the arithmetic mean and the standard deviation of all their grades and the same statistics for each of them. Then I compared the grades between them to determine whether the differences were significant. For example, Patricia (the oldest one) had a mean of 16.12, which was not too bad, but Debora (the second-oldest) got 17. Then I would ask myself whether these differences were important. Could they be attributed to Debora's greater effort, or was it just chance? If Debora's 17 was because she had studied really hard, she deserved a reward.

"I also used to record all the 'good things' they were doing, such as keeping their room clean and tidy, helping their mother in the kitchen, or avoiding fighting. Every Saturday we would gather together to count all the good things. If there was a statistically significant increase in the number of the good things, they would obtain some privileges or rewards.

"Of course, my wife and I were quite flexible, which is why the system never worked properly, but still, we had a great time and lots of fun. There were many family situations where I could apply numbers and statistics, always keeping in mind that the important thing was the knowledge my wife and I got from them, and that we could find ways to help our kids to grow up and become good people."

Statistics as a character builder? Why not? Here's how to teach your kids to make their own wise statistical analyses.

A Picture Is Worth a Thousand Words

thirteen.org/edonline/lessons/1000words

A well-done lesson plan that teaches kids how to find different kinds of graphs and analyze them for statistical data.

Adventures in Statistics

mathforum.org/trscavo/statistics.html

A math project involving fifth-grade students and the area of classrooms. Students develop a hypothesis, then use measurement, graphing, computation, and data analysis to present results.

Against All Odds: Introductory Statistics

learner.org/resources/series65.html

A video course in statistics for high-school classrooms

Hotlinks

Against All Odds: Introductory Statistics
learner.org/resources/series65.html

Elementary Statistics
sofia.fhda.edu/gallery/statistics

The Best Stats You've Ever Seen
www.ted.com/talks/view/id/92

and adult learners. Consists of 26 half-hour video programs and coordinated books.

Amazing Applications of Probability and Statistics
intuitor.com/statistics

A collection of articles explaining why you should understand statistics and the laws of probability. "Reasoning based on probability and statistics gives modern societies the ability to cope with uncertainty," says Intuitor. Very teenager-friendly.

Collaborative Statistics   cnx.org/content/col10522

Rice University purchased the rights to this popular stats textbook in order to make it available online for free. The book is intended for introductory college statistics courses for students who are majoring in non-technical fields. Intermediate algebra is the only prerequisite.

Elementary Statistics   sofia.fhda.edu/gallery/statistics

A complete course in elementary statistics, with 12 half-hour video lectures. Lessons include assignments and exams with answer keys.

How Juries Are Fooled by Statistics   tinyurl.com/jurystat

Oxford mathematician Peter Donnelly reveals the common mistakes humans make in interpreting statistics—and the devastating impact these errors can have on the outcome of criminal trials.

Mystic Ball   mysticalball.com

A fun way to teach younger children about random chances. Ask a question and manipulate an actual "Magic 8-Ball" via the Web.

Percent and Probability   mathleague.com/help/percent/percent.htm

Definitions and examples of statistics problems—with answers.

Statistics Online Computational Resource   socr.ucla.edu

An interesting software tool for probability and statistics education. Applets provide visual representations of experiments in statistical measurement.

Technology PoW   mathforum.org/tpow

Java applets allow students to work out statistical problems, submit their answers to public view, and check them against hints and solvers. Good use of colorful graphics.

The Best Stats You've Ever Seen   www.ted.com/talks/view/id/92

A fascinating demonstration of the application of stats to real-world problems. Click the link on the right to see Rosling's animations of statistical data. The second talk is even more interesting than the first.

Mathematics

Chapter 7

Art Appreciation

Hotlinks

Artist Study
squidoo.com/
cmartiststudy

Dick Blick Art Lessons
dickblick.com/lessonplans

Incredible Art Department
princetonol.com/
groups/iad

Student Art Lesson Plans
art-rageous.net/
Art-Plans.html

The Arts Videos
tinyurl.com/artsvid

I GREW UP in a house of artists. My mother majored in art before becoming an art educator in the public schools. My brother attended an arts college on full scholarship and is now working as an architect. Both of my sisters surround themselves with beauty. Their homes, their clothes, their dinner parties are all exquisite. Even my husband, the painter, has astonishingly good taste.

Me? It seems I took after my father—the Boeing engineer who believes green plaid slacks look swell with a red plaid tie. In June. At a wedding.

That's why I was so pleased to find a treasure trove of art resources online.

As my kids and I have considered these resources and discussed art and artists, I've noticed a swelling sense of . . . well, if not taste and culture, at least a dislike of polyester and plaid.

I've also come to see the very real benefits of teaching children about art. Oh, not the kind of "art" that I learned in school—not the kind where we became really, really good at coloring inside the lines.

As our family has considered various artists and discussed what constitutes "art," I've seen in my growing children a sense of the visual and an appreciation for good taste.

Here's Joan Zielinski, an artist, a retired art instructor in the public schools—and my own mother—on the benefit of having your children learn about art: "Teaching the arts—and visual arts in particular—reaches and uses intelligences that traditional pencil/paper activities, which form the bulk of most school activities, don't reach. Teaching the arts gives success to many who otherwise don't do as well in school. Students who are schooled in the arts score much higher on college-admissions tests than those who have not been schooled in this important field. One reason is that we teach the whole child in this way, not just one small part of the child. The child is able to develop more of his or her brain by being trained in the arts."

How should parents teach their children the arts? "It doesn't mean that at Thanksgiving time we teach the child how to cut out paper turkeys and that at Christmas we make green and red paper chains . . . though there is a place for these activities.

"To do a complete curriculum, it's important to study the great masters, both past and present. Both parents and children should learn how to analyze great works of art. Become familiar with the vocabulary of the visual arts, so that its usage becomes a part of your kids' vocabulary as much as any other part of their speech. Such concepts as texture, line, contrast, color, and space are necessary for understanding art.

"By studying great works of art, the child will be learning about great artists as well as about the periods of time and the place in which the artists created their work."

My mother is also keen on incorporating art into other curriculum areas. "There are many wonderful resources for finding out about the stories of artists' lives. Sometimes these ideas will fit well into a social studies curriculum so that everything dovetails together and a large unit of writing, history, geography, reading, and art can be coordinated." It's not just the artistically inclined who will benefit from the following resources. Even the art-impaired can learn to find beauty through an understanding of artistic principles.

In this chapter, you'll be introduced to art history and appreciation, crafts, design, drawing, painting, sculpture and ceramics, and visual arts. You'll find related humanities resources for dance, drama, and other performing arts in Chapter 11. We start here with general tools for teaching and understanding art.

Art Index   art.pppst.com

An index of art-related PowerPoint presentations that teach the elements of art. One of the sections, The Isms, teaches about Cubism, Impressionism, Pointillism, Realism, and Surrealism. Another discusses art media: crayon, paint, fabric, yarn, clay, paper, stone, wood, and metal.

Art Junction   artjunction.org

An outreach project of the Art Education Program of the University of Florida. Art Junction provides activities and projects for teaching drawing, painting, and art appreciation.

Artist Study   squidoo.com/cmartiststudy

Learn how Charlotte Mason taught art. She suggested that a different artist be studied consistently for an entire term—up to twelve weeks. During that time, at least six different works of art by that same artist should be studied.

Arts Ed Net   getty.edu/education

Lesson plans, scope and sequence, curriculum ideas, online galleries and exhibitions, discussion area, reading room, and much more. This is a must-visit site if you're teaching the arts.

Arts Lesson Plans   tinyurl.com/artlps

Fine arts lesson plans designed by classroom teachers. Most are easily adapted to homeschooling programs.

ArtServe   rubens.anu.edu.au

An eclectic collection of art resources surveying art history, different periods and styles, architecture, art prints, and various visual arts.

Art Appreciation

Dick Blick Art Lessons   dickblick.com/lessonplans

Amazing art projects with photographs, illustrations, and plans for re-creating. Sculptures, paintings, projects, glasswork, textiles. Gorgeous.

Imagination Factory   kid-at-art.com

Set your imagination loose at the Factory. The Art Lessons come in drawing, sculpture, painting, holidays, printmaking, fiber arts, collage, marbling, and crafts flavors. Or click the Flat Stanley link for art activities to decorate your own Flat Stanley project.

Incredible Art Department   princetonol.com/groups/iad

The name might be a bit over the top, but it's certainly worth a visit—if only for the Matisse Mixed Media Portrait lesson. Start with the Lessons link, which houses a large collection of good lesson-planning ideas, then investigate the Art History and Free Time Activities links in the left-hand column for games and even more teaching ideas. From Princeton University.

Integrated Art Lessons   cameronartmuseum.com/lesson_plans.php

A collection of 20 PowerPoint-based unit studies that integrate art with language, math, science, and social studies. The artwork is stunning.

KinderArt—K12   kinderart.com/teachers

Lots of lesson plans in every form of art media including kitchen art, architecture, crafts, painting, printmaking, sculpture, and textiles. A very good resource.

Living with Art   tinyurl.com/artliv

Very interesting PowerPoint presentations to teach Visual Arts and two courses in Art History, along with a number of other humanities topics. See completed projects and a syllabus, too.

Spiral Art Education   uic.edu/classes/ad/ad382

Click the Cool Curriculum link for access to interesting art ideas and full lesson plans for topics such as "Autobiographical Comics" and "Headline Poetry."

Student Art Lesson Plans   art-rageous.net/Art-Plans.html

A substantive collection of lesson plans written by a high-school art teacher. One of my favorites is Your Life as a Movie, where kids consider movie posters, and then imagine a poster advertising a movie of their lives.

The Arts Videos   tinyurl.com/artsvid

A large collection of educational videos that teach art and culture. One series, for example, explains Art in the Western World. Another demonstrates how to connect with the arts. From the Annenberg CPB series.

ThinkQuest: Arts & Entertainment   tinyurl.com/artsande

Each year Oracle sponsors a competition where teams of students create educational websites that teach a particular academic subject. These Art sites cover the spectrum.

Art History and Appreciation

FOR THOSE WITHOUT any particular inclination to create art, this is the fun part: learning to appreciate it. Art appreciation and art history are easy subjects to teach for free. The reason? Museums love us.

Liz deForest from Santa Monica, California, lives near the Getty museums. "Entry is free," she notes, "and they have fine art, modern art, and architecture. They have it all. The science center here has free admission, too. In fact, most museums have free days, and last year the Hammer Museum was free all summer. We saw the Abstract Expressionist exhibit there. The Los Angeles County Museum of Art is always free for students and has free admission days for adults as well."

Saprina Bowman has been traveling the world with her family. She found a way to take advantage of free teaching moments during a recent trip to Chicago. "Some of the mu-

Art: From the Greek *artios* (fitting, even). Created works of aesthetic value.

seums have free days. Even Paris has many places (including the Louvre) that are free admission on the first Sunday of the month. We didn't spend enough time in the Netherlands or London to discover what free learning experiences they have there, but the amount of time we spent there was worth every penny!"

Sarah Bull, a Wisconsin homeschooler, notes that in her area, the local artisan communities open up their homes for art tours. "This only costs us the gas to drive to each home," she says. "There is a day in the fall when the majority of national museums have free admission, as well. The closest for us is three hours away. The Smithsonian and several museums over the nation participate on this day. Last year we went to the Great River Museum in Dubuque, Iowa. Again, all it cost us was the gas to go. We camped and made it a vacation as well."

Studying great artists—learning about the symbolism and the milieu and the techniques of a work of art—brings about those great "aha!" moments that we enjoy so much as parents and teachers.

One of the best things to do when you are teaching art is to take your little ones down to the public library when it's quiet and pull out some of the oversized art books that contain colored plates of beautiful artwork.

My mother again: "Of course, my favorite activity is studying artists first and then taking kids to a local art museum where they can be surrounded with the works of that artist. They can drink in the atmosphere there.

"In addition, most art museums have terrific educational programs where groups of students can work with docents and produce their own works of art at the museum. You can be put on the mailing lists of all the museums in your area to keep up on what's happening in the field of art.

"Working to make art an integral part of the curriculum you teach, not just one hour every Friday, will help your children develop to their best potential."

Hotlinks

Artlex Art Dictionary
artlex.com

Artsology Investigations
artsology.com

The Last Supper
tinyurl.com/artlast

Web Gallery of Art
www.wga.hu

Art Appreciation

On Vision

Vision: the art of seeing
things invisible.

—Jonathan Swift

Ann M. Glass, from Everson, Washington, is a homeschooling mother of two. She has made Friday her family's art day. "We take most of the morning, since we have dropped other subjects for the day. We study an artist and a composer. For the artist, we learn about his life and what he was known for, talk about his paintings (ideally, we've been able to find pictures at the library or off the Net), and then try our hand at that style of art. For the composer, again, we learn about his life and listen to and discuss his music. We also learn about different kinds of instruments and styles of music."

As you prepare to introduce your own children to art appreciation, consider the following resources. Some are games; some are visual; all are educational.

A Lifetime of Color   alifetimeofcolor.com

The best part of this website isn't the lesson plans—though those are excellent. It's the Technique Demos, where students learn skills such as Contour Drawing, Thumbnail Sketches, and Two-Point Perspective.

Art and Music Lesson Plans   tinyurl.com/artles

For grades K through 7, a nice collection of high-quality art-appreciation lesson plans with titles such as "The Art of Studying Art" and "Art and Artists: An Appreciation for Fourth Grade."

Art Images for College Teaching   arthist.cla.umn.edu/aict/html

Art from around the world. The Ancient link has art from prehistoric Europe, and ancient Rome, Greece, and other locations. Click the non-Western link for access to representative art from Africa, China, India, Indonesia, and the Americas.

Artcyclopedia   artcyclopedia.com

Browse an immense database of artwork by the artist's name, medium, subject, nationality, or movement. Study the work of famous painters,

Leonardo da Vinci

Born to an unmarried peasant woman, young Leonardo was taken into his father's house in Florence and raised as a legitimate son. There he learned reading, writing, and arithmetic, although he didn't become a serious student of Latin for many years. It appears that he was a talented artist from a young age, inasmuch as he was apprenticed to a Florentine artist at the age of fifteen. During his apprenticeship he learned painting, sculpting, and the technical and mechanical arts. By the age of twenty he had joined the local painters' guild, but he continued studying in his master's workshop for five more years.

glassmakers, engravers, inventors, sculptors, potters, and so much more.

ArtLex Art Dictionary   artlex.com

A lexicon of art terms, presented in a very clean and easy-to-use format. Follow the Shortcut links in the left column to find longer articles, with illustrations and examples, for art terms such as Surrealism, silkscreen, and Neoclassicism.

Artsology Investigations   artsology.com

Click the link to Investigations for more than 30 investigations into art questions such as How Do Artist Depict Motion? and What Did Zeus Look Like? Each investigation has numerous examples of artwork that demonstrates a principle.

Check the Value of a Painting   tinyurl.com/artval

That old painting in the attic could pay the college tuition, say the authors of Learn2, a collection of illustrated multipart tutorials. Links on the right lead to related How-To's.

EW Art History   ewart.sbc.edu

Video discussions of several pieces of well-known art—in just a minute. Beautifully presented, with amusing narration.

Art Appreciation

Matisse & Picasso   matisse-picasso.com

All about the gentle competition between two great artists. Lesson plans are supported by a teachers' resource guide and a collection of the artists' paintings.

National Gallery of Art   nga.gov/education/classroom/loanfinder

Holy cow! Free educational materials, on loan from the National Gallery of Art. Borrow teaching packets and slides in unlimited quantities. All you pay is return postage at book rates. Degas, Rembrandt, Toulouse-Lautrec, Picasso . . . just awaiting your order.

The Artchive   artchive.com/ftp_site.htm

This eye-opening resource gathers together in one place every significant piece of the Western world's artwork and all the major artists, painters, sculptors, photographers, even the ancients.

The Last Supper   tinyurl.com/artlast

An amazing undertaking: high-resolution photography of Leonardo's most fragile masterpiece. See how 16 billion pixels lets you examine details of the fifteenth-century mural you've never seen before. Watch the video to see how it was done.

Web Gallery of Art   www.wga.hu

Here it is. All the art. A virtual Louvre of everything by anyone worth studying. Zoom in to see the works in great detail. This one's a real treasure.

Webmuseum, Paris   ibiblio.org/wm/paint

A gallery of online artwork from such masters as Cézanne, Manet, Monet, Jan van Eyck, and Botticelli. Each section contains biographical information that contributes to understanding the artwork.

Crafts

CRAFTING DRAWS FAMILIES together, and gives home-schooling homes a fun atmosphere for learning. North Carolina homeschooler Terri Vitkovitsky recommends setting up a "craft center" supplied with crayons, markers, colored pencils, construction paper, old stickers, glue, old wrapping paper, and buckets of Styrofoam letters/objects. She lets her younger kids have free access to create. "They practice skills on their own, and their pride when you hang up their project is a wonderful reinforcement for them and encouragement for future 'work,' " she says.

> **Craft:** From the Old English *cræft* (strength). Artistic creation requiring manual dexterity or skill.

I do two crafts, and I do them very well. I sew. It's no longer economical to sew, so I don't do it often, but I know how to sew. And I make scrapbooks and cards. I use rubber stamps, colored pens, fancy scissors, and all sorts of other little doodads that allow me to build memory albums for my family.

I've just about gotten my entire extended family hooked as well. On the first Sunday of each month, we have a family gathering and drag out my "stamping" boxes. Photos and cutters and rubber stamps and ink pads and interesting paper I've collected burst from boxes. We clear a long table and go to work.

What started as a moms' activity, though, is turning into a kids' activity, as our little ones clamor for access to the paper goods. Now if I could just get them to neatly label my four thousand unlabeled photos . . .

Whether your crafts decorate your home or just give you an excuse to sit with the kids and poke clay buttons with a fork, crafting builds creativity in a happy, lighthearted way that all kids enjoy. Here are some resources to get you started.

Art Supply Recipes   easyfunschool.com/IndexArt.html

Make your own art supplies! This incredible collection of art projects from scratch are a combination of fine arts and kitchen science that will fascinate your kids.

Art Appreciation

Hotlinks

Art Supply Recipes
easyfunschool.com/
IndexArt.html

Craft Ideas for Elementary Kids
mycraftbook.com

Danielle's Place
daniellesplace.com

KinderArt
kinderart.com

CraftBits   craftbits.com
A bra purse. Seriously. This site has hundreds of fun craft projects for older kids and adults—several of which are probably a little tasteless, even if they are amusing.

Craft Ideas for Elementary Kids   mycraftbook.com
Great collection of craft ideas organized by occasion and by age group. We're looking enviously at the Chinese lantern and the button treasure box.

Craft Recipes   kidschalkboard.com/crafts.html
Recipes for all sorts of craft materials: paint, bubbles, putty, dough, clay, glue, papier-mâché, and crystals. When you get to the end of the list, click the Art Activities link for even more good ideas.

Danielle's Place   daniellesplace.com
What a resource for crafters. In addition to the huge collection of crafts for teaching Christian principles, the site is loaded with resources for teaching history, culture, and other academic topics by using crafts.

DLTK's Crafts for Kids   dltk-kids.com
An extensive collection of printable children's crafts, Christian printables, coloring pages, holiday projects, and educational themes. Companion sites **dltk-bible.com, dltk-teach.com,** and **dltk-holidays.com** add even more crafts to the array.

FamilyFun Arts and Crafts   familyfun.go.com/arts-and-crafts
Need crafts for a holiday? To decorate a kid's room? This site is filled with more than 1,500 colorful lesson plans for toddlers to eight-year-olds.

Instructables: Step-by-Step Collaboration   instructables.com
Half science; half crafting. Instructions for making hundreds of projects. Add your own cool project ideas.

KinderArt   kinderart.com

Ever consider covering a table with finger paint and letting the little ones go nuts? Then this is the site for you. Crafts, drama, folk art, painting, sculpture, printmaking, and dozens of other topics, each with its own lesson plans and instructions.

Make Your Own Copy Machine   kidskreate.com

Lots of educational craft ideas. One project even has Instructions for making a homemade hectograph with boric acid and gelatin. Cool.

Make Your Own Travel Games

momsminivan.com/sew-travel-game.html

If you find yourself car-schooling, here's your best resource: 101 car travel games you make yourself. Start by making a checkerboard bag to hold the checker pieces. Then create aluminum foil sculptures, string figures, or a cootie catcher. That oughta keep your car-seated kids entertained.

Stitchify   stitchify.com

This popular blog will inspire in you a love for the textile and fiber arts. The interviews with fiber artists are enlightening and the tutorials are helpful.

Design

AS A CONCEPT, design incorporates everything from the composition of a photograph to the structure of la cathédrale de Notre Dame. It involves the principles I used in college to lay out newspaper and magazine pages and the concepts Martha Stewart uses to arrange a tray of cookies.

Fundamentally, design involves a principle called the Fibonacci sequence—the "golden mean" observed by the Greeks and explained by a fellow named Fibonacci. All of

Design: From the Middle French *designer* (to designate). To create or construct according to plan.

Art Appreciation

these people observed a natural phenomenon that demonstrates that beauty can be quantified. The principles of design are useful in understanding every form of design: artistic composition, interior design, architecture, newspapers, web pages.

The resources in this section explain not only Fibonacci but also other composition and design principles as they're used in art, architecture, newspapers, websites, and interior design.

Art & Learning to Think & Feel   goshen.edu/art/ed/art-ed-links.html

What would happen if we stopped giving suggestions? This art teacher advises educators to stop suggesting and stop showing. It only encourages imitation, and discourages imagination. Though the entire site is fascinating, click the Elements and Principles link from the Table of Contents to find design concepts that teach balance, harmony, unity, and opposition.

Design: Journalists' Toolkit   jtoolkit.com/design

Click first on the Fibonacci diagram for a graphic representation of the golden ratio used in all good design, from nature to HGTV to the shape of your computer screen. Then examine the other lessons designed for multimedia and online journalists.

Flower Arranging 101   floralcraftresource.com

What the pros know about designing floral arrangements. After learning about tools of the flower trade, follow the link to Floral Design Instruction.

Google SketchUp   sketchup.google.com

Designing a house or a deck or any other 3D object is easier with computers. Google SketchUp is free software that you can use to create, export, and present 3D models. Free tutorials and training classes teach the technique.

Graphic Design Course   artlex.com/graphic.design.html

Graphic arts assignments for a high-school design course.

Art Appreciation

Hotlinks

Art & Learning
goshen.edu/art/ed/
art-ed-links.html

Design: Journalists' Toolkit
jtoolkit.com/design

Home Decorating 101
homedecoratingsense
.com/decorating-101.html

Heritage Education Architecture   histpres.mtsu.edu/then/architecture

How to teach architecture. This site teaches the teacher, with vocabulary, teaching tips, and really good classroom activities.

Home Decorating 101   homedecoratingsense.com/decorating-101.html

The principles of interior design begin with balance, emphasis, rhythm, proportion—all the same elements that constitute any other good design. This online "class" teaches all about color, lighting, and design styles.

Home Portfolio   homeportfolio.com

Design tours, great American homes, and pages of fast-loading room designs that will inspire. See the Dream Portfolio link for the grand tour.

Make an Ikebana Floral Arrangement   tinyurl.com/ikebana

An illustrated multipart tutorial on Japanese flower arranging. Follow the links to the right for related How-To's.

Sense and Sensibility   sensibility.com

Click the Research link to view vintage images of clothing designs from 1795 to 1959. Here's proof that all the best clothes happened in the 1940s.

Typographic   rsub.com/typographic

All about font design. History, a timeline, a gallery of fonts, a glossary, and more.

Drawing

I HAVE A couple of budding artists in my house. There's no need to teach them to draw. One son already loves drawing; another is completely obsessed. He carries a backpack stuffed with paper and pencils and notebooks every time he leaves the house, even if he's only going over to visit the neighbors. Inside the house, he carries around a clip-

Draw: From the Old Norse *draga* (to draw or drag). To create a likeness or picture with lines.

board with his latest project and can be found anytime—day or night—crouched under a table or behind a door, tongue between his teeth, "fixing" his newest drawing.

Whether your little darlings are future Gary Larsons and Mort Druckers or have already made their artistic "mark," here are some resources they'll enjoy.

Arty Factory   artyfactory.com

A surprisingly good site with free art lessons that use many different media. Create pencil portraits, draw animals, work on perspective, learn to design logos, and much more.

Chunky Monkey's Cartoon Lessons

chunkymonkey.com/howto/drawinglessons.htm

What would you like to draw? A monkey? Bugs? Fish? Lessons here, both video and written, teach younger kids the basics of cartooning. Send your kids' artwork to the developers, and they might post them to the kids' page of the site.

Draw and Color with Uncle Fred   unclefred.com

For younger children, Uncle Fred teaches quick, easy-to-emulate demonstrations of cartoony art. Cute.

Drawing Glossary   tinyurl.com/artfog

From Harvard University, an interlinked glossary of the language of drawing. There's your spelling list for your drawing unit study.

Drawing Lessons from Toad Hollow   toadhollowstudio.com

Gradation and smoothing are two of the techniques taught in this collection of more than 20 drawing lessons. Follow the Free How-To link at the top of the page.

DrawSpace   drawspace.com

How often do you get free art lessons from a former police sketch

Art Appreciation

artist? The author of this outstanding site offers dozens and dozens of beautifully illustrated lessons on every conceivable drawing technique and skill. Requires free registration.

Figure Drawing Lab   drawinglab.evansville.edu

Leonardo spent a great deal of energy studying the proportions of the human figure. Your task is a little easier. Learn from master artists the techniques for drawing anatomy. This is a graphics-intensive art course for older kids and teens.

How to Draw   princetonol.com/groups/iad/links/how_to_draw.pdf

An ebook with step-by-step lessons for drawing the human body: the eye, a man's face, anime bodies, length and proportion . . . These are good, basic lessons.

Learning How to Draw

tinyurl.com/learndraw

Surprising, well-done lessons on learning how to draw for nine- to fourteen-year-olds hoping for careers in the arts. The first lesson explains, with diagrams, how to hold a drawing pencil properly. Another has children drawing a city street to learn about perspective.

Online Etch A Sketch   ohioart.com/etch/gallery.action

A gallery of amazing drawings using the popular children's toy. Click the Let's Sketch link for an online version, where you use arrow keys in place of dials. Great fun.

Pastel Resources   artshow.com/resources/drawing.html

Working with pastels is a tricky business, but a group of Pastelists has joined forces to show how it's done. Learn about pastels and their history, and see a demonstration of how to work with pastels in your own drawing. Click the Drawing link for other tutorials.

Hotlinks

Arty Factory
artyfactory.com

Drawing Lessons from Toad Hollow
toadhollowstudio.com

DrawSpace
drawspace.com

Portrait Tutorial
portrait-artist.org/
bearsclover-portrait

Art Appreciation

Art Appreciation

Portrait Tutorial　portrait-artist.org/bearsclover-portrait

This artist remembers that when he was a teenager, he "needed inspiration, some guidance, and some basic advice on materials to use, things to strive for and to avoid, and basic portrait tips." So now he's providing to others what he didn't have. These art lessons offer comforting, useful advice to new artists.

Painting

Paint: From the Latin *pingere* (to tattoo). To depict an image using liquid pigments.

WE ONCE LIVED on the fourth floor of a cement building in Taipei. Out back was a long cement balcony that extended the length of the house. In the center of the balcony was a small drain.

Guess how my children learned to paint? I kept them supplied with all the essentials: watercolors, tempera paint, finger paint, and their favorite, colored chalk. Afternoons—winter or summer—would usually find my kids out on the back balcony dressed in "something washable," with their chalk and paint and big brushes, decorating the cement wall.

Whenever it became overcrowded, we'd go out back with a few buckets of water and a scrub brush, and they'd soon have a fresh new canvas. They'll be well qualified when they graduate from the school of "try it and see how it works." I assume they're in good company. The Irish painter Francis Bacon was self-taught and became well respected for his artistic satire. My kids may not end up famous artists, but they've got a good start at knowing how it feels to paint. The following resources may inspire your kids to a lifetime of painting.

Another Look at Finger Painting　fingerpainter.com

Childhood doesn't count if you never get to finger paint. Find here beautiful examples of finger-painting techniques that will satisfy the artistic urge in painters of every age.

Art Studio Chalkboard

www2.evansville.edu/studiochalkboard

From the Painting link at the top, learn how to stretch a canvas, prepare a painting ground, choose correct tools, and start painting with oils, acrylics, and tempera. The Drawing link has equally good resources.

Artgraphica Art Lessons artgraphica.net/free-art-lessons

Guest artists teach techniques such as oil and watercolor painting as part of this collection of nicely illustrated art lessons. See, for example, how one artist used blocking techniques to create a painting called *The Tranquil Sea.*

Artpad Digital Canvas artpad.art.com/artpad/painter/

An online painting tool that's significantly changed from the silly Paint tool that came with your computer. This one uses a brush to apply paint that actually looks like paint. Frame the result and mail it off to someone who'll enjoy your art.

Chinese Brush Painting asia-art.net/chinese_brush.html

Those beautiful wall hangings you find in Asian décor originate with a form of painting called ink and wash. The calligraphy requires years of training, but simple brush painting is probably within the capacity of most children. Here's where you can learn how.

Decorate Eggs tutorials.com/08/0891/0891.asp

Learn2 is a collection of multipart tutorials with cartoon illustrations. This five-part lesson teaches egg decorators how to hollow out an egg and make wax patterns to create beautiful ornaments. Links on the right lead to related How-To's.

How-To Guide to Airbrushing airbrush.com/how-to-guide.aspx

Airbrushing is a painting technique that demands special equipment, but if you have access, this is a great resource for tutorials and tips

Hotlinks

Art Studio Chalkboard
www2.evansville.edu/
studiochalkboard

Artgraphica Art Lessons
artgraphica.net/
free-art-lessons

Painting Lessons
johnlovett.com/class.htm

Pigments Through the Ages
webexhibits.org/pigments

Art Appreciation

Art Appreciation

from real airbrush artists. Even if you don't have the equipment, the site's worth visiting for inspiration. You could always airbrush the old-fashioned way: blowing paint through a straw.

Oil Painting Lessons   artpapa.net

Three free lessons teach kids how to paint using oils and classical techniques. Illustrations give step-by-step directions.

Paint with a Marble Finish   tutorials.com/07/0754/0754.asp

Faux painting is a fun activity for the whole family. This site provides an illustrated multipart tutorial. Follow the links to the right for related How-To's.

Painting Lessons   johnlovett.com/class.htm

Lovett is an Australian artist who generously provides free watercolor lessons online. Start with the Tips for Beginners lesson before tackling advanced techniques such as painting on location.

Pigments Through the Ages   webexhibits.org/pigments

Paint without pigment is just a gloppy gray mess. Learn how pigments were made historically, and how they're used in modern painting techniques. Nice artwork illustrates the concepts.

Susie Short Watercolors   susieshort.net

Watercolorist Susie Short offers up tips for tackling techniques such as creating water droplets with paints, and transferring drawings to watercolor paper. The step-by-step demo of how to paint a watercolor rose is typical of the high educational value of this resource.

The Joy of Painting   bobross.com

It's that crazy-haired, soft-talking painter guy from educational TV, here to share a few painting techniques while trying to shill books and supplies. Click the How-To Projects link.

Sculpture and Ceramics

SCULPTURE INSPIRES. WHETHER carved marble or bronze casting or gold-leafed monument, there's something "larger than life" about seeing heroic historical figures and dramatic events carved out in three dimensions.

Sculpture also inspires children. Homeschooling mom Keithena Kibbe from Goodyear, Arizona, explains how sculpture keeps her five children interested in art. "Music and art have a real impact on my children," she says. "They all are very inspired. Right now, my six-year-old really wants to sculpt like Michelangelo. A lot of working with clay and banging on rocks is going on. And my five-year-old daughter is sure she will grow up to be a singer!"

Keithena has made this foundation part of her combined art and music curriculum. "We always do art and music events as a unit study," she says. "This year we did a short four-day unit on Monet, and at the end of the week we visited his showing at the local art museum.

"Because four of my children are very young, we haven't selected a music program yet, but our church has many, many resources and lessons. My sixteen-year-old son takes guitar and bass lessons twice a week, so I expect that most of the music will be taught there. Everything else we do will be in unit studies."

In this section we examine sculpture in many kinds of media: paper, clay, wire, wood—even pumpkin! When your little clay benders and paper folders and knife wielders need inspiration and direction, the following Internet resources will come in handy:

Goshen College Ceramics

goshen.edu/art/DeptPgs/CerLinks.htm

If you have access to a kiln, you're most of the way to discovering ceramics. Here's inspiration from a college art prof. Though college-level art classes are challenging,

> **Sculpt:** From the Latin *sculpere* (to carve). To shape or mold with artistry and precision.

Art Appreciation

Hotlinks

Papier-Mâché Resource
papiermache.co.uk

Polymer Clay Spot
jaedworks.com/clayspot

The Pumpkin Gutter
pumpkingutter.com

The Sculpture Studio
thesculpturestudio.com

the lessons on this site—on topics such as Cleaning & Working Safely—easily transfer to younger kids.

How to Make a Piñata   wikihow.com/Make-a-Pinata

Nine steps to your next birthday party. Create colorful paper sculptures you fill with treats and hang up for the amusement of blindfolded bat swingers. Note the links at the end of this article to similar art projects.

Museum of Art Education   sdmart.org/education-plans.html

The San Diego Museum of Art has created a collection of art lesson plans for projects that can be developed from inexpensive materials and are easy to integrate into a variety of disciplines. Three-dimensional portraits and bookmaking are among the many projects available here.

Orihouse: Knotology   tinyurl.com/artorig

Knotology is what happens when you plait, fold, or weave strips of paper into sculpture. You've seen the puffy stars and candy-wrapper woven bracelets. Now investigate this gallery of amazing artwork that follows simple geometry to create astonishing artifacts.

Paper Crafts for Kids   themes.pppst.com/papercrafts.html

PowerPoint presentations that teach paper crafts. One of the sections, How to Make Paper Kites, teaches kites and balloon making. Another discusses paper airplanes. Fold on!

Paper Toys   thetoymaker.com/2toys.html

Toys that move, math toys, gift boxes, animal toys. Fold 'em up, and it's playtime.

Papier-Mâché Resource   papiermache.co.uk

Papier-mâché works best if you live in a dry climate—or near a heat vent. At this site you'll find lessons on how to create papier-mâché sculpture, along with inspirational galleries of artist-made creations. Gorgeous!

Polymer Clay Spot   jaedworks.com/clayspot

Learn the basics of working with this pliable, blendable polymer that can be blended like paint and fired like clay. Techniques and answers to FAQs are also included.

Teaching Innovative Wire Sculpture   tinyurl.com/artinn

Can your kids turn a spool of wire into art? They'll be able to after they learn about this article. The links immediately above the article go to several additional wire-sculpture resources.

The Pumpkin Gutter   pumpkingutter.com

Jack-o'-lanterns in my house were good, but they never looked like this. One guy, one month a year, one amazing gallery of carvings. From produce.

The Sculpture Studio   thesculpturestudio.com

Wood carving and stone carving tutorials that provide basic instruction, with photographs, of getting started as a sculptor.

Willard Wigan's Art in Miniature
slideshare.net/sscholle/willard-wigan

Wigan's miniature art—much of it small enough to fit comfortably in the eye of a needle—is wondrous. Your children will be astonished, and perhaps inspired to follow suit.

Art Appreciation

Visual Arts

PHOTOGRAPHY IS MY favorite visual art form. Not only is it one I can be good at without knowing how to make a recognizable ear, but it's also one that has the capacity to be the most poignant, the most memorable, for future generations of our family.

Homeschooler Cheryl Northrup, a Lamar, Colorado, mother of seven, explains how she schooled her son in the vi-

Visual art: From the Latin *visus* (sight). The production of images.

sual arts. "We bought the book *How to Draw*. We didn't do very much with it, unfortunately. Then we had a teacher come to our house and teach several kids from our homeschooling group. That was a fair experience. Art is like anything else; if they are really going to progress, there needs to be some regularity, and we had a hard time fitting it in.

"Now that we are in Lamar, my mother is here. She taught art in the public schools for twenty-two years, and comes over and tutors my kids twice a week. My son painted a full-sized mural on his bedroom wall of a tropical rain forest. That was his project for nearly a year. She has had them doing ceramics, life drawing, still life, and landscapes in pencil and watercolor, and now my fourteen-year-old-son is doing art merit badges (art, architecture, sculpture). For us, it's perfect. And homeschooling gives us the flexibility to stay with it all day if they still feel inspired. They have done some very nice work and have discovered an audience in the county fair, where they have even won some premiums.

"We have also done art appreciation à la Charlotte Mason. I have purchased several art books with great works in them, some with artist bios included. Those have been very good. The Art for Children series is particularly good. Because of my mother's influence, my children have been to many museum showings as well."

Visual arts is the catchall category for art that defies categorization. It is murals, photography, graphic arts, stained glass, collage, and more. The following resources will help your children learn more about the visual arts:

Hotlinks

Art of Stained Glass
art-of-stained-glass.com

Artist's Toolkit
artsconnected.org/toolkit

Basic Art Lessons
home.att.net/~tisone/
lessonpg1.htm

Urban Curators
urbancurators.com

3D Painted Rooms   2loop.com/3drooms.html

Mind-blowing interior paint projects that look like three-dimensional art, depending on where you stand in the room. Your kids will stare.

Art of Photogravure   photogravure.com

Beautiful imagery using the historic art of photogravure. Learn about the history, and the process, of creating images using a method that has nearly disappeared.

Art of Stained Glass   art-of-stained-glass.com

Suddenly, I'm dangerous. I watched the Instructional Videos on this site, and started thinking I actually knew something about working with stained glass. (Fortunately, I recalled a stained-glass cutting venture in college, and remembered that I'm a klutz.) Inspiration for glass workers and wannabes, like myself.

Artist's Toolkit   artsconnected.org/toolkit

Want to see an animated explanation of the difference between geometric and organic shapes? How about animations of explaining warm and cool colors? This video-heavy site is full of lessons for learning about visual elements and principles.

Basic Art Lessons   home.att.net/~tisone/lessonpg1.htm

Lessons for the visual arts, to help kids improve their observation skills. Learn about negative space, collage, color, and patterns with step-by-step teaching instruction.

Color Theory   tinyurl.com/artcol

A very good resource for the basics of color. Simple principles about how to mix, match, and use colors in visual art.

Escher for Real   tinyurl.com/artesch

Dutch artist M. C. Escher is famous for his crazy artistic illusions. Now see how computer scientists are trying to re-create those illusions out of real-life objects.

Fractals   math.rice.edu/~lanius/frac

Learn about fractals, those fascinating geometric shapes that repeat at ever smaller scales to produce irregular shapes.

Art Appreciation

Jasc Paint Shop Tutorial
huntfor.com/photography/tutorials/paintshoppro.htm

Free video lessons for using one of the most popular graphic arts programs. The tutorial provides 24 lessons.

Make Your Own Kaleidoscope   krazydad.com/kaleido

It's only a digital kaleidoscope, but enter the address for any photo, and this fun little toy will turn it into a graphic, which you can then export, if you like. It's a good, quick lesson in digital imaging.

Movie Title Screens Gallery   shillpages.com/movies/index2.shtml

Love the movies? You'll be fascinated by this collection of movie titles and logo designs from thousands of commercial movies. It's interesting to note how typefaces reflect their time period.

Understanding Color   rgbworld.com/color.html

How color plays a role in our lives. This site examines the properties, theories, meanings, and effects of color. Psychology, science, art—color is part of lots of academic areas.

Urban Curators   urbancurators.com

An amazing collection of photographs of framed urban settings. It's inexplicable. See it. Believe it. Do it yourself.

History Highlights

MY FAVORITE PART of homeschooling: teaching my young ones about history. Helping them find their place in their extended family, community, and world. To me, history is what makes us human. History is how we remember who we are, and why we matter.

An appreciation of history creates in children a love for those who were heroic, and an aversion to evil.

The more children understand of history, the better perspective they have for handling the present. A real understanding of history equips kids for living well in the real world.

Here is how a historian from Missouri, who now works as a political consultant, answers the question "What is history?"

"I have studied history for as long as I remember, and the only answer I have ever come up with is that it is everything! I know that is vague, but let me expand for a moment.

"What are we if not history? Our lives are long and full of experience. We yearn for more and more experience, more knowledge, more joy, every moment that we live. But once it is lived, it is gone. What would we be if we could

Hotlinks

Alternatime
tinyurl.com/hisalt

Historical and Cultural Contexts
learner.org/interactives/historical

History Wizard
historywiz.com

Internet History Sourcebook Project
www.fordham.edu/halsall

History

not remember, could not live, over and over, in a past moment? Why would we yearn for more if we could not remember anything before? We all wish to believe that we are living for today and looking toward the future, but in fact we spend most of our time in the past. The history of us, our personal history, our cultural or intellectual or geological history are integral parts of why we live and hope and dream.

"To study history is to take the extra step from simply remembering and appreciating to trying to understand what came before. Perhaps we will make better choices. In any case, it is pure pleasure when it is felt as a precious personal memory. This is what I feel.

"When I find an old turn-of-the-century book in which Bobby has written, 'I love Susie,' I believe I can feel what Bobby felt when he scribbled those words. When I walk along a battlefield or a historic way, or in one of those old houses, I half expect those who strode through, so long before, to turn the corner and offer to talk with me awhile. I believe I feel as they felt when they were there, and I am stronger and more comfortable with my being because of that feeling.

"We cannot study the future, and the present changes too fast to lend itself to anything more than criticism. The past is all we truly own and are capable of understanding. It is everything we are."

Studying history also provides children a connection with the larger world around them. For Colorado homeschooler Cheryl Lemily, it's one of the best things about educating her kids. She says she loves when her kids really "get" a topic she's studying with them. "We were recently studying the Revolutionary War," she says. "After watching some DVDs and reading some books on the subject, my oldest son and I began exploring the Internet for information. We came across a name he recognized from the DVDs (Phillis Wheatley), and my son started jumping up and down pointing at the screen shouting 'Oh, oh, I know her!' I couldn't believe how excited he was. This is a child who rarely gets excited about anything (except video games). Also, my then four-year-old was in the restroom at a local restaurant when he began rambling on about George Washington. Tears instantly welled up in my eyes as I said,

'You do listen, you really do!' He said matter-of-factly, 'Of course, Mommy.' He never actually sat down with us when we were doing our study, but was always within earshot. I never knew he was listening."

In this chapter, you'll be introduced to American history, the American West, ancient and medieval history, family history, modern American history, the history of religious education, state history, and world history.

First, though, are some great tools for teaching history from multiple eras.

Alternatime   tinyurl.com/hisalt

A very large collection of timelines of history, science, arts and literature, pop culture, and science fiction. How large is it? There are four timelines covering recent Iraq history, and three covering the Great Depression.

BBC: History   bbc.co.uk/history

Let the BBC tell you about all of history—ancient and modern—from a British perspective. The Greeks, Romans, Egyptians, Vikings, people of the Indian subcontinent, and Anglo-Saxons are explored. There's so much here one hardly knows where to begin. Documents, essays, videos, timelines . . . Oh, just go take a look. It's wonderful!

Best of History Websites   besthistorysites.net

Annotated lists of links to hundreds of history lesson plans, teacher guides, activities, games, and quizzes. Link categories: prehistory, ancient/Biblical, medieval, American, early modern Europe, World War II, art, oral, maps, lesson plans, games, and research.

Dynamo's History for the Home
bbc.co.uk/education/dynamo/history

History fun and games from the BBC for younger learners. Find out how people lived a hundred years ago. Music, animations, and more will entertain.

On History

History is philosophy learned from examples.

—Thucydides, Greek historian

History

Generations in History   tinyurl.com/genhist

Do you cringe when your children ask what life was like before television? Whether you remember Lincoln? Although it's part of a commercial site, this particular page is helpful in teaching your children how to get a sense of historical perspective—even if it does get surprisingly unhelpful at the end.

Historical and Cultural Contexts   learner.org/interactives/historical

Become a document detective! Use your sleuthing skills. Figure out when and where historical events took place by examining primary sources and making an educated guess to pinpoint them on a map and timeline. Test your document expertise and analytical skills by answering questions.

History Activities & Crafts   abookintime.com

This site is primarily about reading recommendations for teaching history, but click the Crafts link at the top of the page for access to resources for "American" crafts and "world" crafts to supplement your lessons.

History & Government   tinyurl.com/hisgov

Award-winning websites that teach history and social studies subjects such as world and U.S. history, law, and politics.

History Lessons and Activities   easyfunschool.com/IndexHistory.html

What makes this site so much fun is the suggestions for activities that bring history alive. Plan a Sumerian feast, engage in some good ol' Egyptian brickmaking, or create a Greek fresco. That's some fine learnin'.

History/Social Studies Forms   tinyurl.com/hisfor

Printable forms and worksheets for everything historical, from the ancient world to the Great Depression.

History Toolkit   dohistory.org/on_your_own/toolkit

The How to Create a Timeline link is just one of many useful tools at this site for amateur historians who want to contribute to the making of history. The Step-by-Step Guide to Oral History is also a treasure chest of good advice.

History Wizard   historywiz.com

This award-winning site is rich with multimedia and text to teach every period and place. The site is divided into three main categories—Ancient, Medieval, and Modern—each of which contains hundreds of resources.

Internet History Sourcebook Project   www.fordham.edu/halsall

A nicely organized collection of historical texts, some of which are actually hosted here but most of which are links to other hosts. These are transcripts of primary source documents, making them fairly reliable as a research source. Ancient, medieval, and modern history are thoroughly addressed.

Kids LearnOutLoud   kids.learnoutloud.com/Kids-Free-Stuff

"I have a dream." "Give me liberty or give me death." Find here free podcasts and audio and video resources for kids and teens. The history podcasts are a good resource, but many of the other resources on this site—literature, arts, social science, and others—are also historical in nature. Orson Welles and The Mercury Theatre, for example, will delight students of modern history.

Our Timelines   tinyurl.com/tlunit

A unit-study idea involving creating a timeline as a history project. This homeschooling family made its own history timeline, and has the photos to prove it.

Printable Timelines and Worksheets
worksheets4teachers.com/timelines.php

All sorts of timeline makers, including a worksheet for deciding what to put on a timeline of your own life.

History

American History

America: Named after the Italian explorer Americus Vespucius.

Hotlinks

Activities at the Library of Congress
myloc.gov

Freedom: A History of US
pbs.org/wnet/historyofus

U.S. History Foldables
tinyurl.com/artfold

U.S. Presidents
tinyurl.com/hisusp

U.S. Time Periods
tinyurl.com/artust

YOUR KIDS KNOW the Revolutionary War came before the Civil War, right? But do they understand the social and economic forces that brought about each conflict? The most important part of learning history is not dates and names: it's reasons and responses.

A New Jersey history teacher, John J. Leddy Jr., explains why it's important that your children learn history: "Knowing your history won't ensure a salary increase or win you a prize, but it will add a new dimension to your life. You are no longer trapped in the present. Both the past and what may be likely to happen in the future are open to you. Reading history gives wings to your mind. Dates and places take on new importance.

"Imagine for a moment that you have found yourself standing in a field. To the unaware, it is a field like any other. But this field is very different to people who know their history; to them it is known as Gettysburg."

For Kentucky mom Jessica Murphy, studying local history during a family trip is just another fun aspect of homeschooling. "We took a field trip to a festival, Taste of Cincinnati. It is free to walk around but costs money to eat and try the different foods. There was a cooking demonstration that we watched. The festival was in downtown Cincinnati, so we walked around the area and talked about the buildings and what they were used for. We went to a

Americus Vespucius

The man we know as Amerigo Vespucci was taught at his boyhood home in Florence by his uncle, who schooled him in the humanities. When he was only twenty-five, the famous Italian family the Medicis hired him to be their spokesman to the king of France. In 1491 he went to Spain on Medici family business and became associated with the man who outfitted Columbus' ships. Five years later, Vespucci was managing the shipfitter's agency, and the following year he began making voyages of his own.

---

popular area called Fountain Square. We talked about Memorial Day and what it means to us as Americans and what the National Anthem and the American flag mean to our country."

She says she learned that planning is key to making field trips worthwhile. "I am not so good at planning things. We are a very spur-of-the-moment family, so it is a little difficult. We could have learned a lot more about the history of Cincinnati, Fountain Square, and The Taste of Cincinnati—why it was started, what the fountain means and the different parts, how old the buildings are and what they are made of, as well as the architecture, but that may be a little deep for a five- and seven-year old.

"In the future, I need to get more information before we go, if I can. I think they learn more that way than talking about it after the fact. The light goes off when they see it after they learn about it."

Raylene Hunt, a home-educating mom of two from Maine, advises studying history according to your child's timetable. "Follow your children's interests. Last year's history for my son was based on various early presidents. He was very interested in the biographies of these men, so that was our history."

This section covers the history and institutions of the United States of America. These resources give your children access to information on everything from the first European contact with North America to the early part of the twentieth century.

History

Colonial Williamsburg Freebie

Call 888-223-5080 for a free scenic calendar and information packet on Colonial Williamsburg.

You'll find related resources later in this chapter covering the American West, modern American history, and world history. You can also find information about American prehistory in the anthropology and multicultural education sections of Chapter 10. Also in that chapter is an entire course on civic duty, which might well be taught concurrently with the American history lessons.

Ready to teach American history? Here are your best bets:

1492 Exhibit   sunsite.unc.edu/expo/1492.exhibit/Intro.html
A history exhibit on Columbus's explorations from the Smithsonian. Lots of information here.

Activities at the Library of Congress   myloc.gov
The Library of Congress in Washington, D.C., sponsors this educational adventure through American history. Kids can play Knowledge Quest, a game that lets them examine the library's collection of historic objects, conquer challenges, and claim rewards. Regularly updated with new lesson plans and online activities.

American Advertising Galleries   scriptorium.lib.duke.edu/adaccess
Images and database information for over 7,000 advertisements printed in U.S. and Canadian newspapers and magazines between 1911 and 1955. Full-color magazine advertisements promote beauty and hygiene, radios and televisions, transportation, and even the war effort.

Comic History of the United States
librivox.org/comic-history-of-the-united-states-by-bill-nye
Bill Nye—not the Science Guy but rather, a nineteenth-century journalist—presents U.S. history from the first European settlement through the Civil War. This is an audio recording of the book.

Digital History   digitalhistory.uh.edu

Government- and university-sponsored site chock-full of great links. Includes an online U.S. history textbook, learning modules, classroom handouts and worksheets, learning activities, e-lectures, online virtual exhibits, and links to hundreds of primary sources and history reference materials.

Duke's Rare Book and Manuscript Library

library.duke.edu/specialcollections

Digitized collections of rare books, historical documents, photographs, and personal correspondence. Of particular note under the category Civil War Women is the series of Rose O'Neal Greenhow letters where she argues with William Seward and reports to Jefferson Davis her meeting with Robert E. Lee.

Fact Monster United States   factmonster.com/us.html

Child-sized articles on U.S. history, population, race and ethnicity, laws and other American Studies topics.

Freedom: A History of US

pbs.org/wnet/historyofus

Watch the 16-part series from PBS. Includes excellent supplementary materials, such as teaching guides, workshop videos, and biographies. You could spend days here and never see it all.

Home of Heroes   homeofheroes.com

Dedicated to the belief "that freedom is not free," author Doug Sterner spent two years writing 12,000 web pages for his Home of Heroes website. This compilation commemorates the soldiers, sailors, and airmen who put other people first; who believed in something strongly enough to risk their lives.

Best Homeschooling Moment

My best homeschooling moments? My daughter got an A+ on her high school Constitution test; my son passed all his multiplication/division facts.

—Angela Petersen, homeschooling mom of two, Marseilles, Illinois

History

National Historic Landmarks   cr.nps.gov

A virtual tour of national historic landmarks. Web classes, lesson plans, and many more useful, educational tools. Sponsored by the National Park Service.

Primary Sources and Activities   archives.gov/education/lessons

A collection of fascinating lesson plans on American history from the Constitutional Convention to Watergate and beyond. Produced by the National Archives and Records Administration.

RadioLovers   radiolovers.com

Before the Internet, before television, this is how the great-grandparents got their media fix. Listen to hundreds of old-time radio programs and turn on your imagination. Comedies, dramas, mysteries, variety shows, westerns, music, and more. The radio programs your kids might love: the sci-fi/superhero tales of Batman, Buck Rogers, Flash Gordon, Frankenstein, and others.

Teaching with Historic Places   cr.nps.gov/nr/twhp

Properties listed in the National Park Service's National Register of Historic Places enliven history, social studies, geography, civics, and other subjects. Create your own lessons, or use on-site lessons to educate your kids of middle-school age.

Field Tripping

We would like to go to Monticello later this school year to learn more about Thomas Jefferson.

—Angela Jones, stay-at-homeschooling mom of two, Dry Fork, Virginia

Today in History   memory.loc.gov/ammem/today

Each day provides multiple history lessons, with old pictures, additional links, and explanations of important historical events from the Library of Congress. Make it your homepage.

U.S. History Foldables   tinyurl.com/artfold

History lapbooks with photos of how they're assembled. These printables cover essential knowledge for U.S. history to 1877. Print and play.

U.S. Presidents   tinyurl.com/hisusp

Scholastic publishes this collection of articles, biographies, and speeches designed for primary- and middle-school ages. Very readable. The articles ask questions such as Can a President Be Too Strong? and What Makes a Great President?

U.S. Time Periods   tinyurl.com/artust

Hundreds of free resources for teaching history, courtesy of the U.S. government. Posters, sound recordings, poetry, artwork, and much more. A real treasure.

American West

WHY IS THE American West a separate section in this book? Much of early American history focuses on the East Coast. From Plymouth Rock to the War Between the States, the bulk of the geographical United States was unexplored.

If that had been the end of it, the United States and Canada would both be bit players on the world stage. It was the opening of the West, and the transcontinental contact, that made the two North American countries so powerful. That, and the attitude that developed concurrently with the Westward expansion, combined to make the North American bloc of Canada and the United States the most potent political and military force in world history.

East Coasters, Midwesterners, Mountain Westers, or West Coasters, your children are affected by the Westward expansion.

Are you prepared to help your children appreciate their great Western heritage? Use these excellent online resources to teach your kids about the opening of the West. Happy trails!

West: From the Latin *vesper* (evening). The direction in which the sun appears to set.

Hotlinks

An Uncommon Mission
www.kn.sbc.com/wired/
mission

Legends of America
legendsofamerica.com

Things to Do at Home
americanhistory.si.edu/
kids/athome.cfm

History

History

Oregon Trail Freebie

Get a free educational resource guide from the National Historic Oregon Trail Interpretive Center. Call 541-523-1843, or order from **tinyurl.com/bl6cjt.**

An Uncommon Mission
www.kn.sbc.com/wired/mission

The history of each of the California Missions as depicted in the art and words of a traveling priest. Each mission page is illustrated with artwork, has historical information, and gives additional resources.

Laura's Prairie House   laurasprairiehouse.com

Fun activities that supplement the Little House books. Make a corn-husk doll, and learn how the pioneers used plants for food and medicine. An affectionate page about Laura Ingalls Wilder, pioneers, and the Westward expansion.

Legends of America   legendsofamerica.com

A well-collected and well-categorized group of links to Native American resources, the Old West, ghost towns, vintage photos, and just plain American history. Enjoy the forums where visitors share ghost stories and legends.

Lewis and Clark Base Camp   nationalgeographic.com/lewisclark

Kids can travel westward across America with Lewis and Clark in this online exploration. Or see gorgeous photographs of expedition sites taken by photographers from National Geographic.

Little House Lapbooks   lapbooklessons.ning.com/LittleHouse

Beautifully rendered lapbook to supplement Laura Ingalls Wilder's *Little House in the Big Woods* book. Watch the video for an inspiring lesson on lapbooking and literature.

Mormon Trail   lds.org/gospellibrary/pioneer

Travel all 1,300 miles of the Mormon Pioneer Trail beginning in Nauvoo, Illinois. Each stop along the trail contains artwork, historical information, and related journal entries from those who made the journey.

New Perspectives on the West   pbs.org/weta/thewest

Study guide to supplement the PBS documentary series. Includes lesson plans, biographies, old-timey maps, an interactive timeline, and transcribed documents. Fascinating. Worth visiting with or without watching the actual documentary, which may be available at your local library.

Oregon Trail   isu.edu/~trinmich/oregontrail.html

Diaries and memoirs are just part of the story of the largest corridor to the western United States, the 2,000-mile Oregon Trail. See what the pioneers lived through, and hear what modern historians have to say.

The Gold Rush   pbs.org/wgbh/amex/goldrush

The 1849 Gold Rush inspired more than just the naming of a football team. It impelled a mass migration across a continent. This PBS report documents the stories and struggles of the first forty-niners.

Things to Do at Home
americanhistory.si.edu/kids/athome.cfm

Track the buffalo or build a sod house, in two of the many activities on this site. Each of these resources is very in-depth, and would make a good foundation for a full unit study. Sponsored by the Smithsonian's National Museum of American History.

Trailblazers   trailblazers101.com

Though Lewis and Clark get the credit for being the first non–Native Americans to open the West, it was earlier explorers and fur traders who made the initial inroads. Read the full story, with illustrations, here.

Best Homeschooling Moment

When we were camping we went to historical grounds that contained part of the original Oregon Trail. We walked grounds that original settlers and Native American Indians walked. At the end of the week with no TV, no computer, no radio except to catch the weather, and no pool or playground, you might think we would be going crazy. It was the best week ever. We weren't ready to come home. We learned so much as a family that week. Homeschool is not just for kids anymore!

—Melinda Penberthy, homeschooling mom learning as she teaches, Pevely, Missouri

History

Ancient, Medieval, and Renaissance History

YOUR KIDS ARE sure to find something to love about ancient history. If it's not the heroic legends of Arthurian knights, it will be the plays and romance of the Renaissance.

Medieval: From the New Latin *medium aevum* (Middle Ages). The period from the collapse of the Roman Empire to the Renaissance.

This section covers world history, from 6,000-year-old Chinese civilization, through the Babylonian, Egyptian, and Israeli cultures, to the Greeks, the Romans, and the Mesoamericans. You can find related resources in the anthropology section of Chapter 10, which covers prehistory and archaeological findings, as well as in the world history section later in this chapter, which begins with medieval and Renaissance-era world history.

Following are some of the best educational resources on the Internet for teaching about ancient history, both near and far.

Ancient and Lost Civilizations

crystalinks.com/ancient.html

Impressive artwork accompanies the stories of the ancient world. It's an excellent source for most cultures, but in particular for ancient cultures ignored by most: Maori, Inuit, Clovis, Mesoamerican, and others.

Ancient Cultures: An Odyssey Through Time

differentways.org/services/mod_ancient.html

A lesson plan to help nurture the connection between today's students and the human cultural heritage. Uses various "wheels" (Wheel 1: Exploring What You Already Know) to accommodate individual learning styles. This resource is designed for the classroom, but because of its individuality, will work especially well in a homeschool setting.

Ancient Egypt Lesson Plans for Teachers

dia.org/education/egypt-teachers

Activities such as mixed media design using hieroglyphs will help your kids walk like an Egyptian. The Detroit Institute of Arts (DIA) provides a variety of cross-curricular activities for grades 4 through 8 based on the theme of Ancient Egypt. Includes math teacher-created plans.

Ancient Greece Resources   ancientgreece.com

The history, mythology, culture, and geography of the Hellenic world, taught with essays and a handful of charts.

Ancient History   ancienthistory.mrdonn.org/#ours

So much good stuff here, it's hard to find a starting place. Unit studies? Debates? Ancient myths? Just dive in.

Collapse   learner.org/interactives/collapse

Why do civilizations collapse? Explore the collapse of four ancient civilizations to discover lessons that might prevent our own collapse.

Early Modern Culture   eserver.org/emc

An electronic seminar—an online academic journal, really—containing works of art, college-level essays, and discussions of Renaissance studies. It may be over the heads of most teens, but the academic information is solid, and probably useful as background for parent instructors.

Exploring Ancient World Culture   eawc.evansville.edu

What makes this site so useful is the readings from ancient civilizations: Plato's *Crito* on the Greek page, *The Art of War* on the Chinese page, *The Papyrus of Ani* on the Egyptian page, and other documents of great civilizations.

History for Kids   historyforkids.org

Way too many advertisements, but the content is very, very good. Ancient history, with illustrations and photos, written at a child's level.

Hotlinks

Ancient History
ancienthistory.mrdonn
.org/#OURS

Collapse
learner.org/interactives/
collapse

Exploring Ancient World Culture
eawc.evansville.edu

History

The Families of the Gods   www.windows.ucar.edu

Visit any page on the site and from the menu bar at the bottom visit Myths or History & People to access illustrated history pages on ancient mythology and cultures. The Family Trees are particularly useful if you're confused by the complicated relationships of ancient mythical deities.

The History of the Peloponnesian War   tinyurl.com/hispel

A free audio recording of the Greek Thucydides classic.

Women in the Ancient World   womenintheancientworld.com

What kept grooms in the ancient world from changing their minds before marriage? That and other questions about the roles of men and women are answered on this site about the status, role, and daily life of women in the ancient civilizations of Egypt, Rome, Athens, Israel, and Babylonia.

Family History

Family: From the Latin *familia* (household). Those related to an individual by blood or marriage.

IS THERE A more important aspect of history than what your children can learn about their own family? Whether your ancestors were kings or paupers, there's a lesson in it for your children.

Genealogical research has come into its own over the past two years. Not only have technological advances changed the nature of archiving documents; online resources have also made it possible for large extended families to work together to conduct research and share information.

Our extended family gathers together one Sunday a month to work on genealogy, family histories, and scrapbooks. The younger kids play with their cousins and dads, and the women and older children sit around the table with scissors, rubber stamps, and adhesive to mount photos on scrapbook pages and compare genealogical research. Now that we have scanners and good-quality color printers, we even swap photos and print out copies on the spot.

This section on Family History includes resources for genealogy and personal history. If you are working across curricula, consider the possibility that genealogical research can teach technology, writing, reading, and foreign languages.

No matter how you view it—as an academic exercise or as a means for drawing families together—genealogy works.

All About Me Museum   tinyurl.com/hisaam

Personal history is a big part of family history. This unit study helps younger children complete a comprehensive project that help them see themselves as a living part of history

Capturing the Past   byub.org/capturingpast

Capturing oral histories is fun for the entire family. This site walks users through the four steps of interviewing family members.

Cyndi's List   cyndislist.com

The consummate resource for genealogical research. Bet you can't think of anything that's not here.

FamilySearch   familysearch.org

Not only is this the largest repository of family records anywhere in the world; it also provides a course in how to conduct family history research. H6911

FamilySearch Indexing   familysearchindexing.org

Interested in providing a bit of community service without ever leaving home? Perhaps you and your children would enjoy volunteering to extract and preserve historic documents. You'll find here a list of projects currently under way.

Getting Started   cyndislist.com/educate.htm

Part of the astonishing Cyndi's List, an index of tens of

Hotlinks

Capturing the Past
byub.org/capturingpast

FamilySearch
familysearch.org

Rootsweb
rootsweb.com

History

thousands of genealogy sites, this page explains how to get started on family history.

Guide to Family History Research
arkansasresearch.com/guideindex.htm

A how-to guide for getting started in the rewarding hobby of family research. The first page of this tutorial lists lots of reasons for looking into your own genealogy: medical, simple curiosity, preserve the past, find your ethnic heritage, and many others.

Oral History Guidelines   history.com/classroom/oralhistguidelines.pdf

From the History Channel, an 18-page handbook on conducting oral history interviews. It's probably a little formal for talking to Grandma, but interviewing is a basic life skill that transfers to many disciplines.

Personal Ancestral File   ldscatalog.com

From the Search box, type PAF, short for Personal Ancestral File—an incredible piece of software you can download and use for free. PAF tracks everything you could ever want to remember about your family: all the usual dates and locations information, of course, but also nearly unlimited space for photos, documents, and stories.

Plan a Family Reunion   tinyurl.com/hispfr

The best way to create a family history is to interview your relatives. And what better way to get those relatives together for an interview than to have a family reunion? Here are the seven steps to reuniting your extended family.

Rootsweb   rootsweb.com

Search the WorldConnect Project, where thousands of users have contributed genealogical information on some half a billion family names. So far. Somehow, you're related to someone on this database.

Scrapbook Journalizing   tinyurl.com/hisser

The writer says that even if she hasn't caught up the baby books, her kids always have an updated account of their lives. "Journalizing is an enjoyable way to develop a love for and mastery of writing, learn to read (pleasurable exposure to print, print and more print), and a record of self-discovery." Great advice for implementing a notebook-based curriculum.

The UnWritten library.thinkquest.org/C001313

Instructions for saving photo stories for the future. Let your kids collect old family photos, then print out the worksheets for the photo-story kit to turn photos into history.

Modern American History

STILL SHAKEN UP over 9/11? The Vietnam War before your time? What can you tell your kids about the Gulf War? If those subjects are tough, how will you teach them about the New Deal? The Depression? Prohibition? The Monroe Doctrine? Expansionism? From World War I to the present, these are the forces that shaped modern American life. Check out the following sites to improve your own knowledge and find teaching ideas and materials.

> **Modern:** From the Latin *modo* (just now). Of contemporary or recent origin.

A Nation Remembers time.com/time/911

A tribute to the heroes and victims of the 9/11 attacks. Photoessays and art describe the impact of that terrible day.

American Cultural History kclibrary.nhmccd.edu/decades.html

The twentieth century is all here, decade by decade. The site was prepared by a college reference librarian and includes short essays and photographs.

American Memory memory.loc.gov/ammem

From the Library of Congress, primary source materials—photographs and multimedia, mostly—on the history and culture of the United

History

States. Learn, for example, about the history of America's performing arts, advertising, military, and immigration, A teacher's link provides lesson plans and activities for teaching the materials.

Cold War Museum   coldwar.org

It wasn't all Elvis and moon landings. The Cold War defined politics and much of the world economy for nearly half a century. The Cold War museum documents it with teaching articles and activities.

Face to Face   itvs.org/facetoface/flash.html

Lessons that compare the internment of Japanese Americans after Pearl Harbor with the treatment of Arab and Muslim Americans after the tragedies of September 11. It opens with video interviews and transcripts. Students can explore these civil liberties issues through discussion, through becoming the enemy, and through artistic expression.

Fact Monster Timeline   factmonster.com/yearbyyear.html

Pick a year in the twentieth century, and learn about world and U.S. events, economics, sports, entertainment, achievements in science, and significant deaths that occurred that year. Very encyclopedic.

Famous Speeches   history.com/media.do

Churchill, Roosevelt, Kennedy . . . This video collection documents great speeches and historical moments in the twentieth and twenty-first centuries.

Hotlinks

A Nation Remembers
time.com/time/911

American Memory
memory.loc.gov/ammem

Famous Speeches
history.com/media.do

History News Network   hnn.us

A newsmagazine that seeks "to expose politicians who misrepresent history. To point out bogus analogies. To deflate beguiling myths. To remind Americans of the irony of history. To put events in context. To remind us all of the complexity of history."

History of Technology for Kids
www.fcc.gov/cgb/kidszone/history.html

The U.S. government started the Internet. It might as well

be the one to document its history. Written for children, this site contains interesting historical information about the Internet, as well as cell phones, cable, television, and other technologies. Click the links on the left to find answers to FAQs, as well as a very nice history of satellite technology.

New Deal Network   newdeal.feri.org

The New Deal was Roosevelt's answer to the Depression. It's still controversial, though this site—sponsored by the Roosevelt Institute—doesn't acknowledge it. Nevertheless, the archives and lessons here give kids a good understanding of the difficulties Americans faced in those black times. See, for example, the lesson plan entitled Dear Mrs. Roosevelt, which presents letters to the First Lady during the Great Depression.

The Authentic History Center   authentichistory.com

From the Civil War period to the present, artifacts and sounds from American popular culture. Consider, for example, the loveliness of Disco Barbie from the 1970s, or the Red Cross's Y2K pamphlet from the nineties.

Triangle Factory Fire   www.ilr.cornell.edu/trianglefire

The 1911 fire in the Triangle garment district of New York shocked a nation and changed the course of the Industrial Revolution. The Cornell University exhibition uses historical photos and articles to bring the tragedy home.

State History

I GREW UP in the Seattle area, and every year, on my birthday, my father took me out for a day to do anything I wanted to do. Nearly all my birthday trips involved a visit to downtown Seattle, where we would visit the farmers' market, walk to the piers on the waterfront, and best of all,

History

State: From the Latin *status* (condition). Political subdivision of a nation.

Hotlinks

America's Story
americaslibrary.gov

Perry-Castañeda Maps
www.lib.utexas.edu/
maps/histus.html

Postcards from America
postcardsfrom.com

Roadside America
roadsideamerica.com

take the tour of Seattle's historic underground, the first floor of the city that existed before fire consumed most of the wooden buildings in town.

Today you can ask me anything about Seattle history. Those childhood trips made me an expert, and as a result, I learned to love my hometown.

Terri Vitkovitsky from Camp Lejeune, North Carolina, also uses local sites to teach hands-on history. "Visit local monuments, statues, and historical markers. Could be the person who founded your city—perhaps a soldier who made a difference—sparks further exploration."

Perhaps your state requires you to teach your children local history. Or you may simply be fond of the place you live, and believe your kids are better off knowing about those who made it what it is today.

In either case, the Internet is ready to help. The following resources do a great job explaining the history, and in some cases the law and other information, for every state in the United States and in one case, for every province in Canada.

50 States Activities & Games   50states.mrdonn.org
History games, unit studies, and lessons about each of the states, from educator Mr. Donn.

50 State Quarters Program   usmint.gov/kids/coinnews/50sq
The U.S. Mint has released quarters for all fifty states. Learn their history—and other fascinating facts about each state. Free lesson plans suggest ways to teach state history using the coins.

America's Story   americaslibrary.gov
Discover the stories of America's past. Start with Explore the States for history of individual U.S. states. Then meet famous Americans or jump back in time with a brief timeline, and background information

Stonewall Jackson

Orphaned at a young age, Thomas Jonathan "Stonewall" Jackson had little formal education. He grew up in the homes of relatives and, in 1842, received his appointment to West Point. He did poorly at first, but he eventually graduated and gained his commission as a second lieutenant in the Army. It was during the Mexican War that he first met General Robert E. Lee, the future commander of the Confederate Armies, and his noteworthy military future was set. Prior to his orders to return to the military, the future Civil War hero taught natural philosophy at Virginia Military Institute.

explaining each element of the timeline. Children in grades 3 through 8 will enjoy the site.

Canadian History   collectionscanada.gc.ca/caninfo/ep097.htm

It's provinces, not states, but the history's just as interesting. This government-sponsored site begins with historical information for the entire nation, but page down to find provincial histories and resources. Under British Columbia History, for example, the Cariboo Gold Rush link takes kids on a gold-mining expedition to an old mining town, with photos and stories.

Our 50 Great States   homeschooling.about.com/c/ec/1.htm

An email course, where you'll receive email lessons, at the rate of two per week, about each of the states from Delaware to Hawaii, in order of their admission to the Union.

Perry-Castañeda Historical Map Collection
lib.utexas.edu/maps/histus.html

Historical maps of U.S. states and territories show migration, battles, Indian tribal areas, and early boundaries.

History

Postcards from America   postcardsfrom.com

From each state: five postcards and commentaries, from a family that visited every state over the course of a year and wrote postcards to share their travels. Click the Teachers link for activities and educational ideas.

Roadside America   roadsideamerica.com

Mostly historic, always fun. For each U.S. state and Canadian province, find crazy roadside attractions and learn about legendary phenomena such as the Jersey Devil, Salt Lake's Gravity Hill, where your car rolls *up* the hill, and the Big Teepees found across the western states.

State and Local Government on the Net   statelocalgov.net

Government-sponsored sites for every state and territory, as well as most of the counties and cities. The categories with red triangles are the ones without advertising.

State Unit Studies   tinyurl.com/histate

Facts and information about every state. Click the U.S. map for the state of your choice, and learn about its capital and geography.

The US 50   theus50.com

Articles about the history of each state, combined with facts, tourist attractions, and other good information.

US State Unit Studies   easyfunschool.com/IndexStateUnits.html

Unit studies teach state history across the curriculum. Includes suggestions for building mini-museums, creating a portfolio, and other good educational activities.

History

World History

HOW DID I teach my kids about the history of the world? I packed them up and moved them to China.

You may want to pursue a different route.

Whatever you teach them of world history, you will make them better, and better-educated, people.

Scott Schickram is an avocational historian in Houston. He believes an understanding of world history is critical to becoming an educated, contributing member of society. "My understanding of history helps me understand current events," he says. "But the most important benefit is the appreciation of what a great nation we live in here in the United States."

He suggests that one of the most interesting ways to learn history is to get to know great historical figures. "In preparation for the future, I think high school students should study biographies of famous people. History is really a history of people, not just dates. By reading the biographies of Washington or Franklin, I've learned to appreciate the events they helped shape. It also made me realize they were human beings like myself. Often their problems were far worse than any I face."

One homeschooling mom of four from the Jacaranda Tree Learning Co-operative in Hawkes Bay, New Zealand, says studying history ought to be an ongoing enterprise. "I have heard it said that children ought to cover history four times in their education, and it bears consideration. Initially, it should be covered chronologically from beginning to end to provide a framework for detailed studies later.

"It need not be onerous either—what about audio timelines, living books, documentaries, interviewing others, museum visits . . . ?"

The following resources introduce the history and institutions of world civilizations. (See also the related sec-

World: From the Old English *woruld* (human existence). All matters related to the affairs of the human race.

Hotlinks

Electronic Passport
mrdowling.com

History For Kids
kidspast.com

School History
schoolhistory.co.uk

History

tions on social issues, minority education, and anthropology in Chapter 10.)

BBC History   tinyurl.com/hisbbc

Animated lessons for a number of world cultures—the Iron Age Celts, Vikings, the Indus Valley, and many more.

Castles on the Web   castlesontheweb.com

One mom writes: "Wonderful site to build a unit study around; take your pick of topics: English history, medieval times, King Arthur, and more. This site has links, photos, free greeting cards, tours, book lists, medieval studies, and heraldry. It's all to do with castles. It even has a question-and-answer section and a list of contacts for vacationing in castles—one can only dream!"

Electronic Passport   mrdowling.com

Short articles with great illustrations on many, many aspects of world history. Start with time and space, and continue through prehistory all the way to the World Wars. For middle-school ages.

History for Kids   kidspast.com

A graphics-heavy site full of fun games, quotes from important people in history, and best of all, twenty well-illustrated lessons in ancient and modern world history. For younger and middle-grade kids.

Hyper History   tinyurl.com/hishyp

Five thousand years of history in one pretty picture. See how civilization developed from the Sumerians to World War II and beyond.

Medieval England   tinyurl.com/hisorb

A nine-chapter text on English history. Covers medieval British history from the fall of Britain to the War of the Roses.

Misconceptions About the Middle Ages   tinyurl.com/hismiss

A collection of articles disputing popular myths about the Dark Ages. Were you aware, for example, that far from being hacks, medieval physicians shared the belief of modern doctors that many diseases were caused by immoderate living?

PPST World History   worldhistory.pppst.com

PowerPoint presentations that cross wide swaths of world history. Includes collections of presentations such as the Byzantine Empire, the Anglo-Saxons, the Industrial Revolution, and Terrorism.

School History   schoolhistory.co.uk

World history taught from an English perspective. But every lesson plan is replete with activities, essays, links, and writing tasks. Downloadable PowerPoint presentations, worksheets, and online quizzes are available with many lessons.

The Holocaust and World War II   tinyurl.com/hishol

Anne Frank brought a human face to the horror of the Holocaust. This Scholastic series explores her life and larger questions about the Holocaust with a collection of articles aimed at primary- and middle-school ages. Very readable.

The Western Tradition   learner.org/resources/series58.html

Annenberg presents Western history in video form. This series includes 52 half-hour programs, beginning with the dawn of history and covering the scope of Western civilization.

World History   studystack.com/category-33

Online flashcards—including the space to build your own—that reinforce the study of world history. Some of the card stacks here include Ancient Persia facts, Mayans-Aztecs-Incas, and the Russian Revolution. Uses traditional flashcard format, as well as games and other tools for teaching.

History

Chapter 9

Music Marathon

I SPENT TEN years in piano lessons. And practiced for half an hour a week.

During my lesson.

I don't know why my mother paid for this exercise in futility.

It wasn't until I became an adult and had to play the piano for Sunday school that I actually learned to play. I'll never get an invitation to play Carnegie Hall, but I can manage to get through the sheet music without too much trouble. I hope that modest ability—and the fact that my husband is a musical genius—qualifies us to teach music.

Well, okay . . . And also the fact that we have access to so many good resources for teaching music, including musicians in our community and on the Internet who are unfailingly generous with advice and suggestions.

Shelly and Ryan Simmons are among them. At the time of our interview, Shelly was the music cataloger at the University of California at San Diego and a student in music psychology. Ryan played associate principal bassoon in the San Diego Symphony. They offer some good advice to parents who are looking for ways to teach their children to appreciate music: "Our best recommendation is for parents to realize that everyone can be a musician, and everyone can

Hotlinks

Classics for Kids
classicsforkids.com

Free Children's Music
freekidsmusic.com

Musical Mysteries
tinyurl.com/musbee

Science of Music
exploratorium.edu/
music

sing. The reason people think they can't do these things is that they feel there is a level of education or expertise needed to even try.

"Start young children off with simple rhythm exercises: clapping to the beat on the radio or CDs, using different hands for different beats, learning to count with the rhythms. Anyone can do this. There are great rhythm instruments to be had at any local music store: blocks, fish, sanding blocks, and so on. Every local guitar and drum music shop has these rhythm instruments, and for under $30, a parent can get one lesson in their use if absolutely necessary. Children through elementary school can use these as accessories to the radio, piano, CDs, or other music.

"Another extremely easy but effective (and fun) exercise is for the parent or teacher to either play piano or put on a classical, jazz, or other music recording and have the children dance to the music. A great example is choosing ballet music and having the kids pretend they are butterflies emerging from cocoons, or trees in the wind.

"These simple yet effective exercises are both fun and imaginative, and allow the participants to feel that they are interpreting and making music. This then should be followed by age-appropriate music lessons with a local professional, if desired—piano lessons being the most beneficial."

Ryan and Shelly endorse the resources at the Music Educators National Conference (**menc.org**) for parents and other educators of children. They also recommend a site called Music Games (**bobchilds.co.uk/mtrs/games.htm**) as a helpful resource for music teachers.

Those are only the beginning of the dozens of great resources available for free to parents who are teaching music. Sarah Bull, who homeschools in Wisconsin, uses community resources to teach music. "We do music at the park or squares. Several of the communities in our area have one concert per week or month that offers free entertainment from jazz and rock 'n' roll to symphonies. They usually last about an hour, and are great for teaching our children culture, music, and fine arts."

Homeschoolers find lots of novel ways to incorporate music education into their curriculum. Kentucky mom Jessica Murphy uses music to encourage fitness in her kids. "We turn on the radio or get out the tambourines and march or jump around. This is great, fun exercise, too; we have dance competitions even though we have no formal dance training. It's fun, and it covers PE, too! My seven-year-old likes to make up songs and sing, so I have been trying to get her to write them down. As soon as we can get a keyboard and learn to play, we will try to put them to music."

In this chapter, you'll be introduced to music appreciation, theory, musicianship, and vocal music.

We start, though, with some general tools for teaching music.

Arts   tinyurl.com/musdis

A collection of worksheets (with solutions) from Discovery School. Most cover music studies, but there are also a couple of fun Theatre worksheets.

Classics for Kids   classicsforkids.com

Listen to radio programs, learn about composers, play music games, and use lesson plans to teach children all about classical music. Designed for elementary ages, with impressive graphics and very useful teaching resources.

Energy in the Air   library.thinkquest.org/5116

Sounds from the orchestra. This site explains how sound is made and what it looks like when it is recorded.

Free Children's Music   freekidsmusic.com

Just fun, fun, fun songs for children. High-quality tunes—better than most of the music they hear on children's television—that will have your kids snapping their fingers and singing along.

Learn2 Read Music   tinyurl.com/mustut

An eight-part tutorial, with illustrations, that teaches notes, clefs, where notes fall on the keyboard, time signatures, and all the other basics of reading music.

Lesson Plans for Music   lessonplanspage.com/Music.htm

Hundreds of lesson plans, organized by grade level. Lessons are submitted by classroom teachers, but most can be adapted to home-schooling.

Music Education at DataDragon   datadragon.com/education

A basic introduction to reading music, musical genres, and music history.

Music Lesson Plans   tinyurl.com/musles

Lessons in music for grades K through 12. Lessons such as I'll Be Bach and Pure Funk teach many musical styles.

Music Through the Ages   music.pppst.com

Hundreds of PowerPoint presentations that supplement your music lessons. Covers the entire spectrum of music instruction, with sections on subjects such as Musicians, Musical Instruments, and Music Journal Topics—and that's just the beginning.

Musical Mysteries   tinyurl.com/musbee

This Irish site is filled with games and educational fun that teach concepts such as sound, rhythm, and mood. Learn, too, about a range of orchestral instruments.

Performing Arts Encyclopedia   loc.gov/performingarts

Lots of podcasts of lectures and performances sponsored by the Library of Congress. Find here digitized items from the collections of scores, sheet music, audio recordings, films, photographs, and other materials.

Science of Music   exploratorium.edu/music

Do your kids know why their voices sound so great in the shower? How opera singers manage to sustain a note so long? The science of music explains it all with online exhibits, movies, and questions.

Music

Using Music in the Classroom   tinyurl.com/muscla
Research-based evidence that music is an aid to learning. Includes suggestions for using sound as an aid to teaching.

Music Appreciation

IN OUR HOME, Dad is the music nut. There seems to be nothing he doesn't know, and there are few instruments he doesn't play, so the kids get much of their musical education just through osmosis.

Cheryl Northrup is a bit more focused. "The arts have a high priority in our homeschool," says the homeschooling mother of seven from Lamar, Colorado. "When we lived in Denver, we could get tickets from the public schools to go to ballets, symphonies, plays, and opera, all for six dollars or less.

"Now that we're in a small town, we have taken our children, from a very young age, to community concerts and high-school performances. The quality of these programs can be outstanding, especially in the larger schools. I found, though, that in the cities you had to be more careful about the play being produced. The public schools there are much less conservative than here.

"To prepare for these experiences, we read the stories of the opera or ballet, and sometimes listen to some of the music ahead of time.

"We don't forbid any kind of music in our home except that with explicit lyrics; however, the children are very aware of what we approve of and don't. They all have personal copies of good classical music, so there is always an option. One son in particular fell in love with Gilbert and Sullivan, so I buy those for him whenever I find one I can afford. In addition, all six living children have had lessons in various instruments, including piano, violin, and bassoon."

Homeschooler Ann M. Glass from Everson, Washington,

Appreciate:
From the Latin *appretiare* (to appraise). To understand the value or worth of a thing.

has found that music has a soothing effect on her two children. She keeps her home filled with the sounds of music: "We play classical quietly in the background during school, and everything else—gospel, jazz, children's, band, and more—is played at all other times."

Ann sometimes takes her sons to concerts as well. To prepare them for the experience, they spend time in advance of the event discussing and listening to the type of music they'll hear at the concert. She is also teaching them concert etiquette and has five rules for behavior during concerts:

- Sit quietly with hands and feet to yourself. Listen and learn.
- Stay in one place without standing up.
- Follow the action with your eyes.
- Help others by setting a good example.
- Show appreciation with applause, not yelling or shouting.

Has this experience had any impact on her boys' artistic or musical ability? "Yes!" she says. "My five-year-old tends to be a bull in a china shop, a one-man demolition squad. But he is extremely gentle with musical instruments. He handles them with reverence and awe! He has developed good timing and has a good sense of rhythm. He is looking forward to beginning piano lessons when he can read and write."

All the education has paid off with her older son as well. "My seven-year-old was at the dentist listening to the music and exclaimed that it was Mozart. I'm still trying to convince the dentist that the child is not a prodigy! Both boys can listen to a piece of music and tell you something about it: the composer, the style of music, and the instruments used."

With the following helpful online resources, your chil-

Hotlinks

Essentials of Music
essentialsofmusic.com

Exploring the World of Music Videos
learner.org/resources/
series105.html

Music Teacher's Resource Site
mtrs.co.uk

Sound Reasoning
cnx.org/content/col10214

Musically Appreciated

Q: An unfortunate man went to work in a mine and, on his first day, fell down a mine shaft. When he finally hit the bottom, what musical note was he singing?
A: A-flat minor, of course!

dren can be musical "prodigies" as well. Here's a short course on music appreciation that will soon have them listening to and analyzing music and composers, and understanding music history:

Classical Composers' Archive

spight.physics.unlv.edu/picgalr2.html

An archive of biographies sorted by nation, year of birth, and other criteria. The best element of this resource is the clickable timeline, where you can see when all the classic composers lived, in chronological order.

Dismuke's Virtual Talking Machine   dismuke.org

Wonderful recordings of vintage music, supplemented by a radio program and a blog that teaches children to appreciate early-twentieth-century music.

Essentials of Music   essentialsofmusic.com

Basic information about classical music. This site includes information on musical eras, biographies of composers, a glossary, and many audio clips.

Exploring the World of Music Videos

learner.org/resources/series105.html

A large collection of educational videos that teach music appreciation. One, for example, discusses the transformative power of music. Others demonstrate rhythm, melody, and timbre. From the Annenberg CPB series.

Jazz for Young People   tinyurl.com/musjaz

Several lessons, with printables and audio clips, that teach the history of jazz. Satchmo's "Hello Dolly" is not to be missed.

mFiles   mfiles.co.uk

More than just downloadable music, this site features articles about and songs by modern and classical composers such as Bach and

Beethoven, along with sheet music and audio files. The moving cursor lets you follow along with the sheet music as you hear the song played.

Music Appreciation   tinyurl.com/musapp

Oklahoma Homeschooler program presents a free unit study incorporating a music notebook, biographies of famous musicians, research on famous composers, and the relationship between math and music.

Music Teacher's Resource Site   mtrs.co.uk

Great free resources for teaching music to kids ages four to sixteen. Musical rounds, tips for teaching, and really good lesson plans.

NEA Jazz in the Schools   neajazzintheschools.org

Jazz is the quintessential American music form, and kids love hearing it. Here's the key to teaching it. Amazing step-by-step online lesson plans with teaching tips, videos, student activities, and links.

Noisy Learning   cnx.org/content/col10222

An online course with 11 loud but fun music education lessons that teach younger children about sound, rhythm, and culture. The first lesson, "Percussion Fast and Cheap," has children using their own bodies as percussion instruments: hand claps, foot stomps, tongue clicks, and more.

Online Music Encyclopedia   library.thinkquest.org/10400

Biographies of well-known composers and well-illustrated articles describing various musical instruments. You'll also find a pretty good collection of MIDI files.

Silver Burdett Making Music Series   sbgmusic.com/html/teacher

Everything there is to know about teaching music at the elementary level: two different scope-and-sequence recommendations, entire scripts for children's musicals, and best of all, reference articles that teach about instruments, composers, cultures, history, musical styles, and well-known performers. Such fun.

Music

Sound Reasoning   cnx.org/content/col10214

A full-scale music appreciation course for older learners. Incredibly in-depth, with audio examples of the principles being taught. This one is very, very good.

Stand Up and Sing   tinyurl.com/mussta

For middle- and high-school ages, this Library of Congress site uses lyrics and images of popular sheet music to show how music reflects the political, social, and economic conditions existing during a particular period of time—in this case, the era of industrialization and reform in the United States.

Music Theory

I WAS ASTOUNDED to discover that when he was a Beatle, Paul McCartney couldn't read music. I suppose good looks, attitude, innate talent, and luck must compensate for other failings! For the rest of us—those who'll never find work as "the cute one"—the musical world is more approachable when we're better educated.

To call themselves educated, your kids really do need to know at least the basics of musical notation. They should know what an octave is. They should understand the difference between a treble and a bass clef. They should recognize a quarter note, and know how many beats in a measure. They should be able to find middle C on a sheet of music and on a piano. And they should be able to conduct a simple song in 4/4 time.

If their aspirations are somewhat higher, they'll certainly be better off if they learn to read, compose, and improvise music.

This section presents resources for teaching your children the basics of reading, composing, improvising, and notating music. They'll learn scales, signatures, and other elements of the language of music. Your children might not compose the

Theory: From the Greek Greek *theōriā* (contemplate, look at, consider). To develop a conception or mental framework for understanding a subject.

next "Hey, Jude," but they might—at least—be able to read it when someone else does!

An Online Course in Songwriting   euronet.nl/users/menke/songs.html

A songwriter's handbook. The page is unattractive, but the material is very well written. Learn about writing music and lyrics from a Dutch guitarist/songwriter.

Cyberfret   cyberfret.com/composition

The free guitar lessons are a bonus, but click the Theory and Composition links on the left for in-depth lessons on music theory, songwriting, and ear training for guitarists.

G Major Music Theory   gmajormusictheory.org

Not just free sheet music, though there's plenty of that. It's everything a child—or adult—needs to know to be music-literate. Chapter one of the Music Theory Workbooks begins with the keyboard and treble clef. The final chapter of the Harmonic Dictation section uses Verdi's "Grand March" from *Aida* to teach the secondary dominant chord progression.

Introduction to Music Theory   cnx.org/content/col10208

A 10-lesson course in music theory. Learn where octaves come from (it's a frequency thing). Play an ear training game. Discover how to form chords. Very good information for middle- and high-school-aged musicians.

Music Theory   musictheory.net

An animated course in music theory. The first lessons teach the basics of staffs, measures, and time signatures. The advanced lessons delve into complex subjects such as inverted triads and Neapolitan chords. Includes "trainers" to teach listeners to distinguish types of chords and intervals.

Hotlinks

G Major Music Theory
gmajormusictheory.org

Introduction to Music Theory
cnx.org/content/col10208

Music Theory
musictheory.net

Online Music Theory Tutor
childrensmusicworkshop
.com/musictheory

Music Theory for Songwriters   chordmaps.com

Songwriters have to understand the language of music in order to compose worthwhile melodies and lyrics. This site approaches music as a parallel to language, and in 16 lessons, helps kids understand the basics of music composition.

Music Theory I   mibac.com/Pages/Theory/Main_Theory.html

Simple, well-diagrammed explanations of dozens of theoretical principles, listed in order from simple to difficult. Click the Music Theory II link (top left) for concepts that are even more advanced.

Online Music Theory Tutor

childrensmusicworkshop.com/musictheory

These music theory lessons begin with simple staff, clef, and ledger line tutorials, and continue through building and using advanced chords, triads, and inversions. Other features include trainers and utilities such as a staff paper generator and a chord calculator.

Special Subjects in Music Theory   cnx.org/content/col10220

This is the fourth theory course from Connexions. Teaches advanced concepts such as transposition and syncopation, as well as the scales used in non-Western music. For grade 8 and older.

Theory Flashcards   musicards.net

Customize your own music flashcards to teach notes, key signatures, intervals, triads, and much more. Students can roll their mouse pointer over a flashcard to see the correct answer.

Theory on the Web   smu.edu/totw/toc.htm

An online theory course that moves rapidly from the basics to fairly advanced theory. By the eighteenth lesson, users will understand how to write inverted chords, parts, and nonchord tones. Whew. The site is illustrated with images and MIDI files. It's sponsored by Southern Methodist University.

Wolfgang Amadeus Mozart

Perhaps the most famously homeschooled student in all the world is Mozart, the remarkable child prodigy who was taught by his father. When he was just four years old, Mozart was picking out chords and playing short pieces on the harpsichord. By the age of five, he was composing concertos and playing at the Bavarian court in Munich. Shortly after that, he was performing in Vienna and enjoying the beginnings of his worldwide fame as a composer and musician.

The Basic Elements of Music   cnx.org/content/col10218

This, the first of four Connexions music theory courses, teaches early elementary students about rhythm, pitch, and the textures of music.

Understanding Basic Music Theory   cnx.org/content/col10363

The third of four music theory courses from the Connexions site, this one teaches common notation, along with an introduction to the physics behind music theory.

Musicianship

CHILDREN ARE natural musicians.

Many mothers swear that their children respond to music even before they're born.

Shortly after her birth, my youngest daughter would sometimes be weeping with all the usual frustrations of babyhood, but when someone would begin playing soft piano music, she'd immediately stop and listen, rapt, to every note.

The moment children gain control over their little hands and feet, they begin to use floors, pans, tables, and cabinets as percussion instruments. And eventually every instrument in

Instrument: From the Latin *instrumentum* (tool, implement). A device for creating or performing music.

the house gets played—no matter how badly—by any child who has access.

Teaching children to play music is mostly a matter of allowing their natural fascination to find a disciplined course. The following resources will go far in helping you direct that course. Here are some of the best Internet sites for teaching children to play musical instruments. These sites focus on technique, and include many resources for free sheet music.

Chordie   chordie.com

For guitar players and vocalists, a massive collection of guitar tabs, guitar chords, and song lyrics, most of which are submitted by users.

Drum Lessons Database   drumsdatabase.com

Drum lessons with inspirational videos—you must watch the hip-hop drummers, for example—and giveaways. The database of lessons is immense and includes every conceivable style.

Easy Music Lessons   easymusiclessons.com

Click the Free Lessons link on the left for online video drum, bass, and guitar lessons. These are basic, of course, but they provide a great introduction to technique.

Hotlinks

Easy Music Lessons
easymusiclessons.com

MusicU
musicu.com

Piano Lessons
pianotricks.com

**Reading Music: Common
Notation**
cnx.org/content/col10209

Lester S. Levy Collection of Sheet Music
levysheetmusic.mse.jhu.edu

You won't find "Hit Me Baby One More Time" on this site, but that's probably not a bad thing. This collection does house more than 29,000 pieces of music, focusing on popular American music from the period 1780 to 1960. The entire collection is indexed on this site; search for a catalog description of the pieces. You'll also be able to see—and print—an image of the cover and each page of public-domain music.

Linkware   linkwaregraphics.com
Free music flashcards, graphics, and worksheets.

Maran Student Library   maran.com

High-quality books illustrated with color photography teaching piano and guitar. Other books in this series focus on non-musical topics: yoga and weight training, algebra, dog training, cooking, computers, and crafts. Worth bookmarking.

Metronome Online   metronomeonline.com

An online metronome that you can set by tempo or by mood. Read the collection of articles to learn how to use metronomes in practicing a musical instrument. The site also has a button that plays a tone at 440Hz for tuning instruments to the A above middle C.

Music Rack   sheetmusic1.com/music.rack.html

Staff paper, sheet music, worksheets, and tests. Great material for reinforcing music lessons.

MusicU   musicu.com

Have any aspiring professional musicians in your home? MusicU is a quick education on how to make it in the music biz, with dozens of articles and other resources on such topics as Home Demo Recording, Music Business Attorneys, and Ten Tips for Building Stronger Songs.

Mutopiaproject   mutopiaproject.org

Classical sheet music, all free and legal.

My Piano   my-piano.blogspot.com

Our favorite site for free sheet music. The legal ones are arrangements that have been composed, without words. There are thousands in the gray area of sheet music "shared" by users.

Online Piano Lessons   free-online-piano-lessons.com

Learn how to form piano scales, piano chords, arpeggios, and modes for the piano. This is a theory-heavy course for students who have a year or two of piano practice under their belts.

On Creativity

Creativity is more than just being different. Anybody can play weird—that's easy. What's hard is to be as simple as Bach. Making the simple complicated is commonplace—making the complicated simple, awesomely simple— that's creativity.

—Charles Mingus, American jazz composer and pianist

Pathway to Dreams   cnx.org/content/col10326

Got a dream? This online self-paced course teaches kids—and adults—to reach their artistic goals, whether in music or any other art form.

Piano Lessons   pianotricks.com

Whether your children are absolute beginners, or a piano-playing experts, these free lessons will help them improve their game.

Reading Music: Common Notation   cnx.org/content/col10209

Some people play instruments without ever reading a note. The rest of us, though, rely on our music reading skills to get us through. This 14-lesson course teaches the basics of musical notation to would-be musicians.

Start to Play   guitarstartplay.com

Online guitar lessons. Start by learning to tune your instrument, and move through chords, strumming, and finger picking (arpeggio).

Texas School Music Project   tsmp.org

Click the Keyboard and Theory links at the top of this page to find excellent instructional tools for young jazz pianists. Other links teach the basics of nearly every instrument in the band and orchestra—including invaluable choir instruction for vocalists.

Video Guitar Lessons   freeguitarvideos.com/lessons.html

Video lessons that teach everything from tuning a guitar to advanced arpeggios. Site includes more than 90 free video lessons, and several additional text-only lessons.

ViolinMasterclass   violinmasterclass.com

With narrated videos and written explanations, this very well done site offers up violin classes for learners of all ages. Classes are taught by a very nice man with a very thick accent.

Vocal Music

IS THERE ANY need to teach children to sing?

Heaven knows, I spend enough energy trying to get some of my kids to stop singing!

Despite my ongoing struggle for some peace and quiet in my noisy house, I recognize that there are plenty of times when disciplined singing not only benefits an individual voice but also teaches the entire group of children to listen to one another's voices in order to harmonize and modulate their singing.

The only thing I haven't been able to teach effectively is the long rest!

The following resources will help you teach vocal music and turn your little angels into a heavenly choir.

Sing: Akin to Dutch *zingen*, German *singen*, Icelandic *syngja*, Gothic *siggwan*, Danish *synge*. To create music with the voice.

Canto Gregoriano   interletras.com/canticum

The history, characteristics, pronunciation, and other aspects of Gregorian chant. Much of this site seems to be a literal translation from the Spanish, but it's very informative nevertheless.

Center for Church Music   songsandhymns.org

Classic hymns with sheet music and audio files for singing along. Each song includes a hymn history and a devotional that invites contemplation.

Choral Conducting Suggestions
worshipandchurchmusic.com/choralsuggestions.html

Conducting a choir is hard work. Here's a list of 42 ideas for making it all a bit easier.

Choral Public Domain Library   cpdl.org/wiki

CPDL is one of the world's largest free sheet-music sites, with some 10,000 pages of musical scores for choirs and vocalists.

Hotlinks

HamieNet
hamienet.com

Music Learning Materials
lds.org/churchmusic

Video Voice Lessons
tinyurl.com/vidvoice

Music

Ear Trainer   good-ear.com

When you play the piano, you need only hit the right keys. When you sing, though, you've got to hit the right intervals. Good Ear helps singers learn how to hit musical intervals correctly.

HamieNet   hamienet.com

An amazing tool for accompanying soloists. Pick a song, tempo, key, and even which instruments are available by deleting tracks. Then download the results to a CD.

How to Sing   wikihow.com/Sing

Advice from vocal coaches about correct posture, proper breathing, warming up, and other techniques for aspiring singers.

Jeannie Deva Voice Studios   jeanniedeva.com

Free voice lessons that teach expanding vocal range, eliminating register break, avoiding vocal blow-out, the mind-body connection, and effective lead vocals.

Mama Lisa's World   mamalisa.com/world

Fun tunes and sheet music for popular nursery rhymes and children's songs from around the world. Sing along with the little ones.

Music Learning Materials   lds.org/churchmusic

Click the link to Learning Materials for access to a well-done video course on conducting music, as well as lessons on teaching songs to children, accompanying others, adding variety to group singing, and learning music symbols and terms.

Video Voice Lessons   tinyurl.com/vidvoice

Learn how to sing better and improve your voice with voice exercises, tips and techniques, and other vocal training and basic singing instruction from a professional music-theory teacher. There are 28 videos in this series. On the right, find links to hundreds of additional voice-training videos.

Chapter 10

Social Studies Skills

I REMEMBER, WHEN I was in the sixth grade, spending half the school year studying Central and South America.

But we didn't study Central and South America, exactly. Our teacher decided, instead, to have each student pick an individual country and study it. At the end of the school year—the plan went— we would each do a presentation on our country, and somehow, magically, we'd all be educated about Central and South America.

So for several months I spent every waking moment worrying about "my" assigned country. I read every encyclopedia article, copied out all the entries in every book I could find, and searched every available magazine for the tiniest mention. I drew topographical maps and political maps. I traced the native costumes and photocopied pictures of local pottery. Then I wrote a turgid, boring report about my assigned country.

When it was all over, I couldn't have told you the name of any other country in all the rest of the Western Hemisphere. But I was the world's leading sixth-grade expert on a forgettable little place called French Guiana. Somehow, I don't think my experience was the best possible way to learn about another culture.

Hotlinks

Fact Monster Social Studies
tinyurl.com/hismon

MIT Social Sciences
tinyurl.com/ssmit

PBS Social Studies
pbs.org/teachers/
socialstudies

Worksheets to Go
tinyurl.com/sswtg

On Learning

Whoso neglects learning
in his youth,
Loses the past and is
dead for the future.

—Greek tragic dramatist
Euripides (484 B.C.–406
B.C.), *Phrixus*

The real goal of a social studies education is, in the words of the National Council for the Social Studies (**www.ncss.org**), to teach students "the content knowledge, intellectual skills, and civic values necessary for fulfilling the duties of citizenship in a participatory democracy."

What I learned from that experience was simply that I absolutely, unequivocally, completely loathed French Guiana.

When it came time to teach my own kids about our southern neighbors, I took an entirely different tack. Listening to the *Evita* CD piqued their interest. Silly competitions ("Want this jelly bean? Name the biggest country in South America") got them searching the globe. Earnest discussions about Cuban politics got them thinking.

And guess what? All my kids know how to find French Guiana.

In this chapter, you'll be introduced to resources for teaching about business management, civics, cultures, current events, economics, geography, psychology, and social issues.

We begin, though, with resources that cover the entire spectrum of social studies.

Arts and Culture Lesson Plans   tinyurl.com/ssarts

A large and eclectic collection of lesson plans covering many areas of history, society, and culture. One lesson, "In My Other Life," asks children to consider what it might feel like to grow up in an Asian, African, or Latin American country. Another, "My Piece of History," helps children create an exhibit of historical items from their own homes.

AskERIC Social Studies Lesson Plans   tinyurl.com/sseric

Many, many lesson plans in all areas of the social studies curriculum.

EW Social Studies   tinyurl.com/ssedu

A collection of lesson plans covering general social studies, civics, current events, economics, geography, government, history, holidays, psychology, regions and cultures, and sociology.

Fact Monster Social Studies   tinyurl.com/hismon

Child-sized articles on government, geography, and general social studies topics.

MIT Social Sciences   tinyurl.com/ssmit

Highlights for High School provides resources from MIT to improve social studies instruction at the high school level. Watch video demonstrations, study for AP exams, and sample college coursework.

New York Times Crossword
nytimes.com/learning/teachers/xwords/archive.html

All sorts of fun social studies–oriented crossword puzzles, on topics such as economics, civics, geography, and history. Tough but educational.

PBS Social Studies   pbs.org/teachers/socialstudies

Choose a grade level and a subject for PBS lesson plans. Topics include anthropology, archaeology, civics, debate, econ, and ethics. Many lessons have video clips from PBS programs.

Social Studies at PPPST   pppst.com/socialstudies.html

PowerPoint presentations that teach subjects across the curriculum: ancient history, U.S. states, holidays, world history, patriotic symbols, world geography, American history, civil rights, continents, U.S. government, economics, countries, elections, religions, regions, Native Americans, psychology, and Black History Month.

Social Studies Classroom Resources   eduplace.com/ss

Under the Classroom Resources for Teachers section find social studies activities, bilingual resources, current events, graphic organizers such as timelines and idea charts, monthly themes, outline maps, shape-book patterns, spelling lists, and instruction on using the Web.

Social Studies

Social Studies Lesson Plans

eduref.org/cgi-bin/lessons.cgi/Social_Studies

Social studies lesson plans covering many curriculum areas. Learn about using an abacus, the Bill of Rights, archaeological methods, and many others.

Social Studies Online   classroom.jc-schools.net/SS-units

Lesson plans, worksheets, activities, and scope-and-sequence recommendations for a range of social studies topics, including maps, current events, culture, econ, geography, civics, and history. The link to processing skills has resources that teach kids how to learn.

Social Studies Videos   learner.org/resources/browse.html?discipline=7

A large collection of educational videos that teach many social studies topics. One section, for example, explains Teaching Geography. Another probes beliefs and biases about the Constitution. From the Annenberg CPB series.

Worksheets to Go   tinyurl.com/sswtg

A collection of social studies worksheets (with solutions) from Discovery School.

Business and Industry

Business: From the Old English *bisignis* (busy + ness). Being engaged in trade or commerce.

LEMONADE STANDS AND dog walking will probably be your kids' first foray into the business world. Who can blame them? The lure of entrepreneurship is compelling. Who wouldn't want to be his own boss, set his own hours, and take all the profits of a successful business?

Unfortunately, some 50 percent of small businesses fail within the first five years.

Help your junior entrepreneurs stay on the winning side of the ledger by teaching them the basics of business early on.

In this section, we consider resources for accounting and business management. You'll find a related section on economics later in this chapter, and another section on personal financial management in Chapter 14.

Accounting Dictionary   investorwords.com/bysubject.html

A glossary of business and accounting terminology, with more than 3,200 vocabulary words.

BNet   bnet.com

Your business-minded teenagers will want to make this one their home page, especially if they're considering studying business in college. In the Business Library section, find the Encyclopedia of Business and other good study materials.

Business Letter Writing   tinyurl.com/ssbs

Everything your kids need to know about writing and formatting business letters. Includes reproducibles and a lesson plan.

Business Studies
bbc.co.uk/schools/gcsebitesize/business

Learn how business works overseas with business lessons from the BBC. Much of this information applies in every free economy.

My Own Business   myownbusiness.org

This free online course on starting your own business covers Deciding on a Business, Business Plans, Basic Computer and Communication Tools, Organization and Insurance, Location and Leasing, Accounting and Cash Flow, How to Borrow Money, E-Commerce, Buying a Business or Franchise, Opening and Marketing, and Expanding and Handling Problems.

Hotlinks

My Own Business
myownbusiness.org

Net MBA
netmba.com

Simple Studies
simplestudies.com

Small Business Administration
sba.gov

Write a Business Plan
tinyurl.com/plabus

Social Studies

Net MBA   netmba.com

Short, easy-to-read articles on every subject covered by college-level business classes. Get a solid overview of accounting, economics, finance, management, marketing, operations, statistics, and strategic management.

Obtain a Business License   tinyurl.com/tutbus

An illustrated multipart tutorial on licensing a new business. Follow the links to the right for related How-To's.

Simple Studies   simplestudies.com

Free accounting lessons with diagrams, illustrations, related exercises, and a glossary.

Small Business Accounting Assistance   businesstown.com

A collection of short articles on the basics of dozens of business subjects: accounting, advertising, finance, taxes, time management, and much, much more.

Small Business Administration   sba.gov

The SBA is the go-to place for anyone who wants to start a small business. It's very likely that you'll find the SBA, or its sister organization, the Small Business Development Council, in your own community, where helpful mentors will teach you how to get your business off the ground—for free. Get started by clicking the Small Business Planner link at the top of the page.

Work-at-Home Moms   wahm.com

Just the place for moms and families that need to produce income from home. Ideas, message boards, and advice for starting family home businesses.

Write a Business Plan   tinyurl.com/plabus

Writing a business plan is the first step to starting a successful business. Here's how. Learn2 is a collection of multipart tutorials with cartoon illustrations. Links on the right lead to related How-To's.

Civics

I'VE ALWAYS BEEN fascinated by government and the law, but it wasn't until I was in law school at a British university that I actually learned to appreciate the American political system.

As I studied English legal systems and began to understand the roots of much of American law, I became increasingly aware of the brilliance of the U.S. Constitution and the system of government it empowers. I appreciated the Constitution even more when I learned, during my English Constitutional Law course, that England doesn't even have a document called a constitution. You can imagine how tough that made things at test time!

Unfortunately, the subject of civics—government, law, politics, citizenship—is given short shrift in many school curricula. As a homeschooler, you have the freedom to be sure your own children are well schooled in the workings of government and in their duties as citizens.

Gilbert Scott Wolfe, a senior planner for the city of Westlake Village, California, worries that too many teachers aren't teaching children what they need to know about civics. "I'm very happy to hear that education in government and civics is taken seriously by educators in the homeschool arena," he said. "I have seen that in many schools, the subject is glossed over or taught more as history than as a subject that has meaning for every citizen today. There is yet hope for our future!"

I asked how his civics education affects his daily life. "I'm an urban planner," he responded, "and the basic education I acquired in civics classes is actually used on a day-to-day basis. Knowledge of the relationships among federal, state, and local levels of government is very important in determining which programs and policies we can

Civics: From the Latin *civicus* (citizen). Study of the rights and duties of citizenship, and the function of government.

Social Studies

Hotlinks

America Rock
schoolhouserock.tv/America.html

Cyber Nations
cybernations.net

Project Vote Smart
votesmart.org

World Law
jurist.law.pitt.edu/world

implement at the city level and which we might be precluded from enacting by state or federal law.

"A general knowledge of the Constitution is also important. Because planners write many local laws, we need to know how the Constitution serves as the basis for all of our laws at every level of government, as well as how various constitutional amendments protect the rights of citizens."

Parents who want to educate their children about civic duties, citizenship, the legal system, and American government can get plenty of help. This section describes the complex political institutions, laws, and customs through which the function of government is carried out. These resources will get your kids on track for political and civic involvement.

You'll find related sections on legal issues related specifically to homeschooling in the section on legal issues in Chapter 2. Sections on American history, the American West, and modern American history are located in Chapter 8.

America Rock   schoolhouserock.tv/America.html

Here are those beloved old Schoolhouse Rock videos—with the classics "I'm Just a Bill," "No More Kings," and other favorites. Lyrics and animations are included.

Cato Institute   cato.org

Prizing freedom and liberty above all other principles, the Cato Institute's politics are decidedly libertarian. But the information found under the For Students link will provide thought-provoking discussion no matter what your political leanings. The page has offerings in many academic disciplines: economics, history, law, natural and physical sciences, philosophy, and, of course, political science.

Community Helpers
teach-nology.com/teachers/lesson_plans/history/comm

Lesson plans that teach kids about what makes a community.

Cyber Nations   cybernations.net

An educational game that teaches the effects of various forms of government. Create a nation anywhere in the world and decide how you will rule your people by choosing a government type, a national religion, an ethnicity, a tax rate, a currency type, and more in this new geopolitical, nation, and government simulator.

Democracy Project   pbskids.org/democracy

PBS presents several excellent resources for introducing children to the structure and duties of local, state, and federal government. For grades three to six. Three of the resources—How Does Democracy Affect Me, President for a Day, and Inside the Voting Booth—have accompanying lesson plans for instilling in your kids a sense of civic duty.

Fold an American Flag   tinyurl.com/sscivs

There's a right way and a wrong way. This illustrated multipart tutorial shows you how. Follow the links to the right for related How-To's.

Government Web   usa.gov

Bills itself as "Government made easy." This is the portal to all U.S. government websites. Links to every federal agency and most state, local, and tribal government agencies. You know it's all there, because it even includes the top-secret NSA, the No Such Agency.

Law Library   law.jrank.org

An encyclopedia of easy-to-read articles about virtually every important legal decision in U.S. history. If you're a Judge Judy fan, you'll fall in love with the Law Library. Straightforward, no-nonsense law.

Our Government   tinyurl.com/ourgov

Understand the three branches of U.S. government, learn how a bill becomes law, and read historical documents.

Patriotism   patriotism.org

Read up on the origins of holidays such as Presidents' Day, Labor Day, Citizenship Day, Columbus Day, and other patriotic U.S. holidays.

Social Studies

Civics Freebie

Helping Your Child Become a Responsible Citizen explains the values and skills that make up character and good citizenship. Call 877-4-ED-PUBS and request product number ED004454H.

Patrick Henry

Fiery orator and Bill of Rights campaigner Patrick Henry was a home scholar. He was tutored at home by his well-educated Scottish father, who was trained in the classics. Henry did attend a local school for a short time, but the future lawyer and governor of Virginia was mostly self-taught. Henry's memorable words "If this be treason, make the most of it" and "Give me liberty or give me death" were a catalyst to the American Revolution.

Project Vote Smart   votesmart.org

Click the Political Resources link on the left to find lesson plans and dozens of other aids for teaching your kids the inner workings of government. Government 101 promises you'll never be embarrassed on national television by questions about how the U.S. government operates. It's all here.

Robert's Rules of Order Revised   constitution.org/rror/rror—00.htm

If you're running a club or an organization, you need to know Robert's. Likewise if you run for any public office that involves meetings. Near the bottom of this page is a formal Plan for the Study of Parliamentary Law. It's a bit thick, but it does address the topic systematically.

The Official Robert's Rules of Order Site   robertsrules.com

These are the rules under which every assembly, congress, and legislature operates. The question-and-answer forum is particularly useful.

Wacky Patent of the Month   colitz.com/site/wacky_new.html

Primarily a site about how to work through the legalities of obtaining a patent, but the Wacky Patents submitted over the years are particularly amusing.

World Law   jurist.law.pitt.edu/world

Is your future Eagle Scout working on a Citizenship in the World merit badge? Here's the place to learn about international law, treaties, agreements, and issues.

Culture and Society

THE STUDY OF US! What's more fascinating than all the history, culture, and language of human beings? Anthropology, sociology, and multicultural education are similar disciplines. Whereas sociologists study contemporary societies, anthropologists examine societies that existed in the ancient past and societies that are less technologically advanced than their own. Multiculturalism describes ethnic communities in a larger society.

This is how Ann M. Glass, a homeschooling mother of two in Everson, Washington, introduces anthropology and other research-worthy topics into her homeschooling: "My sons are five and seven, and this is the third year that we've done research-type learning," she says. "At first we used books. The boys chose the topic, and I broke it down into manageable chunks. Our resources were the library, our own personal library, interviews, and the Internet. My oldest would read the information aloud. The boys would dictate to me what they wanted written. As my older son became more proficient in writing, he began to do some of the writing for himself.

"Our first topic was snakes. (Ugh!) We tacked white construction paper with headings on it all over the house. As we came across information, we wrote it on the paper under the correct heading, using various colors of Sharpie pens. In addition to the research, we also read stories, watched videos, and happened upon a snake in our garden who was shedding his skin right in front of us!

"After we completed our book, I pasted the pages back to back. (If you write on both sides of one sheet, the ink leaks

Culture: Culture, from the Latin *colere* (to care for, guard, or cultivate). The customs, attitudes, and beliefs characteristic of a particular social or ethnic group.

Social Studies

through.) Then I hole-punched the pages and hooked them all together with metal rings.

"The second year the boys chose the whole continent of Africa. Like a foolish, enthusiastic mom, I agreed. (Do you have any idea just how big Africa is?) We pretty much did the same thing with Africa that we did with snakes. We divided the continent into its regions and compared the regions. We also tried new foods, played African games, and learned some Swahili. It was very much like a unit study, except we did a lot of reading and writing, as well as map work. This, too, was laminated and made into a book.

"This year we chose the Philippines. Instead of a book, we bought a large three-ring binder and divided it into sections: geography (maps, climate, land, provinces), missions and beliefs (Protestantism, Catholicism, Islam, and animism), history (heroes, World Wars, presidents, symbols), culture (people, way of life, festivals, work, leisure pastimes), fauna (mammals, reptiles, sea life, insects, birds), and flora (edible and inedible)."

Your own approach to multiculturalism, anthropology, and sociology may not be as wide-ranging, but no matter how you address it, the subject is immense, and it's well worth the effort to make it interesting.

In this section, we consider resources for multiculturalism, anthropology, and sociology, including ancient and modern cultures and social groups. You'll find a related section on social issues later in this chapter, and a section on world history in Chapter 8. In Chapter 11 you'll find a section on world languages.

Adopt an Elder   anelder.org
A program that provides food, simple medicines, clothing, fabric, and yarns to help Navajo elders live on the land in their traditional lifestyle.

Hotlinks

Adopt an Elder
anelder.org

Inanimate Alice
inanimatealice.com

People & Society
nsf.gov/news/overviews/
people

Primitive Ways
primitiveways.com

Social Studies

Booker T. Washington

It was intense poverty that kept emancipated slave Booker T. Washington from gaining a formal education, but that didn't stop him from wanting to learn. The ambitious young man was born into slavery. At the age of nine, after his emancipation, he began working in a salt furnace, and later toiled in a coal mine. At sixteen, he enrolled himself in an agricultural institute and worked as a janitor to pay his expenses. Perhaps the most visible and influential African American of the nineteenth and early twentieth centuries, Washington founded what is now Tuskegee University.

Allyn & Bacon's Sociology Links   abacon.com/sociology/soclinks

This collection of resources is particularly useful because it helps to explain what sociology is: The Miscellaneous Discipline.

Black History Month   biography.com/blackhistory

Celebrate Black History with this great resource that provides timelines, biographies (of course), quotes, and fast facts on notable blacks in U.S. history.

Chinese Fortune Calendar   chinesefortunecalendar.com

Feng shui, lunar calendars, the *I-Ching*, and more fun topics.

Citizen's Guide to Surviving Police Encounters

tinyurl.com/civicrights

Did you know that more than half of citizen encounters with police occur during traffic stops? Don't let your teenagers get behind the wheel of a vehicle without understanding their civil rights, and knowing how to respond to police requests during a traffic or street encounter, or when they get a knock on the door from police or CPS workers. Flexyourrights.org created this video—which does contain some mildly crude language—to educate teens and parents.

Social Studies

Government & PoliSci   learnersonline.com/weekly/subject/gov.htm

Web quests on topics such as presidential advertising, copyright law, and the death penalty. Extremely well done, with photographs, links, explanatory text, and illustrations.

Inanimate Alice   inanimatealice.com

Follow Alice as she grows up from an eight-year-old girl in Northern China through her life in Italy and Russia, and more. This award-winning site contains beautifully animated stories that help children understand what it means to live in other parts of the world.

Kulture Kidz   aakulturezone.com/kidz

Your source for biographies, reading materials and lesson plans for Black History Month, mostly, but the site includes plenty of resources for other observations: Asian-Pacific, Hispanic, and Native American heritage celebrations.

Multicultural America   everyculture.com/multi

An encyclopedia of articles about virtually every ethnic and cultural group in North America. Did you know there's an ethnic group called English-Americans?

Musical Travels for Children
cnx.org/content/col10221

An online course for children that introduces interesting aspects of music in other cultures. Learn about music native to Europe, Asia, Africa, the Americas, and Australia with these thoughtful, in-depth lessons.

Native Tech   nativetech.org/games

Learn to appreciate Native American handicrafts from the Eastern Woodland Indian peoples. Beadwork, pottery, metalwork, and other technologies, along with recipes for dishes such as Pemmican Soup and Wild Peppermint Tea.

Field Tripping

The little town we lived in here in New Mexico gave the kids a tour of the jail and showed them what happened when they had to arrest people. (I loved that one. The kids were little angels for over a month afterward.)

—Jackie Schlageter, homeschooling mom of eight, Oscuro Township, Carrizozo, New Mexico

---

People & Society   nsf.gov/news/overviews/people

An overview by the National Science Foundation: "Out of fascination and need, people have always studied people. When curiosity is backed by scientific methods, we get fascinating insights into human behavior, origins, societies and economies."

Primitive Ways   primitiveways.com

A gallery of things very, very old. Ancient uses of fire, flint, musical instruments, technology, and much, much more.

Resources For and About Multiethnic Americans
ipl.org/div/pf/entry/48507

A collection of resources that discuss or were written by biracial and multiracial Americans, and that deal primarily with ethnic identity. This tutorial from the IPL's pathfinders series is a good guide for further research.

Save Sociology   savesociology.org

Argues against politicizing the discipline of sociology and for restoring it to scientific, not political, inquiry.

Sociological Subjects   sociosite.net/topics

Social Problems and Solutions is the general heading for this collection of resources for every subject under the aegis of sociology. Click the Society link at the bottom of the page to see themes listed in categories.

The Antislavery Literature Project   antislavery.eserver.org

This resource seeks "to increase public access to a body of literature crucial to understanding African American experience, US and hemispheric histories of slavery, and early human rights philosophies." It is home to a great number of videos, as well as literature, historical documents, and even guides for teaching about slavery in American history.

Teaching Tips

Reading, reading, reading! I don't bother with textbooks. We love reading aloud, personal reading, and audiobooks. My daughter has developed an interest in government by reading Orwell.

—**Aimee Nusz**, teacher and fellow student of two, Amarillo, Texas

Social Studies

Current Events

DO YOUR KIDS know what's going on in the world?

Naturally, nobody knows everything that's going on. Newspaper and television news editors struggle all the time with trying to decide which of all the world's events most deserve space or time in their medium. In the same way, homeschooling parents get the privilege of deciding which of all the thousands of issues being discussed around the world, which of the millions of events going on every day, deserve time and space in their homeschooling curricula. Popular music? Movie stars? Substance abuse? The extramarital intimacies of celebrities?

Naaahhh . . . you've got more discernment than that! When your kids study current events, they can do so in a framework that encourages them to understand the reasons wars happen, the real issues behind the political "sound bites," the "correct" side of the abortion issue—in short, anything you decide to expose them to.

Current: From the Old French *courre* (to run, course). Events in progress at the present moment.

A knowledge of current events is more than simply being able to recite the events of the day. When children thoroughly understand current events, they understand how those events affect the way people live.

Here's how we do it in our house: Every day, each kid is expected to read one non-fiction article and prepare to report on it orally. From time to time we have "speech" class, during which each child gives an impromptu talk on any subject we assign. The only ground rules: You have to speak for the entire time period (which varies according to the age of the child), and you have to tell us something we didn't know. The assignments are sometimes very specific, but lately we've gone to vague assignments, on topics such as "circles" or "light." For two minutes or so, the child speaks on the assigned subject, usually with hilarious results. They've all become quite adept at drawing analogies between the assigned topic and serious subjects about which they actually know something.

The resources in this section suggest fun ways to teach current events. They also provide sources for the news stories that explain the events that children need to be aware of in order to converse intelligently around anybody's dinner table! (See related sections on social issues later in this chapter and on modern American history in Chapter 8.)

All You Can Read   allyoucanread.com

Links to the websites of pretty nearly every newspaper on the planet.

CNN Education   cnn.com/studentnews

The classroom edition of CNN. Includes Ten Questions & Newsquiz, Learning Activities, and "One-Sheets," explanations for young readers of events in the news.

C-SPAN in the Classroom   www.c-spanclassroom.org

If they're going to learn about the world around them, your kids can't do better than to learn what's going on in the halls of Congress. C-SPAN provides video clips, discussion questions, student activities, graphic organizers, worksheets, and quizzes for teaching kids what's currently happening in government.

HappyNews   happynews.com

"Real news, compelling stories, always positive." One story, for example, proclaimed "10-year-old Scholar Takes Calif. College by Storm." Citizen journalists from around the world contribute current stories of virtue, goodwill, and heroism. Happy News also sponsors essay competitions with cash prizes.

New York Times Learning Network   nytimes.com/learning

The Gray Lady, online and just for kids. Daily lesson plans discuss current events in the news. Special sections for parents, teachers, and students will be of particular interest to homeschooling families. Get your kids up-to-date on the news around them.

Hotlinks

All You Can Read
allyoucanread.com

CNN Education
cnn.com/studentnews

C-SPAN in the Classroom
www.c-spanclassroom.org

Professional Cartoonists Index
cagle.msnbc.msn.com/teacher

Social Studies

News for Students, Resources for Teachers   cnnfyi.com

Top stories written by CNN journalists, working in collaboration with teachers, to be appropriate in vocabulary and content for junior and senior high school students. Many stories are accompanied by quizzes, discussions, or activities.

NewsHour Extra   pbs.org/newshour/extra

The Daily Buzz, and Student Voices, along with regularly updated lesson plans, teach kids to think about current events. From PBS.

Online Newspapers   tinyurl.com/sscur

An extensive but not complete list of U.S. and overseas newspapers.

Professional Cartoonists Index   cagle.msnbc.msn.com/teacher

Editorial cartoons are the most memorable way to analyze and understand current events. Here you'll find lesson plans for every grade level, along with the best of today's editorial cartoons. Lots to talk about with your kids.

Science Friday   sciencefriday.com

NPR provides a weekly broadcast of science topics in the news. From this page listen to podcasts of the programs, or click the Teachers link at the top for access to related discussion ideas, activities, and curriculum standards.

Time for Kids   timeforkids.com/TFK

Time magazine for kids, published weekly throughout the traditional school year. Includes worksheets, mini-lessons, and graphic organizers to help teach kids to be news-savvy.

WebCurrents   learnersonline.com/weekly/subject/art.htm

Web quests tied to current events. Quite well done, with photographs, links, explanatory text, and illustrations.

Economics

OVER THE COURSE of a college semester, I read and sweated and agonized over economics, struggling to incorporate the philosophical "social" part of the science with the quantitative mathematical part. Eventually, one of my study buddies came to my rescue by explaining that the philosophical part meant that economics was a squishy science that really couldn't be quantified. All the math was just more philosophy; there is no real, measurable way to define the relationship between supply and demand.

Oooohhhhhh . . .

Once I understood the principle, the nature of my study changed. I stopped worrying about formulas and definitions and began considering the philosophy. If I couldn't measure the effects of the "invisible hand," I could certainly observe it in commerce and politics and even my own personal finances. Once I understood what it was I was looking at, I saw it in everything around me. When George Bush described Ronald Reagan's economic plan as "voodoo economics," I had the grounding to form my own opinion. When the air traffic controllers struck, I had an opinion about how they should be confronted. None of it required math. It was all about the principle.

Anthony Davies is an assistant professor of economics and finance at Pittsburgh's Duquesne University and a strong supporter of homeschooling. He explains why it's important for children to understand the principles behind economics: "Economics is not a discipline that teaches one what to think," he says. "Rather, economics teaches one how to think.

"To master economics is to look at the world through eyes that are fundamentally altered. The economic thinker sees human actions as the results of motivations tempered

> **Economics:**
> From the Latin *oeconomicus* (orderly, methodical). Study of the production, consumption, and distribution of goods and services.

Hotlinks

CyberEconomics
ingrimayne.com/econ

Federal Reserve Education
federalreserveeducation
.org/fred

Hip Pocket Change
usmint.gov/kids

Money Rock
schoolhouserock.tv/
Money.html

Social Studies

John Quincy Adams

The sixth president of the United States was schooled on the run. The son of President John Adams, John Quincy spent much of his childhood traveling on diplomatic missions with his father. At the young age of fourteen, he became private secretary to the American envoy in St. Petersburg, Russia.

by constraints. To the economist, all actions—no matter how irrational they appear—have a rational explanation if one simply takes the time to understand the motivation of and constraints placed on the actor.

"For example, the economist is not surprised when an increase in the minimum wage leads to lower earnings among minimum-wage workers. The economist knows that firms will respond to the increased cost of labor by—where possible—replacing workers with machines."

Dr. Davies clarifies the reason for my own frustration in economics class, and explains how you can prepare your middle- and high-school–aged children for their first college-level encounter with economics: "The best preparation for studying economics," he says, "is at least one course in practical calculus. By 'practical' I mean that the student need not spend overly much time on learning why calculus works the way it does, but rather that the student be able to wield calculus like a tool—to be able to 'speak' in equations as one might speak in English. Easily 80 percent of economics students get caught up in the vagaries of graphing and mathematical manipulation such that they rarely get to delve into the more meaty issues of economics."

When it comes to practicality, says Scott Schickram, director of product development at Ranger Insurance in Houston, a solid economics education beats all. "Every day we are faced with decisions concerning what to buy, where to live, and who to work for. These are important decisions.

"In studying economics, I've learned that it's important to find the right information, consider different options, and not make decisions without considering all the choices. Fortunately, information can be found to help make good decisions about purchases or job choices.

"Economics has also made me realize how important it is to save and invest for the future. Seeing how different countries have grown their economies and become prosperous reminds me that 'compound interest' works and is one of the greatest miracles in the world."

Whether you're teaching younger kids about being wise consumers, educating your middle-school–aged children about supply and demand, or introducing older kids to stock market analyses and economic indicators, these great resources will be useful. You'll find related resources under the Business heading earlier in this chapter, and under Financial Management in Chapter 14.

AmosWEB   amosweb.com

Whimsical economics? Look to AmosWEB for lots of fun economic learning, such as Ask Mr. Economy and Gloss-arama. The Free Lunch Index, for example, measures the state of the economy by asking visitors where they got their lunch today.

CyberEconomics   ingrimayne.com/econ

A complete online textbook on micro- and macroeconomics. From basic supply and demand to government and economic policy.

Department of the Treasury Learning Vault   treas.gov/education

Get a sense of how the Treasury plays a role in the economy with these articles on the history, functions, and collections of the U.S. Treasury.

Econ Handouts   tinyurl.com/ssecon

From a university student learning center, printable handouts to reinforce business and economics learning. Many handouts include problem sets with answers. Handouts cover economics, accounting principles, and finance.

Federal Reserve Education   federalreserveeducation.org/fred

Educational resources from the U.S. Federal Reserve. Order free videos and econ publications, or visit resources such as the Federal Reserve Kids Page, where students can learn all about how the Fed regulates money supplies.

Foundation for Teaching Economics   fte.org

Lesson plans, a Hot Topics newsletter, and other resources. The best part: Free economics courses for teachers—not for kids. Registration requires a refundable $150 deposit.

Google Earth   earth.google.com

Your neighborhood, from above, and from the street. Kinda creepy.

Great Economics Lessons   ecedweb.unomaha.edu/K-12

Click the Classroom Lessons links for access to econ lessons such as Homer Price—The Donuts, or Popcorn Economics, which teach economics through children's literature and other easy-to-find resources. The National Standards links outline a complete course in economics for every grade level.

Hip-Pocket Change   usmint.gov/kids

A government-sponsored site designed to generate interest in coins, the United States Mint, and U.S. history. Kids who've argued that you should use plastic to buy them expensive toys will benefit by learning the beauty of cold, hard cash.

KidsBank   kidsbank.com

Your elementary-aged children will love learning about money, banking, and economics with these cartoon characters. Easy-to-read, lots of fun.

Math and Money   factmonster.com/mathmoney.html

Ever wonder how coins are made? The econ portion of the math-centric site is filled with articles teaching the history of money, the public debt, and important vocabulary words relating to economics.

Money Rock   schoolhouserock.tv/Money.html

The old Schoolhouse Rock videos are back, this time teaching economics and the money system. "This for That," for example, teaches about the barter system, and "Making $7.50" teaches about budgeting an allowance. Includes the lyrics and animations.

National Council for Economic Education   ncee.net

The NCEE provides lesson plans and other resources as part of its Campaign for Economic Literacy. Click the Resources link at the top for access to the free educational materials.

Planet Orange   orangekids.com

Interactive graphics and games for studying earning, spending, saving, and investing. Pick a guide, cross a desert, barter a sandwich.

STAT-USA/Internet   stat-usa.gov

The government generates all sorts of statistics, but nearly all of them have to do with two subjects: Population and the Economy. This is where kids can go to find research from the U.S. Department of Commerce on business, trade, and economics.

The Great Depression   stlouisfed.org/greatdepression

Do your kids appreciate the hardships their ancestors experienced in the Depression years? Here is a full high-school curriculum that teaches economic principles and history that may—if we're smart—prevent a repeat of one of the blackest periods of history.

What Is a Dollar Worth?   sensato.com/1921/01cpi.htm

How much could a dollar buy in the past? The Consumer Price Index measures the value of money. Pick any two years, from 1913 to today, for a quick comparison.

Geography

Social Studies

Geography:
From the Greek *geographia* (earth + map). Study of the earth and its physical features.

IF YOU WERE to name a country or a state, most of my kids could find it on the globe.

It's not because they're particularly smart (although I like to think they are). It is, frankly, because they've been there. Or if they haven't, they know somebody who has. Nothing brings geography home like bringing geography home! Geographers study the earth and its life, as well as the physical, economic, political, and cultural factors that have affected each.

Why is it important to study geography? T. Ulysse, a professor of geography in Brantford, Ontario, answers, "It is essential that citizens be well educated in the field of geography in order to participate fully in the improvement of their society. There are many important issues upon which the ordinary person must make choices every day. A good education, particularly in the field of geography, will go a long way toward providing future citizens with the tools to find their way in the vast jungle of modern society.

"Of course, I am speaking of a well-balanced program of geography in which each student is given ample opportunities to:

Hotlinks

Awesome America
awesomeamerica.com

The World Factbook
cia.gov

Xpeditions
nationalgeographic.com/
xpeditions

Your Visited Countries
world66.com

- develop his or her independent and critical thinking
- develop an appreciation for the multicultural nature of the society in which he or she lives
- understand the interaction and the interdependence that exist between human beings and the rest of the natural world
- understand that each of our actions affects our physical as well as our social environment

A basic understanding of geography is a critical component of your children's education. Not only will it earn them a spot on *Jeopardy!,* it'll also help them find their way across the country or around the world, knowing where they're going and why it's worth the trip.

The following geography resources look at the world up close and from far, far away. (You'll find related sections on Earth Science in Chapter 12 and on state history in Chapter 8.)

Arctic & Antarctic   nsf.gov/news/overviews/arcticantarctic

An overview by the National Science Foundation: "Earth's polar regions may seem like mirror images. But each is a unique environment with features we are still trying to understand, and each affects the rest of the globe."

Awesome America   awesomeamerica.com

Incredible photographic journey through all fifty U.S. states. State facts, trivia, and links to resources such as state parks. Worth visiting, though, just for the incredible photos.

Color Landform Atlas of the United States   fermi.jhuapl.edu/states

A very cool map site. Shaded relief maps show landforms of each U.S. state. You'll also find satellite views of most states, as well as 1895 maps. Includes external links to newspapers, weather, and more.

Earth At Night   tinyurl.com/ssgeo

If you're doing a unit study on space, or would just like to see what the world looks like at night, you'll love this site. The difference between North and South Korea is fascinating. And look how much brighter Hong Kong and the east coast of Taiwan are than the rest of China! This is a very, very cool site. Teach geography with the supporting information at **tinyurl.com/ssgeo2.**

Earthcam   earthcam.com

Links to live video cameras all around the world. Your kids can see cameras in China, Russia, and other exotic sites around the world. Supervise your kids: some of the cams are located at less-than-savory locations.

Social Studies

Flags of the World   crwflags.com/fotw/flags

Learn about the flags of the different countries of the world, their history, and their cultural significance. And learn a new vocabulary word: vexillology—the study of flags.

GeoBee Challenge   nationalgeographic.com/geobee

Each day, 10 new quiz questions from the National Geography Bee. Are your kids ready to compete?

Getty Thesaurus of Geographic Names   tinyurl.com/ssget

Places all around the world, and their hierarchical relationship to other places.

Map of the World   tinyurl.com/mapworld

Part of the Encarta reference suite, which includes a dictionary and an encyclopedia, this clickable atlas of the world will center the globe on any point, or zoom in to a single portion of the map.

Mr. Nussbaum Social Studies   mrnussbaum.com/circumcode.htm

Geography games and resources that teach landforms, U.S. and Canadian geography, and world geography. You'll also find here excellent resources for teaching U.S. history.

Online Map Creation   aquarius.geomar.de/omc

Create custom maps. You have to know the latitude and longitude to set the boundaries, then check the boxes for political boundaries, rivers, cities, topography, and bathymetry, or tectonic features. Define locations and create labels. Once the maps are formed, zoom in or out, or define a new map center by clicking. Print out the "projections" page so your kids can learn about Mercator, Equidistant, and other ways of drawing a round planet on a flat surface.

Perry-Castañeda Map Collection
lib.utexas.edu/maps

On Finding One's Path

Do not go where the path may lead; go instead where there is no path, and leave a trail.

—Ralph Waldo Emerson

Social Studies

Perhaps the best map collection anywhere. You'll find here world and regional maps of historical events, current events, themes, weather, roads, topography, and anything else you could ever want to see mapped.

Read a Topographical Map
tutorials.com/04/0453/0453.asp

An illustrated multipart tutorial on finding your place on a topographical map. Follow the links to the right for related How-To's on using road maps, map folding, using a compass, and more.

Strange Maps   strangemaps.wordpress.com

Who owns Nevada? That's just one of the questions answered in this collection of unusual maps that illustrate all sorts of interesting data in the form of geographic maps.

TerraServer   terraserver.com

The best photos in town—*any* town! The USGS has photographed your house, your grandma's house, and the White House. Name your town, see a picture.

The World Factbook   cia.gov

If the CIA has experienced some bad PR over the years, perhaps the *World Factbook* will go some way toward fixing the agency's rep. Click the link on the right to find the authoritative go-to place for in-depth information on every country on the planet, updated twice a month with new statistics, maps, and information that only the CIA has the resources to compile. The most interesting part of each country's description is at the end, under the heading "Transnational Issues." There you'll get the skinny on the CIA's opinion of what sorts of troubles are brewing in the nations of the world.

We Travel in a Boat and in a Car   bright.net/~double/travel.htm

A great idea for geography: "Travel" with your family to see the world

National Geographic Bee

Write National Geographic Bee, National Geographic Society, 1145 17th Street NW, Washington, D.C. 20036-4688. The annual registration deadline is mid-October.

Social Studies

using homemade maps. Keep a journal of your travels. Visit the author's homepage for more great homeschooling tips.

Where's Yours?   wheresyours.com

Where's your favorite place? Active travelers share photos and stories of the greatest places on earth. The site sponsors contests with expensive giveaways.

WHTour   world-heritage-tour.org

Step inside a three-dimensional view of famous destinations around the world. London's Kew Gardens and Jerusalem's Dome of the Rock are among the many sites available for viewing.

Xpeditions   nationalgeographic.com/xpeditions

From *National Geographic,* lesson plans, activities, maps, and geography news for teachers and students. Suggested curriculum standards describe what kids should know at various grade levels.

Your Visited Countries   world66.com

A great resource for armchair travelers, with some 80,000 articles about more than 20,000 destinations, written and updated by real-life travelers. Register (it's free) and get access to do-it-yourself maps of states, provinces, and countries you've visited.

Psychology

ONE OF MY dearest friends and I spent a semester of high school researching the psychology of children's drawings.

We visited preschool and kindergarten classes and asked children to draw pictures of their families.

Then we compared their drawings with some information we found in a book, and wasted about an hour of class time psychoanalyzing their artwork. "This child is abused," we proclaimed, "because the mommy in his drawing has no arms." "This child feels divided from her family, because she drew herself in the bottom corner."

Oh, we were a dangerous pair.

If you want to raise children who are less arrogant than we were, closely supervise their access to the following resources. (Related information is located in Chapter 13, under Mental Health.)

American Academy of Child and Adolescent Psychiatry
aacap.org

Assisting families in understanding developmental and behavior disorders in adolescents. The Facts for Families links covers numerous disorders in lay terminology.

Classics in the History of Psychology   **psychclassics.asu.edu**

Books, books, books. Here you'll uncover the full texts of many historically significant public-domain documents and books from the scholarly literature of psychology. Sort by author or topic.

Encyclopedia of Mental Disorders   **minddisorders.com**

They're all here: NPD, BPD, OCD, PPD, PTSD . . . who knew there were so many ways for people to be dysfunctional?

High School Psychology   **apa.org/ed/curriculum.html**

Curriculum activities and articles from the American Psychological Association. In Light-Dark Sensory Adaptation, for example, students wear an eye patch to discover how the body adapts to changes in environment.

Kids Psych   **kidspsych.org**

Fun psychology games for very young learners.

Psych Humor   **psych.upenn.edu/humor.html**

Lots of psychology jokes and bumper stickers to lighten up your studies.

Psychology:
From the Greek *psukhikos* (soul) and *logia* (study). The study of an individual's behavioral characteristics.

Social Studies

Hotlinks

Encyclopedia of Mental Disorders
minddisorders.com

Kids Psych
kidspsych.org

Psychology Encyclopedia
psychology.jrank.org

Psych Site   abacon.com/psychsite

Activities, teaching tips, quizzes, and a psychology dictionary.

Psychology: A ConnecText   dushkin.com/connectext/psy

The Internet component of a McGraw-Hill psychology textbook, this site conveys a great deal of useful information on the basics of psychology. Read about important theories, people, and studies related to the field.

Psychology Encyclopedia   psychology.jrank.org

Twenty-two volumes of psychology filled with articles on every subject from Abnormal Psych and Addictions to Withdrawal Behaviors and Word Association Tests.

Psychology Presentations   pppst.com/psychology.html

PowerPoint presentations that teach general psychology. One of the resources, "Introduction to Psychology," provides nearly an entire course in the subject. The Psychology Lesson Plans near the bottom of the page discuss social skills, self-esteem, friendship, kindness, feelings and emotions, critical thinking, ethics, violence, fads, multiple intelligences, problem solving, family life, and general psychology.

The Psychology of Emotions, Feelings, and Thoughts
cnx.org/content/col10447

An online "textbook" teaching students to distinguish between emotion and logic, and to understand thoughts, feelings, depression, and other psychological concerns.

The Teaching of High School Psychology
apa.org/ed/natlstandards.html

What the APA believes high school students should know about psychology as a prerequisite to graduation.

What Is Psychology?   tinyurl.com/sswhat

The first two lessons of this university-level online course are free. It's a good way to sample the subject.

Social Issues

THERE ARE PERSISTENT social problems and controversies in the world.

How will you teach your children about feminism and abortion and poverty? What about world hunger? Human rights abuses? Response to natural disasters? How will the next generation solve problems that our generation continues to struggle over?

They'll be able to do it because we'll teach them how. We'll give them a social conscience, and train them to think about solutions. When our children take over, they'll be well equipped to make the world a better place.

The following resources are a great start for their social education. (See related sections on community service, and values and standards, in Chapter 4; and the section on minority education earlier in this chapter.)

Contemporary Studies

school.discoveryeducation.com/lessonplans/constudies.html

Lesson plans from the Discovery Channel on racism, population, genetic engineering, and other pressing issues of the day.

Cyberschoolbus   un.org/Pubs/CyberSchoolBus

A site for educating children about international issues and the United Nations. Includes news, briefings, and other information about the organization.

FBI Public Official Corruption Reporting

reportcorruption.fbi.gov

Why is public corruption one of the FBI's top investigative priorities? Find out why corruption matters, and learn about election fraud and other law enforcement issues.

FindLaw Legal News   legalnews.findlaw.com

Brief news items about civil rights, crime, politics, tort law, decisions before the Supreme Court, and much more. It's a

Social Studies

> **Social:** From the Latin *socius* (companionship). That which arises from living in communities and groups.

Hotlinks

FindLaw Legal News
legalnews.findlaw.com

Slate Explainer
slate.com/id/1787/
landing/1

**Southern Poverty Law
Center's Tolerance**
tolerance.org

Social Studies

solid foundation for discussions about current political controversies.

Innocence Project   innocenceproject.org
No discussion about the death penalty is complete without consideration of the Innocence Project, and its success in securing the release of more than 200 death-row inmates.

National Peace Essay Contest   usip.org/ed/npec
A scholarship contest for high school students. Every year, American high school students write analytical essays on a topic relating to world peace. Winning essayists could qualify for prizes worth as much as $10,000.

Slate Explainer   slate.com/id/1787/landing/1
An interesting attempt to explain the background to issues currently in the news. It's regularly updated with new, and always fascinating, explanations.

Social Issues Reference   social.jrank.org
Learn from an entire encyclopedia of articles on social issues from abortion and AIDS to welfare and working families. Another set of articles addresses social trends, such as uses of free time, population statistics, religious affiliation, and crime.

Southern Poverty Law Center's Tolerance   tolerance.org
Fight bigotry. The website houses diversity educational materials for parents, teachers, kids, and teenagers. The teen resources include writing competitions where kids can earn gift cards and money for their writing.

TED's Global Issue   ted.com
TED is an annual summit on . . . well, any subject that fascinates. Click the Global Issues link on the left to watch broadcasts of the talk of a lifetime from interesting writers, academics, scientists, and artists.

The Affirmative Action and Diversity Project   aad.english.ucsb.edu

The pros and cons of affirmative action as a means for enforcing social equity and ending racism. Sponsored by the Department of English, University of California, Santa Barbara.

US Civil Rights in the 1960s   ted.coe.wayne.edu/sse/units/civil.htm

A 16-day unit study on the beginning and growth of the civil rights movement.

Women's History   tinyurl.com/hiswom

Scholastic publishes this collection of biographies and articles aimed at primary- and middle-school ages. Very readable.

Chapter 11

Humanities Home

I WAS CONTEMPLATING the other day the notion of senses. You'll agree, I think, that most of us experience the world with five physical senses. Many have suggested that intuition is a sixth sense. But how, I wonder, do you account for some other "senses"?

How do you explain rhythm? I watch my youngest child at twenty-one months dance and skip and twirl every time she hears music with a beat. She stomps her little feet and bounces her shoulders and pumps her arms in time to the music. How does she know how to do that? And how is it that we can discern beauty? What gives some people a sense of harmony or balance or aesthetics? Why do even young children know the difference between young and old, clean and dirty, pretty and ugly? Why do people cry or smile or feel joy? How do we know whether or not a thing is funny? What makes a sense of humor? What causes sensitivity? And why can't dogs dance?

The humanities. It's what makes us human. It's everything and anything to do with the arts. It's language. It's poetry. It's literature and music and painting and sculpture. In other chapters of this book, we look specifically at certain segments of the discipline called Humanities: Chapter 5 introduces language arts, Chapter 7 examines the visual arts, and Chapter 9 covers music. In this chapter we look at the

Hotlinks

Arts and Letters Daily
aldaily.com

Arts for the Classroom
pbs.org/teachers/arts

National Standards for Arts Education
tinyurl.com/artstand

other arts: dance, drama, foreign language, forensics, journalism, philosophy, and religious studies. This chapter begins, though, with great resources that cover the entire spectrum of humanities education:

American Treasures   lcweb.loc.gov/exhibits/treasures

Humanities treasures from the Smithsonian. View galleries of resources that illustrate memory, reason, and imagination.

Arts & Humanities   tinyurl.com/edworldarts

A collection of lesson plans covering art history, foreign languages, language arts, literature, dance and music, and visual arts.

Arts and Letters Daily   aldaily.com

If you love the humanities, here's your new homepage. It's a daily newspaper chock-full of articles on philosophy, aesthetics, literature, and language.

Arts Edge   artsedge.kennedy-center.org

The Kennedy Center provides a collection of lesson plans for the visual arts, theater, dance, and music for students in grades K through 12. As an example, the lesson "A Deeper Shade of Purple" teaches second graders to identify purple, discover color mixing, and create a purple portrait.

Arts for the Classroom   pbs.org/teachers/arts

Lesson plans, activities, and videos for teaching the entire humanities curriculum. One example: "Dancing into History" has kids conducting research on the Great Depression and producing a dance that communicates the events and human emotions of this era.

Discovery Fine Arts   tinyurl.com/discfinearts

Fine arts lesson plans from the Discovery Channel. Ask your local library to order the accompanying videos.

Eduplace Activities   eduplace.com/activity

A fairly large collection of activity-based lesson plans organized by

Humanities Freebie

Creative Partnerships for Prevention provides arts and humanities ideas for innovative learning activities for youth. Call 877-4-ED-PUBS and request product number ED001363P.

curriculum area. Some of the categories are drama, media, journalism, poetry, dance, storytelling, and visual arts. But there's more: unusual categories such as social skills, pets, sequence of events, growing up, heroes, and folk legends . . . and that's just the beginning.

Geoffrey Chaucer Website

courses.fas.harvard.edu/~chaucer

Literature, history, culture, and language all collide in this resource that exposes students to the Middle English of Chaucer.

Humanities Interactive   **humanities-interactive.org**

Humanities exhibits that incorporate galleries of photos, essays, games, and best of all, teaching guides.

Humanities Lecture Series   **hallcenter.ku.edu/~hallcenter/video**

Video archives of guest lecturers speaking at the University of Kansas Hall Center for the Humanities.

National Endowment for the Humanities   **edsitement.neh.gov**

The best of the humanities. The NEH presents lesson plans and other resources in art and culture, literature and language arts, foreign languages, history, and social studies. Each lesson includes graphics, resources, and tips for teaching the subject.

National Standards for Arts Education   **tinyurl.com/artstand**

Curriculum standards for dance, music, theater, and visual arts, for grades K through 12.

Picturing America   **picturingamerica.neh.gov**

America's artistic heritage can be the basis for teaching. Once you've entered the site, click the Themes link for illustrated lessons on leadership, freedom and equity, democracy, courage, landscapes, and creativity.

The Lost Museum   **lostmuseum.cuny.edu**

An interactive investigation of what was once America's most-visited museum—until 1865, when it mysteriously burned to the ground. Play Nancy Drew and try to solve the mystery of who set the fire, or explore the virtual reconstruction, essays, and classroom lessons to find clues.

Dance and Performance Art

MY MOTHER DREAMED of turning her daughters into ballerinas, so at the age of three I was enrolled in ballet class.

I loved it. I'd skip and turn and whirl in the basement of the local Anglican church until, finally, it came time to practice for our annual recital.

Eagerly I'd drag my mommy to my dance classes, and we'd wait outside the "studio" door for the previous class to be dismissed. It was a dark, dingy place, that basement hallway, with low ceilings and bare lightbulbs, but I didn't care! I was going to be in a recital, with my four-year-old ballet partner—a partner who was always late to class.

On the day of our dress rehearsal, my mommy took me early to dance class, and I stood there in that basement hallway, dancing circles around my mother, waiting for my partner to show up so that I could go practice my little dance.

As we stood there in the basement that day, a noisy delivery truck drove around the side of the church to the holding area near the top of the stairs to deliver some metal chairs.

It seems they were somewhat less graceful than the dainty little girls who arrived at ballet class early and stood around the basement hallway waiting for their partners.

Crash! Bang! Slam! The drivers dropped an entire pallet of metal chairs on the bare cement floor, and several of them came crashing down the stairs.

Perform: From the Old French *perfournir* (to finish). To present entertainment before an audience.

Humanities

Hotlinks

How to Dance
wikihow.com/Dance

PE Central Dance Lessons
tinyurl.com/pedance

The Step Aerobics Page
turnstep.com

My mother says I didn't miss a beat.

Hearing the horrendous crash of metal chairs falling down a flight of cement stairs, I turned to her and asked, "Is that my partner?"

Clumsy children or graceful dancers, your children will get—at the very least—some cultural literacy out of these free resources. With any luck, they'll also be inspired to dance. These sites discuss dance, as well as resources for the performing arts in general. You'll find related information in the drama section later in this chapter and in Chapter 9.

Ballet History   androsdance.tripod.com/history

Lots of articles about dance technique, history, and biography, as well as feature articles about ballet.

Blast Dance   bbc.co.uk/blast/dance

Educational site from the BBC provides support, inspiration and advice for young dancers.

Dance Teacher Magazine   dance-teacher.com

An online publication for dancers. Lots of articles on teaching, dance styles, business, and health.

Dancer   dancer.com/aboutpointe.php

All about pointe shoes, health and safety, expert advice, and more for ballet dancers and the people who love them. This is a commercial site, but the educational materials are worthwhile.

First Ballets   ballet.co.uk/contexts/first_ballets.htm

Interesting essays about ballet standards such as *Swan Lake, Sleeping Beauty, The Nutcracker,* and *Giselle.*

Free to Dance   pbs.org/wnet/freetodance

From a PBS special—probably available through your local library—lesson plans and more documenting the development of modern dance as an African-American art form.

Humanities

Serge Lifar

The famous Russian dancer was a self-taught success. Born in 1905, Lifar taught himself the intricacies of the ballet and grew up to become a teacher, choreographer, director, and dance historian. In 1929 he created the title role in George Balanchine's *The Prodigal Son*. Lifar was the principal dancer and ballet-master of the Paris Opéra in the thirties, forties, and fifties. He is known for his own works, the 1950 ballet *Phèdre*, and his 1969 oeuvre, *Le Grand Cirque*.

Great Performances   tinyurl.com/greatperform

Your local library probably has DVDs of the PBS series. Use these lesson plans in conjunction with the DVDs to teach appreciation of such classics as *Swan Lake* and *The Nutcracker*, as well as other musical and cultural performances.

How to Dance   wikihow.com/Dance

How not to make a complete and utter fool of yourself on the dance floor. Boys: It's step-touch, not step-hop-hop-overbite-thumbs-up.

PE Central Dance Lessons   tinyurl.com/pedance

Dance lessons in more than a dozen categories. Also find a link to National Dance Standards.

Street Dance Australia   tinyurl.com/stredan

In the left column of this guide to Latin dance are links to articles, on-line books, and "dance survival guides" that teach choreography, appreciation for dance, and how to prevent injuries when you are the one dancing.

The Step Aerobics Page   turnstep.com

Aerobics dancers and teachers alike will enjoy learning from more than 16,000 patterns submitted by users. Step, aquatic, cycling, quad step, and many other styles are covered.

Humanities

Waltz   **tinyurl.com/tutwaltz**

An illustrated multipart tutorial for the easiest ballroom dance. Follow the links to the right for related How-To's on wedding etiquette.

Drama

ONE OF THE best things we ever did with our children was take them to see a live performance of *A Christmas Carol.* The performance was part musical, part drama, and part slapstick. The kids loved it!

There's no better way to get your children really involved in a work of literature than to let them see it live.

If you have a house full of children, you've got a great opportunity to act out some of the dramatic fiction and historical work you've read in other parts of your curriculum.

Drama: From the Greek *dran* (to act). The portrayal of life or situations on the stage or in film.

Joshywa Schrader, cofounder of the Colorado Art Theatre in Denver, has some suggestions for getting your children involved in the dramatic arts. "The way I motivate people with little or no theater experience is by using one simple word. I use the same word for adults and children. The word is 'play.'

"Children love to play, and adults are normally too self-conscious about trying something new, so all we do for a while is play.

"I understand it sounds strange. The reason I use this approach is that a lot of people do not realize that when they are playing . . . they are acting! Think of when children play Doctor, or House, or Cowboys and Indians. They are at the first stages of developing characters. They are, in fact, already practicing the art of theater.

"So I first assign them a scene in which they will play. Literally, play. Once they have developed their own characters through their playtime, we only have to develop those characters, and then they are on their way. They feel comfortable, because in a lot of aspects, they are not performing."

The following resources will inspire you and your family in teaching

Humanities

film and theater in your homeschool curriculum. (Related resources on literature and public speaking are in Chapter 5.)

Audition Tips   rehearsalroom.com

Click the Working Actor link on the left for acting and audition tips, or the Director's Notes for articles by a director who discusses his professional life.

Big Book of Skits   macscouter.com/skits

A huge collection of ideas for skits—particularly under the Big Book link. You'll be happy to have this one for your next camping trip.

Blast Film   bbc.co.uk/blast/film

Film school for aspiring filmmakers, courtesy of the BBC. Includes advice from industry experts, and the lowdown on filmmaking.

Drama Collection   drama.eserver.org

A collection of plays, modern works, and classics, along with articles on dramatic criticism.

Drama in Education   tinyurl.com/dramaed

A page of questions and answers for teaching drama. Lots of inspirational ideas.

Drama Lessons Galore
childdrama.com/mainframe.html

A very enthusiastic collection of lesson plans, essays, sample plays and monologues, and curriculum suggestions. For grades K through 12.

Film and Television   filmtv.eserver.org

Works in film, television, and other media studies. Links, articles, and more resources, from the e-server collection.

Independent Lens Online Shorts Festival
pbs.org/independentlens/insideindies/shortsfest

Short films by independent filmmakers. Watch them

Hotlinks

Big Book of Skits
macscouter.com/skits

Puppetools
puppetools.com

**The Basics of
Screenwriting**
tinyurl.com/
basicscreenwriting

**Theatre Education
Database**
tedb.byu.edu

Humanities

Humanities

Best Homeschooling Moment

Being told by a veteran drama teacher that she can always tell the home-educated children in speech and drama exams. They stand out.

—Work-at-home mom of four from Jacaranda Tree Learning Co-operative, Hawkes Bay, New Zealand

---

before showing them to kids, of course, but short films may inspire the budding filmmaker in your home.

Learner Interactives Cinema
learner.org/interactives/cinema

For high-school–aged learners, write your own dialogue for a scene or put yourself in a producer's shoes by managing the production of a film.

Puppetools   puppetools.com

The Internet Puppet Utility. Everything you could possibly want to know about puppetry: patterns, articles, and radio programs. It's a commercial site, but it's packed with free resources.

Screen-it   screenit.com

Entertainment reviews for parents. The operators of Screen-it are a husband-and-wife team who review movies, videos, and CDs for content. The MPAA's movie rating system is egregiously inconsistent; Screen-it is astonishingly consistent. The writers categorize material into 15 categories (such as violence, language, and nudity), so that parents may make informed decisions about what is and is not appropriate for their children. Warning: Screen-it often contains movie spoilers. Is that a bad thing?

Teaching Theatre   edta.org/publications

A quarterly publication for drama educators. Learn about acting, directing, playwriting, and technical theater.

The Basics of Screenwriting   tinyurl.com/basicscreenwriting

From the American Film Institute, a five-lesson course on screenwriting for beginning writers. Clips from well-known films illustrate the lessons.

Theatre Education Database   tedb.byu.edu

Unit studies and lesson plans that teach many aspects of theater, from acting and auditions to voice and diction. Click links at the top of the page.

Foreign Language

WHEN MY OLDEST child was eighteen months old, we moved to Taiwan. I'd had a few weeks of intensive Chinese instruction before we arrived, so I was able to at least buy groceries and find the correct bus.

To maintain my visa, I had to enroll in a Chinese-language class—something I was actually looking forward to. After all, I'd studied French for four years and assumed I'd have no trouble picking up a third language. So off I went to my daily Chinese class, while my baby spent the better part of his days playing with the Chinese children in our little neighborhood. I worked and worked. He played and played. Within two months, guess who was the fluent Chinese speaker in the family?

Eventually, my baby became so fluent at Chinese that he refused to speak English at home. As a consequence, my Chinese had to improve if I wanted to speak to my own son.

Mark Thorne is a fourth-year Latin student at Southwest Missouri State University. He has at least a passable ability in seven languages. Upon graduation, he hopes to become a professor of Latin and ancient history. A strong supporter of homeschooling, Mark offers this encouragement to parents teaching their children another language: "Having come this far, I can truly attest to how good it feels to know something of another language. It's a very liberating feeling, because you no longer feel mentally confined to this continent."

As you might expect, he believes Latin is particularly useful for people who are getting started in language studies.

Foreign: From the Latin *foranus* (outside). That which is unfamiliar or non-native.

Humanities

"Even the most basic knowledge of history and languages of the past is incredibly useful," he says. "For starters, a study of Latin forces students to look carefully at their own language, both at its structure and at how it works. They communicate more clearly and effectively when they are more sensitive to how languages function.

"It has been said that just under half of English vocabulary comes from Latin (albeit largely through French); knowledge of Latin, therefore, can sometimes help you figure out what words mean, even if you have never heard or read them before. This has obvious benefits for someone taking such tests as the SAT, ACT, or GRE.

"Latin comes in really handy when traveling. It allows you to read what's written on medieval paintings, on tombstones, beneath statues of famous heroes, on cornerstones of buildings, and even on the backs of paper money!

"Latin is the foundation of all Romance languages. If you speak or come into contact with anything related to French, Italian, Spanish, Portuguese, or Romanian (and if you speak English, that includes you), Latin matters to you whether you realize it or not. Valete!"

When your baby is ready to speak—or sign—another language, these resources are here to help:

American Sign Language Browser
commtechlab.msu.edu/sites/aslweb
Video demonstrations of hundreds of ASL vocabulary words.

Babel Fish Translation   babelfish.yahoo.com
This is where I go to double-check my college French and my bad Chinese before humiliating myself in public. For good measure, it also translates Dutch, German, Greek, Italian, Japanese, Korean, Portuguese, Russian, and Spanish.

Hotlinks

Babel Fish Translation
babelfish.yahoo.com

Before You Know It
byki.com

Ethnologue
sil.org/ethnologue

LiveMocha
livemocha.com

Transparent Language
transparent.com

BBC Languages   bbc.co.uk/languages

Explore in-depth studies in French, Spanish, Italian, German, Portuguese, Greek, and Mandarin—and a smattering of other languages, such as Polish and Urdu. From the BBC.

Before You Know It   byki.com

Free software for learning any of more than 60 languages. Includes learning activities such as multiple choice matching, pronunciation, and dictation. Quite advanced, given its price. Such a bargain.

Ethnologue   sil.org/ethnologue

An encyclopedia that catalogs all of the world's 6,912 known living languages. Discover what's spoken where by how many. It's a fascinating study.

Foreign Language Lesson Plans   tinyurl.com/hflles

Foreign language lesson plans designed by classroom teachers. Most are easily adapted to homeschooling programs.

Foreign Language Videos   tinyurl.com/hflvid

A large collection of educational videos that teach students how to speak a foreign language. One series, for example, explains Spanish speaking and listening skills. Another explores French culture, and others teach teachers how to teach. Spanish, German, and French are covered. From the Annenberg CPB series.

GCSE Bitesize   tinyurl.com/bitesizelang

Lesson plans for teaching Welsh, French, German, and Spanish, from the BBC. For teens. The plans include listening skills, mock exams, and tips for speaking, reading, and writing.

Greek and Latin Studies   tinyurl.com/hflcla

Answers the question, Why study Greek and Latin and the classical humanities? The Latin Teaching Materials section is flawless. If you're teaching the classics, you must have this resource.

Humanities

Ignite the Fire   ignitethefire.com/foreignlang.html

Free foreign language courses online for ages three through college. There are eighty different languages here. It's well worth checking out.

Internet Activities for Foreign Language Classes   clta.net/lessons

Language-learning activities for learners of ten different languages. Many are useful in any language.

Japanese Online   japanese-online.com

Register—yes, they do ask weird questions—and get access not only to a free Japanese language course, but also to a really well-done English-language math course based on the placement tests administered to Japanese students.

Language Flashcards   studystack.com/category-6

Online flashcards—including the space to build your own—that reinforce foreign language learning. Covers more than a dozen languages. Uses flashcards, games, and other tools for teaching.

Latin/English Dictionary   humanum.arts.cuhk.edu.hk/Lexis/Latin

Pretty straightforward. Enter a Latin word (or portion thereof), and get an English word in return.

Latin Pronunciation   tinyurl.com/latinpro

A review of books that explain Latin pronunciation. It's YOO-lee-us KYE-sahr, not JOO-lee-us SEE-zer.

Literacy   t2literacy.notlong.com

Presentations and handouts from teacher workshops on foreign language instruction. The first lesson, "A Meaningful Approach to Teaching a Foreign Language," helps teachers give context to language instruction, giving the task some relevance in everyday life.

LiveMocha   livemocha.com

Learn a language for free, with help from native speakers. An incredible resource. And pitch in to teach someone else a little English.

MIT's Foreign Languages   tinyurl.com/hflmit

Highlights for High School provides resources from MIT to improve language instruction at the high school level. Watch video demonstrations, study for AP exams, and sample college coursework.

School Languages   tinyurl.com/schoollang

Resources from the BBC for learning Spanish, French, and Gaelic. For older students.

Speaking Languages   richmond.edu/~terry/Middlebury/guidelines.htm

An online course in teaching a foreign language and measuring proficiency.

Technology and Language Instruction   tinyurl.com/techlang

It's a How-to-Teach tutorial that focuses on language learning, but the lessons here apply to every subject. The Checklist for Speaking Proficiency will help you determine your child's language level.

Tex's French Grammar   laits.utexas.edu/tex

Extensive French grammar lessons with illustrations, audio files, and interactive exercises. All with an unexpected Texas twist.

Transparent Language   transparent.com

Click the Languages link at the top of the page to access free resources for learning the basics of more than 100 languages, from Afrikaans to Zulu.

Public Speaking

IF YOUR CHILDREN ever take you seriously when you tell them they can grow up to be president or prime minister, you'd better get them ready to become public speakers!

I love the observation of English philosopher John Stuart Mill, who said of his taciturn countrymen, "Among the ordinary English . . . the

Forensics: From the Latin *forensis* (public forum). The study of formal debate; argumentation.

habit of not speaking to others, nor much even to themselves, about the things in which they do feel interest, causes both their feelings and their intellectual faculties to remain undeveloped, reducing them, considered as spiritual beings, to a kind of negative existence."

Homeschooled children have a unique challenge when it comes to learning the skills of effective public communication. Without a handy public forum, opportunities for public speaking have to be conscientiously arranged. At the same time, though, those who are raised in larger families also have a unique opportunity to practice their interpersonal communication skills nearly every waking moment. Fortunately, there actually are opportunities for even young children to take a deep breath and stand up in public to speak:

- Field trips: You might require your children to ask a certain number of intelligent questions of their guide.
- Public meetings: Your civic-minded children can be encouraged to go before a town council to request consideration of a particular issue.
- Auditions: Your children might be interested in auditioning for a part in a local play or a church choir or other performing group.
- Service organizations: Your Scout or Camp Fire Girl or 4-H'er can find a multitude of opportunities to organize an activity or event that requires him or her to stand before a group and speak.
- Church: If your congregation doesn't encourage youngsters to address either the youth organization or the entire congregation, perhaps it's time you had a word with your priest, rabbi, or minister.

How better to understand their faith than for youngsters to prepare to teach someone else what they've learned?

This section covers effective oral communication, speech, and debate. The following online resources will

Hotlinks

Oral Presentation Advice
tinyurl.com/oralpres

The Debatabase
debatabase.org

Youth Model Governments
tinyurl.com/modelgov

Humanities

have your children up and speaking publicly in short order. See related information in the section on logic and critical thinking in Chapter 4, and under Civics and Social Issues in Chapter 10.

Anecdotage   anecdotage.com
Need a clever story to open a speech? Here's your resource. It's a collection of amusing anecdotes—most of them probably true—from famous folk with a wit.

Debate Central   debate.uvm.edu
It's a comprehensive resource for argumentation, persuasion, public speaking, and debating. The site uses videos and other curriculum materials to teach forensics.

HumorMall   humormall.com
How-To's, free jokes, and tips for comedians and public speakers who use humor.

Oral Presentation Advice   tinyurl.com/oralpres
The instructions on how to give a bad talk are particularly amusing.

Preparing Effective Oral Presentations
kumc.edu/SAH/OTEd/jradel/effective.html
How to make effective oral presentations, with visual aids. A good tutorial.

Selected Lessons in Persuasion   cnx.org/content/col10520
For high-school students, a four-lesson unit on the art of persuasion. Lessons include handouts, activities, and texts.

The Debatabase   debatabase.org
The arguments for and against hundreds of debate propositions. Join in by helping edit the debate wiki.

Tips for Effective Presentations   tinyurl.com/epresentations
How to prepare, how to present, and how to create visual aids. Quite useful.

Humanities

Abraham Lincoln

The best-loved president in U.S. history had very little formal education. As a boy, he is reported to have said, he attended school "by littles": a little now, a little then. In all, the future attorney and politician had no more than a year's formal education, but he was known for his willingness to walk for miles to borrow a book. And by the time he was an adult—despite having been raised by parents who were barely literate themselves—he was able to read, write, and multiply a bit. The few books Lincoln did read, he absorbed thoroughly.

Write a Speech   tinyurl.com/forens

Prepare beforehand, and public speaking is easy. Learn2 is a collection of multipart tutorials with cartoon illustrations. Links on the right lead to related How-To's.

Youth Model Governments   tinyurl.com/modelgov

There's no better forensics and civics experience for teenagers than the Youth and Government programs offered through your local YMCA. Except, perhaps, Model UN, Model Congress, or Junior State. Most programs welcome homeschoolers.

Youthful Voices Competition   sfoc.info/youth/index.php

It's an annual competition for young public speakers in the Carolinas. Competition organizers ask, "Did you ever imagine that you could share the stage and tell your stories with some of the best-known storytellers in the country . . . maybe even the world?"

Journalism

I BECAME A journalist because I thought I could change the world. At the beginning of my career, I was full of optimism and hope. I expected that my deep sense of right and wrong—and my sharp-tipped pen—

would somehow right all the injustices in the world and make humankind happier and better.

Over the years I've grown a thick layer of cynicism about my profession. I've found that few reporters are willing to admit to having biases—worshiping, as they do, at the altar of "objectivity." Yet they filter their news choices through a net that screens out or mocks any point of view that doesn't adhere to their own worldview—all the while protesting that they're simply being objective. It was an argument I engaged in frequently while in J-school. My professors didn't see it the same way. Journalism has to be objective, they'd insist. "Why?" I'd ask. The only answer I ever got: Because Sears won't advertise in controversial newspapers, and Sears pays the bills.

So American journalism limps along, pretending objectivity while being completely unable to avoid taking a stance.

Case in point: Because journalists tend to be low-paid, many are the second earner in a two-income household. This situation often means that their children end up in low-level day care facilities. Even so, I was a little surprised to see a major news story in a very conservative newspaper decrying the evils of a government that doesn't provide free day care for two-income families.

The author of the story, who found a multitude of sources supporting what was clearly her personal concern, gave just a cursory, derisive nod to the idea that many working families are just as passionate about wanting a break from their tax burden so they can stay home and raise their own children.

That's why I appreciate the British view of journalism. Objectivity is rarely the goal. Publications are openly biased. They make no pretense of being able to adequately represent the argument against whatever issues they support. Readers know what they're reading and choose their publications accordingly.

Journalism:
From the Middle French *journal* (daily). The collection, writing, and presentation of news and opinion.

Hotlinks

CyberCollege
cybercollege.com

High School Journalism
highschooljournalism
.org/Teachers

Journalism Lesson Plans
tinyurl.com/jlessons

Video 101
video101course.com

Humanities

Fortunately, for my vision of how journalism ought to operate, the Internet is making it possible to economically produce any kind of publication: opinionated, outrageous, intelligent, investigative, heterodox, orthodox, devout . . . all of it espousing a particular worldview, and all of it causing readers to actually think about their beliefs and perspectives.

Alex Johnson, an editor and producer for MSNBC.com when we interviewed him, makes use of his journalism training every day. The Redmond, Washington–based, journalist says that although he can't answer for other people, "I can tell you how I use my journalism background in daily life.

"I'm essentially a shy, quiet person. But that won't fly if you're a reporter, whose job—when you break it down—is to confront people and ask them questions they don't want to be asked. Learning how to do this has made it a lot easier for me to deal one-on-one with people in general.

"Since journalists are trained to find ways to keep people talking, you become more adept at conversation, because you know how to listen. If you can't listen attentively, you'll never be a good reporter. If nothing else, being a journalist means you can always find someone to talk to!"

If your children are ready to gain a journalism education of their own, here's help. Related resources for developing research skills are found in Chapter 4. You'll also find links to writing and reading materials in Chapter 5. The following resources cover print, broadcast, and electronic journalism.

Ask a Reporter   nytimes.com/learning/students/ask_reporters

Reporters from the *New York Times* answer questions. Click the link to Frequently Asked Questions, and page up to find which reporters are attached to which beats, so that you can direct your questions to the appropriate person.

CyberCollege   cybercollege.com

Free online lessons in mass communications, and film and television production. The opening page is less than impressive, and you might be tempted to rush past it. But dig around. You'll find scores of fascinating lessons in studio and field production, as well as the history of the media. This is a fabulous, completely illustrated online course in journalism.

Dow Jones Editing Exercise   freep.com/legacy/jobspage

How to get a job in journalism. Click the Toolkit link, then the Dow Jones Editing Test link to find a really tough editing test that every prospective journalist ought to study.

FactCheck   factcheck.org

Lying politicians—it's tautological. And FactCheck proves it. FactCheck is the lie detector for politicians on both sides of the aisle. There'll be no more bogus tales of tax cuts or clean living—not if the journalists at Annenberg have any say. FactCheck is a great model for any aspiring journalist who needs to learn to check facts before publishing tall tales.

High School Journalism   highschooljournalism.org/Teachers

The American Society of Newspaper Editors sponsors this resource for teenage journalists. Though it's heavily public-school–oriented, the resources and contests are more inclusive. Give your high-school–aged kids good resources, tools, and ideas to jump-start them in journalism. Lesson plans cover every area of a journalism curriculum.

Journalism Lesson Plans   tinyurl.com/jlessons

Regularly updated journalism lesson plans from the *New York Times*.

Journalism Unit Study   easyfunschool.com/article2120.html

A unit study that will work for many age groups and give your children a real sense of being a journalist.

Media, Music, and the Arts   tinyurl.com/musocw

Highlights for High School provides resources from MIT to improve journalism and other humanities instruction at the high school level. Watch video demonstrations, study for AP exams, and sample college coursework.

Newsroom Jargon   tinyurl.com/deseret

Part of a series of journalism articles celebrating the sesquicentennial of the *Deseret News*.

Professor Gibson's Wonderful World of Editing   web.ku.edu/~edit

Grammar rules and other goodies. It's editing from A to Z, spelling, words for the wise, and lots and lots of excellent editing resources.

The Newspaper Clipping Generator

tools.fodey.com/generators/newspaper/snippet.asp

A fun tool for making your own mock newspaper clipping. Name your paper, write your headline and story, and you've got a genuine-looking news clip.

The Slot: A Spot for Copy Editors   theslot.com

A copy editor's dream site. Learn what a copy editor is, and read Bill Walsh's Sharp Points columns and his blog about editing errors he's found in major newspapers. It'll make you feel better about your own small errors.

Video 101   video101course.com

Journalism is less and less about newspapers, and more and more about broadcast. This online video editing course—one of the best you'll find on any subject—is used by schools around the country. It incorporates video clips and animations that illustrate the principles being taught in the lessons. Your aspiring journalist will enjoy working through these modules.

Philosophy

THE DISCIPLINE CALLED philosophy crosses several curriculum areas. From Greek beliefs about logical thought to Heidegger's and Sartre's existentialist revolt, philosophy covers logic, reason, art, communication, reading, writing, critical thought, and theology.

Steve Naragon was an associate professor of philosophy at Manchester College in Manchester, Indiana, when we interviewed him. He has a theory about how philosophy is useful in everyday life: "Studying philosophy brings with it a great many advantages," he says. "Studying philosophy sharpens your ability to understand and evaluate arguments, to make fine conceptual distinctions, and to clear up any number of misunderstandings that result from a misuse of language or logic. In this regard, philosophers can be quite handy to have around.

"Philosophy helps instill us with humility, both moral and intellectual; ever since Socrates, it has been demonstrating to us how little we actually know about a great many things (with the lesson that we ought not to be too self-satisfied, nor push our views on others too vigorously). Philosophy helps us debunk much of the nonsense offered up to us by the wider culture. Philosophy can help us find some ground or center for our beliefs and our sense of self, and it can help us articulate and act upon our particular conception of the good. If the Socratic claim that 'the unexamined life is not worth living' rings true for you, then philosophy is indispensable."

The following resources will help you get a handle on philosophy: (See related resources in Chapter 4 under logic and critical thinking, and under values, standards, and ethics.)

Philosophy:
From the Greek *philosophos* (lover of wisdom). The discipline that considers core logic, aesthetics and ethics.

AskPhilosophers   askphilosophers.org
More than 2,000 questions and nearly 3,000 answers to such philosophical questions as What do we owe to people who don't yet exist? Caution: Site is hostile to religion.

Classics Online   classics.mit.edu
Some 500 works by Homer, Aristotle, Plato, and other classical philosophers. And it's all searchable.

Hotlinks

Classics Online
classics.mit.edu

Internet Encyclopedia of Philosophy
utm.edu/research/iep

No Dogs or Philosophers Allowed
nodogs.org

Humanities

How to Write a Philosophy Paper   tinyurl.com/howtophi

For precollege philosophers, a three-part essay on writing philosophic essays.

Internet Encyclopedia of Philosophy   utm.edu/research/iep

The oldest online philosophy encyclopedia, this one is written at a more accessible level than the Stanford EoP.

No Dogs or Philosophers Allowed   nodogs.org

Videos and more for a popular philosophy-oriented television program. The author claims to have learned philosophy by driving a cab.

Philosophy at EServer   philosophy.eserver.org

Writings by modern and classical philosophers. The Humor link is highly recommended. Articles, texts, and more resources, from the e-server collection.

Philosophy Lesson Plans   eduref.org/cgi-bin/lessons.cgi/Philosophy

Philosophy lesson plans designed by classroom teachers. Most are easily adapted to homeschooling programs.

Philosophy Slam   philosophyslam.org

The Kids Philosophy Slam seeks to give kids a voice and to inspire them to think by participating in a competition to create art, essays, or other media regarding a philosophical question posed each year. Homeschoolers are welcome to participate.

Philosophy Study Guides   sparknotes.com/home/philosophy

More than eighty guides to every major philosophy topic, from Plato's *Apology* through Thoreau's *Walden*. Each guide includes study questions and answers.

Philosophy Talk   philosophytalk.org

Since early 2004, weekly podcasts produced by a couple of Stanford philosophy profs. Easy listening.

Stanford Encyclopedia of Philosophy   plato.stanford.edu
The second-oldest encyclopedic resource for philosophic research. Start with Abstract Objects, and months later, finish by learning about Zombies. Seriously. It's written at a more scholarly level than the Internet EoP.

Religious Education

THIS MAY BE the single most significant factor in most people's decision to homeschool: the desire to make a spiritual education part of their children's academic experience. In one survey, well over half of all homeschoolers described themselves as "Biblically based Christians."* Add to that mix the large numbers of other faithful who are homeschooling members of other Christian denominations, Jews, Bahá'ís, Sikhs, Hindus, Muslims, and even Wiccans and Pagans—and it's clear that spirituality is a big factor in most families' home education.

Religion:
Associated with the Latin *religre* (to tie fast, rely). Reliance on a supreme being or supernatural influence.

Researcher Brian Ray has discovered that providing a solid religious foundation may be the most important factor in the decision to homeschool, after providing kids a good education. "Most homeschoolers list two or more reasons for homeschooling, and at least 60 percent (whether agnostic, Christian, Jew, or Muslim) would put transmitting values, beliefs, and worldview to their children as one of these." Ray's research demonstrates the broad span of the homeschooling community. The community, he writes, includes "conservatives, libertarians, and liberals; low-, middle-, and high-income families; black, Hispanic, and white; parents with Ph.D.s, GEDs, and no high-school diplomas."

* See our website, **hsfree.com,** for citations for this and other statistics and references in this chapter.

Humanities

Hotlinks

Interfaith Calendar
interfaithcalendar.org

Internet Sacred Text Archive
sacred-texts.com

Studylight
studylight.org

Your Guide to the Religions of the World
bbc.co.uk/religion/religions

Religion is indisputably a major influence on the homeschooling movement. That's a good thing, say people who have considered the alternatives. Henry Simmons, head of the Presbyterian School in Richmond, Virginia, explained in a recent radio broadcast the effect of ignoring or downplaying the teaching of religious philosophies and doctrines: "What happens when religion is cut out? What happens when we try to create a world that is perfectly secular, that has no religion, has no place for God, has no place for a community of faith? First of all, we're creating a strange world in terms of humankind." Simmons worries that the practice of teaching secular lessons—lessons without a religious foundation—undermines the well-being of individuals and the health of our society.

"What is going to sustain you when the things that society prized and rewarded you with, or for, fall away? When you no longer are handsome or beautiful, when you don't have physical strength? When you, perhaps, don't have the same quickness of wit or whatever, and don't dress as well? Can't do all the things society does? Can't play a good game of golf? What's going to sustain you? What's going to sustain you as an individual? And what's going to sustain you and me together? That thing is the knowledge that there is something that is deeper than us or that transcends us, that we are related to in some real and powerful way."

For Dr. Anthony Davies, assistant professor of economics and finance at Pittsburgh's Duquesne University, education that neglects morality is without substance. The economist calls himself a strong supporter of homeschooling and explains why:

"I support homeschooling because I believe that young minds cannot be taught without the background of moral context. Knowledge, no matter how we might wish otherwise, is not independent of morality. It

Humanities

is an incomplete and hollow education that speaks of truth without addressing how one should respond to that truth.

"What good does it do for our children to learn of history without learning that this or that person behaved well or poorly, and so should or should not be emulated? What good does it do for our children to learn of science without learning that the ability to act is not, of itself, license to act? What good does it do for our children to learn if they are not taught that it is truth that is absolute and opinion that is relative? It is precisely the moral context that homeschooling can and does bring to education. It is this context that, in its fruition, marks the difference between knowledge and wisdom."

Susan D. Clawson homeschools five children in Clearfield, Utah. She says her religious faith sustained the family during their years in the military, and the variety of religious associations her children have made has been beneficial to their own spiritual development. This is what she says about how she has educated her own children about religious faiths other than her own: "We have friends from various religions and some who claim no religion at all. Having been moved around with the military in their early years, my two older boys had a wide variety of playmates: all different religions, ethnic backgrounds, and cultures.

"When we look up something on a map as we're reading the newspaper or *National Geographic* or listening to the news, we'll talk about the people who live there. Their religion, their food, their manner of dress, and other aspects of their lives are discussed, all informally. I wouldn't say that we've ever undertaken a formal survey of world religions, but it sounds like a fascinating area of study!"

In her homeschooling, Susie has developed her own religion curriculum: "We live our religion twenty-four

New Views

Moses led the Hebrew slaves to the Red Sea, where they made unleavened bread, which is bread made without any ingredients. Moses went up on Mount Cyanide to get the Ten Commandments. He died before he ever reached Canada.

—Alleged response given by a sixth-grader to a history exam question

Humanities

hours a day. Our conduct is based on what we believe. We're active participants in worship services in our church, in its youth programs, men's and women's groups, and so on. We use this as a springboard of sorts. We help our children understand that what we learn at church is to be used in our lives, to serve and love others, and not to judge. Our faith is big on building bridges with other faiths and cultures. Instead of dwelling on our differences, we find links between our similarities, still holding on to our beliefs. We're helping our kids to learn to live this way by doing it ourselves."

The history of religion is stormy—but virtually everyone agrees that a better understanding of unfamiliar religious faiths can't help but improve your children's own level of spirituality. Where it reinforces their faith, they benefit, and where it causes them to ask questions, you're there to respond.

The following resources are of two types: comparative and explanatory. The comparative religion links avoid the name-calling and controversy that is so easily found on the Internet. They focus instead on the facts about various religious movements and faiths, and compare them in a matter-of-fact manner you're sure to find refreshing.

The explanatory sites represent the doctrine, history, or theology of the world's major religious movements. For the most part, they are scholarly in nature and avoid material of a proselytizing nature. If you're inclined to teach your children how the rest of the world lives its beliefs, here's a start. (Related resources on ethics, morals, standards, and values are found in Chapter 4.)

Adherents   adherents.com

An amazing site. All studies of comparative religion should begin here. A compilation of some 43,000 records documenting the membership of more than 4,200 religious faiths.

Blue Letter Bible   blueletterbible.org

The word-for-word concordance/translation tool makes BLB a keeper. Several verses comes with links to corresponding hymns.

Christian Classics Ethereal Library   ccel.org

It's a digital library of hundreds of classic Christian books selected "for edification and education." Includes the Bibles and commentaries, as well as works by early Church fathers and more recent writers.

Faith & Reason   pbs.org/faithandreason

PBS takes its shot at reconciling science and religion. Listen to audio discussions of Science and Religion in Dialogue.

Interfaith Calendar   interfaithcalendar.org

So it turns out that almost every day is a holiday—or a holy day—for someone, somewhere. As I write, for example, we're at the intersection of holidays observed by the Orthodox, Hindu, and Muslim faiths. And next week it's the Catholics' and the Jains' turn.

Internet Sacred Text Archive   sacred-texts.com

An archive of more than 1,400 books about religion, mythology, folklore, and the esoteric. Read the *Koran,* the *Tao Te Ching,* the *Kitab-i-Aqdas,* or the *Rig Veda.* A mind-bending collection.

Learn About Greek Mythology   wingedsandals.com

Take the tour with Hermes the messenger god, through a magical place filled with awesome gods, daring heroes, and fabulous monsters. Navigate through Greek history, geography, and mythical beings.

Religious Education Links   crickweb.co.uk/links-re.html

Well-done flash presentations that teach basic information about Christianity, Hinduism, Islam, and Judaism. Click Stages 1 and 2 tabs on the menu bar to find other high-quality resources for religious education.

Religious Movements Homepage   tinyurl.com/relmovements

Intelligent conversation about new religious movements.

Religious Studies Glossary   ccat.sas.upenn.edu/~rs2/glossind.html

Can you tell your *Bavli* from your *Gemara*? While you are studying Judaism, Christianity, and Islam, this glossary of terminology will prove helpful.

Humanities

Religious Tolerance   religioustolerance.org

Very ecumenical, this site welcomes, and seeks to include, people of any, every, and no faith by setting out to disseminate accurate information about every form of theology. Accurate is, of course, in the eye of the beholder, but generally speaking, the site is reasonable and helpful.

Studylight   studylight.org

For depth of commentary, and access to Hebrew, Greek, and Strong's, nothing beats Studylight for in-depth Bible study. Search by word, topic, or specific scripture reference. Studylight lets you choose the translation (presently 47 options, including the Vulgate and two Spanish editions) and the commentary. The Hebrew and Greek concordances I find particularly useful in trying to discern on my own the Author's original intent.

Western Religions   mrdowling.com/605westr.html

Short articles with great illustrations on Judaism, Christianity, Islam, and how religion affects conflict in the Middle East. For middle-school ages.

Science Scholarship

W HEN MY SIBLINGS and I were children, we got all our best science lessons hands-on. Our parents had a family membership to the local science center, and the four of us used it as the family playground whenever our parents had business downtown.

Homeschooling families find lots of ways to make science fun and educational for their children. Terri Vitkovitsky from North Carolina says she can't even begin to count the number of science experiments that happen in her home during a regular week. "Kids playing with things—liquids, bubbles, blocks, pulleys, dirt, clay, and all the rest—trying to investigate *on their own* how and why things work."

Wyoming mom Kathryne Thompson says sloppy science experiments make for good learning. "With science, keep it as fun (read messy) as possible."

Joyce Dumire, a homeschooling mom in Akron, Ohio, has found dozens of science activities for her teenage son. Among their projects: kite flying; rocket building and launching; visiting a city waterworks; city park activities; visiting state parks as they traveled; ripping out and changing a flower bed, replanting it, and redesigning it for

Hotlinks

Junk Science
junkscience.com

Robert Krampf's Science Education
krampf.com

Sci4Kids
ars.usda.gov/is/kids

Science Buddies
sciencebuddies.org

Science Rock
schoolhouserock.tv/
Science.html

On Intelligence

Intellectual growth should commence at birth and cease only at death.

—Albert Einstein, 1879–1955.

plants, sun, and water flow; taking apart a computer and rebuilding it; talking with a landscape architect; doing lots of home experiments based on a book she picked up from a homeschool fair; and checking the local county extension office for activities, letting her son pick things he enjoyed, and finding a way to make them into a lesson.

Joyce's extended family took up spelunking as well. "We camped out near the caves (preparing was part of home economics) and learned about the rocks, formations, animal and plant life, and history of the area."

Ann Crum homeschools two children in central Arkansas. Living out in the country, with goats, chickens, and a garden, makes for some great laboratory experiences, she says. "The kids have learned so much about reproductive biology, conservation, animal husbandry, ecology, agriculture, nutrition, diseases, parasites, and good stewardship from our animals and garden. Last spring their project was a section of our vegetable garden. They had to plot the area, estimate the crop production, choose vegetables and flowers that would grow well here, and keep a journal of their activities. They even had to figure the cost of seeds and soil amendments and weigh that against their projected harvest. We also included a small course on composting, which is a scientific adventure as well.

"Basically, what I strive for is not necessarily for my children to learn a lot about a particular scientific or math discipline, but to learn how to use the scientific method in all areas of their lives. To learn to explore and be curious. Along the way, they learn to apply science to real life." Real life is what science is all about. The resources in this chapter will help you teach your children all the hard sciences: anatomy, archaeology, astronomy, biology, botany, chemistry, earth science, ecology, physical science, scientists, technology, and zoology.

We start this chapter with general tools for teaching all different kinds of science:

101 Science   101science.com

Yes, it's a linkfarm, but it's so well organized that the categories themselves are a lesson in science. Links are overwhelming, with connections to 20,000-plus science resources.

125 Questions   sciencemag.org/sciext/125th

Top 125 questions science has tackled—and may or may not have answered. Questions are as varied as Are we alone in the universe? Can researchers make a perfect optical lens?

BJs Science Resources

camillasenior.homestead.com/resources.html

Nearly 300 science printables in biology, motion, flight, physical science, fluids, optics, water, electricity, astronomy, and cell systems.

COSI's Online Activities   tinyurl.com/cactive

Science experiments, online. Travel to a star, conduct surgery, parachute without crash landing. With these wonderfully presented interactive animations, kids learn how science applies to real life.

Discovery Channel Videos   dsc.discovery.com/video

Endless science videos from Discovery Channel programs. Space, earth, technology, history, animals, survival—it's an easy way to impart scientific learning.

Education Overview   nsf.gov/news/overviews/education

An overview of science by the National Science Foundation. Discusses how learning takes place and what teachers need to know.

EdWorld Science   tinyurl.com/edsci

A collection of lesson plans covering general science, agriculture, chemistry, history of science, life science, physical science, process skills, natural history, and space science.

Science Freebie

Learning Partners: Let's Do Science! suggests ways parents can help their children see that science is everywhere. Call 877-4-ED-PUBS and request product number ED001442P.

Science

Science

Everyday Mysteries   loc.gov/rr/scitech/mysteries

The Library of Congress answers questions such as Why does hair turn gray? and Why is the ocean blue? Sort of an "Everything You Ever Wanted to Know About Agriculture, Anthropology, Astronomy, Biology, Botany, Chemistry, Geography, Home Economics, Meteorology, Motor Vehicles, Physics, Recreation, Technology, and Zoology."

Free Science Lectures   freesciencelectures.com

A large collection of video lectures on science topics. Covers most areas of the science curriculum.

Helping Your Child Learn Science   ed.gov/pubs/parents/Science

A really great foundation for teaching science. Of particular note: the Concepts link, which teaches the nine basic principles of science. If your children understand these concepts and their applications, they've learned the basics of science. You'll also learn a lot from the information under Activities in the Home, and Activities in the Community.

Junk Science   junkscience.com

This site purports to uncover faulty scientific data and analysis, much of which appears to further special agendas. Your little scientists will enjoy reading about Freud and ice cream and lots of other pseudoscientific stuff. Go directly to the bottom of the page for the best resources: Short Course is a free on-line class in the scientific method. And don't miss the Archives or the Videos.

K–6 Science Refreshers   nsdl.org/refreshers

Build your content knowledge or provide a quick refresher just in time to teach a topic. It ain't cheating. It's "preparing."

LiveScience   livescience.com

Blogs, articles, videos, quizzes, and more. Like its sister site, Space.com, this graphics-heavy website is too com-

---

Science Freebie

Helping Your Child Learn Science provides practical information to support science learning at home. Call 877-4-ED-PUBS and request product number ED004451H.

plicated to navigate, but click the Sitemap link at the very bottom of the page to see a well-organized view of articles about everything scientific. Current hot topics include animals, Antarctica, birds, climate, cloning, dinosaurs, DNA, earthquakes, environment news, evolution, fish, global warming, history info, hurricanes, insects, inventions, memory, monkeys, nanotechnology, nature, ocean, penguins, reptiles, robots, science, sea, sharks, tornadoes, tsunami, viruses, volcanoes, weather, and wildlife. That pretty much covers science, right?

Paso Partners   sedl.org/scimath/pasopartners
Science unit studies for kids K through 3. Lessons cover subjects such as the five senses, the human body, and simple machines. Includes Spanish translations.

Robert Krampf's Science Education   krampf.com
Homepage for the fantastic "Experiment of the Week" newsletter and fascinating science videos. The site includes information on "watt" is electricity, the million-volt electric show; the nuts and bolts of lightning; burning questions, the science of fire safety; energy transformations; and more.

Sci4Kids   ars.usda.gov/is/kids
How fun is this? Click on any object in a complex graphic and find stories to match. Learn about weird science, plants, insects, transportation, and so much more. From the USDA.

Science and Technology   factmonster.com/science.html
Articles that teach many science topics. Inventions, science projects, animals, weather, space, transportation, and the human body are all explained.

Science Blogs   scienceblogs.com
Central location for learning what scientists are discussing among

---

Free Smithsonian Publication

Torch, a monthly newsletter from the Smithsonian, and *Inside Smithsonian Research*, are available to the general public for free. Contact the museum's Office of Public Affairs at 202-633-2400 to be added to the mailing list.

Science

☆ *Best Homeschooling Moment*

Our best homeschooling moments come when we are exploring science and nature firsthand, and those moments in real life when my children compare life to something they heard in the Bible.

—Kristene Brooks, a disciple training four disciples, Boerne, Texas

themselves. Blogs are organized into five categories: technology, brain and behavior, education and careers, politics, and medicine and health.

Science Buddies   sciencebuddies.org
Science fair preparation, from start to finish. Covers everything from the scientific method to suggestions for research projects.

Science E-Books   eduplace.com/science/hmsc
In addition to the grade-specific lessons, this site incorporates graphic organizers, glossaries, games, and bibliographies for teaching across the science curriculum. For learners in grades K through 6.

Science Fair Central

school.discovery.com/sciencefaircentral

A great soup-to-nuts handbook for students, with project ideas, a science fair organizer, and advice for parents. There's even a science fair competition for your kids to enter.

Science Lesson Plans

eduref.org/cgi-bin/lessons.cgi/Science

Science lesson plans designed by classroom teachers. Most are easily adapted to homeschooling programs.

Science NetLinks   sciencenetlinks.com

Everything you need to teach science—interactive activities, lessons, benchmarks—all sortable by grade level and science subject.

Science Rock   schoolhouserock.tv/Science.html

The old Schoolhouse Rock videos are back, this time teaching nine different science subjects. The "Body Machine" teaches anatomy, "Interplanet Janet" is a video about the solar system, and "Greatest Show on Earth" teaches about the weather. Includes the lyrics and animations.

Science Teachers' Resource Center chem.lapeer.org

Labs, activities, teaching tips, worksheets, and more for teaching chemistry, biology, and physical science.

Science Videos tinyurl.com/scivid

Lots of educational videos that teach science across the curriculum. One section, for example, explains Teaching High School Science. In another, students watch scientists investigate how microbes affect our world. From the Annenberg CPB series.

Singing Science acme.com/jef/singing_science

Better than Schoolhouse Rock, dozens and dozens of great songs about science topics. Such fun! Your kids will love this one!

Teachers' Domain teachersdomain.org

Register (it's free) to get access to a very large collection of science lesson plans from WGBH, the public television station. Lesson categories are earth and space, engineering, life science, and physical science.

Visionlearning visionlearning.com/library

Science lessons in modular form. Each module discusses a science principle in great depth, using text, pictures, vocabulary links, and diagrams.

WebCurrents Science learnersonline.com/weekly/subject/science.htm

Web quests. Extremely well done, with photographs, links, explanatory text, and illustrations.

Anatomy

THE KNEE BONE'S connected to the . . . leg bone . . . or something like that.

From the time they first start talking, kids get a thrill out of naming parts of their own bodies.

Anatomy: From the Greek *anatome* (dissection). The study of the structure of the body.

Now it's time to take it to the next level. Anatomy teaches children to appreciate not just the names of body parts but also the complexity of their own bodies. Through anatomy, kids learn how their bodies are structured while discovering the fascinating qualities of eyeballs, hair, toenails, and all the other things that make them, physically, who they are.

These Internet resources provide a better anatomical foundation than anything your kids would ever hear in a classroom, because they let kids examine real photos of real bodies. The Visible Human Project, for example, may be the single most amazing science project in the world. So here they are, the resources for an online anatomy class. (For related resources, see the human development section in Chapter 13 and the biology section, which includes genetics, later in this chapter.)

Hotlinks

Atlas of the Human Body
tinyurl.com/humatlas

Gray's Anatomy
bartleby.com/107

Human Anatomy Online
innerbody.com/htm/
body.html

Normal Anatomy
tinyurl.com/normanat

Atlas of the Human Body   tinyurl.com/humatlas

This American Medical Association site describes more than 40 elements of the nervous, circulatory, digestive, endocrine, reproductive, skeletal, muscular, lymphatic, respiratory, and urinary systems. Includes detailed drawings of anatomical features, such as sense organs, fetal development during pregnancy, and the effects of stroke.

Gray's Anatomy   bartleby.com/107

Don't know what's where? This illustrated text from *Gray's Anatomy*—the book, not the TV show—will set you straight.

Habits of the Heart Lessons
smm.org/heart/lessons/top.html

Eleven illustrated lesson plans for teaching the cardiopulmonary system. Includes links, charts, materials lists, and everything else you need to teach the science of the heart.

How the Body Works   kidshealth.org/kid/htbw

Animated, easy-to-read illustrations of how the body works. Your younger children will enjoy it. Hear a heart beat, go inside a human ear, or listen to hiccups and learn what causes them.

Human Anatomy Online   innerbody.com/htm/body.html

Examine ten body systems, or search by topic. As you mouse over various body parts, the corresponding explanation appears in a side window. Very useful site for teaching anatomy to middle and upper ages.

Hypermuscle   med.umich.edu/lrc/Hypermuscle/Hyper.html

What happens when you use your muscles? Find out at this site that illustrates muscles in various stages of work.

Illustrated Encyclopedia of Human Anatomic Variation
tinyurl.com/anavar

If your child hopes to get into medical school, these lists of health topics are probably worth consulting. And click the link to Anatomy Atlases for beautifully drawn graphics.

Neuroscience for Kids   faculty.washington.edu./chudler/neurok.html

Click the Explore link to find dozens of illustrated articles on neuroscience, written for kids. Learn about the brain, the spinal cord, and sensory systems. You'll also find here experiments, activities, games, and answers to frequent questions.

Normal Anatomy   tinyurl.com/normanat

Using slices from the Visible Human Project, kids can examine cross sections of the human body and test their own anatomical knowledge.

The Brain from Top to Bottom   thebrain.mcgill.ca

This McGill University site teaches about the human brain, using graphics and text to address such diverse topics as physiology, memory, emotions, movement, senses, mental disorders, development, language, and dreams and consciousness. Written in both French and English.

Science

The Human Heart   fi.edu/learn/heart

The Franklin Institute of Science provides this online tour of the heart. Written for middle-school and older children.

Archaeology and Paleontology

I ONCE HEARD of a kid who didn't care about dinosaurs. Naaah. Just joking.

Paleontology and archaeology are fundamentally related. They involve the two things kids—especially kids of the male variety—love best: dinosaurs and digging in the dirt.

Danish Geologist Susie Mathia describes the many kinds of scientists who examine the Earth and the things in it. Generally speaking, geologists study the bedrock to determine the location of certain attractive raw materials (such as sand, water, minerals, and coal) and to estimate their quality. "As you can imagine," she says, "geologists work in many fields. As a professional, I examine rocks with respect to structure, mineral composition, and chemistry. The result of such an examination aids in ore exploration.

"Other scientists examine the underground for petroleum, and they have the title petrologist. Scientists looking for water have the title hydrogeologist.

> Archaeology:
>
> From the Greek *arkhaiologia* (antiquities + study). The systematic study of material remains.

Geologists working with soft materials such as sand, gravel, and clay are called sedimentologists.

Geologists also work with earthquake predictions (seismologists), and volcanic activities and the building of our planet (volcanists).

"A certain type of geologist examines the development of life on Earth—everything from human beings to bluefish, dinosaurs, trilobites, insects, and mammals. This sort of geologist has the title paleontologist. Some consider paleontologists more related to biologists than to geologists. A paleontologist knows about the ecosystem and environment of a certain group of now-extinct animals/ living forms."

If you want to give your favorite dirt diggers some purpose, the following resources will be helpful. See the related section on anthropology in Chapter 10, and another related section, earth science, later in this chapter.

All About Dinosaurs
enchantedlearning.com/subjects/dinosaurs

For younger children, an illustrated, easy-to-read resource about dinosaurs. Lots of fun facts.

ArchaeOlogy   ology.amnh.org/archaeology

A very kid-friendly site for learning about an archaeologist's work. Incas, a Spanish mission, and an ancient city are all subject to digging and exploring.

Archaeology at Jamestown   historicjamestowne.org/learn

An archaeological adventure, where kids can work the way an archaeologist works, digging artifacts, cataloging them, and trying to work out their age. The Jamestown lesson plans will help your children discover the ancient world around them.

Chaos in Prehistory   tinyurl.com/prehistorychaos

A rather advanced argument that linear accounts of prehistory may be flawed.

Dilophosaurus! A Narrated Exhibition   tinyurl.com/dinodiscover

Take a guided audio tour of the discovery of the Dilophosaurus, by the Berkeley paleontologist who made the find.

Dinosaur Dig   sdnhm.org/kids/dinosaur

From the San Diego Natural History Museum, play dinosaur games, or discover how, where, and what you need to know about finding fossils.

Hotlinks

Dinosaur Dig
sdnhm.org/kids/dinosaur

Heritage Education Archeology
histpres.mtsu.edu/then/archeology

NPS Archaeology
nps.gov/archeology

Science

Heritage Education Archeology   histpres.mtsu.edu/then/archeology

How to teach archaeology. This site teaches the teacher, with vocabulary, teaching tips, and really good classroom activities.

NPS Archaeology   nps.gov/archeology

The For Kids link on the right is great for young explorers, or click Research in the Parks for the National Park Service's resources about archaeological efforts in the United States. The Coso Rock Art feature, for example, describes the best-preserved, largest concentration of prehistoric art in North America. Learn about the people who created a quarter-million drawings on rocks. And the Earliest Americans feature is a must-see for anyone interested in pre-history.

Prehistorics Illustrated   prehistoricsillustrated.com

Crowded with dinosaur illustrations, news, and other information about the prehistoric world.

Astronomy

TWINKLE, TWINKLE, LITTLE star . . . Here I am with seven kids and a busy life, and I still wonder what you are!

The science of astronomy has many facets: planetary and solar systems, black holes, rocketry, aviation . . . in short, the whole universe. It can all be a little mind-boggling.

Fortunately, there are a lot of resources available to you to help get your children thinking about things beyond the tops of the trees. One way to get kids interested in astronomy is simply to get them out looking, says Brad Kirshenbaum Sr. Brad is the head of the astronomy department at St. Robert Bellarmine in Omaha, Nebraska. He says his goal as a teacher is to get people interested in astronomy, but he worries that astronomy intimidates some people into thinking that it is a very difficult job, profession, or hobby. "So many times each

Astronomy:
From the Greek *aster* (star) and *nomas* (wander). The study of matter beyond the earth's atmosphere.

year," he says, "I will be outside with my eight-inch LX200 telescope (which attracts a lot of attention), and people walking by will stop and ask what I am looking at and if they can have a look. I always say yes, and take them to some very eye-pleasing objects such as Saturn, Jupiter, the Orion Nebula, or Sagittarius to grab their attention. When they ask questions, I try to keep them interested with 'down-to-earth' responses. When I see their excitement, it is a very exhilarating feeling."

A real education in astronomy can open doors—space shuttle doors, even—for people who pursue it. Mike, a Houston-based instructor for the International Space Station and a NASA employee at the time of our interview, says he uses his astronomy education every day. "Both the space shuttle and the space station use instruments for navigation that require sightings of specific stars. We have to be able to recognize those stars and where they are in the sky to do star sightings.

"A great deal of my job also involves understanding orbital mechanics, since this governs how objects orbit the Earth. A basic understanding of astronomy is a must for me to determine that our training simulators are 'traveling' correctly in simulated space."

Ben Fillmore was a post-grad student in astronomy at University College, London, when we interviewed him. He says a working knowledge of astronomy also has a lot of practical applications. "It is used for everything from predicting the financial growth of various markets to catching today's speeders. The programs used in data extraction in astronomy are essentially the ones used in predicting the NASDAQ and the Financial Times Index. The theory of special relativity leads to the programs used to operate police speed guns and calculate the criminal's speed. Public knowledge on the subject is not too hot. Although movies and documentaries make people aware of the dangers our planet faces, many take a comical view of what astronomers do. But if anyone discovers an asteroid that could hit the Earth or observes a coronal mass

Hotlinks

Astronomy Picture of the Day
apod.nasa.gov

Google Sky
google.com/sky

Space
space.com

Science

ejection (from the sun) heading right toward us, we could someday save the human race."

If you want to get your kids looking skyward, the following great resources can help. Related resources on weather and atmosphere are in the earth science section, later in this chapter.

Adventures of the Agronauts   ncsu.edu/project/agronauts

Illustrated astronomy for younger kids. It's an online curriculum focusing on space biology. Fun, interactive, and free!

All About Space   enchantedlearning.com/subjects/astronomy

Though the overall site has become very commercialized, Enchanted Learning's science pages are still chock-full of good lesson material. The astronomy section is particularly useful, with good graphic illustrations of each of the planets and other celestial bodies. Includes a very well done illustrated astronomy dictionary.

Asteroids   tinyurl.com/astroast

A multimedia tour of space, with lots of background information and photos of asteroids and other discoveries. A good introduction.

Astronomy & Space   nsf.gov/news/overviews/astronomy

An overview by the National Science Foundation: "Astronomy may well be the oldest science of all, seeking answers to questions such as: 'Where did it all come from?' and 'Are we alone?' "

Astronomy Picture of the Day   apod.nasa.gov

Each day features a different image or photograph of our fascinating universe, along with a brief explanation written by a professional astronomer. The archives go back to 1995.

Eye on the Sky   eyeonthesky.org

Click the Our Star link to find "Making a Solar Eclipse Book," the culminating activity for a sun-and-eclipse unit study. It's a good model for making subject-specific notebooks.

FAA Education & Research   faa.gov/education_research

Want to study the physics of air and flight? Click the Student Resources link to find aeronautics and space activities such as coloring books, experiments, games, and word puzzles. In the Kids Corner you'll find advice for making parachutes and windmills.

Google Sky   google.com/sky

Google and a group of observatories have teamed up to map the sky. The whole thing. View it telescopically, and see it again at different wavelengths, as though you had X-ray or infrared vision. Breathtaking.

Largest Known   techdo.com/images/largest-know-star.htm

"Okay, so, Mom? How big *is* the sun?" "Well, dear, I'll show you. Click here." An amazing visual demonstration of exactly how small and insignificant the earth is in relation to other objects in the universe. Startling.

Space   space.com

The graphic version of this important website is overly complex, but click the Sitemap link at the bottom of the page to see the well-organized view. The Top 10s and Space Trivia categories will be particularly useful to homeschooling families. The Space Images and Video section will fascinate young astronomers.

On Science

The important thing is to not stop questioning.

—Albert Einstein

The Nine Planets   nineplanets.org

A tour of the solar system, where kids can learn mythology, history, and current scientific knowledge about each of the planets, moons, and other objects in our solar system. Learn why Pluto is no longer a planet.

The Universe   history.com/minisites/universe

Episodes from the History Channel series that demonstrate in ways your kids will understand how very, very large and complex our universe is.

Biology

Science

Biology: From the Greek *bio* (life) and *logia* (study). The science of living organisms.

FROM ASTRONOMY (WHICH deals with some of the biggest things in the universe) to biology (which deals with some of the smallest): microscopes, DNA, RNA, cellular material, and everything else required for the study of living systems.

Peggy Klass, a high-school science teacher in southwest Missouri, says studying biology teaches kids much more than simple facts about the structure of cells or frogs. "Through the study of biology and the scientific method, kids can internalize a way of questioning and examining facts that readily transfers to everyday life.

"We want to become informed, well-rounded citizens, capable of asking relevant questions. A population that blindly accepts the majority of information given on network news programs and in mainstream newspapers will become a society without freedom. We have a responsibility to question information and seek the facts. The structure of biological inquiry facilitates the expansion of the mind and appreciation for the magnificent beauty and continuity of life around us."

Jessa Jones, who was a pre-doctoral graduate student in human genetics in Baltimore, Maryland, agrees. "I use my knowledge of biology all the time. In fact, I can remember first becoming interested in biology when my high-school teacher explained how it is biologically impossible for any shampoo to repair split ends, despite what they may claim.

"Here are some biology-related questions that might be of interest in the real world: Does that Atkins low-carbohydrate diet really work? Why are all calico cats female? How do the trees know that it is autumn and therefore lose their leaves? How is this antibiotic going to make me better, and why do I have to take all of it? Why is it that ultraviolet radiation causes cancer, but microwaves

Hotlinks

Biology Lessons for Teachers
www.biologylessons.sdsu.edu

Cells Alive
cellsalive.com

Rader's Biology4Kids
kapili.com/biology4kids

Virtual Frog Dissection
tinyurl.com/frogdis

do not? Why am I lactose-intolerant? Why does a woman's chance of having a baby with Down syndrome go up as she ages, while her husband's does not? Why do my legs get really sore after I run? How do nerves really work? Is it true that I should wait thirty minutes after eating before I swim?

"I can use the general principles of biology to answer each and every one of these questions. Studying biology is studying how life works, how people work, what makes you, you! What could be more interesting than that?"

The following resources on biology, genetics, and the life sciences will teach your children how life works. Related resources on human anatomy are in the anatomy section earlier in this chapter; links to culture and anthropology are in Chapter 10, and information on human development is found in Chapter 13.

Biology Lessons for Teachers
www.biologylessons.sdsu.edu

Students at San Diego State University developed this collection of biology lessons. The lessons are very thorough, though the site is still under construction.

Biology Overview   **nsf.gov/news/overviews/biology**

An overview by the National Science Foundation: "A bat, a mushroom, a blade of grass—they're easy to identify as 'life.' But what about a cold virus or mold? Biologists are life's detectives, discovering what 'alive' really means."

Cells Alive   **cellsalive.com**

Oooo, icky! Your microscope, online. Watch animations on bacteriological growth, and find lots of information on cells. A must for the biology student.

Field Tripping

Nature studies are at our fingertips: we live on an 80-acre farm. Picking blueberries or strawberries is a great little trip. Fishing is great for a variety of reasons: life cycles, food chain, seasons, fish, safety, boating, swimming.

—Rebecca Lynn Miller, homeschool mom who wants better life options for her kids, Hudson, Florida

Science

History of Life Through Time   tinyurl.com/histlife

The science of living things has changed since you were a kid. Animal, vegetable, and mineral just doesn't cut it anymore. Learn how all animal and plant life is classified, you metazoan, you.

Life Science Curriculum   eequalsmcq.com

"If it stinks, it's chemistry; if it's slimy, it's biology; and if it doesn't work, it's physics." Free curriculum, amazing graphics, emailed lab notes. An excellent starting point for studying life sciences.

MIT Biology   tinyurl.com/biomit

Highlights for High School provides resources from MIT to improve biology instruction at the high-school level. Watch video demonstrations, study for AP exams, and sample college coursework.

On-Screen DNA   tinyurl.com/dnascreen

Free software that teaches about DNA using 3-D graphics. Includes test questions.

Rader's Biology4Kids   kapili.com/biology4kids

Your kids will enjoy learning about cells, biochemistry, and other biology topics from this well-illustrated, colorful site.

The Parent Company   parentcompany.com

Science kits for Christian families seeking to reconcile evolutionary biology with creation doctrine.

Tree of Life   phylogeny.arizona.edu/tree/phylogeny.html

Kids need to know what scientists are saying about the relationships between earth's different life-forms. This site traces the branching classification that shows the assumed relationships between all living organisms.

Virtual Frog Dissection   tinyurl.com/frogdis

Oh, yuck. Frog guts. At least you don't have to touch it. Examine the dissection from any angle with this animated science project.

Botany

"EVEN IF I knew that tomorrow the world would go to pieces," Martin Luther King Jr. once said, "I would still plant my apple tree." The science of botany teaches children how plant life germinates and grows, how plants are differentiated, and how they are related. Agricultural science teaches children everything from growing a small window garden to managing the family farm.

Richard Marcley is a research scientist and a homeschooling dad living on Vashon Island, near Seattle. His teenagers participate in a program that encourages self-study and that uses parents and professional resources to teach.

Richard studied environmental science in college and now does research for Weyerhaeuser, the paper company. "The work I do is hardcore fundamental science concerned with how wood fibers made up of sugars and lignin (a material similar to crab shells) react in and to water, and how the chemicals we put in that fiber soup affect the many kinds of paper we make. To do this work, I must understand the scientific method and must have learned the basic skills of chemistry, biology, statistics, engineering, and the like.

"Science is an art," he says, "and it really helps if you are creative and can think out of the box. I believe the best people in any field have broad interests, a characteristic that helps them see relationships and draw conclusions that those too close to a subject just might be blind to. That's what all the geniuses say!"

Richard finds that he uses very few of the facts he learned while studying environmental science. But he doesn't regret his studies. On the contrary, he believes any of the sciences can teach the same basic principle: "The beauty of environmental science, like all of the hard sciences—chemistry, biology, physics, and the like—is that it teaches you the scientific method."

> **Botany:** From the French *botanique* (herb). The study of the life and structure of plants.

Hotlinks

Bet the Farm
tinyurl.com/betfarm

Botany Basics
extension.oregonstate
.edu/mg/botany

The Great Plant Escape
tinyurl.com/greatplant

Field Tripping

Go on nature walks, to any woods or marsh or trail. Learn about the kinds of trees, bird identification, plant identification, and if you're lucky, local animals.

—Terri Vitkovitsky, homeschooling mom of five, Camp Lejeune, North Carolina

"Science is linked by some fundamental rules known as the scientific method, honed skills of observation and an honest search (corny but true) for the truth. Science enables many folks to communicate regardless of language because we all speak the same fundamental language of science."

Your little farmers and scientists will have fun finding out about flora with the following resources. Related resources on weather and atmosphere are in the earth science section, later in this chapter.

Bet the Farm   tinyurl.com/betfarm

Perhaps the toughest job in the world is being a successful farmer. It's hard work, and you don't control most of the variables. Your kids will begin to appreciate the contribution of farmers with the help of this game that lets them play at being farmers, making serious decisions about crops and resources.

Botany Basics   extension.oregonstate.edu/mg/botany

Free online course that teaches plant growth, anatomy, life cycles, photosynthesis, and everything else a beginning botanist needs to know.

Discovery Plants   school.discovery.com/lessonplans/plants.html

Botany lesson plans from the Discovery Channel, for grades K through 12. Many libraries carry or can obtain the accompanying DVD.

Integrated Science Class Notes   tinyurl.com/scinoted

From a Utah schoolteacher, notes and PowerPoint presentations for a seventh-grade course in botany and biology. Click the 8th Grade link to the left for similar materials in earth sciences.

Nature Studies Lessons and Activities
easyfunschool.com/IndexNatureStudies.html

Making beet dye, growing popcorn, and creating paper from plants will help your children appreciate the wonders of nature. Try Stupid Vegetable Tricks for a fun season of growing.

Plants & Animals   www.suite101.com/plantsandanimals

A very comprehensive collection of articles on all things living. The horticulture articles are categorized into botany, desert/water-wise gardens, flower gardens, houseplants, landscaping, organic gardens, plants and bulbs, vegetable gardens, and water gardens.

Plants Database   plants.usda.gov

From the USDA, everything there is to know about vascular plants, mosses, liverworts, hornworts, and lichens of the U.S. and its territories. A feature called Plant of the Week will give focus to your botany studies. Or search by state to find the plants native to your home.

The Great Plant Escape   tinyurl.com/greatplant

Plant science for grades 4 and 5. Help Detective LePlant and his partners Bud and Sprout unlock the amazing mysteries of plant life. The teacher's guides will help get your kids thinking like scientists.

The Great Sunflower Project   greatsunflower.org

Tracks bees. Once you are registered, they will mail you sunflowers to plant to attract the bees that the program is tracking. A wonderful science project that the whole family can do!

Tomatosphere   tomatosphere.org

Mails you tomato seeds that are in control groups. You plant the seeds, track the progress, and then report your findings online. The project Tomatosphere is sponsored by several large agricultural companies.

Worm Watch   naturewatch.ca/english/wormwatch

Grubby, grubby worms. Such fun. Learn all about how they contribute to soil ecology and sustain agriculture. The Virtual Worm tour gives an inside look at

Field Tripping

We love going to the James River and to local walking parks. They love nature and at the Monticello Walking Park, they learned to identify different plants and trees.

—Denise Walker, homeschooling mom of two, Virginia

the inside of a worm. Links at the top of the page go to Plant Watch and other science resources your kids may enjoy.

Chemistry

Chemistry:
From the Middle Latin *alchymista* (alchemist). Scientific study of the composition, structure, and properties of an organism or substance.

CHEMISTRY IS THE study of the basic physical elements that make up everything around us. A good working knowledge of chemistry principles helps not only professional chemists but also people who cook and clean and paint.

Kari Farrell Matthews is a math and chemistry teacher in Rossville, Illinois. She's married to a farmer, and she explains how a good knowledge of chemistry affects their lives. "Chemistry is an amazing thing. It is a science that describes everything around us. Why do we sand wood, cook hamburgers, put bleach in our white laundry loads? Why does soap work? What causes sickle-cell anemia? Why does bread smell so good while it is baking? How do batteries work? Chemistry answers these questions.

"My husband uses chemistry on the farm all the time. When he is trying to determine the best kind of fertilizer to buy, or when he is looking at analysis reports of soil samples from his fields, he must use his understanding of chemistry to make the best choices for the farm.

"Not many people are farmers, of course, but most people do basic household chores, like cooking and cleaning. Understanding chemistry helps us make good decisions when we are unsure about what to do next. For instance, chemistry explains how to get a grass stain out of pants. My knowledge of the chemical makeup of the things in my home and on the farm comes into play every day."

Chemistry is a career choice for Doron Wolf, a chemical engineer who lives in Israel. He explains how his knowledge of chemistry affects his work each day. "Chemistry and biology are the main issues when talking about environmental engineering," he says. "I can't design waste treatment without involving chemical or biological considerations. Let's say wastewater from a plant contains caustic soda (NaOH) from cleaning and some organic solvents (such as MEK and acetone). How do you treat them?

"If you don't know chemistry and biology, you can't give the right answer. The correct answer is: First you remove the caustic soda with an acid like chlorine, to get salt with water. Then you treat the solvents with microorganisms or activated carbon that removes them.

"I also use my chemistry at home. Let's say you are cleaning your kitchen. There are many cleaning chemicals used in the process. On a product label, you might find, 'Contains caustic soda, ammonia, citric acid, hydrochloric acid, organic solvents, and more.' If you don't know some chemistry, you don't understand the meaning of those words, and your lack of knowledge can make your cleaning less efficient or can even cause an accident.

"This is not the main problem, however. The main problem begins when people try to combine chemicals to get better results—or so they think. If you mix an acid-based chemical like common chlorine bleach with ammonia, you cause a reaction that releases toxic vapors of ammonia gas. A little knowledge of chemistry might help."

Ready to try your hand at chemistry? The following resources will help.

A Case of Murder: A Forensic Science Unit
tinyurl.com/forsci

Microscopes and chemical agents help students unravel a forensic mystery.

ACS Education   **tinyurl.com/amchem**

The American Chemistry Society's Education site is the portal to the national Chemistry Olympiad, and to resources for teaching chemistry to kids in grades K through 12. Lots of activities, periodic tables, and *ChemMatters* magazine.

Hotlinks

Chemistry Comes Alive
tinyurl.com/chemed

Fun-Based Learning
funbasedlearning.com

Reeko's Mad Scientist Lab
reekoscience.com/
experiments

Chem4Kids!   chem4kids.com

An easy-to-understand introduction to chemistry. This site is written humorously, with eye-catching illustrations. Your elementary-aged learners will enjoy the material.

Chemistry & Materials   nsf.gov/news/overviews/chemistry

An overview by the National Science Foundation: "Most of what you touch, taste, hear, or smell every day in the modern world is the direct or indirect result of research in chemistry or materials science—an effort that never ends."

Chemistry at MIT   tinyurl.com/chemmit

Highlights for High School provides resources from MIT to improve chemistry instruction at the high-school level. College-level coursework will prepare your university-bound teens.

Chemistry Comes Alive!   tinyurl.com/chemed

Things explode. Things dissolve. Things ignite. These free videos from the *Journal of Chemical Education* explain and demonstrate chemical reactions.

Chemistry Handouts   tinyurl.com/chemho

From a university student learning center, printable handouts to reinforce science learning. Many handouts include problem sets with answers. Handouts cover chemistry, with additional printables on the metric system and measurements.

Chemistry Hypermedia Project   tinyurl.com/chemhype

Basic chemistry principles, including a review of math concepts required to solve chemistry problems.

Discovery Forensic Science

school.discovery.com/lessonplans/forensics.html

A group of lesson plans from the Discovery Channel that teach chemistry as an applied science: detective work.

Carl Wilhelm Scheele

Like so many other successful people, German chemist Carl Scheele was entirely self-taught. Scheele was apprenticed to a druggist, but in his spare time he conducted his own experiments. Although he's not well known—mostly because he was slow to publish his findings—he made some of the most significant discoveries in human history. In 1772 he discovered the existence of oxygen (he called it "fire air"), and later he discovered chlorine, glycerine, hydrogen sulfide, and several types of acid.

Fun-Based Learning   funbasedlearning.com

Chemistry games to teach equations, along with a quiz to teach the elements, lesson plans, and games that teach algebraic principles.

Learn About Chemistry   reciprocalnet.org/edumodules

Ever wonder about the chemical structure of diamonds? Salt? How about Advil? View common molecules in three dimensions, or learn more about crystals and chemicals in everyday life from the chemists at Indiana University.

Reeko's Mad Scientist Lab   reekoscience.com/experiments

Dozens and dozens of homespun chemistry experiments, sorted by skill and by these categories: atomic/electric, chemical reaction, chemistry, cohesion, floatation, geometry, inertia/momentum, light, motion energy, pressure, sound, and miscellaneous. Oh what fun!

WebElements: The Periodic Table   webelements.com

Learn everything there is to know—at least, everything normal people want to know—about the chemical elements. Click on the element name; another page pops up with text, audio, graphics, cartoons, history . . . Good stuff.

What's That Stuff?   tinyurl.com/whatstuff

What exactly is in lava lamps? Chewing gum? Cheez Whiz? The products you use in everyday life have fascinating chemical histories. Read all about it.

Earth Science

Earth: Related to the Hebrew *'erets* (world) and the Aramaic *'araq* (world). The geographic formation of the planet.

GEOLOGY ROCKS. JUST ask the kid who's found her first agate. Or the one who pounds a rock on the sidewalk and observes it break apart in layers.

This section considers resources for the study of earth processes, earth science, and geology.

Jenn Sides, who lives in southeastern Pennsylvania, is nearly ready to graduate from college with her degree in environmental geoscience. Although she's not yet a professional scientist, she finds many opportunities in daily life to use her knowledge of geology. "I just look around me and see the wonder of it all," she says. "It sounds silly, but I like the fact that I can look at an outcrop of rock and know its history.

"I also like knowing what mechanisms are at work around me. For instance, just recently I had a friend who wanted to buy a new house. She was looking at a nice new development near where I live, but I warned her that the property was smack in the middle of a floodplain for a little stream that ran through the area. I also knew that the soil would hold the water for a while. Lucky for her, she listened and bought elsewhere. Hurricane Floyd nailed us not too long after, and had she bought that house, she would have been floating in the middle of the little stream, because it flooded its entire floodplain!"

Geology has other important practical applications. Sharon D. Pérez-Suárez is a graduate student at the Uni-

Hotlinks

Experience Science
eduplace.com/
science/hmxs

Geography4Kids
geography4kids.com

USGS Science Education
education.usgs.gov

versity of Florida investigating a midocean volcanic ridge in the Caribbean plate. The ridge is spreading, and Sharon is studying its magma chamber, part of her research into the effects of volcanic eruptions on the environment.

During her internship she studied sulfur dioxide clouds in the ozone formed by volcanic eruptions. Because gases play an important role in eruptions, she says, it's important to know the amount and composition of gases in magma chambers before an eruption occurs. When volcanoes erupt, they spew sulfur dioxide into the stratosphere, where it gets converted to aerosols, which absorb ultraviolet light and cause global climate change. In her research, she found a mathematical relationship between the total mass of erupted sulfur dioxide and the occurrence of volcanic activity.

Thomas Ferrero, a consulting engineering geologist in Ashland, Oregon, explains how his work makes the world a better place for many people. Every day, he says, he shows mining companies, government agencies, engineers, architects, construction contractors, home owners, and others how to solve large and small problems having to do with the earth. He teaches people how to do everything from drain a basement to stabilize a foundation on an unstable slope or prevent soil erosion.

"I have located valuable mineral deposits," he says. "I have found groundwater where others failed. I have stopped landslides. My work is always varied and interesting. I love what I do for a living." The school of hard rocks—er, knocks—is now online. The following resources cover the study of earth processes, earth science, and geology. (Related resources are in the archaeology section, earlier in this chapter.)

Experience Science eduplace.com/science/hmxs

For K–6 learners, modules—lessons—in life, earth, and physical sciences. As an example, the Terrarium Habitats module teaches terrar-

---

Field Tripping

Visit a beach. There's lots to learn about the animals that inhabited the shells we find, about how sand is made, and the tides.

—Terri Vitkovitsky, homeschooling mom of five, Camp Lejeune, North Carolina

Science

ium planting while explaining producers, consumers, predators, decomposers, and food chains.

Geography4Kids!   geography4kids.com

An easy-to-read, well-illustrated primer on earth sciences, including Earth Structure, Atmosphere, Hydrosphere, Biosphere, BGC Cycles, and Climates.

Mineral Information Institute   mii.org/teacherhelpers.html

Colorful PDF-formatted downloads that teach about minerals and lots of other science-related topics. Great for unit studies.

Plymouth State Weather Center   vortex.plymouth.edu

Weather-forecasting tools. From the Tutorials links on the left, click a resource such as Cloud Boutique, where kids can learn about cloud formations with pictures and descriptions.

Science Lessons and Activities
easyfunschool.com/IndexScience.html

Try these fun science experiments at home. Dozens and dozens of experiments will engage your kids in making edible rocks, blue clouds, homemade tornadoes, and a sundial in a pot. Living science is learning science.

On Scientific Inquiry

Some people see things as they are and say why; I dream things that never were and say why not?

—Robert F. Kennedy, quoting George Bernard Shaw

Sea and Sky   seasky.org

The graphics at this site are extremely colorful and show real pictures of the seas and sky. Here are but a few things that will enchant your kids: Sea Games, Sea News, Aquarium Resources, The Ocean Realm, Ocean Explorations, Sea Lab, Sea Gallery, Sea Links, Sky News, Astronomy Resources, The Cosmos, Space Exploration, Sky Lab, Sky Gallery, Sky Links, and Sky Games. The entire site is a pleasure to explore.

The Image   theimage.com

Images of gemstones and minerals, along with notes from a geology course. The site also hosts information about digital photography techniques.

USGS Science Education   education.usgs.gov

Geography and geology lesson plans from the U.S. Geological Survey, along with a wealth of other educational resources, including free posters.

Weather Channel Kids   theweatherchannelkids.com

"Explore the weather like never before" is this site's slogan. Online games to teach kids about heat waves, droughts, hurricanes, tornadoes, floods, thunderstorms, and windstorms. The Epic Conditions link has great videos of athletes challenging snow, rocks, whitewater, and other natural phenomena.

Field Tripping

Longwood Gardens in Pennsylvania has lots of info and it is great for kids to work on all types of lessons.

—Joanna Francis, homeschooling mom to a child with ADD and a preschooler, Newark, Delaware

Science

Environmental Studies

ENVIRONMENTAL STUDIES COVER lots of subject matter, including plant and animal ecologies, environmental education, and, for our porpoises—er, purposes—oceanography.

How does the ocean affect the environment? Maria Therese Greenfield, a graduate student doing volunteer work in England's oceans, explains, "The marine environment is undoubtedly one of the most hostile and productive environments on this Earth," she says. "It's also one of the least understood."

Maria believes that any person who deals with the sea in any form should have a basic understanding, "to learn to respect its power and life-giving attributes. The world would be a lot colder place without the oceans, as heat is stored in them during the summer months and released during the winter."

This is how she teaches schoolchildren about the sea and its power: "Initially, I start with local oceanographic phenom-

Ecology: From the Greek *oikia* (dwelling) and *logia* (study). The relationship between organisms and their environments.

Hotlinks

**EPA Environmental
Kids Club**
epa.gov/kids

How to Compost
howtocompost.org

Where You Live
epa.gov/epahome/
commsearch.htm

ena—such as tides, waves, pollution, currents, storms, temperature, and survival techniques. Then I go on to the global, such as tsunamis, hurricanes, El Niño, seawater, hydrothermal vents, and information on the oceans themselves.

"With the activities taking place out of school hours, it can be difficult to keep the children's interest. Field trips, where kids can see what they are being taught, also help. One of the children I taught told me, 'I thought the ocean was wet, salty, and dead; now I think it's dangerous but cool!' It made me realize that I've been doing some good, without scaring anyone away from the ocean."

Your children can have the same appreciation for the world around them. Get started teaching with the following resources. (Related resources are in the biology section, earlier in this chapter.)

Community Design Lesson Plans
planning.org/resourceszine/Lessons.html

Design your own community with help from lesson plans by the American Planning Association. Learn what makes good communities and lousy communities.

Demand Debate   demanddebate.com

CO_2 levels rise and fall—this site claims—in response to, and not in advance of, global temperature changes. Perhaps the sky is not falling after all?

Earth & Environment
nsf.gov/news/overviews/earth-environ

An overview by the National Science Foundation: "Our planet gives up its secrets slowly. But every year we learn more about its oceans and air, its restless continents, its myriad ecosystems, and the way living things interact with their environments."

Environmental Education Resource Kits

audubon.org

Contact your local chapter of the Audubon Society for access to free educational materials. Many chapters will donate or lend tools, books, kits, and other materials related to bird-watching and environmental awareness. Nearly every chapter also sponsors free community lectures.

EPA Environmental Kids Club   epa.gov/kids

The Environmental Protection Agency offers free educational posters and other materials.

How to Compost   howtocompost.org

Information on composting as it relates to gardening, science, and biology.

If Trees Could Talk

foresthistory.org/education/curriculum

A 10-module, middle-school curriculum that asks and answers questions as diverse as the 8,000-year history of conservation and how trees improve neighborhoods. Other parts of the Forest History Society's Educational Outreach Program include great articles from the society's *Green Teacher* magazine and a teacher's guide.

Mother Earth News   motherearthnews.com

How to live sustainably. Start by composting, driving electric cars, and gardening organically. Graduate to—oh, say, homeschooling your own kids.

Waters Journey: Everglades   theevergladesstory.org

The world's most ambitious wetlands and ecosystem-restoration project is under way, and this site keeps track. Includes lots of educational resources.

Science

Field Tripping

I want to go to a recycling plant to show how things get recycled, products made from recycled products, and so forth.

—Terri Vitkovitsky, homeschooling mom of five, Camp Lejeune, North Carolina

Field Tripping

I consider our trips to the beach, mountains, and various parks over the years to be great field trips. I love botanical gardens. The ones in Bellevue, Washington, as well as the Seattle Arboretum were favorites when we lived in that area.

—Liz deForest, housewife and homeschooling mom of three, Santa Monica, California

Where You Live   epa.gov/epahome/commsearch.htm

Read EPA data about your local community. Enter your zip code and surf your watershed, or learn about local hazardous waste sites. Also interesting is the daily forecast of the expected intensity of ultraviolet radiation from the sun.

Physical Science

THE PHYSICAL SCIENCES are all the processes you had to learn formulas for when you studied science. In this section we cover physics and the properties of physical objects, including the study of matter, energy, force, and motion.

There's no need, of course, to teach your young children the mathematics of physics. They're born scientists who, given the space, will spend their entire childhoods investigating gravity and motion and that unmovable object called parents.

Susie Clawson, a homeschooling mother of five in Clearfield, Utah, has found ways to teach the physical sciences without having to rescue the good china before it gets tossed from the deck. "Science is something that often gets pushed aside at our house," she says. "We love doing experiments, but it is usually something that gets put on the back burner and then forgotten.

"We started a science group with a couple of other homeschooling moms and their kids. We decided to keep it in our local area so that it wouldn't get to be a burden to drive great distances.

"Once a month we meet at one of our homes, and the hostess leads the day. We really have no rules for which topics we're doing, but usually it is something that our children have expressed an interest in pursuing in great detail.

"This week is my turn, and we're starting with some basic physics. We're also going to do some weather. My daughter is a Girl Scout, and she wanted to work on some experiments

Physics: From the Greek *phusikos* (nature). Study of the interactions between energy and matter.

for a badge. Also, one of the other kids in the group just finished a weather study, and he's going to share his stuff with us."

You'll enjoy getting physical with the helpful resources below!

101 Physics Facts   tinyurl.com/101facts

Here's one of the 101 facts you should know: Radioactive half-lives cannot be changed by heat or pressure. Here's another: Physics is fun.

Differential Equations   sosmath.com/diffeq/diffeq.html

Review material and easy-to-understand explanations of differential equations, which are used in physics to calculate rates of change of continuously changing quantities.

Energy Home   eon-uk.com/EnergyExperience/85.htm

Another Brit site, this one giving animated lessons in energy. Students follow the lessons to learn what energy is, where it comes from, how it's used—or wasted—and how to use it safely.

Engineering   tinyurl.com/ocweng

Highlights for High School provides resources from MIT to improve engineering instruction at the high-school level. Watch video demonstrations that explain engineering principles.

Engineering Overview   nsf.gov/news/overviews/engineering

An overview by the National Science Foundation: "Engineers bridge the gap between what the mind can imagine and what the laws of nature allow. They work at the outermost frontiers of electronics, manufacturing, bioengineering, structural design and more."

Fermilab Science Education   ed.fnal.gov

Click the Students link up top for a very large, very well done program of classes, activities, and resources that teach physical science.

Hotlinks

101 Physics Facts
tinyurl.com/101facts

Engineering
tinyurl.com/ocweng

How Stuff Works
howstuffworks.com

The Physics Classroom
tinyurl.com/phyclass

Will It Blend?
willitblend.com

Science

Pierre Curie

French scientist Pierre Curie was homeschooled. His doctor father taught him at home, and by the time young Pierre was fourteen he was passionate about mathematics, particularly spatial geometry. A few years later he finished college and began working as a laboratory assistant at the Sorbonne, where he met his future wife, Marie. The two of them were awarded the Nobel Prize for physics in 1903.

The Educators link has field trips, study units, workshops, and classroom projects. Really top-notch stuff.

High School Physics   intuitor.com/physics

Intuitor calls physics the "Neglected Science." The site carries good articles to fix that problem: "Why Take Physics?," "Which Physics Program Is Right for Me?," and others.

High Speed Exploding CDs   powerlabs.org

Blow stuff up! Shock things! Turn everyday objects into weapons! All sorts of dangerous science experiments await you. One of my favorites: powerlabs.org/cdexplode.htm, where those ubiquitous AOL CDs explode as they spin at high speeds. Cool!

How Stuff Works   howstuffworks.com

My younger kids loved this one so much they made it their homepage. How Stuff Works explains how toilets flush, how telephones get sound, how your automobile turns gasoline to motion, and pretty much everything else you've ever wondered. Spend some time considering the mechanics of animals, auto, business and money, communication, computer, electronics, entertainment, food and recipes, geography, health, history, home and garden, people, science, and travel. Fascinating.

Machines and How They Work   tinyurl.com/macwork

A theme study on machines—games, lessons, projects, and worksheets.

Music, Waves, Physics   cnx.org/content/col10341

For advanced physics learners, an online course in the concept of waves as seen in sound. A solid understanding of calculus is a prerequisite. The course is very well done, with illustrations, definitions, and other tools for advancing understanding.

Nanoscience   science.pppst.com/nanoscience.html

PowerPoint presentations that teach principles of very, very small science. One of the lessons, "What is Nanoscience?," explains the difference between microtechnology and nanoscience. Another discusses nanoscience in nature.

Physics   tinyurl.com/ocwphy

Highlights for High School provides resources from MIT to improve physics instruction at the high school level. Watch video demonstrations, study for AP exams, and sample college coursework.

Physics Lessons   physicslessons.com

Online experiments and quizzes that illustrate concepts such as mechanics, measurement, heat, light, electricity, and fluids.

Physics Overview   nsf.gov/news/overviews/physics

The National Science Foundation provides an overview of the science of physics: the blue of the sky, the colors of the rainbow, the fall of an apple, the motions of the moon. What's happening here? Why do things work this way? This is a good starting place for understanding the breadth of physical science.

Physics 2000   colorado.edu/physics/2000

An interactive journey through modern physics with Colorado University. Have fun learning visually and conceptually about twentieth-century science and high-tech devices. Explains Einstein, basic principles of waves, quantum mechanics, polarization, and the periodic table, and more in an easy-to-read format that will make a scientist out of your most truculent child. To get to the tutorials, click the Science Trek link.

Science Projects   energyquest.ca.gov/projects

Tons of science projects—most of which you can do at home—to teach physical science. Lemon Power, for example, uses a lemon to make a voltaic battery and power a digital watch.

The Atoms Family   www.miamisci.org/af

The Atoms Family at the Miami Museum of Science grabs the attention of your student with its creepy play on words. Learn about energy conservation, kinetic and potential energy, properties of light, and other principles of physical science.

The Exploratorium   exploratorium.edu

There's so much to love about this site, but click the Educate link at the top to access amazing hands-on science activities and "Science Snacks" such as candymaking, pinhole projectors, paper airplanes, and rain sticks. These projects will turn your kids on to the fun of science.

The Physics Classroom   tinyurl.com/phyclass

Click the Physics Classroom link for an online tutorial written for high school students, or visit the Laboratory for projects that demonstrate principles of physical science.

Will It Blend?   willitblend.com

It started as an advertisement for a high-end blender; now it's just fun. The website films the blender tearing into rake handles, Rubik's Cubes, marbles, and everything else. The Try This at Home section makes for good kitchen science.

Scientists and Inventions

FROM THE MOST quantitative to the most qualitative: We move now from hard science to fun scientists. In this section we discover scientists and inventors, inventions, the history of science, and science careers.

Homeschooling and science are a natural fit. Little Alexander Bell (the "Graham" was added later) was schooled at home for most of his youth. He spent two years in high school, graduated at fourteen, and became a music and elocution teacher. Later he became a resident master at Weston House Academy, where he began studying sound. His great invention changed the way the world communicates. After he invented the technology that is still used in modern telephone communications, he continued working as a teacher and a scientist for the rest of his life.

And he's just one of dozens of well-known scientists and inventors who were schooled at home.

Do your budding scientists need inspiration? The following resources teach kids about scientists, mathematicians, and inventors and help them become junior inventors on their own.

Ancient Inventions   tinyurl.com/siinvent

An exhibit of several dozen ancient inventions. Ancient technology changed the way people live, just as it changes lives in modern times.

ASEE Engineering K–12 Center   engineeringk12.org

Information for K–12 students and educators interested in learning about engineering. The Students link introduces engineering and explains how to become an engineer. The Educators link provides lesson plans for such activities as building a strong bridge out of paper. (Click the How Do I Use link on the left.)

Science

Scientist:
Related to the Latin *scientia* (to know). One who is trained in the study of a particular field of inquiry.

Hotlinks

Eric's World of Science
scienceworld.wolfram
.com

Lemelson Center
invention.smithsonian.org

The Science Toy Maker
sciencetoymaker.org

Eric's World of Science   scienceworld.wolfram.com

Biographies of more than 1,000 scientists and mathematicians. Or click the tabs at the top of the page for definitions of thousands of words related to chemistry, physics, astronomy, and math. Consider this your science glossary.

Exploring Leonardo   mos.org/sln/Leonardo

When it comes to teaching the physics of machinery, textbooks just don't cut it. But this Museum of Science website shows the operations of levers, wedges, wheels, axles, screws, pulleys, gears, chains, and more. The site includes a helpful lesson plan for teaching machine science.

On Failure

I haven't failed—I've found 10,000 ways that don't work.

—Thomas Edison

Invent Now   invent.org

The place for inventors and inventions. From the menus at the top, find contests for kids, or browse the Inventors Hall of Fame. The Workshop menu teaches users how to patent an invention.

Inventing Is Kid's Stuff   cspace.unb.ca/nbco/pigs/invent

Turn "things that bug you" into an invention with this unit study that has kids brainstorming, creating, and advertising their inventions.

Invention Dimension Games   web.mit.edu/invent/g-main.html

Games and trivia that teach kids about inventions and inventors. Or click the Inventor's Handbook link for an 11-chapter text on how to patent and market an invention.

Lemelson Center for the Study of Invention and Innovation   invention.smithsonian.org

The Smithsonian's Lemelson Center seeks to encourage inventive creativity in young people. Click the Centerpieces link for exhibits and activities that teach about inventions and creativity.

Science Toys You Can Make with Your Kids   scitoys.com

Make toys at home with common household materials—often in

only a few minutes—that demonstrate fascinating scientific principles. Study radios, heat engines, and solar batteries.

The Science Toy Maker   sciencetoymaker.org

A brightly colored page of toys you can make at home to learn scientific principles. Or submit your own toy inventions!

Technology

IF YOUR CHILDREN are to be competitive in the world they grow into, technology and computer science may be the most critical areas of all for them to understand. But it's not just for their future that kids should understand technology. New research has demonstrated that kids who have more Internet access earn higher scores on standardized reading tests after six months, and higher grade point averages one year and sixteen months after the start of the study than did children who used it less. More time spent reading, given the heavily text-based nature of web pages, may account for the improvement.* Other researchers found that children who are adept Internet users get less caught up in television and talk shows than those who aren't. And they hear and see more science and news programming than those who don't use the Internet.

Being Internet-savvy has plenty of practical applications, as well. Lillian Haas, who homeschools two children in Audubon, New Jersey, says the Internet is turning her kids into better learners. "My son uses both the library and the Internet to do research. If he needs help focusing his search, either my husband or I will help. He generally doesn't write down his results, and I don't ask him to, because when he is researching something, it's for his own purposes. He does what he wants to with his information."

Technology:
From the Greek *tekhnologia* (craft + study). The practical application of scientific knowledge.

* See our website, **hsfree.com,** for citations for this and other statistics in this chapter.

Homeschooler Joyce Dumire has enrolled her teenage son in two Internet-based classes, algebra and geometry. Technology helped her son be better educated in other ways, too. "I found older friends and relatives with special skills who shared time with my homeschooled son. One is a computer specialist who keeps the systems running for a large company; my son now is very good with computers. Another loves music and showed him how to work sound boards, which taught him science, math, and music."

In Susie Clawson's home, the technology-oriented learning has been a little more casual. "I had wonderful visions of my kids using all these interactive sites I'd find," says the Clearfield, Utah, mother of five. "But the reality in our house is that they each use the Internet for their own personal pursuits and rarely for homeschool. Usually their use has something to do with their favorite books or cartoons. They use the Internet when they do art. Both of my older boys are into cartooning, especially Japanese-style cartoons. They copy pictures from different sites as practice."

These are some of my favorite sites on the Net for learning about the Net—as well as the rest of the technological revolution your kids are a part of. Whether your kids want to learn to build a website, care for hardware, or learn programming, these resources will be helpful. (See related tools in the Internet safety section of Chapter 2, and the computers section of Chapter 6.)

Hotlinks

Clean Your Computer
tutorials.com/05/0554/
0554.asp

**Computer Science Study
Guides**
sparknotes.com/cs/

How to Make a Website
wikihow.com/
Make-a-Website

Broadband Security FAQ   dslreports.com/faq/security

How-To's for nearly every computer security question. Your junior hackers will be fascinated.

Clean Your Computer   tutorials.com/05/0554/0554.asp

Electrical equipment attracts dust and dirt. Here's how to clean it without killing it. Learn2 is a collection of multipart tutorials with cartoon illustrations. Links on the right lead to related How-To's.

Computer Languages History

levenez.com/lang/history.html

See a graphic representation of the history of programming with this timeline of the development of different computer languages.

Computer Science Study Guides

sparknotes.com/cs/

Guides to every computer science subject from C++ fundamentals and arrays through hash tables and sorting. Includes vocabulary lessons, and problems and solutions for each subject.

Computing Overview

nsf.gov/news/overviews/computer

An overview by the National Science Foundation: "The Internet, Google, and web browsers show how past progress in computing affects our daily lives. The cutting-edge systems under design now will have an enormous impact on society—and science."

Do It Yourself Web Site   mcli.dist.maricopa.edu/diy

The very best place around for teaching your kids about the Internet. If you want to learn how to build your own websites, your best route may be Maricopa Community College's Do It Yourself.

How to Make a Website   wikihow.com/Make-a-Website

Look to Wikihow for instructions to solve tens of thousands of life's problems. From this page, learn about website creation, HTML, FTP, and other acronyms that will bore your computer-illiterate friends.

Killer Sites   killersites.com

Video lessons on designing websites. The sample lessons are free, and very informative. The commercial resources are a bit pricey.

Nanoscience Overview   nsf.gov/news/overviews/nano

An overview by the National Science Foundation: "Nanoscience is the

Motivation

We don't motivate our kids, they motivate themselves. Enthusiasm is highly contagious; let your kids catch it from you!

—Darnia Hobson, unschooling mum of three, New Zealand

Science

ability to manipulate atoms and molecules. This fast-moving field is transforming our ability to custom-design objects and processes at sizes smaller than 1/1000th the width of a hair."

Picnik   picnik.com

Photo-editing tools, from the Web. Quick, easy to understand. Not as advanced as some commercial products, but it'll do all the basic photo editing you might require for scrapbooking or blogging.

Put File   putfile.com

Wow. Sort of a combination Photobucket and YouTube, Put File permits unlimited uploads of all your media files—photos, videos, audio, and flash. Incorporate the stored files into the websites you build. File sizes up to 200M are permitted, and multiples files can be uploaded at once. You get to choose whether to make your uploads public or private. It's my new favorite storage depot.

Technology   learnersonline.com/weekly/subject/tech.htm

Web quests on tech subjects such as Satellite Systems and High-Speed Broadband. Extremely well done, with photographs, links, explanatory text, and illustrations.

Technology Worksheets   tinyurl.com/techwork

A collection of technology and computing worksheets (with solutions) from Discovery School.

The Principles of Beautiful Web Design
sitepoint.com/article/principles-beautiful-web-design

Starting with principles for designing a business card, this tutorial shows with examples and graphics how to design websites to attract a reader's eye. It's a full education in design principles.

Top Ten Mistakes in Web Design   useit.com/alertbox/9605.html

Updated from year to year with new mistakes, reflecting the use of new technology. The old pages lists are still entertaining.

Science

Web Page Authoring   sofia.fhda.edu/gallery/html

An online course in web page authoring. There are 22 lessons, along with corresponding assignments.

Webopedia   webopedia.com

Even geeks have trouble keeping up with all the lingo. Can you define tech terms like blawg? Candela? Foobar? Haptic? This online nanodictionary can help.

Zoology

WHICH OF YOUR children intends to grow up to become a veterinarian?

Any kid who ever fell in love with a dog or a gerbil has entertained the thought.

That's why the study of zoology has the potential to be so much fun. Zoology is the science of animal life and includes a sub-branch called entomology. It's a bug's life.

It can also be your kids' life. Larissa Nituch, a zookeeper and zoology student in Montreal, explains how: "The best way to prepare for a career in zoology is to volunteer, volunteer, volunteer! Anyone over the age of sixteen can volunteer his or her time at most animal shelters, wildlife rehabilitation centers, veterinary offices, and zoos. This is the best way to get valuable experience with animals and will greatly increase your chances of getting a job later on. You should also take any animal- and science-related classes available at your school, and read all the books you can get your hands on. It is sometimes difficult to get into this field, but if you are dedicated and work hard, there is no doubt that you will succeed!"

Not sure you can teach science? Jim Sherrard, an environmental coordinator in Plano, Texas, has some inspira-

> **Zoology:** From the Greek *zôion* (living being). The study of animal life.

Hotlinks

Animal Info
animalinfo.org

Cornell Lab of Ornithology
birds.cornell.edu

What's That Bug?
whatsthatbug.com

tion for you: "I am most passionate in my belief that teaching is one of the highest callings to which we can aspire; certainly it is one of the most rewarding. It is the one profession where one person can contribute and make a quantum change in society." About his job as a zoologist, he says, "I have been fortunate as a zoological professional to have traveled the Earth. I have seen firsthand the degradation of the rain forest in South America; man's inhumanity to man in dealing with the indigenous inhabitants; and the staggering, awesome, humbling vastness of the Amazon River. Being a zoologist in the corporate environment, I have had the unique opportunity to teach and bring man closer to his environment—even if only for a fleeting second."

Terri Vitkovitsky, a homeschooling mom of five from North Carolina, uses the world around her to teach zoology. "Just the other day we had a wonderful cockroach in our house (part of living in coastal Carolina). I tried to catch it but was unsuccessful and it slipped away and hid. My kids (oldest eight years old) decided to take on the mission that I saw as fruitless. They lured the roach out with a flashlight shining thru a cardboard paper towel tube and got it with shoes strapped to their hands. When I asked how they thought to do this (never having thought of this myself or seen it), my eight-year-old's reply was 'Mom, everybody knows that cockroaches are nocturnal.' He had used this information to realize that the roach would seek out the dark and the bright light would force it from its hiding place where they would be able to get it. This is one of the many cases where I learn more from them than they do from me."

Whether it's antelope or ants, beetles or bears, houseflies or horses, your child will find something of interest in these whinny-ing resources:

Animal Info   animalinfo.org
A searchable database of endangered mammals, along with photographs and information about what is being done to save them from extinction.

Free Video Insect Zoo

With Planet Insect, you can tour the O. Orkin Insect Zoo at the Smithsonian Institution's Museum of Natural History. Call 800-563-4687 to order a copy.

Bugs and Insects   tinyurl.com/scbugs

Scholastic publishes this collection of articles aimed at primary- and middle-school ages. Very readable.

Cornell Lab of Ornithology   birds.cornell.edu

Ornithology is for the birds. Nest cams; a video collection of natural sounds of birds, frogs, and mammals; and All About Birds, a complete guide for bird-watchers.

Educating for Conservation

www.fws.gov/educators

Click the Conservation Library link for great publications such as Homes for Birds, a complete how-to on building bird habitats in your backyard. Or click the Video link to access free wildlife videos. And that's just the beginning of this great site run by the U.S. Fish and Wildlife Service.

How to Care for Fish   aquariumfish.net

One fish-loving mom reports that she goes to this site "a lot!" Get tons of information about how to raise fish without killing them.

Learn About Wiggly Worms   tinyurl.com/aworms

A theme study on worms—games, lessons, projects, and worksheets.

Mr. Nussbaum Science   mrnussbaum.com/zoocode.htm

Games, videos, and other educational tools for learning about all sorts of animals: sharks, birds, mammals, insects, penguins, and others. This site also has sections for learning about biomes, habitats, bacteria, and the periodic table.

Scholastic Animals   tinyurl.com/schanimals

This very readable collection of articles from Scholastic is aimed at primary- and middle-school ages.

☆ *Best Homeschooling Moment*

I was sitting at the dining room table looking out the sliding-glass window when my nature boy appeared with a swallowtail butterfly crawling up his shirt onto his face. I got the camera in time and took a photo while it was on his nose!

—Diana Malament, a mom homeschooling one with two graduated, Gaithersburg, Maryland

Science

Science

Best Homeschooling Moment

As a bird built its nest outside our back door window, we watched it lay eggs, the babies hatch, the parents both feed, and the birds emerge. That was a good homeschooling moment.

—Kristene Brooks, a disciple training four disciples, Boerne, Texas

Tasty Insect Recipes   tinyurl.com/schbugs

Is it science or is it health? The Department of Entomology at Iowa State University offers up such delicacies as Banana Worm Bread, Chocolate-Covered Grasshoppers, and Mealworm Fried Rice. Eat up! Hey, you never know when the next famine will hit.

Waterford Game & Activities

waterfordpress.com/entergame.html

Seriously well-done games, activities, and printables for studying dozens of animals. The page also includes a few tools for studying geology, plants, and weather, but animal studies make up the bulk of these resources.

What's That Bug?   whatsthatbug.com

Send in a mug shot of the mysterious critters under your house and ask the Bugman to identify them.

Chapter 13

Health Handbook

I SUPPOSE WE'RE a typical family when it comes to health. One son is a vegetarian. My older daughter is an athlete. Another son works at McDonald's. And so it goes.

Health education ain't what it used to be.

Where your childhood was spent learning about jumping jacks and cigarettes and eating your apple a day, your children face a world with food pyramids and aerobics and D.A.R.E. programs and HIV. Substance abuse, gerontology, untreatable viruses and infections, abortion—they're all part of the new face of health education, which today comprises physical fitness, personal hygiene, and the development of lifestyle practices that improve the quality of life.

Sometimes health is best learned by seeing a parent's good example. "Much of health is caught not taught," observes a homeschooling mom of four from Hawkes Bay, New Zealand. "Set the example in your household. Make sure you and your children get out for a walk or a run at the park—this is 'school,' too, even though they are having fun!"

Jody O'Donnell, from Columbus, Ohio, is a nurse

Hotlinks

Health Education Network
tinyurl.com/healthed

HHMI Catalog
hhmi.org/catalog

Online Health Science Curriculum
tinyurl.com/teachhealth

The Office of Science Education
science-education
.nih.gov

who homeschools two of her seven kids. She explains how she incorporates health lessons as a natural part of her complete homeschooling program: "My daughter was with me through my last pregnancy and delivery and wrote a paper on it. This pregnancy was different from the others; I was diagnosed with gestational diabetes, so that was a little more to research.

"If my daughter reads a book, she writes a report. Right now she is reading a series of books and will write summaries of what she reads. We place everything in a file for her end-of-the-year evaluation.

"My oldest is a good kid, and I feel blessed to be spending this time with her. The house is cluttered, but the kids have fun!"

In this chapter, you'll be introduced to resources on community health, drug abuse education, human development, mental health, nutrition, personal health, physical education, and safety and first aid. First, though, we visit some resources that address a wide variety of health topics:

☆ *Best Homeschooling Moment*

Another parent asked him if he liked homeschooling. My son replied, "Oh, yes. Public school wasn't as interesting, and I didn't learn as much in a month there as I do in a day here. Plus I can sleep late, and the cafeteria food is much tastier!"

—Darlene Pineda, an intelligent, liberal family person, Elizabeth City, North Carolina

BAM! Body and Mind   www.bam.gov

From the CDC, an online comic book that answers kids' questions on health issues and recommends ways to be healthy, safe, and strong. Become a Disease Detective; create an activity calendar, or learn survival skills. Includes a Teacher's Corner with middle-school classroom activities based on national education standards.

Children's Health Encyclopedia
healthofchildren.com

Brilliant. An easy-to-read encyclopedia that covers five areas of health: immunizations, drugs, procedures, diseases and disorders, and development. Very accessible, written in clear English with recommendations for further reading on nearly every subject.

Health and Sports

learnersonline.com/weekly/subject/health_pe.htm

Web quests on topics such as national fitness, donating blood and *E. coli* outbreaks. Extremely well done, with photographs, links, explanatory text, and illustrations.

Health Archive

educationworld.com/a_tsl/archives/health.shtml

A collection of lesson plans covering environmental education, family life, mental health, nutrition, our bodies, safety, sex, STDs, AIDS, and substance abuse.

Health Education Network   tinyurl.com/healthed

Lesson plans that teach health topics such as nutrition, disease prevention, conflict resolution, and body image, for grades 3 through 12.

Health Lesson Plans   eduref.org/cgi-bin/lessons.cgi/Health

From the Educator's Reference Desk, lessons plans on health topics such as body systems and senses, chronic conditions, consumer health, environmental health, family life, human sexuality, mental health, nutrition, process skills, safety, and substance abuse prevention.

HealthU   healthu.com

Online video courses taught by doctors and university lecturers with interviews, graphics, quizzes, and transcripts. The courses cover vascular health, weight loss surgery, ulcerative colitis, multiple sclerosis, psoriasis, lymphoma, chronic myeloid leukemia, leukemia, heartburn, insomnia, and breast cancer.

HHMI Catalog   hhmi.org/catalog

The Howard Hughes Medical Institute offers free DVDs and videos on health and science topics. Select from such titles as Seeing, Hearing

---

☆ *Best Homeschooling Moment*

When my daughter wakes up each morning when her own body tells her it is time to get up and she looks at me every morning and says, "You're the best mom in the world and thanks for taking me out of school. What are we going to do today?"

—Melinda Penberthy, homeschooling mom learning as she teaches, Pevely, Missouri

---

Health

Health

Field Tripping

During camping trips we have studied nature, searched out animal tracks, even worked on swimming. (We also learned how to warm up someone who stayed in a cold pool too long and had blue lips.)

—Saprina Bowman, proud mom of two homeschooled boys, Baumholder, Germany

and Smelling the World or Genes and Gender: The Process of Becoming a Male or a Female.

LifeWorks   science.education.nih.gov/LifeWorks

Think you have a future doctor in the house? Explore careers in health and medicine with this resource from the National Institutes of Health. Kids can browse more than 100 career descriptions, and begin as early as the eighth grade to prepare for admission to a medical school.

NIGMS Publications   publications.nigms.nih.gov

More free publications from the NIH. Order health booklets on topics such as research, cell biology, and chemistry. Or view the publications online at no charge.

NIH Curriculum Supplement Series
science.education.nih.gov/supplements

Supplement your health curriculum with these teaching guides from the NIH. Download them, or request free printed editions of guides such as Cell Biology and Cancer or The Brain: Our Sense of Self.

Online Health Science Curriculum   tinyurl.com/teachhealth

A cross-curriculum collection of well-organized health lesson plans and more than 300 interdisciplinary activities to teach about blood, bones, the brain, the cardiovascular system, diabetes, forces and motion, and more. Sponsored by the University of Texas.

The Office of Science Education   science.education.nih.gov

Do your kids love getting mail? Sign them up to receive free health booklets from the National Cancer Institute. Titles such as *The Good News About Fruits & Vegetables* will keep them running for the mailbox, and learning about health, all at the same time.

Community Health

THERE WAS A time, just a few years ago, when the medical and scientific community was optimistic about someday finding cures to all the world's ills.

That's all changed now. Not only are all-new diseases—including new and quickly mutating strains of hepatitis—making an appearance, but also some of the old standbys are proving intractable. Resistant strains of certain viruses and other microbes have developed in recent years, and physicians are observing that some diseases that once seemed imminently treatable are, in fact, incurable.

Moreover, certain diseases and conditions—heart disease, AIDS, lung cancer, fetal alcohol syndrome, for example—are simply beyond the reach of the medical community as long as people continue the behaviors that facilitate the conditions.

Jens Query, a doctor of internal medicine at a university in Münster, Germany, says there are many reasons for teenagers and children to take an interest in health and in disease prevention: "First, the best therapy for a disease is to prevent the disease. One of the best examples is the incidence of lung cancer. Since the 1980s, the United States and other countries have spent millions of dollars for cancer research. The results might have been better if the government had closed down cigarette production and supported the workers. This will be an important time for children and teenagers who smoke, because they are in the beginning stages of smoking. Unfortunately, it's very difficult to convince them of the danger posed by smoking, because they will not see the risk, and the cancer does not appear until years later.

"Another point of prevention will be adipositas (obesity). It's a very important issue because young people tend

Health: From the Old English *hal* (hale, whole). The condition of being sound of mind and body.

Health

Hotlinks

AdkPathCourse
adkpathcourse
.blogspot.com

Merck Manual
merck.com/mmhe

Virtual Surgery
edheads.org

to eat only fast food and sweets. Adipositas is an important risk factor for several diseases, including diabetes and heart failure. Yet the number of obese people is growing, so it is very important to teach young people the problems associated with this condition.

When you're looking for ways to teach your children the fundamentals of health, the following resources will come in handy. They deal with medical issues, epidemiology, disease control, and prevention; some offer specific information on AIDS, HIV, and STD education.

Your children may not be ready to cure cancer, but with these resources at hand, they'll certainly be able to keep themselves healthy. These links teach kids about vaccines, diseases and disorders, epidemics, and disease prevention.

AdkPathCourse   adkpathcourse.blogspot.com

An illustrated online course describing diseases and disease processes. It's in blog form, so begin at the end and work your way forward.

Infection Detection Protection   amnh.org/nationalcenter/infection

Click the Prevention Convention link for 10 tips on preventing infection diseases. Or let your junior detectives solve the Microbe Mystery to learn about epidemiology.

Merck Manual   merck.com/mmhe

The home edition of the *Merck Manual,* the world's most widely used textbook of medicine. The book covers all sorts of diseases and disorders, including diagnosis, symptoms, and treatment.

Patient Education   www.asahq.org/patientEducation.htm

Is someone in your family facing surgery? These FAQs from the American Society of Anesthesiologists will answer lots of questions about what goes on in the operating room. On the right, find a coloring book for children called "My Trip to the Hospital," a 29-page PDF workbook for children who will be going to the hospital.

Health

Tell a Cold from the Flu
tutorials.com/07/0706/0706.asp

An illustrated multipart tutorial discusses symptoms and prevention. Follow the links to the right for related How-To's on other health topics.

The Great Pandemic   **1918.pandemicflu.gov**

Great background for a unit study on medicine, this site explains the story of the 1918 outbreak of the Spanish flu, which killed an estimated 675,000 Americans and 30 to 50 million people worldwide. Learn about the medical system in the U.S. in 1918, then click the link to the U.S. government's avian and pandemic flu site.

Vaccines for Children   **cdc.gov/vaccines/programs/vfc**

A federally funded program that provides vaccines at no cost to children who might not otherwise be vaccinated because of inability to pay.

Virtual Surgery   **edheads.org**

Perform surgery by conducting a virtual hip replacement or a knee replacement. Kids can use virtual tools such as the scalpel and bone saw, or view images from actual surgeries. This site also provides a safety lesson with a crash scene investigation, and teaches about weather and machines.

Community Health Freebie

Antibiotic Resistance Fact Sheet explains the dangers of misusing antibiotics, and how it creates drug-resistant supergerms. Call 1-888-878-3256 and request item number 534R.

Health

Drug Education

ALCOHOL ADDICTION CAUSED Russ Taylor to lose his job, his children, his home, and for a time, even his freedom. He even gave serious consideration to suicide. While he was undergoing a battle with Hodgkin's disease, he told me this chilling tale of the effects of substance abuse: "My story," he says, "is one of alcohol abuse. I didn't know it at

Health

Drug: Related to the Middle English *drogge* (from dry, as in dried plants). Chemical substance affecting central nervous system, resulting in changes in behavior or physiology.

the time; being a product of the 1950s, when alcohol was a part of life, I thought the drinking was normal. It was the way I grew up. Drinking and driving were a part of tolerant society . . . and condoned."

When Russ was a teenager, his father was a heavy drinker. "The attitude he conveyed to my friends and me," says Russ, "was 'if you need to party, you do it in front of me.' I understand his thought process, though I don't condone it now." Russ says that in his teen years, drinking made him feel competent, as though he "fit in" and was "cool." The truth, he says, was different. "What it really did was lead to my feelings of isolation, being unaccepted, having a small circle of friends, and becoming a dropout my senior year."

He pulled his life together enough to attend college and marry. In the beginning, the drinking was mostly under control. When his eldest child was three, however, his marriage began to crumble, and after his wife left home with his two children, he began drinking more heavily. Intermittent attempts to overcome the addiction were unsuccessful, and over the course of nearly two decades his condition deteriorated to homelessness and a period of incarceration, with his sons bouncing between foster homes and sometimes living on the streets or in shelters. There's no happy ending to this story. Russ's life is beginning to come together now, despite crushing debt and continuing worry about being able to support himself. He's trying to rebuild a relationship with his sons, even as he faces a disease that is often fatal.

Russ is now a strong supporter of homeschooling and urges parents to teach their children the dangers of addictions: "Abuse of any substance—be it alcohol, illicit drugs, or nicotine—has a profound effect on your physical, emotional, and spiritual well-being," he says. "Alcohol is a depressant, stripping away self-esteem, damaging

Hotlinks

Above the Influence
abovetheinfluence.com

Mothers Against Drunk Driving
madd.org

The Truth
thetruth.com

brain cells, and killing vital organs such as the liver. Society has become less tolerant of drunks, and the legal consequences of a drinking and driving offense can exceed $2,500 or more, plus there's the risk of incarceration.

"Use of illicit drugs, even marijuana, exacts a heavy financial and legal toll, too. In most states, simple possession of an illegal substance can warrant incarceration for two years or more. On the physical side, illicit drugs physically affect all organs of the body in varying degrees, and in some individuals, the small effects of one drug lead to cravings for more powerful ones.

"Nicotine is one of the hardest drugs to get away from. In most cases, addiction is instantaneous. Smoking-related consequences are among the top three killers, and include cancer, heart and vascular problems, and fires. Health costs for the care and treatment of smokers are extremely high; most insurance companies triple your premium for coverage. And if you smoke in your home and then try to sell your home, a lot of people will not buy it.

"Today's teens are under constant pressure to conform to the desires of their peers, and substance abuse is one of the negatives that the youth of today cannot escape. You can turn on the television and see alcohol and drugs being used, and alcohol advertised on sports events, all giving the concept that it is cool to use. What is not shown is the grief, the pain, and the sickness that these substances cause with prolonged use . . . nicotine included."

Kathy Bohon was trained as a certified drug and alcohol counselor. She is now a stay-at-home mother of three living in Georgia. She explains the critical need for teaching children about substance abuse, even if they're homeschooled: "Homeschooled kids may face less risk of peer-induced substance abuse than other children, but they will one day enter college and be exposed to the high-pressure alcohol and drug culture common among young adults. Entry-level jobs are also a high-risk environment. Children should understand the health risks and techniques for avoiding pressure.

Health

The following online resources are the best around for teaching your children the truth of substance abuse.

Above the Influence   abovetheinfluence.com

You've probably seen ATI's television campaigns. These well-done materials are designed to appeal to teens and older adolescents.

Drug Free   drugfree.org

The Partnership for a Drug-Free America provides educational materials for parents and teens. Fact sheets, articles, and videos discuss drugs both illegal and legal.

Mothers Against Drunk Driving   madd.org

Many members of MADD lost a child to a drunk driver. This website is part of the group's mission to stop drunk driving, support the victims of this violent crime, and prevent underage drinking.

NIDA Goes Back to School   backtoschool.drugabuse.gov

The National Institute on Drug Abuse offers free curriculum materials such as posters, pamphlets and teacher's guides. Learn about the science of drug abuse with information on marijuana, opiates, hallucinogens, and other illegal drugs.

Stop Under Age Drinking   stopalcoholabuse.gov

Free government publications on underage drinking, along with ideas for fighting the problem. These resources are designed to help anyone interested in prevention, including parents, community-based organizations, and youth.

The Truth   thetruth.com

An antismoking site funded by the American Legacy Foundation, an organization established out of the tobacco industry settlement. Animated, kid-inhabited site your children will consider fun.

Tips for Teens About Steroids   ncadi.samhsa.gov/govpubs/phd726

Clear facts about the dangers of steroid abuse. Written for teenagers and parents.

TIPS4Youth   **cdc.gov/tobacco/youth**

No smoking here. Educational resources and materials, such as videos, tip sheets, and posters. This is a great starting point for studying the dangers of tobacco for the human body.

Human Development

HOW DO YOU effectively teach something as intimate and important as human growth and development, reproduction, and aging?

Many homeschoolers say they've found practical ways to broach the subject of human intimacy with their children.

Ann Crum homeschools a twelve-year-old daughter and a fourteen-year-old son in central Arkansas. Living in a rural area, she says, has made things easier for her. "Over the course of time, sex ed has come into play not as a specific course but as a part of everyday life. Through the years, we have had pets who have bred and had babies. We have talked openly about reproduction and gestation in those animals.

Development:
From the Old French *des* (un) and *veloper* (wrap). Growth and change in an organism.

"My kids have witnessed breeding and birth and all the processes that occur in the mother animal during the gestation period. We have made it a point not to shelter them from these basic facts of life. We have also made it a strong point that we are humans, not animals, and that we have a commitment to our spouse before we have babies. Although the physical processes are similar, the moral aspects are quite different.

"My children were interested to learn, however, that geese mate for life. So they know that not all animals breed just with any old mate. They have witnessed the loyalty of a gander toward his mate when she is setting eggs or raising goslings and the fact that he will step up and block you from getting near by hissing and spreading his wings.

"We also raise goats, so they became yet another opportunity for hands-on sex ed. We have witnessed the breeding, the birthing, and the

Health

Health

nursing of the kids. My children were impressed at how strong a bond exists between a doe and her kid."

Another component of human growth and development is the aging process. Howard Dombrower is associated with a geriatric care center in Toronto. He believes it's important to teach children about the aging process for several reasons: "Aging affects all of us, and for this reason alone it is important to learn about aging," he says. "It helps us to better understand ourselves."

Another reason? We have some influence over how aging affects us. "Our grandparents and some of our parents are now experiencing age-related changes that affect memory, hearing, vision, skin, the joints in their bodies, their reflexes—even how their heart, lungs, liver, and kidney function. If we are to better understand our parents and grandparents, then it is important to increase our awareness and understanding about these changes."

Dr. Dombrower reminds children that some of the worst effects of aging are not inevitable: "Many of these age-related changes should not be confused with diseases. For example, although it is normal for short-term memory to decline in the elderly, it is not normal for the elderly to lose judgment, long-term memories, perceptual abilities, or abstract thinking."

With the following resources, your own children will be well prepared for the physical changes they experience throughout life:

American Social Hygiene Posters
special.lib.umn.edu/swha/IMAGES/home.html
An American historian began this collection of government-issued posters produced from 1910 to 1970. Most relate to sexual abstinence and family hygiene. Fascinating.

Bare Facts   bbc.co.uk/schools/teachers/barefacts
An excellent curriculum outline for parents to use in talk-

Hotlinks

Bare Facts
bbc.co.uk/schools/
teachers/barefacts

Life's Greatest Miracle
pbs.org/wgbh/nova/
miracle/program.html

Teaching Sexual Health
teachingsexualhealth.ca

**The Multidimensional
Human Embryo**
embryo.soad.umich.edu

ing to their children about sex. The lesson plans and video transcripts will be invaluable. Unfortunately, the videos themselves aren't available to viewers outside the U.K.

Growth Charts   cdc.gov/growthcharts

Help your kids track their height and weight with charts provided by the Centers for Disease Control and Prevention. An educator's guide discusses the proper use and interpretation of the charts.

Healthy Start, Grow Smart

ed.gov/parents/earlychild/ready/healthystart

Have a baby joining the family? These booklets will help your children understand what to expect with their new sibling, and teach them important skills in caring for babies.

How Human Reproduction Works

howstuffworks.com/human-reproduction.htm

Exactly the right amount of information, accurate diagrams, and nothing controversial. A safe and academically sound site for teaching about the human reproductive process in accessible language that's neither too fluffy nor too abstruse.

Internet Pathology Laboratory   library.med.utah.edu/WebPath

If your teens have a medical bent, they may be interested in this on-line textbook of AIDS pathology. Or click the tutorials link to learn about the pathology of various diseases such as cancer, heart disease, and osteoporosis. Twenty or more illustrations for each organ system or general pathology topic, all with descriptions and explanations as you move from one to the next. Sponsored by the University of Utah.

Life's Greatest Miracle   pbs.org/wgbh/nova/miracle/program.html
Beautifully filmed PBS documentary on development in the womb.

Gerontology Freebie

Alzheimer's: Searching for a Cure provides helpful tips about how Alzheimer's is diagnosed, its symptoms, current drug treatments, and lifestyle advice to help prolong mental health. Call 1-888-878-3256 and request item number 551P.

Health

On Aging

Education is the best
provision for old age.

—Diogenes Laërtius, c.
A.D. 200

Each of the eight "chapters" of the documentary runs about seven minutes. Watch how babies grow, from conception to birth.

Pregnancy and Childbirth
methodisthealth.com/pregnancy/anatomy.htm
The anatomy section of a large site on pregnancy and childbirth. Other resources on this site offer in-depth explanations of topics such as planning for pregnancy, pregnancy concerns, and labor and delivery.

Talk About Menstruation   **tinyurl.com/mense**
A narrated, animated diagram of the menstrual cycle will explain menses to your preteen kids. Click the Related Articles link on the right for other good articles about puberty, both male and female.

Teaching and Learning About Aging   **unt.edu/natla**
Research, curriculum, lesson plans, and more for children of all ages. Click the Research link at the top of the page to access the educational materials.

Teaching Sexual Health   **teachingsexualhealth.ca**
A Canadian site for teaching puberty, sexuality, and reproduction. Under the Elementary section of the Student link, your preadolescent children can read simply written answers to basic questions about human development. The Teachers section offers advice and lesson plans for teaching sexual health.

The Multidimensional Human Embryo   **embryo.soad.umich.edu**
Animations of developing human embryos from 22 to 56 days old based on magnetic resonance imaging. Fascinating.

Health

Mental Health

GOOD MENTAL HEALTH makes for a good life. Understanding mental health issues such as depression and an alphabet soup of other disorders makes healthy children more sympathetic, and helps children and adults who are afflicted with these disorders know when and how to seek treatment. In this section, we cover knowledge of self and others, self-esteem, and other mental health issues.

Basil Johnson, a retired forensic psychologist in Roseburg, Oregon, has spent thirty-five years in the mental health field, twenty-two of them as a doctoral-level psychologist with a specialty in forensic psychology. He describes the reasons it's important to teach your children about good mental health:

"It often surprises people to know that 10 percent of the human population will experience a disabling mental disorder at one time during their lives. The extent to which that disorder impairs the victim is often dependent on the severity of the disorder, how willing the victim is to seek and receive treatment, and how the significant others (friends and relatives of the victim) respond to the disorder.

"Fortunately, all mental disorders are amenable to treatment, and treatment is available throughout the United States."

Although she's now been "converted" to homeschooling as a principle, Shari Setter, a Peyton, Colorado, mother of five, started teaching her children at home simply to protect their self-esteem. When her second child was in kindergarten, his teacher informed her that her son had attention deficit/hyperactivity disorder. But her doctor disagreed. "The doctor said he was just a boy! The teacher wanted to hold him back in the half-day kindergarten program. I said no way. We lived on a street with five other

> **Mental:** From the Latin *mens* (mind). Relating to the order of the mind and brain.

Hotlinks

Anorexia Nervosa and Related Eating Disorders
anred.com

Conflict Resolution
tinyurl.com/conres

Mental Health & Behavior
tinyurl.com/mhealth

Social and Emotional Learning
edutopia.org/
social-emotional-learning

kids who went to kindergarten with him. If that wouldn't have been a self-esteem killer, what would have?

"We decided to start homeschooling, and it has since become a personal conviction."

Your homeschooled children are probably more secure, healthier, and more capable than many of their peers. But if they ever have to deal with their own or someone else's depression or bipolar, attention deficit, or eating disorder, familiarity with the information in these resources will be a big help. These resources also address abuse, conflict resolution, and self-esteem. You'll find related information on psychology in Chapter 10 and on marriage and family relationships in the life skills section of Chapter 14.

Anorexia Nervosa and Related Eating Disorders   anred.com

ANRED is a nonprofit organization that teaches about eating disorders and how to recover from them. Educational materials at this site discuss statistics, warning signs, treatment, and other must-know information about body image and disorders.

Conflict Resolution   tinyurl.com/conres

Lesson plans on being a peacemaker, intervening in fights, playing fair, and related issues.

Dunebrook   dunebrook.org/lesson_plans.html

This child abuse–prevention resource sponsors lesson plans that teach kids to express emotion and feel better about themselves.

On Esteem

He who knows others is wise; He who knows himself is enlightened.

—Tao Te Ching

Five Senses   sedl.org/scimath/pasopartners/senses

Kids need a self-image boost? Let them learn about the miracle of their own bodies. For grades 1 through 5, a seven-lesson unit study on the senses integrating math, science, and language.

Man of the House   mothboys.org

Help for young men who don't have a father in the

home. Encourages responsibility, social development, morality, etiquette, and other virtues.

Mental Health & Behavior   tinyurl.com/mhealth

Order booklets and posters that address topics such as depression, domestic violence, bullying, and mental illness.

Resource Toolbox

hooah4health.com/toolbox/toolbox.htm

The U.S. Army Center for Health Promotion and Preventive Medicine offers mental health resources for soldiers; they'll help your family learn about topics such as stress management, suicide prevention, spiritual wellness, and civilian fitness.

Six Seconds EQ   6seconds.org

A website about Emotional Intelligence, the capacity to create positive outcomes in relationships. Includes articles, news, and much more to assist in learning about and improving one's EQ.

Social and Emotional Learning

edutopia.org/social-emotional-learning

Part of the George Lucas Educational Foundation site, these videos discuss emotional intelligence.

Mental Health Freebie

Warning Signs: A Violence Prevention Guide aims to help youth avoid violent situations and even stop violence before it happens. Other free guides discuss warning signs for mental health concerns. Call 800-268-0078.

Health

Nutrition

I DON'T KNOW about you, but I've always found it a little off-putting to be told I am what I eat.

From a macular, cellular perspective, though, it's true. Every single cell in the human body is a product of the food, liquid, air, and other products that get processed by that body. If you consume nothing but crayons and bleach, your body will, in very short order, prove that it's a

Health

Nutrition: From the Latin *nutritus* (to give suck, nurture). Substances that sustain life and promote growth.

product of what it eats, and cease to function. When kids live off Twinkies and Pepsi, they have to consume an awful lot of pastry to try to suck out enough nutrients to sustain life.

North Carolina homeschooling mom Terri Vitkovitsky has advice for teaching kids the most basic truth about nutrition: "Go strawberry (or any fruit) picking. We get to see a farm, a field and how it is set up, how the strawberries grow, because inevitably there are blossoms and all the various stages of the fruit. Actually we usually take it one step further and come home and make jam. I think these kinds of field trips are great, so kids realize strawberries don't really come from cellophane packages at the grocery store."

Ryan Rupp is a baseball player in Leo, Indiana, who did coursework in biology. He says being careful about nutrition changed his ability to compete athletically. "From my own experience I have noticed a huge difference with my gains in the weight room after beginning to take nutritional supplements. I feel that it is nearly impossible to get all necessary nutrients from food that I eat, so I usually take several dietary supplements each day."

He suggests a good way to motivate children to practice good nutrition: "Parents of a homeschooled child will want to find a topic that interests their child and that also relates to nutrition. For example, a child might look up to professional athletes. A professional athlete must maintain proper nutrition at all times or risk losing his or her competitive edge."

Nurse and certified childbirth educator Danielle Leopold has been teaching about human growth and development for fourteen years. She also has a suggestion for parents who want to motivate their children to learn about good nutrition. "Plan a menu for a healthful diet together. Meal planning is an effective way to teach.

Hotlinks

How to Read Food Labels
scientificpsychic.com/
fitness

My Pyramid
www.mypyramid.gov

Raw Food How-To
rawfoodhowto.com

Super Star Nutrition for Kids
tinyurl.com/supereat

"Use balanced diet information and good nutritional guidelines. Have the child plan a week's worth of family menus to understand what goes into making a healthy life."

Joel Drakes, a personal trainer and nutritionist in New York, has been training for more than fifteen years and is certified in fitness and nutrition. Joel says he has seen for himself the benefits of eating nutritiously. "I began exercising and eating properly at around seventeen years old and have never regretted it. I have never been sick, other than the regular cold (if you call that being sick), and have had no need of doctors.

"I recommend that parents get their children involved in some kind of activity, and that they lead by example. Forget the pizzas, french fries, and burgers for now. Consume wholesome foods."

To teach your own kids the importance of consuming whole foods, consider the following resources. (Related resources are in the physical education section later in this chapter and in the life skills section Chapter 14.) These resources discuss food labels, vegetarianism, weight management, and the food pyramid.

How to Read Food Labels   scientificpsychic.com/fitness

There is a great deal of good information on this site, but click the Food Labels link to read a comparison of discrepancies in Nutrition Facts labels from two identical products. What buyers should know—and watch for—when reading those labels. They aren't always accurate.

It's Up to You   bbc.co.uk/northernireland/schools/4_11/uptoyou

Great BBC website teaches nutrition by showing how it relates to success in sports. Colorful animations, tips, quizzes, more. From the Personal, Social, and Health education segment of the U.K. curriculum.

Leafy Greens Lesson Plans   leafy-greens.org

From the North Carolina Department of Agriculture, great lesson plans on nutrition, with a strong bias toward green leafy vegetables.

On Nutrition

It is easier to change a man's religion than to change his diet.

—Margaret Mead

Health

Receive free materials such as book covers, trading cards, brochures, and posters.

Metabolism Calculator   tinyurl.com/metabol

Wonder how many calories you actually consume every day? This calculator considers a person's age, weight, and other factors to determine his or her daily caloric use.

My Calorie Counter   my-calorie-counter.com

An online diet and exercise journal that tracks food intake, water consumption, activity, and weight on a daily basis. This tool charts weight against other factors so your kids can watch how their food intake and activity influence their weight.

My Pyramid   www.mypyramid.gov

The USDA's nutritional "pyramid" guidelines can be personalized to your specific age, gender, and activity level. Help your kids choose the foods and quantities that are right for them.

Raw Food How-To   rawfoodhowto.com

Videos and articles on how to successfully live a vegan raw-food diet. It's extreme; it's amazing. And it's healthy.

Super Star Nutrition for Kids   tinyurl.com/supereat

Lesson plans and activity sheets teach kids to shop for food and prepare nutritious meals.

Personal Health

THE OLD SAW about snips, snails, and puppy dog tails certainly holds true in our family. With five boys, there's hardly an hour in our day when Dad and I aren't asking, "And did you wash those grimy hands?"

Fortunately, puberty seems to have a positive effect on personal hygiene. Whenever there's a dance or some other social event that involves girls, our older boys are found steaming up the bathroom, hanging over sinks brushing their teeth, searching for a new container of deodorant, or carefully pressing their shirts and pants.

Too bad their mother doesn't count as a girl!

That's little comfort, though, to parents whose children aren't yet to the point of obsessing over their own personal hygiene or other personal health considerations. If your children are younger, you may find yourself struggling to teach these principles effectively.

Laurie Welton is a hospital- and clinic-based infectious disease specialist and a professor of medicine in Michigan. She describes the importance of personal hygiene on the health and well-being of your entire family: "A lot of common infections are transmitted from one child to another and then to the whole family by hands. A child sneezes into his hand; then, by not washing his hands, he can spread it to all the other kids and the rest of the family in the same household. The most common infections transmitted are colds, viral gastroenteritis, and even hepatitis A, which is often transmitted by a fecal/oral route if good hand washing is not done around small children." For parents, she offers this advice: "You might try some games to show kids how easy it is to transfer germs.

"Try using something that washes out but is easily passed to another by shaking hands or touching something. You could even make a game of it. Take something sticky (jelly or jam?) in different colors, name a different infection for each color, and let them enjoy themselves in a place away from your good furniture. Let them also brush their teeth with water-soluble black food coloring to let them see what their teeth would look like if they did not brush them."

This section looks at resources for teaching hygiene, personal care, good sleep habits, and dental health.

Hygiene: From the Greek *hugieine* (the art of health). The habits and practices that promote good health.

Health

Hotlinks

Bedtime
facs.pppst.com/
bedtime.html

Open Wide and Trek Inside
tinyurl.com/wideopen

SunWise Kids
epa.gov/sunwise/
becoming.html

Bathtime   facs.pppst.com/bathtime.html
A collection of PowerPoint presentations that teach kids the importance of regular bathing.

Bedtime   facs.pppst.com/bedtime.html
Lots of resources for teaching kids what sleep is, and why they need it.

Food Safety   health.pppst.com/foodsafety.html
PowerPoint presentations that teach kids how to handle food safely and avoid contamination. One of the lessons, "Food Detective," lets kids track down bad habits that cause illness.

Four Steps to a Healthy Smile   oralhealthmonth.com.au/brushing-teeth
Diagram and discussion of proper tooth brushing.

Hand Washing   tinyurl.com/handwash
How hand washing prevents disease. A discussion for older students.

Open Wide and Trek Inside   tinyurl.com/wideopen
Free booklet that teaches younger learners the science of tooth brushing and major scientific concepts relating to oral health.

Sleep Disorders and BioRhythms   tinyurl.com/sleepdep
Part of the NIH's curriculum supplement series, this teacher's guide and multimedia student activities teach teens about the importance of getting adequate rest.

So You Wanna . . . Beauty & Fashion   tinyurl.com/sobeaut
Written for teens and preteens: how to do your makeup, buy a suit, dress better, rent a tux, or lose weight.

SunWise Kids   epa.gov/sunwise/becoming.html
Sign up your homeschooling cooperative to receive a free SunWise Tool Kit. The kit includes curriculum materials from the Environmental Protection Agency for teaching kids about sun safety. The kit includes UV-sensitive Frisbees that turn purple when exposed to UV radiation. Register online at **epa.gov/sunwise** or call 202-343-9924.

Tots Health Corner **tinyurl.com/health**
Fun cartoons that demonstrate healthy habits.

Physical Education

WHEN MY GRANDMOTHER was young, she went with a few friends to Washington, D.C., to work for the 1930 U.S. Census. While she was there, she played basketball and became a member of the national women's basketball team. I still have pictures of her in her bloomers and prim basketball blouse. Unfortunately, I didn't inherit the family jock genes. Those went to my youngest sister, who, at 6'2", is a mean competitor on the basketball court, and spends her weekends and evenings being a jock. She'll outlive me by forty years.

Lisa Williams teaches physical education and coaches softball in Eureka Springs, Arkansas. She has some great ideas for helping kids get enthusiastic about improving their fitness. "To motivate them, I tell them how much healthier PE can make them and how much fun they can have by getting and staying healthy," she says. "All kids are different, so you have to treat them differently when teaching them. Some give up easily; some won't give up trying until they are exhausted. I tell them not to give up and just do the best they can. Nobody is perfect. Keep trying!

"Reward them with something different and fun once in a while. Go hiking, swimming, or fishing as a reward. Kids can have physical education and not even know it! If you're teaching at home, try to have your child get some form of cardiovascular exercise at least three days a week for 45 minutes. Running, jumping rope, cycling, and swimming are a few good examples. Make sure they warm up and stretch before any strenuous exercise. The

Athlete: From the Greek *athlon* (contend for a prize). One who possesses or acquires strength, agility, or endurance.

Health

Hotlinks

Maran Student Library
maran.com

PE Unit Plans
tinyurl.com/peunit

The Runner's Resource
runners-resource.com

Walking
walking.about.com

PE Central website (**pecentral.org**) has all the info you will need to get started."

Howard Martin is a certified fitness instructor and the founder and owner of a fitness consulting firm located in Victorville, California. He also operates a commercial website that promotes exercise. He shares some thoughts about the importance of fitness for youngsters today: "We are meant to move, walk, run, jump, and be active," he says. "Not only does the body want to, but it actually needs to move. It responds in a positive way when we do. The body becomes stronger and more flexible through exercise, and the mind gets a big benefit as well. When we exercise and use proper nutrition, we actually feel better mentally and perform better in such things as memory.

"So become active with your kids. Get them involved in an activity with others. Get them jogging, rollerskating, and participating in sports. This will make a huge difference in their lives. Being fit and healthy is not an accident; it is achieved just like anything else."

For Tristi Pinkston, a Utah homeschooler, sports are her kids' academic motivator. "When I need to motivate them, I frequently use a reward system, such as 'Let's finish up school and then we can go to the playground,' or 'One more page and then you can help me make dessert.' However, much of the time I don't need to do this—they understand the importance of getting it done, and in most subjects, they find school fun, so it's not a hardship."

If you're not yet motivated to "hit the road," these resources will give you plenty of helpful information about physical education, fitness, recreation, sports, and athletics.

On Principles

On matters of style, swim with the current; on matters of principle, stand like a rock.

—Thomas Jefferson

99 Tips for Family Fitness Fun
shapeup.org/pubs/99tips
Great advice for getting your family moving. Tip 99: Build an obstacle course in the basement or garage on a rainy day.

EdWorld Physical Education   *tinyurl.com/eworldpe*

A collection of lesson plans covering games, exercise and movement, and team sports.

Game Time   *nauticom.net/www.dbullock*

A well-organized collection of PE games. The article on "gym" teachers is worth a read.

Maran Student Library   *maran.com*

High-quality books illustrated with color photography teaching yoga and weight training. Other books in this series focus on other subjects, beyond physical education: cooking, algebra, dog training, computers, and crafts. Worth bookmarking.

PE Lesson Plan Page

members.tripod.com/~pazz/lesson.html

A collection of PE lesson plans submitted by college students, with games such as Clean Your Room and Survivor. Most of these games require groups—or large families.

PE Unit Plans   *tinyurl.com/peunit*

Unit studies developed by university PE majors. Teach your kids kayaking and canoeing, or dozens of other sports.

Physical Activity and Health   *cdc.gov/nccdphp/sgr/adoles.htm*

Why your kids need to be fit. A report of the surgeon general, from the Centers for Disease Control and Prevention.

Physical Education at MIT

ocw.mit.edu/OcwWeb/hs/intro-courses/pe

Highlights for High School provides resources from MIT to improve PE instruction at the high school level. Watch video demonstrations that prepare teens for college coursework.

PE Freebie

Handout on Health: Sports Injuries explains what kinds of activities are most likely to cause injuries, how to prevent them, and treatments available. Call 888-878-3256 and request item number 502R.

Health

Physical Education Lesson Plans
eduref.org/cgi-bin/lessons.cgi/Physical_Education

PE lesson plans designed by classroom teachers. Most are easily adapted to homeschooling programs.

Play 60   nflrush.com/health

Peyton Manning and the rest of the NFL are part of the league's youth health and fitness campaign, focused on making the next generation of kids the most active and healthy by encouraging them to be active for at least sixty minutes a day. Tips, activities, and lots of ideas for play.

Sports and Homeschoolers
tinyurl.com/nhensport

Options for homeschoolers who want to participate in organized athletics.

Sports Media   sports-media.org

Dozens and dozens of lesson plans on everything from adaptive PE for disabled children to yoga. Includes topics such as CPR, flag football, orienteering, and self-defense. All grade levels. To access the database for free, you'll have to submit a lesson plan of your own.

Stretch Before Exercising   tutorials.com/05/0503/0503.asp

Learn2 is a collection of multipart tutorials on loosening up, with cartoon illustrations. Links on the right lead to related How-To's on safe exercise.

The Runner's Resource   runners-resource.com

A tool for tracking your long-distance training. Tons of educational information to help your runners avoid injury. A must-read if you're undertaking a running program.

Walking   walking.about.com

Chats, discussions, articles, and links on the subject of walking.

Health

Safety and First Aid

OUR HOME SAFETY program is pretty simple: We all chase the toddler around and make sure she stays out of the Drano. It's sort of a combination fitness and safety curriculum.

There are almost certainly better, more disciplined, ways to approach this subject. Paramedic Barbara Kartchner has some suggestions for teaching first aid and emergency preparedness. She addresses her advice specifically to kids. Here is what she says:

"If any of you are Boy or Girl Scouts, you probably know the motto 'Be prepared.' What does that really mean to you? I think sometimes young people believe that because they are young, they can't handle emergency situations as well as adults can. First of all, let me tell you that some of the best students I had when I taught CPR were the younger people in class, such as in grade school. I think you are not as afraid to try new things, or as embarrassed when you make a mistake learning something, as adults are.

"I would also like you to think about a family member or a good friend being in an emergency situation right in front of you. Let's say they are burned by a pot of boiling water, or fall and break a bone, or become ill enough to need a doctor. How would you feel if you couldn't help them?

"All of the things I described, you could handle and get help for with the proper training. Give yourself credit for the ability to learn new things.

"My daughter Karen worked at our town's swimming pool in the summer as a lifeguard. One day a small boy dove into the pool awkwardly and hit his head. Because Karen had taken first aid training, she and the other lifeguards were able to rescue the child and help him properly until the ambulance arrived. Karen said she didn't have

Aid: From the Old French *ade* (help). To provide assistance or relief.

Health

Hotlinks

Ask a Cop
askacop.org

First Aid Web
firstaidweb.com

Ready.gov
ready.gov

USFA Kids Page
usfa.dhs.gov/kids

time to be scared but almost automatically remembered what to do. She also said she was really glad to be able to do a good job in helping. I hope you will think about being prepared and be confident in learning to do so."

One homeschooling mom, Terri Vitkovitsky from Camp Lejeune, North Carolina, says she uses field trips to teach her kids about safety. "Go visit a local fire station. They usually do lessons on fire safety, plus the kids get to see the fire gear, trucks, and fire station, which is always a big hit. And tour the local police station, where the kids will learn more about safety, rules/laws, and best of all, police vehicles."

The following resources will get you started teaching your kids what they need to know about home safety, personal safety, emergency preparedness, being home alone, and natural disasters.

American Red Cross   redcross.org

Good instructional downloads for natural and man-made disasters. Helps teach about twisters and earthquakes and so on in a way that lessens the fear of the disaster. Click the Preparedness link on the left to download a free coloring book.

Ask a Cop   askacop.org

Materials on virtually every safety topic: Car seats, self-defense, fireworks, guarding against burglary, identity theft . . . It's a very long list. The You Be the Detective section teaches kids to think through situations that might put them in harm's way.

Equipped to Survive   equipped.org/kidprimr.htm

What your kids need to know to survive being lost in the woods. A must-read before your next family camp-out.

Health

Child Safety

Free child safety kit lets parents store a child's identification information—fingerprints, photo, and more—at home. Call 800-742-6780.

Safety Freebie

Primer on Summer Safety explains how to avoid or treat typical summer injuries and illnesses such as sunburn, mosquito and tick bites, bee stings, and heat illness. Call 888-878-3256 and request item number 650M.

First Aid and Safety

education.com/topic/child-first-aid

This site provides good articles about Internet safety for teens, social networking, and protecting your children from strangers.

First Aid Web   firstaidweb.com

A self-guided online CPR course and an online first aid course. Learn what to do when dealing with an emergency for adults, children, and infants.

Home Alone: Are You Ready?

pbskids.org/itsmylife/family/homealone

Homeschooling families don't usually have to deal with the latchkey issue, but if you have as many kids as I do, all of them with their own activities, you know that sometimes being home alone happens. Here's good advice on teaching children to be safe when they're by themselves.

Ready.gov   ready.gov

The Kids link opens a jungle of preparedness advice. Activities encourage kids to prepare their families for emergencies by preparing a supply list, creating a readiness kit, and conducting family discussions about what to do in an emergency. Graphics rich and very well made.

Safety & Practical Living   facs.pppst.com/living.html

PowerPoint presentations that teach safety and child development, One of the lessons, "Fire Safety," includes an in-depth discussion of rules for fire safety: no matches, check smoke detectors, set up an escape drill . . . Another discusses crossing the street safely.

USFA Kids Page   usfa.dhs.gov/kids

Fire safety tips from the U.S. Fire Administration. Kids can study here for the junior fire marshal test, or learn about smoke alarms and escaping from fires.

Buckle Up

Basic Car Seat Safety, a brochure that explains the importance of wearing seat belts and using car seats, from the National Safe Kids Campaign. To order, call 800-441-1888 and order item 3227.

Health

Chapter 14

Graduation Guidance

Y OU'VE RAISED THEM, taught them well, and turned them into good people. Your parenting is never done, but at some point your hands-on role as their primary educator will be.

What's next?

In this final chapter, we look at what it takes to launch your kids into adulthood.

What do homeschoolers do when they finish their secondary education? Research suggests that homeschoolers don't differ greatly from the population at large. In two studies of 232 students homeschooled for an average of seven years who had completed a high-school course of study, 69 percent went on to post-secondary education and 31 percent found jobs. In the general population, those figures differed by only two percentage points.*

Other studies suggest that homeschoolers enter college at an even higher rate than the general population. In the general U.S. population aged eighteen to twenty-four, less than half—46.2 percent—had attained some college courses or higher. At the same time 74.2 percent of the home-educated had attained some college courses or higher.

*See our website, **hsfree.com,** for citations for this and other statistics in this chapter.

Teaching Tips

Start with the end in mind and align all your choices with that focus.

—Work-at-home mom of four from Jacaranda Tree Learning Co-operative, Hawkes Bay, New Zealand

A different study, this one of 20,000 homeschooled children, found that 88 percent of homeschooled children continue their education beyond high school, a figure the report compared with the 50 percent of the general population that do so.

In this chapter, you'll find resources for teaching your child to be a successful adult. Find information on personal financial management, basic life skills, college preparation, earning early college credit (including resources for Advanced Placement), college financial aid, and career planning. We begin, though, by introducing resources for graduating your homeschooled child.

Graduation

FOR SOME FAMILIES, homeschool graduation is an event, with parties, ceremonies, diplomas, and transcripts.

For other families, like ours, graduating from homeschool is mostly a sort of slide into adulthood. The kids "graduate" when they begin attending college full-time or enter the military. Our college-ready kids have taken tests—including the GED—only when doing so advanced their goals. They've provided transcripts and diplomas to military recruiters and college financial aid officers who required them. And so far, with four of four of the older homeschoolers in college, one of whom first entered the military, and all of whom are also working at respectable jobs, there've been no hitches that took longer than about eight minutes to sort out.

> **Graduate:**
> Related to Latin *grdus*, step. Marking a stage of academic completion.

Perhaps we've been lucky when it came to requests for documentation. It's more likely that we knew where to find resources. Here are some of our favorites:

Elective Course Descriptions

oklahomahomeschool.com/courseDesc.html

When it comes to providing transcripts to recruiters and colleges, ex-

Hotlinks

GED for Free
gedforfree.com

Homeschool Diploma Forms
donnayoung.org/forms/high-school.htm

Sample High School Transcript
geocities.com/Athens/2026/transcrp.html

plaining the coursework your kids have completed is simplified with these sample course descriptions from Oklahoma Homeschool.

GED for Free   gedforfree.com

Free online GED prep course covers math, language arts, reading, writing, social studies, science. The 200-page course covers all the key points of the GED, and the developers claim it's comparable to some GED study guides that cost twenty dollars or more at bookstores.

GED Testing Center Locator   tinyurl.com/testloc

Enter your zip code and find a local GED testing center.

Homeschool Diploma Forms

donnayoung.org/forms/high-school.htm

Donna Young helpfully provides forms for your graduating high-schooler. Diplomas, transcripts, and a GPA calculator are all available, along with other information about the basics of homeschooling high-schoolers.

Homeschool Report Card   tinyurl.com/grarep

Printable report card forms to complete by hand, or to use as templates for your own grade reports.

How to Figure a Percentage and Letter Grade

homeschooling.about.com/library/howto/htgrade.htm

In the event grading motivates your kids, here's how to calculate the percentage and letter grade of an assignment or a project.

Recognizing Home School Diplomas   tinyurl.com/diplomarec

A federal law recognizes diplomas issued by homeschooled parents for the purpose of financial aid. This article gives details.

Sample High School Transcript

tinyurl.com/gradtrans

If your children apply to the military, most colleges, or even some jobs, they'll need a transcript of their high-school coursework. It's up to you to provide one. The sample transcript in this page will serve as a good guide.

The Portfolio and Its Use   tinyurl.com/portfoliouse

Though written for parents of younger children, the information in this article applies equally to families putting together academic portfolios for graduating students. "Portfolios enable children to participate in assessing their own work; keep track of individual children's progress; and provide a basis for evaluating the quality of individual children's overall performance."

Teaching Tips

Keep the big picture in mind and find what works for you. You may even have to change methods after a year or two. Keep it fun and it will be worth doing for you and the kids.

—Lori Larsen, family fun with four kids, Auburn, Washington

Personal Finance

TAKEN YOUR CHILDREN grocery shopping lately? Helping a parent find a bargain on apples or bread is often a home-schooled child's first—and most important—lesson in money management. Lesson two comes when the kids argue that you can pay for expensive toys because you still have checks in your checkbook.

How do you teach a child about money management? It's a big topic. The field of personal finance begins with basic topics such as budgeting, banking, financial planning, charitable giving, consumer protection, and investing. As they begin working, your teens will also need to become savvy about payroll taxes, income taxes, employee benefits, health, medical and life insurance, and wills and estate planning. These great tools will get them started down the path to financial success. (Find related resources under the Business and Economics sections of Chapter 10.)

Finance: From the middle English *finaunce*, to settle, pay, finish. Personal financial management and consumer protection.

Graduation

Hotlinks

Consumer Rights & Protection
lectlaw.com/tcos.html

Investing in Youth
philanthropy.ml.com/
ipo/resources

Money Math for Life
tinyurl.com/moneylife

My Money
mymoney.gov

The Mint
themint.org

Basics of Saving and Investing   finra.org/Investors
FINRA'S primer on financial decisions, how markets work, investment choices, investment information, and fraud.

Consumer Rights & Protection   lectlaw.com/tcos.html
An incredible resource for learning all about consumer rights and legal responsibilities.

Fool's School   fool.com/school.htm
The Motley Fool is a first-class investment teacher. Follow their 13 Steps to Investing to become rich, rich, rich . . . slow, slow, slow. I cannot recommend it highly enough.

Investing for Kids   library.thinkquest.org/3096
A very cool site, developed by three brilliant high school students. Very informative, very impressive.

Investing for Your Future   investing.rutgers.edu
A basic investing home study course. Learn about successful financial management with a glossary of terms, study guide, Q&As, and frequent updates.

Investing in Youth   philanthropy.ml.com/ipo/resources
Jump-start your kids' economics education. These lesson plans and activities teach inflation, savings, budgeting, and much more. Sponsored by the Merrill Lynch Family Saving Center. Teach kids the value of money and the basics of saving. The site provides money equivalents activities for the primary grades with printable coin cutouts. In addition, teachers in grades 4 through 12 will find a budget plan game and a savings scrapbook for classroom use. Easily adapted to homeschool.

Making Ends Meet   tinyurl.com/grbudg
A guide to help families get the most from their money. How to set

Graduation

goals, develop a savings plan, evaluate your resources, and put your financial plan into action.

Margin: Borrowing Money to Pay for Stocks
sec.gov/investor/pubs/margin.htm

SEC's primer on how margin works, risks, rules, tips, margin calls.

Money Math for Life   tinyurl.com/moneylife

From the U.S. Treasury, a five-lesson curriculum supplement for middle-school math classes, teaching grade 7–9 math concepts using real-life examples from personal finance.

Motley Fool   fool.com

There's one born every minute, but those of us who invest Motley Foolishly aren't among their ranks. Click the Investing link to get started, then learn the basics of buying low and selling high. Pay yourself first, understand the power of compounding, start early, do something, and never turn down free money. Master the basics, and wealth will follow.

My Money   mymoney.gov

From the U.S. government, a website "dedicated to teaching all Americans the basics about financial education. Whether you are planning to buy a home, balancing your checkbook, or investing in your 401(k), the resources on MyMoney.gov can help you do it better."

Planet Feedback   planetfeedback.com

Be a better consumer. Tell corporate America what you think! Your letters are delivered directly to the appropriate company.

Teaching Your Child About Money   family.go.com/tagsearch/money

Ready to teach your children about budgets, savings, and money management? Here's some great advice.

Finance Freebie

Consumer Action Handbook provides helpful tips about preventing identity theft, understanding credit, filing a consumer complaint, and much more. Call 888-878-3256 and request item number 568R.

Graduation

The Dollar Stretcher   stretcher.com

Income doesn't stretch to cover expenses? Here's the solution. It's a massive collection of advice and tips for being frugal.

The Mint   themint.org

All about budgets, credit, scarcity and stock markets, for grades 6 through 12. From the Kids section, students can learn basic financial management with information on topics such as how banks work, how to decode a paycheck, and how to shop smart.

Tips for Teaching Students About Saving and Investing

sec.gov/investor/students/tips.htm

The SEC—the government body that regulates securities—presents a series of talking points to help kids understand the importance of planning for their financial future.

Life Skills

OF ALL THE skills your children can learn, the skill of making a home has to be the most important. Whether it's cooking a meal, tending a crying infant, repairing a leaky toilet, organizing financial documents, driving safely, cleaning a bathroom, or communicating kindly, home-making is the most basic of adult life skills.

Just as there's no better way to learn a foreign language than to live in a foreign country, you can consider home-schooling a full-immersion course in family life and adult re-sponsibility.

Raylene Hunt, a home-educating mom of two in Maine, agrees. "Remember that your worst day as a homeschool teacher is probably still better than the best day in a public school classroom. Homeschooling prepares children for daily life in adulthood far better than any classroom ever can. Once girls learned to keep house, cook, and care for

Competence:
from the Latin *competere*, to meet, to agree. The basics of getting along in an adult world.

Graduation

children by doing it daily within their families. Now kids have to attend home ec classes that can't possibly cover in a 50-minute class two to five times a week everything they will need to know, whether they remain single or have families."

She advises parents to embrace the variety of experiences available in everyday living to teach important academic lessons: "My advice in any/all subject areas is don't feel limited. If you have a child who has a specific interest, use that interest, exhaust it. Base every subject off it. We've used everything from NASCAR (science, math, social studies, and writing) to the life cycle of the Monarch because we had chrysalises in our yard."

When it's time to teach the theory behind the daily practice of living, these resources will help spark discussion:

AAA Foundation for Traffic Safety   aaafoundation.org
A very comprehensive site on traffic safety. News, research, free materials, even quizzes on "Drowsy Driving," "Drivers 55-Plus," and "Aggressive Driving." This site is sponsored by AAA, and I wouldn't let my teenagers behind the wheel before they had read the material on this site.

Achieving Your Childhood Dreams   tinyurl.com/randydream
This lecture should be required viewing for every adult, and every potential adult, who's ever had a dream. Randy Pausch has already inspired millions. Your kids should be next.

Babysitting   facs.pppst.com/babysitting.html
PowerPoint presentations that teach baby and child care to would-be babysitters. One of the lessons, "A Guide to the Business of Babysitting," explains everything about babysitting, from good business practices to child safety. Another lesson provides a handbook for babysitters.

Hotlinks

Ehow
ehow.com

Marriage Builders
marriagebuilders.com

Mind Tools
mindtools.com

The Natural Child Project
naturalchild.org

Graduation

eHow   ehow.com

Free videos, explaining how to do just about anything. Parenting, personal finance, home and garden, relationships and family, automotive care, and much, much more. Try playing a video a day for the kids as a conversation starter.

Frugal Tips   littlecountryvillage.com/frugal-tips.shtml

Cleaning, saving, reusing, recycling. On the cheap.

Homeschool Curriculum for Life

homeschool-curriculum-for-life.com/organized-mom.html

Homemaking and housecleaning lessons for homeschooling families. By a very organized lady.

Marriage Builders   marriagebuilders.com

Anything you want your kids to know about marriage and family is on this page. Conflict resolution, infidelity, negotiation, meeting emotional needs . . . a thousand more subjects that combined make a thorough course on marriage and family.

Field Tripping

My children are in high school, so I take them in the car for driving lessons, which are free! Here I teach them very important rules of the road. My father is a retired truck driver of forty years, so I have lots of things to pass on to them that I have learned.

—Angela Petersen, homeschooling mom of two, Marseilles, Illinois

---

Mind Tools   mindtools.com

Life skills for adults: Techniques to Help You Think Excellently, Skills for High Performance Living, and Practical Psychology. Includes some Psychometric Tests that are a lot of fun. All the articles on this site are easy to read and convey lots of useful information.

Positive Parenting

positiveparenting.com/resources/resources.html

Really useful articles and tips on parenting. Much better than the usual superficial mishmash of opinions on parenting sites, these articles are filled with practical advice.

Ron and Debbie's Penny-Pinchin' Page

home.att.net/~rsenecal

Ron and Debbie are a couple of self-proclaimed tightwads. In fact, that's one of the reasons they married each other. Here's a compilation of their favorite ideas.

Speed Cleaning Rules & More
thecleanteam.com/rules.cfm

Jeff Campbell, founder of the Speed Team, offers these Speed Cleaning Rules, Clutter Control Rules, and Maintenance Rules. A must-read.

The Natural Child Project   **naturalchild.org**

If you're not already a fan of natural parenting, something on this site will change the way you interact with your children. This site covers, in some depth, attachment parenting, breast-feeding, co-sleeping, abuse, spanking, and dozens of other issues. Wonderfully written.

Teaching Tips

I feel that teaching responsibility for oneself is a number one priority; everything else then falls into place.

—Jenny McComber, real-world educating mom of four, Argyle, Texas

Getting Ahead

THE FUNNY THING about homeschoolers is that they're so uniformly precocious. Every time I meet homeschooled children, I am struck again by their maturity, their civility, and their ability to hold forth intelligently.

Perhaps it's the company of adults that engenders such qualities.

No matter what the cause, the result is that homeschooled children are often in a position to take college classes at an earlier age than average.

The goal here isn't getting them out of the house earlier. The goal is getting them through college economically—securing the best possible education at the lowest possible cost.

If you've prepared your children to participate in academically rigorous coursework, it's a good beginning. Research suggests that the strongest indicator of whether or not your child completes a four-year degree is the quality of his acade-

Advanced: from the late Latin *abante*, in front of. College-level courses and exams for high school students.

Graduation

mic preparation. But you might also consider a couple of programs that can further ease your children's transition to college.

The first is called Advanced Placement—or its alternatives, the International Baccalaureate or the College-Level Examination Program (CLEP). These programs offer college credit for college-level courses and examinations given to children of high school age. The AP program, for example, covers 18 subject areas with 32 courses. If the local school district is cooperative, your kids may want to consider supplementing their home education with an AP class through the local high school, or they may wish simply to take the AP test for college credit.

The second program, offered in several states, is called Dual Enrollment, or Running Start. Basically, pre-college students take an examination, such as the COMPASS, that tests their ability to perform at college level. The three-part exam covers reading, math, and writing, and in most states that accept the test, a high score on two of the three parts makes the child eligible to take classes at a local college for free.

Can't beat the price!

If you're interested in getting your children started early on the college path, these resources will be useful.

Advanced Studies, Part 1   crosswalk.com/511706
A homeschooling family discusses Advanced Placement as a tool for college prep. Also, read a discussion of CLEP in part 2 at **crosswalk.com/511708,** and a discussion of correspondence study and record keeping in part 3 at **crosswalk.com/511710.**

AP Courses and Exams   apcentral.collegeboard.com
Advanced Placement material for high-school students. From the left-hand link, click AP Courses and Exams. The index of Sample Syllabi has models for covering important material for each of the 37 AP subject areas. From the Course Home Pages get access to practice exams, tips, and other information for each topic.

Hotlinks

Advanced Studies, Part 1
crosswalk.com/511706

College Board Tests
collegeboard.com/testing

Crossing Over
crosswalk.com/
homeschool/511700

Eight Ways to Earn College Credit
tinyurl.com/eightways

Asset Test act.org/asset

A college placement test used by about 700 community and technical colleges. Download the student testing guide from the website.

Chemistry AP Exam Prep

jesuitnola.org/upload/clark/ap_exam_prep.htm

All in one place, everything you need to earn those college credits for chemistry.

College Board Tests collegeboard.com/testing

Registration links and background information for AP and CLEP exams, as well as for the SAT and the PSAT exams.

COMPASS Sample Questions cscc.edu/testingcenter/sample.html

The computerized assessment in reading, writing, and math that is part of the admissions process at many colleges and universities. It determines placement levels for each academic area, and allows high-scoring students to advance immediately to higher-level courses, bypassing lower-level requirements. This page prepares students for the test.

Crossing Over crosswalk.com/homeschool/511700

Getting college credit while still in high school is economic, and helps kids get a taste of college at an age when parents are still there to help guide. Here's how one family did it.

Eight Ways to Earn College Credit tinyurl.com/eightways

An explanation of the eight methods for getting college credit early—and often at the expense of the local school district. Dual-enrollment programs such as Washington State's Running Start allow students to enroll in college classes during their high school years.

International Baccalaureate Program ibo.org

Another method for earning college credit while still in high school, the IB program is used worldwide.

College Prep Freebie

KnowHow2Go: The 4 Steps to College explains that college doesn't just happen; it requires preparation. Call 877-4-ED-PUBS and request product number EN 0844B.

Graduation

College Prep

Graduation

Readiness: from the middle English *raedig*, prompt. How to get your homeschooler admitted to a top-notch college.

UNTIL I CAME straight up against it, I didn't put much thought into getting admitted to college. I think my little teenaged mind assumed some sort of fairy princess would come along and take care of all the paperwork for me.

That's how I ended up attending the local community college. It had very nearly an open admissions policy, meaning that I didn't have to do much of anything to be admitted.

But it was a very quick trip from my first day of class to the realization that I really, really wanted to enroll in a "real" school—the big university that several of my favorite adults had attended. And I came face-to-face with the fact that I was utterly clueless about how to get into college. I had to go begging for help. Fortunately, one of those adults knew where to go to get the admissions application and was willing to walk me through the process.

Your kids needn't be as dumb as I once was. All the applications information they could ever want is available online, and most of it is free.

Are they worried about doing well on college admissions tests? If they prepare carefully, there's no need to worry. Homeschoolers typically do very, very well on standardized tests, including college-entrance exams. In fact, children educated at home typically score fifteen to thirty percentile points above public school students on standardized academic-achievement tests, and above average on college-admissions tests—and they do so regardless of their parents' level of formal education or their family's household income. (Factors that have no impact on test achievement are having a parent who is a certified teacher, and living in a state where homeschooling is heavily regulated.)

In this section we consider general university-admissions information, including vocabulary and definitions, and an introduction to college. We cover all the basics of getting into college, from finding a good school, to test prep, to writing an admissions application.

ACE-GED Testing Service   www.acenet.edu/programs/GEDTS

Comprehensive background information from the makers of the GED program. Find contacts, news, history, and articles related to GED testing.

ACT Assessment Tests   act.org

American College Test, the second most used college entrance exam after the SAT. Four sets of questions are available (English, math, reading, and science reasoning), as well as test tips and other resources.

ACT-SAT   act-sat-prep.com

Articles that answer questions such as When Should You Take the SAT? and How Many Times Should You Take the SAT? Test-taking tips and more.

Brainbench Test Center   tinyurl.com/braintest

Lots and lots of free tests. Computing, business, and languages, are just a few of the topics covered.

eLearners   elearners.com

A search tool for online college certificates, courses, online training, and degrees. It's far from a complete listing of all accredited colleges with online programs, but it's a start.

Find a Test   ets.org/choose.html

Educational Testing Service information on AP, CLEP, GRE, SAT, and other standardized examinations.

Mapping Your Future   mappingyourfuture.org

Empower your future! Focus covers all aspects of preparing for college.

My College Guide   mycollegeguide.org

Dear Admission Guru is just one of the many useful resources on this site. Real questions from real students

Hotlinks

Mapping Your Future
mappingyourfuture.org

My College Guide
mycollegeguide.org

Practice Tests
4tests.com/exams/
exams.asp

SparkNotes Test Prep
testprep.sparknotes.com

Graduation

College Prep Freebie

Think College? Me? Now? A Handbook for Students in Middle School and Junior High School encourages middle and junior high school students to begin planning for their college education now. Call FSAIC at 800-4-FEDAID and request publication number 820192.

answered by a real guru. Find the common admissions application. And read about college life.

Overview of Accreditation
ed.gov/admins/finaid/accred

Everything you need to know about what constitutes an accredited educational institution in the United States. Don't find out too late that your child's "college" doesn't qualify for federal financial aid, or grants bogus degrees not recognized by employers.

Practice Tests   4tests.com/exams/exams.asp

What the Internet's for. Free practice exams with scoring and explanations. And this one tests anything: High school exams cover the ACT, COOP/HSPT, the GED, PSAT/NMSQT, the SAT, and TAAS. But there's more: college-credit exams include the AP tests for Biology, Chemistry, and U.S. History, and the CLEP for English, Humanities, Psychology, Math, Sciences, Macro Economics, Management, Marketing, Micro Economics, Social Science, and American Government. Still more: the TOEFL, graduate exams such as the GMAT, GRE, LSAT, and MCAT . . . The list goes on.

SparkNotes Test Prep   testprep.sparknotes.com

Practice tests, notification of upcoming test dates, and online test-prep books for free. Prepare for the SAT, the ACT, AP subject tests, SAT subject tests, the LSAT, and the GRE.

Standardized Tests   studystack.com/category-59

Online flashcards—including the space to build your own—that reinforce college prep studies. Uses traditional flashcard format, as well as games and other tools for teaching.

Test Prep Review   testprepreview.com

Bills itself as "Your Source for Free Online Practice Tests." Practice tests for even obscure admissions exams. You'll want to pay particular attention to the COMPASS, the ACT, the SAT, and the PSAT, of course.

The Student Center   student.com

A social networking site for teenagers and college students. Participants get their very own email address in the student.com domain name. Resources include discussions of student loans, college test prep, and jobs and careers for college students.

Financial Aid

I PAID MY own way through college, and until the last term of my senior year, I did it without taking out a long-term loan. At times it was tough coming up with tuition, and books, and materials. I remember once telling my father that I didn't know how I'd pay for an upcoming term and still keep a roof over my head or food in my tummy.

"Just pay it," he told me. Some advice. But somehow, I did. (And the double-digit size of my pants bears witness to the fact that I didn't starve, either.)

With Pell Grants, scholarships, long- and short-term loans, and, of course, a job, I'm persuaded there's no reason any intelligent, healthy person, with or without a spouse and children, can't go to college. It's not always pretty. I spent a lot of years without health insurance, living in basement apartments, and riding a bicycle. I persuaded an employer to pay my way through law school. Through grad school (where I finally succumbed to the lure of student loans), I managed to keep all my children healthy and happy, even if we did spend an inordinate amount of time in thrift stores.

Now that four of my children are trying to manage college and work,

> **Assist:** From the Latin *assistere*, to help, to stand by. Helping you and your child pay for college.

Graduation

Hotlinks

College Finances
college-finances.com

FAFSA on the Web!
fafsa.ed.gov

Paying for School
mapping-your-future
.org/paying

I've become aware of some other possibilities for getting through. If you're of a mind to help your children through college financially, there are a number of financial aid packages available to you. And the option nobody ever told me about is plenty appealing to my sons: the military. Depending on what programs they consider, there's a possibility of obtaining $40,000 or more in free college money—plus their salary, health insurance, and room and board while they're in the service.

Here's what you and your children need to know about college loans, grants, scholarships, and work programs. And just one more piece of advice, no matter who's footing the bill: When everything seems bleak, and you can't figure out how to cover tuition and books and all your other expenses . . . sometimes, you just have to buckle down and pay it.

College Finances   college-finances.com

Unbiased advice for dealing with student loans, credit cards, calling cards, cell phones, and finances. Good counsel.

FAFSA on the Web!   fafsa.ed.gov

Complete the Free Application for Federal Student Aid, online, and free. Links to lots of government-sponsored financial aid information.

Federal Trade Commission   tinyurl.com/schoolscam

Tips for avoiding scams in education, scholarships, and job placement. From the FTC.

How Homeschoolers Can Earn Athletic Scholarships
crosswalk.com/961782

In consultation with HSLDA, the NCAA clarifies scholarship rules for homeschoolers. Practice jumping through hoops by photocopying the table of contents of your textbooks.

Graduation

Paying for School   mapping-your-future.org/paying

Ten steps for paying for school. A great overview of the entire process, with excellent explanations and resources for each financing option.

Sallie Mae   salliemae.com

The number one provider of student loans also provides a website for calculating your financial aid requirements. The Planning and Preparing for School section of this site is a must-read for prospective students.

SparkCollege   college.sparknotes.com

Click the Financial Aid link for the best, most straightforward advice on college planning you'll find anywhere. The Tax Strategies information is particularly enlightening. Under the Admissions link find concise and helpful information on choosing a college and writing the application essay. Good tips.

StuGeek   stugeek.com

A community for students looking for information on college financing. It seems to be in its early stages still, but it has the potential to be a great resource.

> ### Financial Aid Freebie
>
> Request a copy of the *Student Guide* for the next award year from the Federal Student Aid Information Center. Call 800-4-FED-AID.

Career Planning

WHEN THE GOING gets tough, the tough . . . get a job. One of the joys of homeschooling is that kids can start young building their résumés and accruing valuable experience in the workplace. Jo Zsembery, a New York mom who homeschools twelve children, believes work is fundamental to a child's education: "I think they understand the world turns by work. That is a great lesson. What kind of contribution do they want to make?"

> **Career:** From the late Latin *carrāria*, road, path. Vocational training and employment preparation.

Graduation

Hotlinks

Life Skills for Vocational Success
workshopsinc.com/manual

MyPlan
myplan.com

Planning a Career
mapping-your-future.org/planning

Jackie Schlageter, a homeschooling mom of eight in New Mexico, exposes her kids to the world of work at a young age. She says that when her husband worked as a diesel mechanic, he sometimes brought his children to work with him so that he could show them around the shop and let them see how he works.

In our own family, kids begin working as early as possible. Now that four of the kids are off to college, and one's off to the military, they've found that they're perfectly capable of supporting themselves and paying their own way, simply because they've built résumés that impress prospective employers with their work ethic.

Set your own kids on the path to independence with these career-planning resources. Related resources for your entrepreneurial-minded kids are found under the Business section of Chapter 10.

Careers   knowledgehound.com/topics/careers.htm
Career advice for all sorts of intriguing pursuits: aviator, storyteller, astronaut, actuary, butcher, baker, candlestick mak- . . . oh, maybe not.

Go Get It!   tinyurl.com/gogetit
The BBC explains how to make yourself employable, by brushing up on communication, problem solving, performance, technology, and other skills.

Guiding Your Student Toward a Fulfilling Career
crosswalk.com/homeschool/511742
Resources for Christian parents wishing to guide their students in choosing a career.

I Believe I Can Fly   tinyurl.com/belfly
Foundation for a terrific unit study on "When I Grow Up I Want to . . ." Kids consider careers that interest them, and learn what they must do to prepare.

Life Skills for Vocational Success   workshopsinc.com/manual

Your older teenagers need to prepare for life on their own. This resource makes a great starting point. Click the Employability link to start. Find more than 100 lesson plans for teaching basic life skills. Covers social skills, decision making, employability, money management, transportation, health, family responsibilities, the law, and telephone skills.

Life Works   science.education.nih.gov/LifeWorks.nsf

Career exploration sponsored by the National Institutes of Health. How to prepare for a career in the sciences. Especially useful is the section on preparing for college early.

MyPlan   myplan.com

Helps teenagers plan their future by making well-informed decisions about their education and careers. Read career profiles, job descriptions, educational requirements, and career outlook information. Pick a college based on over 40 criteria, including SAT/ACT scores, location, cost, majors, sports, activities, and more.

Planning a Career   mapping-your-future.org/planning

A 10-step plan for choosing and reaching a career goal. Written for high school and college students. Your older children will find this information very useful.

Teacher's Guide to the OOH
www.bls.gov/oco/teachers_guide.htm

Tips on using the grown-up version of the Occupational Outlook Handbook. Once your kids have found a career interest, they can learn what it takes to pursue the career from the Bureau of Labor Statistics.

Motivation

Teach responsibility for oneself. This goes a long way! Talk about the future and how what you know will help, and about what you need to know to accomplish different things in life.

—Jenny McComber, real-world educating mom of four, Argyle, Texas

---

Graduation

Vocational Education Lesson Plans

eduref.org/cgi-bin/lessons.cgi/Vocational_Education

Career studies lesson plans designed by classroom teachers. Most are easily adapted to homeschooling programs.

What Do You Like?   www.bls.gov/k12

The kids' page from the Bureau of Labor Statistics. Pick an academic area of interest, and learn about careers that match.

Write a Résumé   tutorials.com/07/0768/0768.asp

Learn2 is a collection of multipart tutorial that explains how to write a top-notch résumé. Links on the right lead to related How-To's.

Graduation

Appendix

Curriculum:
Scope and Sequence
Recommendations

		FAMILY YEARS				COMMUNITY
Subject/Age	Preschool	5	6	7	8	9
Basic Education (service, library and media, listening, logic and thinking, reference materials, research writing, study skills, values and decision making. See ch. 4)	Family service, library story time, basic family values	Basic listening and study skills	Children's section of the library	Overview of thinking skills and library reference materials	Community service, library card catalog, decision making	Community service, basic reference materials, intermediate study skills
Language Arts (etymology, grammar, literature, reading, speech, spelling, vocabulary, writing. See ch. 5)	Oral language, reading alphabet with sounds and first words	Oral language, recognition of written words, speech etiquette, writing alphabet	Homo-phones, basic grammatical tenses, reading sentences, basic spelling and vocabulary, writing words	Antonyms, basic punctuation, reading plotted stories, basic spelling and vocabulary, writing sentences	Synonyms, reading short books, speaking in small groups, intermediate spelling and vocabulary, writing paragraphs	Reading books with chapters, intermediate spelling and vocabulary, keeping a journal
Mathematics (basic math, pre-algebra, algebra, geometry, computer math, calculus, trig, statistics. See ch. 6)	Counting	Basic math	Basic math	Basic math	Basic math, keyboarding	Basic math, keyboarding
Art (art history, crafts, design, drawing, graphic, painting, sculpture, visual. See ch. 7)	Crafts, finger painting	Crafts, clay modeling	Crafts, poster paint	Art history, crafts	Design, basic pho-tography	Drawing
History (American, American West, ancient, genealogy, modern American, religion, state, world. See ch. 8)	Family stories, fun-damental religious principals	American history, family stories	American West, family stories	Ancient history, oral family history	Family albums, state history	Journals, world history
Music (composition, analysis, instrumental, vocal. See ch. 9)	Singing	Rhythm	Basic music apprecia-tion, scales	Basic notation, instrumental lessons	Basic vocal skills	Basic music appreciation

AWARENESS			WORLD AWARENESS			LIFE SKILLS	
10	**11**	**12**	**13**	**14**	**15**	**16**	**17**
Juvenile section of the library, note taking, basic research skills	Service to children, non-fiction section of library, listening comprehension, basic research writing, values/ethics	Geriatric service, library periodicals, intro to logic, intermediate research skills	Advanced logic, review of reference materials, intermediate research writing	Adult fiction, outlining, intermediate research writing, decision making	Career-oriented volunteerism, critical analysis, intermediate research skills	Academic periodical section of library, review of reference materials, advanced research skills, advanced study skills	Advanced research writing, college-prep study skills
Word origins, intermediate grammatical tenses, reading and writing poetry, advanced spelling and vocabulary	More word origins, intermediate punctuation, American literature, non-fiction reading, advanced spelling and vocabulary, writing fiction	Grammatical word choice, American literature, reading periodicals, review of spelling and vocabulary	Foreign origins of English words, advanced grammatical punctuation, English literature, independent reading, interpretative speech	Modern usage, English literature, reading adult fiction, improvisational speech	Advanced grammatical tenses, world literature, reading adult non-fiction, expository speech	Style guides, world literature, reading academic journals, extemporaneous speech	Archaic usage, ancient/ Elizabethan/ Jamesian literature, independent reading, debate, college prep spelling and vocabulary
Pre-algebra	Pre-algebra, calculator skills	Pre-algebra, statistical principles	Algebra, spreadsheets	Geometry, computer research skills	Calculus	Trig, programming	Stats, advanced computer programming
Art history, watercolors	Soap and soft media sculpture	Advanced photography	Art history	Design	Drawing, pottery	Acrylics, ceramics	Oils, hard media sculpture
Basic genealogical research, modern American history	Genealogy, basic history of religious faith	American history	Ancient history	American West, religious doctrine	Religious history, state history	Comparative religions, world history	Modern history, comparative religions
Basic composition	Intermediate instrument	Intermediate vocal	Advanced music appreciation	Group vocal	Intermediate composition	Advanced vocal	Advanced instrument

		FAMILY YEARS				COMMUNITY
Subject/Age	Preschool	5	6	7	8	9
Social Studies (anthropology/ sociology, civics, current events/news, economics, geography, minority education, psychology, social issues. See ch. 10)	Basic etiquette, neighborhood geography, integrated playgroups	Problem solving	Basic economics	Children's periodicals	Sociology, local civics, city geography, community involvement, local issues	Reading the news, state geography, state issues
Humanities (dance, drama, languages [including ESL and American Sign Language], journalism, philosophy. See ch. 11)	Free dance, bilingualism in the home	Short skits	Radio news	Folk dancing	Community theatre	Broadcast news
Science (anatomy/ genetics, archaeology/ paleontology, astronomy, biology, botany, chemistry, earth sciences/geology, ecology/marine, physics/physical science, inventors, technology, zoology. See ch. 12)	Experimentation	Earth	Botany	Astronomy	Ecology	Zoology
Health (community health/disease prevention, drugs, human growth/development/ aging, mental health/ self esteem, nutrition, personal health, PE/fitness, safety. See ch. 13)	Free play	Development	Personal health	Nutrition	Mental, noncompetitive sports	Drug education, personal fitness
Graduation (college preparation [advanced placement, college search, college testing, financial aid, admissions], vocational education [careers, resumes, business management], home economics [personal finance, home management, parenting, marriage and relationships]. See ch. 14)	Basic home management					

AWARENESS		WORLD AWARENESS				LIFE SKILLS	
10	11	12	13	14	15	16	17
Regional geography, regional isues	National geography, minority education, national issues	American government, reading adult periodicals, continental geography, issues in the Western world	Anthropology, responsibilities of citizens, world geography, world issues	American government, microeconomics	State government, macroeconomics, minority education	World political systems, behavioral pscynology	Civil rights, intermediate economics, abnormal psychology
Intro to drama	Familiar foreign words	Journalistic style	Dance appreciation, professional theater, intro level language	Foreign language speech, editorials	Foreign language reading, newsletter	Foreign language writing, philosophy	Shakespeare, language fluency
Archaeology	Anatomy	Scientists	Technology	Scientific Method	Biology	Chemistry	Physics
Community health	Human development, competitive sports	Aging, personal health	Drug education, nutrition	Mental health, first aid	Community health		
Relationships	Parenting	Intermediate home management	Personal finance	Advanced home management	Life skills	Vocational skills	College prep

Acknowledgments

To Candace Boelter and Rainy Gadberry, whose research assistance and ongoing encouragement helped get the book off the ground and onto a computer screen: Thank you for your friendship and support.

To Robin, Jacobi, and all the other homeschooling moms who support our education efforts with co-op, homeschool camp, first-Friday hikes, mom's nights out, and driving kids to activities when we're under deadline, bless you. We couldn't have done this book without you. You've made this journey a real joy, and our friendship is as eternal as our gratitude.

To the fabulous members of the Homeschool Reviews list (**tinyurl .com/hsreviews**), who shared their homeschooling joys and their favorite resources, your help was invaluable.

Our gratitude, too, to the Crown Publishing folk who saw this second edition of *Homeschool Your Child for Free* through its long, difficult birth: Heather Proulx, associate publishing manager/associate editor; Cindy Berman, senior production editor; Toni Rachiele, copy editor; and Kevin Garcia, production associate. Your guidance is very much appreciated.

And finally, to Andrew Zack, our brilliant, tenacious agent who makes things happen: Your hard work and firm direction are inspiring. Thank you for taking us under your wing.

Index

Excerpt from
Homeschooling Step-by-Step

Contents

- How long must I homeschool each year?
- Should I have my children tested?
- Who pays for the tests?
- What happens if my child scores poorly?
- Is there an alternative to standardized tests?
- Am I allowed to use the public schools as a resource?
- What is the homeschooling law in my state?
- If I run into legal problems, how do I get help?

Self-test

Worksheet

3   TEACHING STRATEGIES

- How can I teach effectively?
- What are "Teaching Strategies"?
- How do we use these strategies?

Table of strategies

4   APPROACHES AND PHILOSOPHIES

- What are teaching approaches?
- How are these approaches different from the strategies described in Chapter 3?
- Do I need a chalkboard?
- What are the categories of teaching approaches?
- How do I choose an approach?
- How does the Ages and Stages model work?
- How does the model apply to education?
- How do we use these approaches?

Table of Approaches and Philosophies

Self-test

5   CURRICULUM AND MATERIALS

- How do I obtain teaching materials?
- What will I need to get started?
- Do I really need a computer?
- What other teaching aids do I need?
- Which reference materials should I have?

- Should I buy a commercial curriculum?
- If I don't use a commercial curriculum, how will I know what to teach?
- Where do I find inexpensive, quality materials to build my own curriculum?
- What are curriculum exchanges?
- What teaching materials are available on line?
- Are there other sources for non-commercial curricula?

6 GAINING CONFIDENCE

- How do I teach my children?
- Where do I start?
- I don't have a teaching certificate. Am I qualified to teach?
- How will I teach difficult academic subjects I didn't study in college?
- What about laboratory sciences?
- How do I manage such an enormous undertaking?
- Will the PROJECT system work for younger children?
- Will the system work with traditional school-at-home approaches?
- Any cautions before I pull my child out of school?

Self-test

Worksheet

7 A LEARNING ENVIRONMENT

- What is a learning environment?
- What are learning styles?
- How can I know my child's learning style?
- How can learning styles help me be a better teacher?
- How can I know my child's IQ?
- Is my child ready for school?
- What's my child's grade level?
- How do I create lesson plans?
- How do I motivate my child to learn?
- How should we schedule our school year?
- How does the environment of our home influence learning?
- How can I create the best possible learning environment?

Self-test

Worksheet

- What support is available from commercial and government organizations?
- What other support is available in my community?

Checklist

11 GRADUATION GUIDANCE

- What happens after homeschooling?
- How should I prepare for graduation?
- How do I get a diploma?
- What about a transcript?
- What other documentation do I need?
- Should I earn a GED?
- Why college?
- How should I prepare for college admission?
- What if I want to go straight to work?
- Is the military an option?

Checklist

EPILOGUE

APPENDIX A

- Homeschooling Laws, State by State

APPENDIX B

- Ideas for Educational Field Trips

APPENDIX C

- Websites referenced in this book

Index

About the Authors

LauraMaery Gold is the homeschooling mother of seven, a popular homeschooling writer and speaker, and the owner of several online resources for homeschoolers and other educators. She is a volunteer adviser for YMCA youth programs and holds degrees in law, journalism, counseling, and financial planning. The author of more than a dozen books on writing, finance, and technology, she's currently researching a series based on the lives of Biblical prophets. LauraMaery and her husband, Dan, live in the Seattle area, where they spend far too much time shuttling kids to activities.

Joan M. Zielinski is the mother of four—one of whom is LauraMaery. A professional educator for nearly thirty years, Joan is a former Teacher of the Year for the Kent, Washington, School District, who recently retired to undertake volunteer work in literacy education. She and her husband, Stan, breed champion St. Bernards.